THE SLAVONIC & EAST EUROPEAN REVIEW

Volume 91, Number 3 — July 2013

ARTICLES

REVIEW ESSAY

REVIEWS

CONTENTS

The Morphosyntax of Causative Relations in Czech and Upper Sorbian: A Contrastive, Descriptive Analysis

GARY H. TOOPS

Introduction

The present article provides a contrastive, descriptive analysis of causative expression in two closely related, West Slavic languages — Czech (hereafter, Cz) and Upper Sorbian (USo). Although the grammar and the lexicon of both languages have historically been influenced by German (Ger), Cz and USo nonetheless differ in the degree and nature of the influence that the Ger language has exerted upon them over time. A remarkable case in point is afforded by the means employed in contemporary Cz and USo to express not only factitive causative and permissive causative relations (expressed in English [Eng] as 'to have somebody do something' and 'to let somebody do something', respectively) but also curative, or passive causative, relations (expressed in Eng as 'to have something done [by someone]').[1] Of the two languages, USo has no doubt been more exposed and open to Ger linguistic influence, if only because the Sorbian speech community (which includes both Lower Sorbian [LSo] and USo) has historically existed within the confines of a Ger state; consequently, there have been no known unilingual USo-speakers since the 1930s and all native speakers of USo today are bilingual in USo and Ger.

Gary H. Toops is Professor of Russian and Linguistics in the Department of Modern and Classical Languages and Literatures at Wichita State University, Wichita, Kansas.

[1] For an explanation and the history of the synonymous terms 'curative' and 'passive causative', see Gary H. Toops, 'The Syntax and Semantics of Lithuanian Curative Constructions', in Howard I. Aronson (ed.), *The Non-Slavic Languages of the USSR: Linguistic Studies*, Chicago, IL, 1989, pp. 249–82 (pp. 249, 252, and 272, note 2).

Slavonic and East European Review, 91, 3, 2013

Given the contrastive nature of the morphosyntactic analysis contained in this article, it was deemed important that empirical data in the form of Cz causative sentences, on the one hand, and USo causatives, on the other, exhibit as much semantic or syntactic parallelism as possible. An exclusive reliance on online Cz or USo language corpora would have necessarily restricted the various sentence permutations that are necessary to highlight specific morphosyntactic differences not only between (semantically or syntactically) parallel Cz and USo causative constructions, but also between sentence permutations *within* each of the two Slavic languages. Therefore, primary emphasis is placed on sentences drawn from published language sources and linguistic studies as well as on original Cz and USo sentences (and permutations thereof) that have been formulated by, or with the aid of, native speakers, most of them university-level instructors of the languages in question. To the extent that differences in judgements of grammaticality came to my attention in the course of discussing various Cz and USo sentences with native speakers, such differences are duly noted in my discussion of the linguistic material presented below.[2]

Grammatical background

In this article, aspectual pairs of Cz and USo verbs are cited as two infinitives — one imperfective, the other perfective; each infinitive represents a complete and distinct paradigm of finite verb forms (not to mention nonfinite forms such as participles and verbal adverbs).[3] Imperfective verbs in Cz are conjugated for three tenses — a synthetic present (for example, *píšu* 'I write, am writing'), an analytic past (*psal[a] jsem* 'I wrote, was writing, used to write'), and an analytic future tense (*budu psát* 'I will write, will be writing').[4] The conjugation of imperfective verbs in USo is similar, except that in the standard written (or literary) language a synthetic past tense (preterite)[5] also exists, not to mention

[2] A version of this article was read on 6 January 2012 as a paper titled 'Expressing Causative Relations in Czech and Upper Sorbian: A Contrastive Analysis' at the annual convention of the American Association of Teachers of Slavic and East European Languages (AATSEEL) held in Seattle/Bellevue, Washington, USA.

[3] In some treatments of Slavic languages, verbal adverbs are called 'gerunds' or — in the case of LSo and USo — 'transgressives'.

[4] The third-person singular and plural forms of the Cz past tense consist of the verb's *l*-participle alone, i.e., without an auxiliary verb, but are regarded here nonetheless as constituting an analytic, rather than a synthetic, past tense.

[5] In older grammatical treatments of USo grammar, the preterite tense of imperfective verbs is called 'imperfect', while the preterite tense of perfective verbs is called 'aorist'. (Thus, unlike Bulgarian, for example, USo has no perfective imperfect tense and no imperfective aorist.)

an analytic pluperfect and an analytic iterative preterite as well (the USo tense that is formally analogous to the Cz past tense is accordingly termed 'perfect' to distinguish it from the USo pluperfect). Thus the paradigm of USo *pisać* 'to write' includes *pisam* 'I write, am writing' (present), *pisach* 'I wrote, was writing' (preterite), *sym pisał[a]* 'I have written, was writing, used to write' (perfect), *běch pisał[a]* 'I had written' (pluperfect), *bych pisał[a]* 'I would write, used to write' (iterative preterite), and *budu pisać* 'I will write, will be writing' (future).[6] Perfective verbs in Cz are conjugated for only two tenses — a synthetic future (or 'non-past'), which formally resembles the synthetic present of imperfective verbs (see above), and an analytic past tense: *napíšu* 'I will write, will get written, will have written' (non-past) and *napsal[a] jsem* 'I have written, got written, had written' (past). Perfective verbs in literary USo likewise exhibit a synthetic future, *napisam* 'I will write, will get written, will have written',[7] but, again, offer a variety of past-tense verb forms: *napisach* 'I wrote, got written' (preterite), *sym napisał[a]* 'I have written' (perfect), *běch napisał[a]* 'I had written' (pluperfect), and *bych napisał[a]* 'I would write, used to write, would get written' (iterative preterite).[8]

Autosemantic and synsemantic causative verbs in Cz and USo

Like a number of other Slavic languages, Cz and USo may, under certain circumstances, express causative relations by means of contextual implication alone (roughly similar to the causative meaning implicit in Eng utterances of the type *We are building ourselves a new house*, which a speaker may produce in place of a synonymous, explicitly causative construction like *We are having a new house built [for ourselves]*). Related to the contextual expression of causative relations are Cz and USo sentences involving the notion of *giving* something to someone (or taking something to a place) so that a particular action may be performed upon

[6] In contemporary colloquial varieties of USo, as well as in USo dialects transitional to LSo, essentially only one past tense exists — the perfect — so that the USo tense system is practically analogous to that of contemporary standard Cz. Moreover, the USo iterative preterite is fully homonymous with forms of the conditional mood and is obsolete as a past tense in many USo dialects; see Gary H. Toops, 'Aspectual Competition and Iterative Contexts in Contemporary Upper Sorbian', *Journal of Slavic Linguistics*, 9, 2001, 1, pp. 127–54 (p. 137, note 19) for details.

[7] In dialects and colloquial varieties of USo, the auxiliary *budu* (future tense of *być* 'to be') is used to form the future tense of perfective verbs by analogy to the future tense of imperfective verbs, e.g., *budu napisać* in place of *napisam* 'I will write, get written'.

[8] Note that the analytic past tenses in both Cz and USo are formed by means of a so-called '*l*-participle' (or '*ł*-participle') which agrees in gender with the subject. The forms ending in *-a* are accordingly used when the subject is feminine singular.

it. Such Cz and USo sentences incorporate syntagms comparable to Ger ones of the type *etwas in Druck geben* (literally) *'to give something into print' which dictionaries often define as a paraphrase of the explicitly causative construction *etwas drucken lassen* 'to have something printed'.[9] The lexical properties and causative semantics of such constructions in Cz and USo are discussed below. First, however, it is apposite to discuss various morphosyntactic features of the inventories of autosemantic and synsemantic causative verbs that both languages have at their disposal for the expression of causative relations.

Synsemantic causatives are usually termed 'causative auxiliaries' or 'causative helping verbs'. Their causative semantics are syntactically conditioned, and homonyms of such verbs in other syntactic environments (that is, in the absence of infinitive or sentential complements) often express a different lexical meaning. Because synsemantic causatives are by definition helping verbs, they naturally co-occur in predicates with verbal complements that denote actions whose causation by some (overt or implied) Indirect Agent the causative auxiliary verbs express. In addition to the basic meaning CAUSE, the lexical definition of a causative auxiliary frequently (albeit not necessarily) specifies whether the causation in question is permissive (cf. Eng *to let* [*somebody do something*]) or factitive (cf. *Eng to have* [*somebody do something*]).[10] Cz has two causative auxiliaries, *dávat/dát* and *nechávat/nechat*. The causative *dávat/dát* in Modern Cz is completely homonymous with the (autosemantic) verb signifying 'to give' and *primarily* denotes factitive causation. The causative *nechávat/nechat* is completely homonymous with the (autosemantic) verb signifying 'to leave

[9] Cf. Gerhard Wahrig (comp.), *Deutsches Wörterbuch*, 1980 edn, Munich, 1982, p. 1442: *ein Manuskript in Druck geben = drucken lassen, ein Manuskript in Satz geben = setzen lassen, jmdm. etwas in Verwahrung geben = etwas verwahren lassen*. For additional discussion and details, see Gary H. Toops, 'Causative Constructions in the Upper Sorbian Literary Language', *Die Welt der Slaven*, 38, 1993, 1, 102–36 (pp. 107–11).

[10] A third type of causation, assistive causation, is sometimes adduced on the basis of a language like Georgian, which possesses a causative derivational morpheme that is ambiguous with respect to permissive, factitive, as well as assistive causation. Thus the Georgian sentence *Mama shvils ts'erils ats'erinebs* can be translated into Eng as 'The father is letting his son write a letter', as 'The father is having his son write a letter' or as 'The father is helping his son write a letter'. Assistive causativity will not concern us here, as both Cz and USo express this meaning with a verb signifying 'to help' — Cz *pomáhat/pomoct*, USo *pomhać*. Nevertheless, it should be noted that all three Eng translations given here share the semantic property of committing the recipient of the message (that is, reader or listener) to the logical inference that the action denoted by the infinitive complement (*write*) is in fact being performed — either entirely or partly by the direct object *son*, whose semantic status (or thematic role) as a participant in the sentence is that of Direct Agent (or 'Causee').

(be, alone, in place)' and is regularly used to express permissive causation, although in (mostly) colloquial Cz it is also used to express factitive causation; thus *nechávat/nechat* semantically resembles the Ger causative auxiliary *lassen*, which is assumed by some to have promoted the expanded use of *nechávat/nechat* in lieu of *dávat/dát* in the historical development of the Cz language.[11] In contrast to Cz, USo imitates Ger in having only one causative auxiliary, *dać*; unlike Cz *dávat/dát*, causative *dać* in USo is biaspectual (or aspectually neutral) and parallels Ger *lassen* in denoting *either* factitive *or* permissive causation.[12] Because of its biaspectuality, *dać* is only partly homonymous with the USo verb (aspectual pair) signifying 'to give' — *dawać/dać*.[13] Moreover, this biaspectual causative has preterite forms that exhibit desinences characteristic of imperfective verbs (for example, *ja dach, ty daše, wón/wona daše* 'I had/let, you had/let, he/she had/let [somebody do something]')[14] and that therefore differ from some of the preterite forms of perfective *dać* 'to give' (cf. *ja dach, ty da, wón/wona da* 'I gave, you gave, he/she gave'). However, in written USo it is not uncommon to find second- and third-person singular preterite forms of causative *dać* that are homonymous with those of 'donatory' *dać* — a phenomenon which is viewed by some as a literary hypercorrection.[15]

Autosemantic causative verbs are those whose meaning CAUSE, as well as the specific type or nature of the causation (that is, degrees or kinds of impetus or suasion), are inherent in the lexical meaning of the verbs themselves. This meaning is expressed independently of the syntactic

[11] For discussion of how Ger is considered to have influenced the causative semantics of both Cz *dávat/dát* and Cz *nechávat/nechat*, see Gary H. Toops, 'Causativity in Czech: The Verbs *dá(va)t* and *nech(áv)at*', *Canadian Slavonic Papers / Revue canadienne des slavistes*, 34, 1992, 1–2, pp. 39–56 (pp. 41–44, 48–49, and 56).

[12] The USo cognate of Cz *nechat*, *njechać*, is a synonym of USo *nochcyć* signifying 'not to want' (cf. Latin *nōlō*). However, USo has an historically related particle *njech* which encodes jussive and optative meanings (for example, *Njech přińdźe* 'Let him/her come', *Njech je žiwy serbski lud!* 'Long live the Sorbian people!').

[13] Imperfective *dawać* does not occur as a causative auxiliary, but it is often used in USo dialects (like the verb *dawaś* in LSo generally) as a calque of Ger *es gibt* 'there is/are'.

[14] As noted in Gary H. Toops, 'Upper Sorbian Prefixal Derivatives and the Question of German Loan Translations', *Slavic and East European Journal*, 36, 1992, 1, pp. 17–35 (p. 20), the preterite-tense forms of both biaspectual and aspectually neutral USo verbs are formally characterized by the same desinences that characterize the preterite-tense forms of imperfective verbs.

[15] See Gary H. Toops, 'Pushkin in Sorbian: A Contrastive Look at Aspect Use in Literary Upper Sorbian and Russian', in R. A. Maguire and A. Timberlake (eds), *American Contributions to the Thirteenth International Congress of Slavists, Ljubljana, 2003*, 2 vols, Bloomington, IN, 2003, 1 (*Linguistics*), pp. 181–94 (p. 193), and Gary H. Toops, 'Puškin in Sorbian (II): A Further Look at Aspect Use in Literary Upper Sorbian and Russian', *Die Welt der Slaven*, 50, 2005, 2, pp. 241–62 (p. 250, note 17).

environment in which the verbs occur. Thus the lexical meaning of the Eng verbs *to allow* and *to permit* remains essentially unchanged irrespective of whether the complement of either verb is a direct-object noun phrase (for example, *They allowed/permitted us access to the archives*) or an infinitive complement (*They allowed/permitted us to access the archives*). In the latter case, the verbs in question are classified linguistically as *autosemantic* permissive causatives and are thus distinguished from the Eng *synsemantic* permissive causative (causative auxiliary) *to let* (cf. *They let us access the archives*).[16]

Contextual causatives

The term 'contextual causatives' is a translation of Russian (Ru) *kontekstnye kauzativy*, a term introduced by V. P. Nedjalkov in his monograph on analytic causative constructions in Ger.[17] It denotes the linguistic phenomenon of conveying curative, or passive causative, relations by contextual implication rather than explicitly by grammatical means that incorporate productive verbal morphemes or syntagms (for example, periphrastic constructions formed with a causative auxiliary verb and an infinitive or sentential complement).[18] On initial reflection, contextual causatives would appear to be a strictly lexical phenomenon with little, if any, relevance to the grammar of causative constructions. However, as has been previously shown, the use of contextual causatives in Ru is not only conditioned by the semantic properties of reflexive verbs,[19] but also evidenced by the coordinability of both passive-causative and noncausative instantiations of a single verbal lexeme within the same sentence:

[16] It is not necessary to theorize here how the verb signifying 'to give' became grammaticalized as a causative auxiliary in all of today's Slavic languages (nevertheless, for discussion see Toops, 'Causativity', pp. 41–44, and Toops, 'Causative Constructions', pp. 107–11), but it is interesting to note that even the Eng causative sentences provided here could be paraphrased by means of the verb *to give* — cf. *They gave us access to the archives.*

[17] See V. P. Nedjalkov, *Kauzativnye konstrukcii v nemeckom jazyke. Analitičeskij kauzativ*, Leningrad, 1971, p. 20, and V. P. Nedjalkov, *Kausativkonstruktionen*, trans. V. Kuchler and H. Vater, Tübingen, 1976, p. 29. The latter is a Ger translation of the former; the Ru term signifying 'contextual causatives' is rendered in this Ger translation as 'Kontext-Kausativa'.

[18] Note that curatives (passive causatives) are essentially factitive, not permissive; that is, they express the meaning 'to *have* something done', not 'to let something be done'.

[19] Gary H. Toops, 'Russian Contextual Causatives', *Slavic and East European Journal*, 31, 1987, 4, pp. 595–611. For example, the Ru synthetic reflexive *lečit′sja* can be interpreted either noncausatively as 'to treat oneself (medically)' or causatively as 'to have oneself treated', while the analytic reflexive *lečit′ sebja* is interpretable strictly as noncausative — 'to treat oneself'. (With inanimate sentence subjects denoting illnesses, moreover, *lečit′sja* also has passive meaning — 'to be treated').

(1) Ru: Ja sšila plat'e$_i$ u portnichi$_j$, no ona$_j$ ego$_i$ sšila plocho.[20]
I sewed dress at seamstress's, but she it sewed badly
'I had a dress made by a seamstress, but she made it badly.'

As early as 1941, and again in 1954, attention was drawn to the potential curative meaning of various reflexive, albeit formally noncausative, verbal syntagms in Cz.[21] Examples of these — all of which share both formal and semantic properties with corresponding Ru verbs — include the following:[22]

(2) Cz: Právě se holím (u holiče).
just-now REFL I-shave at barber's
'I am getting a shave (= having myself shaved) (at the barber's).'

(3) Cz: Holím se u tohoto holiče pravidelně.
I-shave REFL at this barber's regularly
'I regularly have myself shaved by this barber.'

(4) Cz: Fotografoval jsem se naposled před dvěma lety.
photographed I-have REFL last before two years
'I last had myself photographed (= had my picture taken) two years ago.'

The foregoing Cz sentences, while regarded as grammatical when they were formulated and published by Cz linguists M. Dokulil and F. Kopečný in the mid-twentieth century (see note 21), are often viewed today as ungrammatical by subsequent generations of Cz speakers, who prefer the 'explicit' denotation of causativity by means of the auxiliaries *nechávat/nechat* and *dávat/dát* (see below).[23] Nevertheless, a conspicuous feature of Cz sentences (2)–(4) is precisely that they, *unlike* their morphosemantic analogues in Ru, do find synonymous expression in analytic constructions incorporating causative auxiliaries — here, again, Cz *nechávat/nechat* and

[20] Toops, 'Contextual Causatives', p. 603. Subscripts *i* and *j* indicate coreference.

[21] Miloš Dokulil, 'Morfologické kategorie pasiva ve spisovných jazycích severských ve srovnání se spisovnou češtinou' in L. Zatočil (ed.), *Hrst studií a vzpomínek*, Brno, 1941, pp. 77–99 (p. 82), and František Kopečný, 'Passivum, reflexivní forma slovesná a reflexivní sloveso', *Studie a práce linguistické*, 1, 1954, pp. 224–47 (p. 229).

[22] In the literal glosses, REFL denotes a reflexive voice morpheme (reflexive pronoun).

[23] According to Professor Miluše Šasková-Pierce (born in Prague, 1948) of the University of Nebraska-Lincoln, the use of accusative-reflexive constructions as contextual causatives characterized the speech of her grandparents and is common in nineteenth-century Cz literature (personal communication).

dávat/dát. Thus, the curative meaning of sentence (2) can be alternately (and univocally) expressed as *Právě se nechávám holit*;[24] that of sentence (3) as *Dávám se holit u tohoto holiče pravidelně*; and that of sentence (4) as *Dal jsem se vyfotografovat naposled před dvěma lety*.[25] As in Ru, however, the possibility of expressing curative meaning with noncausative verb forms is confined for the most part to verbs denoting professional services (for example, shaving, cutting hair, taking pictures, repairing shoes; making, mending, laundering or dry-cleaning clothes, and so on).[26] Moreover, this lexical class of verbs need not be reflexive in order to express curative meaning; in the following Cz sentence, the dative reflexive pronoun *si* occurs optionally, as a so-called ethical dative, and does so independently of the sentence's curative meaning:[27]

(5) Cz:	Ivana (si)	šije (šaty)	v	tomto	salónu.
	Ivana (REFL)	sews (clothes)	in	this	shop

'Ivana has (her) clothes made in this dress-shop.'

Sentence (5), above, can in fact be paraphrased as an explicitly causative construction with no change of cognitive meaning, cf. *Ivana (si) dává šít (šaty) v tomto salónu*. Moreover, the reverse process of paraphrasing semantically and/or morphosyntactically passive-causative constructions as formally noncausative ones is also possible in Cz. For example, the curative meaning expressed in the causative 'give'-sentence *Dáváme prát své košile do prádelny*[28] (see below) 'We have our shirts washed at the laundry' can be alternately conveyed by contextual means:

[24] Note that in the absence of the adverbial *u holiče* 'at the barber's', the sentence *Právě se holím* can be read in a noncausative sense — 'I am shaving right now'. The sentence *Právě se nechávám holit* is unambiguously a *causative* sentence, but remains ambiguous with respect to factitive vs. permissive causation (that is, the sentence could mean 'I am letting myself be shaved right now').

[25] The verb *vyfotografovat* is the perfective aspect partner of *fotografovat* and is used here to match the aspect of the perfective causative auxiliary *dal*.

[26] Cf. Toops, 'Causativity', pp. 45–46.

[27] Ibid., p. 46. Indeed, from the standpoint of modern-day Cz usage, it would appear that only nonreflexive and dative-reflexive sentences (that is, those incorporating the dative reflexive pronoun *si*) can function as 'contextual causatives'.

[28] Milan Šára, Jitka Šárová and Antonín Bytel, *Čeština pro cizince. Czech for English-Speaking Students*, 2nd edn, Prague, 1969, p. 359.

(6) Cz: Pereme své košile v prádelně.[29]
we-wash one's-own shirts in laundry
'We have our shirts washed at the laundry.'

In contrast to Cz, contextual causatives in USo are largely unknown. An USo reflexive verb form like *holím se* 'I shave ~ am shaving' in Cz sentence (2), above, for example, can have either a noncausative reflexive or a noncausative passive reading, but not a curative one, cf.:

(7) USo: Runje so pola frizera truham.
right-now REFL at barber's I-shave
'I am being shaved right now at the barber's.' (*or* ?'I am shaving myself ...')
(*not* *'I am having myself shaved ...' *'I am getting a shave at the barber's.')

As demonstrated elsewhere,[30] USo resembles rather Ger and Eng in occasionally conveying curative relations elliptically. The following USo example illustrates how the causative auxiliary *dać*, though absent in the sentence's original formulation, is semantically recoverable:[31]

(8) USo: Ludźo powědachu, zo chce młody hrabja kapałku *natwarić* (*dać*).
'People recounted that the young count wanted *to build* a small chapel (... *to have* a small chapel *built*).'

'Giving' as a means of causation

A second means of expressing causative relations involving professional services in particular (see above) consists of the verb 'to give' (Cz *dávat/dát*, USo *dawać/dać*) and one of the following complements or adverbial modifiers: the provider of the service in question; the place (commercial establishment) where the service is generally rendered (*nomen loci*); or a substantive (that is, deverbal noun) derived from the verb denoting such a service (*nomen actionis* or *nomen acti*). Morphosyntactically analogous

[29] I thank my native Cz-speaking informant Kamil Štumpf (originally of Liberec, Czech Republic) at the University of Leipzig for formulating this sentence and corroborating its causative reading. One anonymous native speaker of Cz found the use of *své* (or *svoje*) 'peculiar', preferring instead the ethical dative pronoun *si* (cf. note 27).

[30] Toops, 'Causative Constructions', pp. 106–07.

[31] The illustrated sentence is modified from Helmut Faßke, *Grammatik der obersorbischen Schriftsprache der Gegenwart. Morphologie / Gramatika hornjoserbskeje spisowneje rěče přitomnosće. Morfologija*, asst. S. Michalk, Bautzen, 1981, p. 216.

constructions with curative meaning are found in a wide geographic spectrum of European languages, ranging from Ger near the western end of the spectrum to Ru at the eastern end, with languages like Polish and Lithuanian (Lith) in between. It is therefore impossible to view either the Cz or the USo causative 'give'-constructions (as I shall call them) as the products of language contact, let alone as the results of specifically Ger influence. Nevertheless, it is worth noting that the corresponding Ru syntagms incorporate the prefix-derived verb *otdavat′/otdat′* 'to hand over, consign' rather than the basic verb *davat′/dat′* 'to give' and so do not represent exact morphosyntactic equivalents of the Cz and USo constructions considered here (the Ru syntagms, moreover, frequently occur with infinitive verbal complements).[32]

Examples of Cz and USo 'give'-constructions that incorporate substantives denoting professional service providers include the following:

(9) (a) Cz: dávat/dát boty k ševci
USo: črije k šewcej dawać/dać
'to give/take shoes to a shoemaker' (that is, to have shoes repaired)
(b) Cz: dávat/dát oblek ke krejčímu
USo: woblek ke krawcej dawać/dać
'to give/take a suit to a tailor' (that is, to have a suit altered or mended)
(c) Cz: dávat/dát hodinky k hodináři
USo: časnik k časnikarjej dawać/dać
'to give/take a watch to a watchmaker' (that is, have a watch repaired)

Such semantically causative 'give'-constructions in both Cz and USo differ formally from noncausative relations of giving in that the service provider is expressed as an adpositional dative (that is, as a dative-case object of

[32] Like Ru, Lith exhibits causative constructions formed with the prefix-derived verbs *įduoti* and *atiduoti* rather than the basic verb *duoti* 'give': cf. Lith *Moteris nori įduoti suknelę pasiūti* 'The woman wants to have a dress made ["sewn"]' (Toops, 'Curative Constructions', pp. 250–51), which corresponds morphosyntactically to Ru *Ženščina xočet otdat′ sšit′ plat′e*. Ju. D. Apresjan, *Leksičeskaja semantika. Sinonimičeskie sredstva jazyka*, Moscow, 1974, p. 209, describes the following Ru syntagms as 'absolutely univocal' ('absoljutno odnoznačnye') in their expression of curative meaning: *otdavat′/otdat′ (obuv′) v počinku* 'to have (shoes) repaired', *otdavat′/otdat′ (časy) v remont* 'to have (a watch) repaired', *otdavat′/otdat′ (kostjum) v čistku* 'to have (a suit) cleaned', *otdavat′/otdat′ (kreslo) na peretjažku* 'to have (an armchair) re-upholstered', *otdavat′/otdat′ (plat′e) v peredelku* 'to have (a dress) altered', *otdavat′/otdat′ (rubaški) v stirku* 'to have (shirts) laundered'. See Toops, 'Causative Constructions', pp. 110–11, note 18, for additional details.

the preposition *k* 'to') rather than as a true, adnominal dative denoting an indirect object. The productivity of such constructions appears limited only pragmatically — that is, by the finite variety of professional service providers that exist in the real world at any given time.[33] As in other 'give'-constructions illustrated below, the direct object also cannot be a reflexive pronoun or an inalienable part of the individual denoted by the sentence subject (for example, one cannot 'give' oneself to a physician to be treated any more than one can 'give' one's teeth to a dentist to be cleaned).

Examples of Cz and USo causative 'give'-constructions that indicate a professional service establishment include the following:

(10) (a) Cz: dávat/dát prádlo do prádelny
USo: šaty do płokarnje dawać/dać
'to take clothes to the laundry' (that is, 'to get one's laundry washed')
(b) Cz: dávat/dát šaty do čistírny
USo: šaty do čisćernje dawać/dać
'to take clothes to the cleaners'' (that is, 'to have clothes [dry-] cleaned')
(c) Cz: dávat/dát auto do lakovny
USo: awto do lakěr(ow)arnje dawać/dać
'to take a car to a paint shop' (that is, 'to have a car [re-] painted')

Causative 'give'-constructions formed with deverbal nouns are exemplified by the following:

(11) (a) Cz: dávat/dát rukopis do sazby/tisku
USo: manuskript do sadźby/ćišća dawać/dać
'to have a manuscript typeset/printed'
(b) Cz: dávat/dát auto do správky/opravy
USo: awto do porjedźenja dawać/dać
'to take a car (in) for repair' (that is, 'to have a car repaired')
(c) Cz: dávat/dát knihu do vazby
USo: knihu do wjazby dawać/dać
'to have a book bound'

Although it is not uncommon for dictionaries to define 'give'-constructions like those listed in example sets (9) through (11), above, as

[33] See ibid., p. 109.

synonyms of passive-causative constructions proper (that is, constructions exhibiting the Cz causative auxiliary *dávat/dát* + infinitive or the USo causative auxiliary *dać* + infinitive), the former do not meet the criteria of strict logical implicature in the same way as true causative constructions do.[34] For example, one Ru-Cz dictionary, in citing the Cz syntagm *dát šaty do čistírny*, parenthetically provides the infinitive verb form *vyčistit*, thereby suggesting that the 'give'-construction and the passive causative *dát šaty vyčistit* 'to have clothes cleaned' are synonymous.[35] However, as various linguists have previously noted,[36] 'give'-constructions in both Cz and USo are only *conventionally* implicative,[37] since they do not necessarily or consistently commit a reader or listener to the logical inference that the action conveyed by the prepositional phrase has actually taken place. By way of illustration, the following Cz sentence conventionally receives a causative reading:

(12) Cz: Jan si dal (čistit) šaty do čistírny.
'Jan took his clothes to the cleaners (to be cleaned).' (that is, 'Jan had his clothes cleaned at the cleaners.')

Nevertheless, the possibility of retracting or contradicting the implication of successful causation remains, as demonstrated by sentence (13), below:[38]

(13) Cz: Jan si dal (čistit) šaty do čistírny, ale pracovníci čistírny (mu) je ukradli.
'Jan took his clothes to the cleaners (to be cleaned), but the employees there stole them (from him).'

Overall, in comparing the above-illustrated Cz 'give'-constructions with the previously described contextual causatives, we see that, while both sentence types express curative meaning, they are implicative in different ways and to different degrees. If the syntactic subjects of contextually

[34] See John Lyons, *Semantics*, 2 vols, Cambridge, New York, 1977, 2, pp. 592–606, and Talmy Givón, *Syntax: A Functional-Typological Introduction*, 2 vols, Amsterdam and Philadelphia, PA, 1984, 1, pp. 118–24.

[35] *Russko-češskij slovar´ / Rusko-český slovník*, ed. L. V. Kopecký and O. Leška, 2 vols, Prague and Moscow, 1978, 1 (*A–O*), pp. 629–30.

[36] Cf. Toops, 'Causative Constructions', p. 108.

[37] H. Paul Grice, *Studies in the Way of Words*, Cambridge, MA, London, 1989, p. 26ff.

[38] As sentence (13) demonstrates, sentence (12) can be nonimplicative even when the infinitive *čistit* 'to clean' occurs in it. The optional occurrence of this verb yields a purposive infinitive, since the Cz sentence *Jan si dal (vy)čistit šaty* is a univocally implicative passive-causative construction signifying 'Jan had/got his clothes cleaned'.

causative sentences are in fact interpreted by a reader or listener as Indirect Agents (that is, Causers) rather than as Direct Agents, then the contextual causatives (to the extent that the verbs are not negated) are necessarily implicative — that is, the action denoted by the verb in each such sentence in fact is, has been, or will be performed. In considering, in contrast, the 'give'-constructions in both Cz and USo, we conclude that their instantiation does not consistently achieve full logical implicature and that they remain, as a class, only conventionally implicative.

Synsemantic causative constructions

Synsemantic causative constructions in Cz consist of the causative auxiliaries *dávat/dát* and *nechávat/nechat* in conjunction with an infinitive complement. When not negated, *dávat/dát* expresses factitive causation, be it curative (*dávat/dát něco udělat* 'to have something done') or noncurative (with a dative Indirect Agent or Causee — *dávat/dát někomu něco udělat* 'to have someone do something'). Curative meaning is expressed by sentences formed with *dávat/dát* + infinitive when they contain no indirect object in the dative case that could be interpreted (or misinterpreted) as a Direct Agent (Causee). Unlike 'give'-constructions, which likewise express curative meaning, *dávat/dát* + infinitive constructions are strictly implicative:[39]

(14) Cz: Jan dal napsat dopis.
Jan 'had' $\text{write}_{\text{INF}}$ letter
'Jan had a letter written.'

(15) Cz: Jan dal zazpívat píseň.
Jan 'had' sing_{INF} song
'Jan had a song sung.'

(16) Cz: Dám si ušít nový oblek.
I-'will have' REFL_{DAT} sew_{INF} new suit
'I will have a new suit made (for myself).'

[39] The subscripts INF, NOM, DAT and ACC, appearing here and hereafter, stand for 'infinitive', 'nominative', 'dative' and 'accusative', respectively. It should be recalled that although infinitive verb forms occur optionally in 'give'-constructions (cf. examples [12] and [13]), they function there as simple purposive infinitives, not as object-governing infinitive complements of the causative auxiliary *dávat/dát*.

(17) Cz: Dal jsem (si) opravit boty.
'Had' I-am (REFL$_{DAT}$) repair$_{INF}$ shoes$_{ACC}$
'I had (the, my) shoes repaired.'

In passive-causative constructions like (14) through (17), above, it is usually, but (for reasons that are not completely clear) not always, possible to express the Direct Agent (Causee) as an adnominal instrumental or as the genitive object of the preposition *od* 'from, by':

(14') Cz: Jan dal napsat dopis ($^{?}$bratrem/$^{(*)}$od bratra).[40]
'Jan had the letter written (by his brother).'
(15') Cz: Jan dal zazpívat píseň $^{?}$sestrou.
'Jan had the song sung by his sister.'
(16') Cz: Dám si ušít nový oblek od krejčího/*krejčím.
'I will have my new suit made by a tailor.'
(17') Cz: Dal jsem (si) opravit boty ševcem/*bratrem.
'I had (my) shoes repaired by a shoemaker/by my brother.'[41]

Although primarily a permissive causative auxiliary, the verb *nechávat/nechat* can be used synonymously in place of *dávat/dát* in sentences (14) through (17) as well as sentences (14') through (17'), above: cf. *Jan nechal napsat dopis, Jan nechal zazpívat píseň (sestrou), Nechám si ušít nový oblek (od krejčího), Nechal jsem opravit boty (ševcem).* The use of *nechávat/nechat* as a factitive causative is viewed by many as a feature of colloquial Cz and is even regarded by some grammarians (in my view, wrongly) as a Ger influence.[42]

[40] According to one native-speaker informant (Miluše Šasková-Pierce, University of Nebraska), *od bratra* in (14') suggests that the letter (*dopis*) in question is a letter 'from' Jan's brother, and instrumental *bratrem* sounds unusual with the causative auxiliary *dal*, which in factitive causative sentences assigns *dative* case to the Indirect Agent (Causee).

[41] The markings $^{?}$ and * before the Direct Agents in the foregoing passive-causative sentences indicate degrees of hesitancy exhibited by native-speaker informants in acknowledging the sentence's grammaticality and in judging the felicity of expressing Direct Agents. While not strictly relevant to the present analysis, it is my informal observation that the felicity of expressing Direct Agents as adnominal instrumentals or as the genitive objects of the preposition *od* increases according to the degree of lexical association that Cz speakers perceive between a given Direct Agent and the action denoted by the infinitive complement. Accordingly, *švec* 'shoemaker' is more often associated with shoe repair than *bratr* 'brother', thus lending itself more freely than *bratr* to being expressed as an instrumental Agent.

[42] See Bohuslav Havránek, 'Die sprachlichen Beziehungen zwischen dem Tschechischen und Deutschen', in B. Havránek and R. Fischer (eds), *Deutsch-tschechische Beziehungen im*

Although USo has only one causative auxiliary verb — *dać* — which, like Ger *lassen*, is polysemous with respect to factitive and permissive causation, direct USo translations of Cz sentences (14) through (17) and (14') through (17') are both possible and eminently idiomatic:[43]

(18) USo: Jan je (wot swojeho bratra) list napisać dał. ~ Jan daše (wot swojeho bratra) list napisać.
'Jan had a letter written by his brother.'

(19) USo: Jan je (wot swojeje sotry) spěw spěwać dał. ~ Jan daše (wot swojeje sotry) spěw spěwać.
'Jan had a song sung by his sister.'

(20) USo: Ja sej dam (wot krawca) nowy woblek šić/zešić.
'I will have my new suit made (by a tailor).'

(21) USo: Sym (wot šewca/wot swojeho bratra) črije porjedźić dał. ~ Dach (wot šewca/wot swojeho bratra) črije porjedźić.
'I had the shoes repaired (by a shoemaker/by my brother).'

In USo, the optional expression of the Direct Agent as a genitive object of the preposition *wot* is unrestricted and parallels the expression of Agents in noncausative passive sentences. In further contrast to Cz, moreover, USo does not instantiate the instrumental case to encode Agents in either passive-causative or noncausative sentences.[44]

Implicative, factitive causative sentences are primarily formed in Cz with the causative auxiliary *dávat/dát* together with an infinitive complement and a Direct Agent (Causee) in the dative case:

(22) Cz: Jan dal bratrovi napsat dopis.
Jan_{NOM} 'had' $\text{brother}_{\text{DAT}}$ $\text{write}_{\text{INF}}$ $\text{letter}_{\text{ACC}}$
'Jan had his brother write a letter.'

Bereich der Sprache und Kultur: Aufsätze und Studien. Abhandlungen der Sächsischen Akademie der Wissenschaften zu Leipzig, Historisch-philologische Klasse, 57, 1965, 2, pp. 15–19 (p. 18); Ronald Lötzsch, 'Zum Ausdruck der Kausativität in den slawischen Sprachen', *Zeitschrift für Slawistik*, 17, 1972, 3, pp. 360–70 (p. 368), and Toops, 'Causativity', p. 49.

[43] The two variants of each USo translation reflect the possibility of expressing past time either by means of the perfect tense or by means of the preterite tense.

[44] The USo use of *přez* + accusative in place of *wot* + genitive for the expression of passive Agents is not unknown, cf. *Šulerjo so nuzowachu wot/přez wučerja tutu knihu čitać* 'The pupils were being forced *by the teacher* to read this book' (Toops, 'Causative Constructions', p. 133). Cf. also Ger *durch* + accusative (*durch den Lehrer gezwungen* 'forced by the teacher'). H. Šewc-Schuster, *Gramatika hornjoserbskeje rěče*, 2 vols, Budyšin, 1976, 2 (*Syntaksa*), pp. 33–34, freely alternates between the USo prepositions *přez* and *wot* for the expression of Agents in passive sentences.

Although this description of the Cz factitive causative is straightforward, certain ambiguities can and do arise. First, the infinitive complement (here, *napsat* 'to write') is often prone to being construed as a purposive infinitive; if the infinitive is so construed, then the sentence, strictly speaking, assumes a noncausative reading: '?Jan gave his brother a letter to write'. Since *napsat* 'to write' is a *verbum efficiendi* and it is not possible to give someone something that does not yet exist, this particular reading, while conceivable, is unlikely; however, substituting *přepsat* 'to rewrite' for *napsat* 'to write' makes a 'donatory' re-interpretation of *dávat/dát* far more likely: *Jan dal bratrovi přepsat dopis* 'Jan gave his brother a letter to rewrite' (in addition to the factitive causative 'Jan had his brother rewrite the letter').[45] Second, since the infinitive *napsat* 'to write' is potentially ditransitive, the dative-case actant *bratrovi* may be interpreted as a Recipient or Beneficiary, rather than the Direct Agent, of the act of writing. If *bratrovi* were so interpreted, then Cz sentence (22) would mean either 'Jan had a letter written *to his brother*' or 'Jan had a letter written *for his brother*'.

From the perspective of morphosyntax, the corresponding USo causative construction is nearly identical to the Cz factitive causative exemplified by sentence (22), above:

(23) USo: Jan je swojemu bratrej list napisać dał. (~ Jan daše … list napisać.)
Jan is own_{DAT} $brother_{DAT}$ $letter_{ACC}$ $write_{INF}$ 'had'
'Jan had his brother write a letter.' ~
'Jan let his brother write the letter.'

With respect to semantics, this USo sentence is ambiguous relative to factitive vs. permissive causation. Nevertheless, the potential, multiple ambiguity described above for Cz sentence (22) does not arise in the case of USo sentence (23). There are several reasons for this. First, the USo infinitive complement cannot be interpreted as a purposive infinitive.[46] Second, in the preterite-tense variant of sentence (23), the causative auxiliary *daše* is distinct from the preterite of the verb 'give' (*da*), so that *Jan daše* cannot

[45] This is confirmed by one native speaker who formulated the following sentence: *Dal jsem bratrovi přepsat dopis, ale on jej nepřepsal* 'I gave my brother a letter to rewrite, but he did not rewrite it'.

[46] To express purpose, one would have to replace the infinitive verb form in USo sentence (23) with the syntagm *k napisanju*: *Jan je swojemu bratrej list k napisanju dał* (cf. Ger *Jan hat seinem Bruder einen Brief zum Schreiben gegeben*).

be interpreted as 'Jan gave'. Third, if the dative-case actant *swojemu bratrej* 'his brother' were intended to be a Beneficiary, it would be expressed today as *za swojeho bratra* 'for his brother'; and if it were intended as a Recipient, it would more idiomatically be expressed as *na swojeho bratra* 'to his brother' (cf. Ger *an seinen Bruder einen Brief schreiben* 'to write a letter to his brother'). Fourth, in both colloquial and 'informal standard' USo, Direct Agents in causative sentences are encoded not by the dative, but by the accusative case, as they are in Ger.[47] These facts are illustrated below by USo sentences (24)(a) through (24)(d):

(24) (a) USo: $^{?}$Jan je swojemu bratrej list *k napisanju* dał.
'$^{?}$Jan *gave* his brother a letter *to write*.'
(b) USo: Jan je *za swojeho bratra* list napisać dał.
'Jan had a letter written *for his brother*.'
(c) USo: Jan je *na swojeho bratra* list napisać dał.
'Jan had a letter written *to his brother*.'
(d) USo: Jan je *swojeho bratra* list napisać dał. (informal standard USo)
'Jan had his brother write a letter.'

One way to obviate the multiple ambiguity of Cz sentence (22) delineated above is to instantiate the causative auxiliary *nechávat/nechat* in place of *dávat/dát*:

(25) Cz: Jan nechal bratra napsat dopis.
Jan$_{NOM}$ 'let' brother$_{ACC}$ write$_{INF}$ letter$_{ACC}$
'Jan had his brother write a letter.' ~
'Jan let his brother write the letter.'

While the Cz causative auxiliary *nechávat/nechat* does not result in the potential ambiguity of the same causative relation that was formulated with *dávat/dát* in sentence (22), at the same time, by virtue of its being primarily permissive, *nechávat/nechat* yields a sentence which, like USo sentence (23), is ambiguous relative to permissive vs. factitive causation. In this regard, it should be noted that part of the ambiguity of Cz *dávat/dát* factitive causative constructions is resolved by the fact that Direct Agents (Causees) in *nechávat/nechat* constructions occur syntactically as objects

[47] See Gary H. Toops, 'Causative Constructions in Colloquial vs. Literary Upper Sorbian', *Die Welt der Slaven*, 57, 2012, 2, 322–32. The concept 'informal standard USo' is introduced there to provide an analogue to that variety of spoken literary Cz known as *hovorová čeština*.

in the accusative, rather than in the dative, case. In other words, owing to their syntactic exponency as accusative objects, such Direct Agents are not prone to being alternately read as Addressees (that is, Beneficiaries or Recipients).

If we reconsider Cz factitive causative sentence (22), above, it is clear that any ambiguity or polysemy that it might exhibit is due to a combination of three factors: (a) the potential purposive reading of the infinitive complement; (b) the fact that the infinitive is specifically a transitive verb; and (c) the fact that the direct object of the transitive infinitive can be alternately read as the direct object of the verb *dávat/dát* when it is interpreted as its (unintended) homonym, meaning 'give'. Essentially, it is these factors that have led some scholars to conclude (incorrectly) that Cz *dávat/dát* is productive as a causative auxiliary only in the formulation of passive-causative sentences (that is, for the expression of curative meaning).[48]

Two corollaries can be drawn from the foregoing observations. First, the fact that a particular causative construction (in this case, the Cz factitive causative incorporating the auxiliary verb *dávat/dát*) is potentially ambiguous *cannot* be taken to mean that it is unproductive. Second, if the infinitive complements of Cz factitive causatives expressed by means of *dávat/dát* are *intransitive* verbs, then the aforementioned factors contributing to the construction's ambiguity (or 'unproductivity') are precluded. Thus, sentence (26), with an intransitive infinitive complement, exemplifies a univocally factitive causative Cz sentence:

(26) Cz:	Policajt	dal	řidiči	fouknout	do balonku.[49]
	Policeman$_{NOM}$	'had'	driver$_{DAT}$	blow$_{INF}$	into breathalyzer
	'A policeman had the driver blow into a breathalyzer.'				

Similarly, even a transitive infinitive complement, provided it is a *verbum efficiendi* (that is, a verb denoting an action which produces or creates an

[48] See Anna-Maria Perissutti, 'Analytické kauzativní konstrukce v češtině', in A. Bičan, J. Klaška et al. (eds), *Karlík a továrna na lingvistiku. Prof. Petru Karlíkovi k šedesátým narozeninám,* Brno, 2010, pp. 355–67 (p. 365). It is appropriate here to quote Perissutti directly: 'The dative causative construction. This is a very rare, marginal construction. The matrix verb *d(áv)at* [sic] [...] is productive in contemporary Cz only in the PCC [= passive causative construction]' (translation mine — GHT). One suspects that, working in the field of corpus linguistics, Perissutti has mistaken frequency of occurrence for productivity.

[49] Perissutti, 'Kauzativní konstrukce', p. 366.

item that has previously not existed),[50] yields a complement that allows for the unrestricted use of *dávat/dát* as a factitive causative, cf.:

(27)	Cz:	Dám	krejčímu	ušít	nový	oblek.
		I-'will have'	tailor$_{DAT}$	sew$_{INF}$	new	suit$_{ACC}$

'I will have a tailor make the new suit.'
(*not* *'I will give the tailor a new suit to make.')

The frequent construction of Cz factitive causative sentences like (28) through (30), below, suggests, in any case, that the possibility of ambiguity in no way disinclines speakers of Cz from instantiating them:

(28) Cz: V kanceláři po semináři jsem dal své sekretářce přečíst své seminární pracovní materiály.[51]
'(While) in the office after the seminar, I had my secretary read the working materials for my seminar.' ~ '(While) in the office after the seminar, I gave my secretary my seminar working materials to read.'

(29) Cz: Petr dal Pavlovi vypočítat složitý příklad.[52]
'Peter had Paul work out a complex problem.' ~ 'Peter gave Paul a complex problem to work out.'

(30) Cz: Petr dal sekretářce opsat pro šéfa závěrečnou zprávu.[53]
'Peter had the secretary copy a final report for the boss.' ~ 'Peter gave the secretary a final report to copy for the boss.'

Indeed, Cz linguists M. Grepl and P. Karlík go so far as to classify Cz sentences like (29) and (30) as ones in which the dative-case objects (here *Pavlovi* and *sekretářce*) perform 'a dual semantic role, namely, [...] the role of "recipient/agent"' (translation mine — GHT).[54]

One temporal property of imperfective *dávat* that is often overlooked by linguists, although it constrains the verb's instantiation as a causative auxiliary, is its general (albeit not absolute) inability to denote progressive action, that is, a *præsens actuale* (including progressive action in the past

[50] Transitive verbs denoting actions that *affect* existing objects (*to read* [a book], *to give* [a present], and so on) are termed *verba afficiendi* and stand in contrast to *verba efficiendi*, which denote actions that *effect*, create, or bring into existence previously nonexistent objects (*to write* [a letter], *to build* [a house], and so on).

[51] Cited by Perissutti, 'Kauzativní konstrukce', p. 366, from the Czech National Corpus.

[52] Miroslav Grepl and Petr Karlík, *Gramatické prostředky hierarchizace sémantické struktury věty*, Brno, 1983, p. 62.

[53] Ibid.

[54] Ibid.

and future) of the causing act. Thus, the contextual causative exemplified as Cz sentence (2), above, cannot generally be paraphrased as a factitive causative by means of imperfective *dávat*. This is shown by the (near) ungrammaticality of sentence (31), below:

(2) Cz: Právě se holím (u holiče).
just-now REFL I-shave at barber's
'I am getting a shave (= having myself shaved) (at the barber's).'
(31) Cz: (*)Právě se dávám holit (u holiče).

Progressive causation can, in fact, be regularly expressed only by imperfective *nechávat*, despite occasional puristic attempts to restrict this verb to the expression of permissive causativity:

(32) Cz: Právě se nechávám holit (u holiče).
'I am getting a shave (= having myself shaved) (at the barber's).'

Along these same lines, Cz informants, when confronted with passive-causative sentence (33), below, generally interpret the imperfective past-tense causative *dávali* in an iterative, habitual sense rather than in a continuous, progressive one:

(33) Cz: Zahraniční zájemci si *dávali* popsat a vysvětlit technické přednosti některých strojů.[55]
'Foreign buyers *would have* (~ *used to have*) the technical advantages of certain machines described and explained to them.'

When native-speaker informants, moreover, are asked to confirm a progressive reading of the above sentence (that is, 'Foreign buyers *were having* the technical advantages of certain machines described and explained to them'), they typically propose substituting *nechávali* for *dávali*: *Zahraniční zájemci si nechávali popsat a vysvětlit technické přednosti některých strojů.*

Thus we see that the verb *nechávat/nechat*, by governing accusative-case objects that express Direct Agents (Causees), obviates potential ambiguities inherent in a variety of factitive causative sentences and that this causative auxiliary also enables or facilitates the expression of

[55] Šára et al., *Čeština*, p. 381.

progressive meaning (i.e., the expression of causing acts in the continuous present [*præsens actuale*], past, or future).[56] Although these two features of *nechávat/nechat* in themselves contribute to the unconstrained construction of factitive causative sentences in Cz, this causative auxiliary exhibits yet another, third morphosyntactic property not shared by *dávat/dát*, namely, the ability to govern not only infinitive, but also sentential complements. Sentences (34)(a) through (34)(c), below, exemplify a factitive causative sentence incorporating *dát* + infinitive, an ambiguously factitive/permissive causative sentence incorporating *nechat* + infinitive, and a primarily permissive causative sentence formed with *nechat* and a sentential complement in the subjunctive mood:

(34) (a) Cz: Dám krejčímu ušít nový oblek.
I-'will-have' tailor$_{DAT}$ sew$_{INF}$ new suit$_{ACC}$
'I will have a tailor make the new suit.'

(b) Cz: Nechám krejčího ušít nový oblek.
I-'will-let' tailor$_{ACC}$ sew$_{INF}$ new suit$_{ACC}$
'I will have/let a tailor make the new suit.'

(c) Cz: Nechám krejčího, aby mi ušil nový oblek.
I-'will-let' tailor$_{ACC}$ that-he me$_{DAT}$ may-sew new suit$_{ACC}$
'I will let the tailor make me a new suit.' (~ ?'I will have the tailor ...')

As has been shown elsewhere,[57] this last morphosyntactic property of *nechávat/nechat* also disencumbers the expression of factitive causative relations when multiple pronominal objects are involved, be they reflexive or nonreflexive. Thus, while the proposition *Hana$_i$ had him drive her$_i$ home* can be felicitously rephrased in Cz as passive-causative sentence (35)(a), below, it is more idiomatically expressed with *nechávat/nechat* and a sentential complement as in (35)(b), despite the latter's potential factitive/permissive ambiguity:[58]

[56] Cz sentences of the type *Dávám dítě spát* 'I am putting the child to bed ("putting the child to sleep")' or *Dávám dítě koupat* 'I am giving the child a bath ("putting the child to bathe")' exhibit direct objects in the accusative case, but they are not causative constructions. Since *dávat/dát* in such sentences is not a causative auxiliary, but rather the lexical verb signifying 'to give, put, place', its imperfective forms can, of course, receive progressive readings.

[57] Toops, 'Causativity', pp. 52–53.

[58] As in Ru example (1), the subscript *i* (also *j*) is used to indicate the coreferentiality of two constituents in a sentence.

(35) (a) Cz: Hana$_i$ se$_i$ dala od něj odvézt domů.[59]
Hana$_{NOM}$ REFL$_{ACC}$ 'had' from him$_{GEN}$ drive$_{INF}$ home
'Hana had herself driven home by him.'

(b) Cz: Hana$_i$ ho nechala, aby ji$_i$ odvezl domů.[60]
Hana$_{NOM}$ him$_{ACC}$ 'let' that-he her$_{ACC}$ may-drive home
'Hana had/let him drive her home.'

While USo *dać* resembles the Cz causative auxiliary *dávat/dát* in not governing sentential complements, the USo morphosyntactic equivalent of Cz sentence (35a), above, is nonetheless eminently idiomatic:

(36) USo: Hana$_i$ je so$_i$ wot njeho domoj wjezć dała.
Hana$_{NOM}$ AUX REFL$_{ACC}$ from him$_{GEN}$ home drive$_{INF}$ 'had/let'[61]
'Hana had herself driven home by him.'[62] ~
'Hana let herself be driven home by him.'

Finally, upon initial consideration of the Cz causative auxiliary *dávat/dát*, it was noted that this verb 'primarily' expresses factitive causation (see above). However, when negated, the causative auxiliary, besides expressing a negative factitive or a negative curative meaning (that is, 'not to have [someone do something]' or 'not to have [something done]', respectively), may also denote a negative *permissive* meaning ('not to let [somebody do something]'). This latter meaning — especially when the Indirect (Causing) Agent is inanimate — is tantamount to a denotation of prevention or prohibition.[63] The following Cz sentence may accordingly be interpreted in at least two ways, as indicated by its English translations:[64]

[59] This sentence is adapted from Toops, 'Causativity', p. 52.

[60] This sentence is adapted from ibid., p. 53.

[61] AUX designates here the past-tense (perfect-tense) auxiliary *być* 'to be'.

[62] As is often the case, the USo causative construction syntactically parallels its direct Ger translation: *Hana*$_i$ *hat sich*$_i$ *von ihm heimfahren lassen*. The idiomaticity of USo sentence (36) is underscored by the existence of an exact morphosyntactic parallel in colloquial USo: *Hana*$_i$ *jo so*$_i$ *wot no dómoj wezć dała* (Leńka Šołćic [Lenka Scholze], personal communication; 'colloquial USo' refers to *serbska wobchadna rěč* as described by Lenka Scholze, *Das grammatische System der obersorbischen Umgangssprache im Sprachkontakt*, Bautzen, 2008). In general, constraints on the occurrence of multiple pronominal objects in USo causative constructions are similar to those found in Ger; for example, 'Hana let him drive her home' can be expressed neither as **Hana hat ihn sich heimfahren lassen* nor as **Hana hat ihn sie heimfahren lassen* (see Nedjalkov, *Kauzativnye konstrukcii*, pp. 4 and 33 for further examples, as well as Toops, 'Causative Constructions', p. 123, note 32, for a fuller discussion).

[63] See Toops, 'Causativity', p. 48, note 25.

[64] See ibid., p. 51. A third, so-called 'modal passive' reading is also possible: 'Peter

(37) Cz: Petr se nedal ostříhat.
Peter$_{NOM}$ REFL$_{ACC}$ not-had/let tonsure$_{INF}$
'Peter did not have (~ get) his hair cut.' (negated factitive/ reflexive curative) ~
'Peter did not let [anyone] cut his hair.' (preventive, i.e., negated permissive)

The same ambiguity is inherent in the USo translation of Cz sentence (37):

(38) USo: Pětr njedaše sej włosy třihać. (~ Pětr njeje sej włosy třihać dał.)
Petr$_{NOM}$ not-had/let REFL$_{DAT}$ hairs$_{ACC}$ cut$_{INF}$
'Peter did not have (~ get) his hair cut.' ~
'Peter did not allow his hair to be cut.'

Other examples of Cz sentences that express the prevention of an action by means of *dávat/dát* + infinitive include the following:[65]

(39) Cz: On mi nedal domluvit.
'He did not let me finish speaking.'
(40) Cz: Tato myšlenka/bolest mu nedala spát.
'This thought/pain did not let him sleep (~ kept him from sleeping).'
(41) Cz: Zvědavost jí nedala nezeptat se. ~ Zvědavost jí nedala, aby se nezeptala.
'Curiosity did not let her refrain from asking.'
(Literally: *'Curiosity did not let her not ask.')

As suggested by the second variant of sentence (41), above, the specific meaning of prevention denoted by the negated causative *dávat/dát* exceptionally allows this verb to govern *sentential* complements (introduced by the complementizer *aby-*) in addition to the infinitive complements

could not be given a haircut ~ Peter's hair could not be cut'. This reflects the semantics of the biaspectual, reflexive modal auxiliary verb *dát se* in Cz, which finds a functional equivalent in the Ger *sich lassen* construction (cf. Ger *Peters Haare ließen sich nicht schneiden* 'Peter's hair could not be cut'). While the cognate USo modal *dać so* exists, its synonym *hodźeć so* is more common. Thus, to Cz *To se dá udělat* and Ger *Das lässt sich machen* 'That can be done', USo usually responds with *To hodźi so činić* (cf. H. Jentsch [Jenč], H., S. Michalk [Michałk], and I. Šěrakowa [comps.], *Němsko-hornjoserbski słownik / Deutsch-obersorbisches Wörterbuch*, 2 vols, 1989–1991, 2 [*L–Z*], p. 11).

[65] Sentences (39) through (41) are reproduced from Toops, 'Causativity', p. 49. For some speakers of Cz, sentence (39), *On mi nedal domluvit*, is somewhat archaic and more felicitously expressed as *On mě nenechal domluvit* 'He did not let me finish speaking'.

by which Cz causative *dávat/dát* constructions are otherwise strictly characterized. Corresponding *dać* constructions in USo, in contrast, do not exhibit sentential complements as syntactic exponents of 'preventive' meaning.

Autosemantic causative constructions

Cz and USo have similar inventories of autosemantic causative verbs that denote either permissive or factitive causation.[66] The Eng glosses provided below for these inventories are approximate, since the semantics of several autosemantic factitive causatives coincide, a fact which results in their being not only synonymous (or nearly so) but, often, intersubstitutable:

(42) *Cz autosemantic causatives*
domlouvat/domluvit 'to talk into (doing something)'
dovolovat/dovolit 'to allow'
nutit/donutit 'to force'
nutit/přinutit 'to compel'
pohnout 'to induce'
přemlouvat/přemluvit 'to persuade'
přesvědčovat/přesvědčit 'to convince'
přimět 'to make (someone do something)'
svádět/svést 'to tempt, entice, lead (someone to do something)'
uprašovat/uprosit 'to implore, prevail upon'
zavazovat/zavazat 'to oblige, obligate, commit'

Several explanations of the above inventory are in order. First, the Cz imperfective causative *nutit* 'to force, compel' is aspectually paired with two suffix-derived perfective verbs, *donutit* and *přinutit*.[67] Prefixed imperfective derivatives of these two verbs exist — *donucovat* and *přinucovat* — but they are often described by native-speaker informants as being or sounding 'artificial'. Nevertheless, they occur in formal writing, particularly in passive sentences denoting general (that is, iterative) and/or negated acts of compulsion, cf.: *Nikdo nemůže být donucován vykonávat vojenskou službu* 'No one can be compelled to perform military service',

[66] Among the autosemantic causatives in either Cz or USo, there is only one with permissive meaning, Cz *dovolovat/dovolit*, USo *dowolećl/dowolić* 'to allow, permit'.

[67] In the view of some native speakers of Cz, *přinutit*, unlike *donutit*, can occur only with subjects that denote *human* Indirect Agents (Causers); I have therefore chosen to gloss *přinutit* as 'compel'. Cf. *Dešť nás donutil* (/??*přinutil*) *zůstat doma* 'Rain forced (/??compelled) us to remain at home'. Where the Indirect Agent is human, *donutit* suggests 'getting' someone to do something, while *přinutit* denotes force or compulsion, cf.: *Matka mě donutila* (/*přinutila*) *jít k lékaři* 'Mother got (/forced~compelled) me to go see a doctor'.

Nikdo z horníků nesměl být přinucován těžit na jednom místě 'None of the miners could be forced to mine in [only] one place'.[68] Second, each of the Cz autosemantic causatives enumerated above may govern either infinitive or sentential complements with no difference in cognitive meaning. And third, the imperfective forms of these verbs are often nonimplicative by virtue of their potentially conative semantics, i.e., the meaning of *attempted* (rather than successfully or completely executed) causation.[69] (Note, however, that the Cz verbs *pohnout* and *přimět*, above, are strictly implicative perfective causatives with no imperfective partners.)

The inventory of autosemantic causatives in the USo literary language includes the following verbs:

(43) *USo autosemantic causatives (literary language)*
dowoleć/dowolić 'to allow'
naręčeć 'to talk into, prevail upon'
nućić 'to force'
nuzować 'to force'
pohnuć 'to induce'
pozbudźeć (~ pozbudźować) / pozbudźić 'to compel'
přeręčeć 'to persuade'
přeswědčeć (~ přeswědčować) / přeswědčić 'to convince, persuade'
zawjazować/zawjazać 'to oblige, obligate, commit'

The USo inventory of autosemantic causatives, above, also requires several explanatory remarks. First, several causatives are unpaired

[68] These sentences are drawn, respectively, from Nejvyšší soud ČR, 'K trestnosti trestného činu vyhýbání se výkonu vojenské služby spáchaného z náboženského přesvedčení', *Rozsudek 6 Tz 144/98* <http://spcp.prf.cuni.cz/judikat/ns144-98.htm> and Martin Mikula, *Základy lomařství*, p. 2 <http://www.volny.cz/martin.mikula/index_soubory/Zaklady%20 lomarstvi. doc> [both accessed 29 April 2012]. According to informants, the past passive participles *donucován* and *přinucován* in either sentence can each be replaced by the simple participle *nucen* (< *nutit*) with no change of cognitive meaning. An online Google search of *donucován*, *donucována*, *donucováni* and *donucovány* on 12 December 2012 produced 22,800, 821, 4,660, and 563 results, respectively; a similar Google search of *přinucován*, *přinucována*, *přinucováni*, and *přinucovány* produced 136, 71, 213, and 38 results, respectively. These results suggest that while the past passive participles of both verbs are in common use, the participial forms of *donutit* are considerably more common than those of *přinutit*. In stark contrast, a search of the plural masculine past passive participle of *nutit*, *nuceni*, alone produced 1,320,000 results.

[69] The conative semantics of imperfective autosemantic causatives is sometimes reflected in dictionaries; for example, Ivan Poldauf (comp.), *Czech-English Dictionary / Česko-anglický slovník*, 1st edn, Prague, 1986, p. 624, defines imperfective *přemlouvat* as 'try to induce | get a p. to' while defining perfective *přemluvit* as 'persuade', 'induce | get a p. to', and 'make (he made me do it)'.

imperfective or perfective verbs: the synonyms *nućić* and *nuzować* signifying 'to force' are both imperfective and thus are not strictly implicative. In contrast, the verbs *naręčeć* 'to talk into', *pohnuć* 'to induce', and *přeręčeć* 'to persuade' are unpaired perfective verbs (*perfectiva tantum*).[70] Second, various bilingual dictionaries of USo cite prefixed, perfective-aspect partners to *nućić* and *nuzować* — among them *donućić*, *ponućić*, *přinućić*, *znućić*, and *přinuzować* — but the existence of such verbs in actual language use is not acknowledged by contemporary speakers of USo.[71] In the Sorbian colloquial language (*serbska wobchadna ręč* — see note 62), moreover, *nućić* (a cognate of Cz *nutit*, see above) does not exist, while colloquial USo *nuzwać* (< *nuzować*) coexists with imperfective (and equally nonimplicative) *cwingwać*, a morphological adaptation (loanword) of Ger *zwingen*.[72] Just as bilingual dictionaries of USo cite artificial, prefix-derived perfective partners to *nućić* and *nuzować*, so some of them also cite artificial, suffix-derived imperfective partners to *pohnuć* 'to induce' and *přeręčeć* 'to persuade' (namely, *pohnuwać* and *přeręčować*, respectively). Third, like the Cz causatives enumerated in (42), above, the USo causatives listed in (43) may govern either infinitive or sentential complements — usually, but not always, with no difference in cognitive meaning (see below) — while imperfective USo causatives may have conative readings as well.

The grammaticality of the following Cz sentences reveals that the complements of autosemantic causatives may be indiscriminately infinitive or sentential. Sentential complements are typically introduced by the complementizer *aby-*, which encodes the subjunctive mood:

(44) (a) Cz: Můj přítel mě donutil/přinutil jít s ním/sebou do kina.
my friend$_{NOM}$ me$_{ACC}$ forced/compelled go$_{INF}$ with him/REFL to cinema

[70] In colloquial USo, the perfective causative *naręčeć* is neither perfective nor causative; rather, it is an aspectually neutral verb signifying 'to address, speak to (someone)' and thus a morphological calque of Ger *ansprechen*.

[71] Some dictionaries also cite secondarily derived imperfective forms of these artificial, albeit theoretically imaginable, prefixal perfectives, among them *donućeć*, *donućować*, *ponućeć*, *přinućeć*, *přinućować* and *znućeć* (see Toops, 'Causative Constructions', p. 130, note 33).

[72] See Toops, 'Colloquial', for details. Being nonimplicative, colloquial USo *cwingwać* corresponds semantically to Ger *drängen* 'to urge (someone to do something)' rather than to Ger *zwingen* 'to force'.

(b) Cz: Můj přítel mě donutil/přinutil, abych s ním šel do kina.
my friend$_{NOM}$ me$_{ACC}$ forced/compelled that-I with him would-go to cinema
'My friend forced/compelled me to go to the cinema with him.'

Because the causative verbs in sentences (44)(a) and (44)(b), above, are aspectually perfective, the implication that 'I went with him (my friend) to the cinema' cannot be retracted or contradicted; this is demonstrated by the infelicity of sentences (45)(a) and (45)(b):

(45) (a) Cz: *Můj přítel mě donutil/přinutil jít s ním/sebou do kina, *ale přesto jsem zůstal doma.*
(b) Cz: *Můj přítel mě donutil/přinutil, abych s ním šel do kina, *ale přesto jsem zůstal doma.*
*'My friend forced/compelled me to go to the cinema with him, *but I stayed home nonetheless.*'

In contrast, substituting imperfective *nutit* for perfective *donutit* or *přinutit* yields sentences that are felicitous:

(46) (a) Cz: Můj přítel mě *nutil* jít s ním/sebou do kina, ale přesto jsem zůstal doma.
(b) Cz: Můj přítel mě *nutil*, abych s ním šel do kina, ale přesto jsem zůstal doma.
'My friend *tried to make* me go (~ *tried to get* me to go) to the cinema with him, but I stayed home nonetheless.'

The imperfective causative's conative meaning is reflected not only in the English gloss 'tried to make' or 'tried to get', above, but also by the fact that sentences (46)(a) and (46)(b) can be paraphrased even in Cz by employing the verb *snažit se* 'to try' in conjunction with perfective *donutit* or *přinutit*, cf.: *Můj přítel se mě snažil donutit/přinutit jít s ním/sebou do kina ..., Můj přítel se mě snažil donutit/přinutit, abych s ním šel do kina ...*[73]

The synonymous USo factitive causatives *nućić* and *nuzować*, both glossed as 'to force', are, somewhat ironically, *imperfectiva tantum* and as such generally convey (in noniterative contexts) no more than attempted

[73] A Google search of the Cz phrase 'se mě snažil donutit' (+ infinitive or sentential complement) on 15 December 2012 yielded 1,020 results; a similar search of 'se mě snažil přinutit' yielded 267 results.

causation. While autosemantic causatives in both Cz and USo govern either infinitive or sentential complements, USo sentential complements may further be predicated either in the subjunctive mood (as in Cz) or in the indicative mood. Use of the indicative mood in USo sentential complements is no doubt the result of Ger influence and characterizes both colloquial and informal standard USo:[74]

(47) (a) USo: Sym jeho nućił tutu knihu čitać, ale wón ju tohodla njeje čitał.
I-am him_{ACC} forced this $book_{ACC}$ $read_{INF}$ but he_{NOM} her_{ACC} still is-not read

(b) USo: Sym jeho nućił, zo by tutu knihu čitał, ale wón ju tohodla njeje čitał.
… that he-would this $book_{ACC}$ read …

(c) USo: Sym jeho nućił, zo wón tutu knihu čita, ale wón ju tohodla njeje čitał.
… that he_{NOM} this $book_{ACC}$ reads …
'I tried to make/force him to read this book, but he still did not read it.'

Sentences (47)(a) through (47)(c), above, are synonymous. Sentence (47)(a) exhibits an infinitive complement; sentence (47)(b) — a sentential complement in the subjunctive mood; and sentence (47)(c) — a sentential complement in the indicative mood. For certain older speakers of USo (for example, those born prior to World War Two), logical implicature can be achieved even with aspectually imperfective causatives like *nuzować*, at least in past time frames, in sentences where the perfect tense of the autosemantic causative (for example, *je nuzował*) is instantiated in place of the preterite (that is, *nuzowaše*),[75] cf.:

(48) (a) USo: Wučer *nuzowaše* šulerjow tutu knihu čitać (… ale žadyn z nich ju njeje čital).
'The teacher *tried to make* the pupils read this book (… but none of them did).'

[74] Cf. Ger sentential complements in the indicative mood after verbs like *veranlassen* 'to cause, induce' and *zulassen* 'to permit, tolerate': *Der Vater veranlasst (/lässt zu), dass seine Tochter mit ihrem Freund ins Tanzlokal geht* (example mine — GHT) 'The father causes (/permits) his daughter to go to the dance club with her boyfriend' (literally, 'that his daughter *goes* …').

[75] See Toops, 'Causative Constructions', pp. 130–32.

(b) USo: Wučer *je* šulerjow *nuzował* tutu knihu čitać (* … ale žadyn z nich ju njeje čitał).
'The teacher *made* the pupils read this book (* … but none of them did).'

Occasionally, USo sentential complements of even perfective causatives (like *přeswědčić* 'to persuade, convince'), if the former are predicated in the subjunctive mood, may constrain the causative verb's strict logical implicature. This is due to a potential *debitive* reading of sentential complements in the subjunctive; therefore, infinitive complements may be preferred.[76] Accordingly, the USo causative construction illustrated by (49)(a) is preferable to that illustrated by (49)(b), below:

(49) (a) USo: Přeswědčich swojeho bratra sej nowy dom natwarić dać (*… *ale wón sej tohodla njeje žadyn natwarić dał*).
'I persuaded my brother to have a new house built for himself (*… *but even so, he did not have one built*).'
(b) USo: Přeswědčich swojeho bratra, *zo by sej nowy dom natwarić dał*, ale wón sej tohodla njebudźe dać žadyn natwarić.
'I persuaded my brother *that he should have a new house built for himself*, but he still will not have one built.'

Concluding remarks

We have seen that Cz exhibits four different types of causative constructions: (a) contextually causative constructions, (b) conventionally implicative 'give'-constructions, (c) synsemantic causative constructions, and (d) autosemantic causative constructions. Since USo has no contextual causatives, it shares with Cz only causative constructions (b), (c), and (d). However, even in Cz the ability of accusative-reflexive constructions (of the type *Právě se holím [u holiče]*) to express curative meaning contextually (that is, 'Right now I am having myself shaved [at the barber's]') now appears to be obsolescent.[77] The 'give'-constructions are the most alike in the two languages, although their productivity is constrained by pragmatic factors. The inventories and morphosyntactic properties of autosemantic causative verbs are very similar in Cz and USo; nevertheless, whereas Cz has two

[76] Ibid.

[77] The apparent obsolescence of Cz accusative-reflexive constructions as contextual causatives stands in stark contrast to those in contemporary Ru, where corresponding sentences of the type *Ja sejčas brejus´* (*u parikmachera*) are subject to no morphosyntactic restrictions (apart from the reflexive pronoun *sebja*) in their expression of curative meaning (that is, 'I am now having myself shaved [by a barber]'). See Toops, 'Contextual Causatives', pp. 604–05, for additional details.

perfective, aspectually unpaired causative verbs (*pohnout* and *přimět*), USo has several austosemantic causatives that are strictly *imperfective* and thus potentially nonimplicative. While autosemantic causatives in both languages govern either infinitive complements or sentential complements in the subjunctive mood, USo also exhibits sentential complements predicated in the indicative mood; moreover, USo sentential complements in the subjunctive mood may receive a debitive reading, which can affect strict logical implicature.

The most complex parallels between Cz and USo, in terms of causative expression, involve the synsemantic causatives. While USo resembles Ger in having only one, biaspectual (or aspectually neutral) causative auxiliary *dać*, Cz has the aspectually paired auxiliary *dávat/dát*. Although the latter is a cognate of USo *dać*, the USo verb imitates the Ger causative auxiliary *lassen* by ambiguously expressing both factitive and permissive meanings and by occurring strictly with infinitive complements. Cz *dávat/dát*, in contrast, is primarily (albeit not exclusively) factitive but, like USo *dać*, also occurs generally with infinitive complements. Both permissive causation and factitive causation in Cz are ambiguously expressed by a second causative auxiliary, *nechávat/nechat*, which occurs (for the most part, optionally) with either infinitive or sentential complements. Both Cz causative auxiliaries — *dávat/dát* and *nechávat/nechat* — are instantiated in passive-causative sentences; such Cz sentences, however, reveal varying lexical constraints on the expression of Direct Agents (that is, 'to have something done *by someone*') in either the instrumental case or as objects of the preposition *od*. In USo passive-causative sentences, which pattern syntactically more like their Ger analogues, such constraints on the expression of Direct Agents (as objects of the prepositions *wot* or *přez*) do not exist.

A Need for Greater Openness: The Countryside in Czech Fiction since 1989

RAJENDRA A. CHITNIS

In *The Country and the City*, Raymond Williams rides a metaphorical escalator back through English literary history, noting how writers repeatedly return from 'the city' to 'the country' to lament the destruction of a better, more 'organic' way of life. The conception of 'the country' is not identical in each case:

> What seemed a single escalator, a perpetual recession into history, turns out, on reflection, to be a more complicated movement: Old England, settlement, the rural virtues — all these, in fact, mean different things at different times, and quite different values are being brought into question. We shall need precise analysis of each kind of retrospect, as it comes.[1]

The persistence of these returns, however, in all urbanized literatures, seems to Williams to reflect 'some permanent or effectively permanent need, to which the changing interpretations speak'.[2] Most basically, 'the country' represents for human beings their origins, an 'other' against which their present state may be measured, both positively and negatively:

Rajendra A. Chitnis is a Senior Lecturer in Czech and Russian Studies at the University of Bristol.

[1] R. Williams, *The Country and the City*, Oxford and New York, 1973, p. 12.

[2] Ibid., p. 289. In his discussion of the 'regional novel', which includes both rural and urban writing, Keith Snell also rejects the notion of decline in favour of cyclicality. He notes that regional-novel publishing emerges most strongly 'during periods when older interior ways of life were being threatened economically, and when changes in familiar and psychological "landscapes" affected even those who were economically secure, who were the majority readership'. K. D. M. Snell, 'The Regional Novel: Themes for Interdisciplinary Research', in idem (ed.), *The Regional Novel in Britain and Ireland, 1800–1990*, Cambridge, 1998, pp. 27–28.

Slavonic and East European Review, 91, 3, 2013

> On the country has gathered the idea of a natural way of life: of peace, innocence, and simple virtue. On the city has gathered the idea of an achieved centre of learning, communication, light. Powerful hostile associations have also developed: on the city as a place of noise, worldliness and ambition; on the country as a place of backwardness, ignorance, limitation.[3]

'The country' may serve as a measure not only of humanity's decline from the ideal, but also of its progress from the primitive. It may not only be advocated, but also tested or mocked as a better way of life, a place of potential escape or source of redemption for 'the city'. A definition of rural writing must therefore include any text for which analysis of the representation of 'the country', as a setting, concept or metaphor, produces a complete interpretation.

'Returns to the Rural' in Czech Literature

Williams's notion of cyclical 'returns to the rural' is exemplified in the history of Czech literature since at least the early-nineteenth-century National Revival. These returns have generally reflected a desire to retreat from excessive openness to alien influences to the strong, comforting embrace of national tradition. In the 1880s, patriotic intellectuals criticized Czech writers for threatening the nation's very existence by abandoning the native literary tradition for superficial imitations of fashionable foreign literature.[4] The 1930s Ruralists responded similarly to the left-wing avant-garde.[5] In the 1950s, in imitation of the concurrent collectivization of agriculture, Czech Stalinist writers seized 'the country' from the predominantly Roman Catholic rural right and enclosed it within Socialist Realism, while during the 1970s Normalization, conformist writers set the 'normality' of the collectivized countryside against the 'abnormality' of the 'Western-inspired' 'reform-Communism' of the 1968 Prague Spring.[6]

[3] Williams, *The Country and the City*, p. 291.

[4] For a discussion of rural fiction in this period, see R. A. Chitnis, 'Putting *Granny* in a Home: Czech Writers and the Village in Kafka's Lifetime', in M. Engel, R. Robertson (eds), *Kafka, Prag und der Erste weltkrieg / Kafka, Prague and the First World War*, Würzburg, 2012, pp. 107–25.

[5] For a discussion of the Ruralists' poetics, see J. Š. Kvapil, *Venkov v současné české literatuře*, Prague, 1944.

[6] Pavel Janoušek argues that, during the Normalization, the rural setting represented for some 'the opportunity to argue that at least in the village, unlike in towns and factories, something visibly new and different and relatively functioning had been created, that is, something like real Socialism'. P. Janoušek, 'Co s tou kolektivizací? Aneb případ zrádné Daniely aneb pokus o Mamuta' (2006), in his *Hravě i dravě*, Prague, 2009, p. 76.

In these periods, the *Ur-Text* of Czech rural writing, *Babička* (The Grandmother, 1855) by Božena Němcová (1820–62) is often evoked, for example, in the 1880s as a model for writers to emulate, or through the 1940 and 1971 film versions. The grandmother, a pious, humble, intuitively patriotic woman who passes on to her grandchildren the model of a self-sacrificing life lived in harmony with Nature and folk wisdom, was presented as a national ideal to which Czechs should return for succour and inspiration, though *Babička* is itself better understood as part of another instance of Williams's 'rural retrospect' in Czech literary history. From the 1890s onwards, rural writers repeatedly try to re-imagine the ideal, closed, rural national space in notionally epic, increasingly anachronistic texts that endeavour to reverse the perceived speed and fragmentation of modern urban literature and life, typified by the monumental novel cycle *Naši* (Our Folk, 1897–1930) by Josef Holeček (1853–1929). Each time, however, the 'return to the rural' is overwhelmed by anxiety. Most writers find the rural ideal only in an unrecoverable past, and view 'the city' — progress, education, economic power — as either the unstoppable cause of the devastation of 'the country' and human beings, or the only source of their recovery.

The Twenty-First-Century Czech 'Return to the Rural'

The present study is devoted to a 'precise analysis' of the 'return to the rural' in early-twenty-first-century Czech fiction, which — as a phenomenon — has gone largely unrecognized by Czech critics, despite producing many of the most admired books of the decade. As in the late nineteenth century, this 'return to the rural' has no single ideological basis, but signals a shift in the preoccupations of Czech literature or the terms in which it explores them. After the fall of Communism in 1989, the countryside had all but disappeared from Czech fiction. A comprehensive survey of 1990s Czech literature makes no mention of it.[7] Then, in 2001, 'the country' suddenly returned in four of the most widely discussed books of the year — by Květa Legátová (b.1919), Jáchym Topol (b.1962), Miloš Urban (b.1967) and Ludvík Vaculík (b.1926) — and the trend continued in the following years.

The authors involved form a panorama of contemporary Czech literature, from those born early in the First Republic (Legátová, Vaculík) to those with no adult memory of the Communist period (Petra Hůlová, b.1979). It includes writers associated with sanctioned fiction (Antonín Bajaja, b.1942), dissidence (Vaculík) and the underground (Topol) under

[7] See L. Machala, *Literární bludiště*, Prague, 2001.

Communism, and writers who emerged only after 1989 — Urban, Radka Denemarková (b.1968), Jiří Hájíček (b.1967) — writers long interested in rural themes (Bajaja, Legátová, Vaculík) and writers who have either moved decisively from 'the city' to 'the country' (Topol) or oscillate between them (Hůlová). Their work, however, seems commonly motivated by a desire to disturb the prevailing, illusorily comfortable stagnation of 'the city, connected perhaps with post-Communist society's perceived failure to break with the myths, attitudes and behaviour of the preceding decades. Unlike their predecessors, 2000s rural writers therefore return to 'the country' seeking not security and stability, but greater 'openness', understood variously as intellectual curiosity, adaptability, empathy, direct contact with Nature, the willingness to revisit prevailing accounts of twentieth-century Czech history or the desire to escape national introversion for the debates of the wider world.

Denemarková and Hájíček present 'the city' as a source of enlightenment and progress. For the others, however, it is a place of homogenized, passive, complacent space of consumerism, convenience, superficial sophistication and illusory security, synonymous with the pro-Western, pro-business, 'global' liberal consensus that dominated the post-Communist Czech political establishment, media and public life. 'The country', by contrast, is forgotten, a place one visits for recreation rather than lives and works. Writers dramatize the rediscovery of 'the country' by showing characters move from 'the city' to 'the country', or by 'moving' the reader to the countryside, sometimes back in time or abroad, where 'the country' exists in a way it no longer does in the Czech Republic. Topol, a 'mystic of Prague', was widely considered in his third novel, *Noční práce* (Night Work, 2001), to have moved himself from the city to the countryside.[8]

'The country' in Czech rural fiction has historically been synonymous with the village. Unlike their late-nineteenth-century counterparts, however, the 2000s writers do not need to dispel urban illusions about idyllic village life, which exists only as an extension of the urban or a festering relic. As Ondřej Horák notes, novelists, like historians, merely investigate the causes of its fate:

> What is the situation in the Czech village and why? Was its structure — especially on the edges of the republic — destroyed as early as 1938, when it became important who was German, Czech or Jewish? Or is today's

[8] L. *Housková, 'Topolova cesta z města'*, *Tvar*, 13, 2002, 3, p. 17.

village more scarred by forty years of Communist unified agriculture? Did November 1989 provide a new impulse for the village, or was it the last nail in the coffin when people began to move to towns for work?[9]

Since the cultural liberalization of the 1960s, writers like Vaculík, in his 1966 novel *Sekyra* (translated as *The Axe*), have blamed the destruction of the village way of life, and the contemporary Czech's definitive separation from the countryside, on the post-war collectivization of agriculture.[10] In an interview published in March 1989, Vaculík's fellow east Moravian, Bajaja, a cattle breeder since 1964, described the change:

> When I started, cooperatives were not yet being merged. Where there had been a village, you had a collective farm. And in some villages there were more private farmers than cooperative farmers. Family, neighbourly relations dominated among ordinary people. There were still farmers working in the cooperatives who had put their property into them. Today it is their children, grandchildren, relatives or completely different people, who have come just to make a good living.[11]

In his view, 'cooperatives are now agricultural-industrial cooperatives. The basic rights of cooperative workers are the same as in industry. Alienation from the soil and from animals is growing everywhere'.[12] This alienation pervades Bajaja's bold 1988 novel, *Duely* (Duels), which echoes the then unavailable *Sekyra* in its portrayal of villages as homogenized, anonymous dormitories, where understanding between generations has broken down.[13]

Vaculík's *Cesta na Praděd* (Journey to Praděd, 2001) is based on a journey that he made in August 1966, as a Prague-based journalist, on horseback and by horse and cart from central Bohemia to north Moravia's

[9] O. Horák, 'Posílám nějaké peníze, s úctou Hitler', *Lidové noviny*, 28 June 2006, p. 20.

[10] In its content and timing, this 'analysis' coincides with the criticism in identical terms of EEC agricultural policy by the emerging ecological movement in the West, exemplified by E. F. Schumacher's *Small is Beautiful* (1973, Czech translation, 2000). The publication of the first major post-Communist historical account of the collectivization coincided with the beginning of the 2000s 'return to the rural' (see K. Jech, *Soumrak selského stavu, 1945–60*, Prague, 2001).

[11] P. Frýbort, O. Neff, 'Literatura má být i zemitá', *Kmen*, 1989, 13, p. 4.

[12] Ibid.

[13] Of *Duely*, Alice Jedličková writes: 'the fathers' generation seems to have vanished. Indeed, because it was this generation which caused the rupture, the generation which, in building better tomorrows, forgot not only their forebears, but also those for whom they wanted to build them'. A. Jedličková, 'Duely bez sekundantů', *Literární měsíčník*, 18, 1989, 10, pp. 140–41 (p. 140).

highest mountain. The text was more than half written in 1966, but not completed until 2001. The narrator says of the villages he sees:

> Neither village, nor town. Neither past, nor future. A loss of memory. The desertion and denial of true origins. The villages in this poor region beside the River Sázava still take their living from the fields, but in 1966 without great confidence in them [...]. Everywhere it is the same and I see it everywhere. I have visited so many such places that they merge for me into one horrendously typical place, a place seen in high fevers or bad dreams. The main village buildings always laid out identically and the same for all the walls, so that to climb over the wall means to find yourself where you were before. It makes no difference whether you speak to no one or everyone. A total loss of long-term memory. They don't know where they have come from, and I don't know where I am.[14]

This homogenization eradicates the natural diversity given by each village's name, the shape of its fields, its trees, the speed of the water in its stream, the views from its windows and doorways: 'The Bohemian village as an artistic living-space, which said something to poets and composers, must be considered a thing of the past.'[15]

For the 2000s Czech rural writers, the traditional idea of the village either no longer exists or repels them as a symbol of ideological propaganda. They are therefore liberated to explore the alternative connotations and uses of 'the country' in early-twenty-first-century literature. The close reading in this study begins with Denemarková and Hájíček, for whom the decay of the village leaves only 'the city'. I then turn to writers who choose instead to look beyond the contemporary ruined village for a more powerful idea of 'the country', located in either the open countryside or the countryside of the past. I end with discussion of two Hůlová novels that serve as commentaries on 'the return to the rural'.

Opening the Past

From Hájíček's *Selský baroko* (Peasant Baroque, 2005) to Denemarková's *Peníze od Hitlera* (Money from Hitler, 2006) to Topol's *Noční práce* and *Kloktat dehet* (2005, translated into English as *Gargling with Tar*), the village serves as an increasingly explicit metaphor for a society that stubbornly rejects openness and enlightenment in favour of reassuring prejudices and

[14] L. Vaculík, *Cesta na Praděd*, Brno, 2001, p. 58.
[15] Ibid., p. 185.

myths. *Selský baroko* still echoes Vaculík's regretful portrayal of the village as a victim of external forces. The novel is set in the author's home region of South Bohemia, paradigmatically idealized by Holeček as the cradle of Czech nationhood, but here beset by unemployment, under-education and alcoholism. Hájíček unequivocally condemns collectivization for devastating agriculture and a once admirable rural way of life, notably in a passage in which the history of the embedding into Czech of the word 'kulak' (the Stalinist Russian label for a land-owning farmer) is implicitly shown to parallel the twentieth-century decline of rural and public life.[16] This decline is encapsulated in the account of a pub that only opens when the landlord gets home from his job in town.

Hájíček's villagers are, however, prejudiced and devious. They mistrust and mock the narrator, Pavel, an archivist and local historian, because of his university education and non-manual profession, and drive away his well-meaning, city-born wife. The 'baroque' political machinations that Pavel uncovers are unchanged between the collectivization and the early twenty-first century. Short of money, Pavel accepts a mysterious commission to establish why, in the early 1950s, three wealthy farmers were imprisoned and lost their land. He discovers that one had made a peasant woman pregnant, but denied paternity. In revenge, she wrote to the police, informing them of the farmers' illegal gambling, and the police seized the opportunity to present their meetings as a plot. In 2004, the woman's illegitimate son is standing for mayor, and his opponents want the information to discredit him. When Pavel refuses to give it to them, it is stolen by Daniela, a woman in their pay, who seduces him.[17]

Daniela embodies the ambiguity of the rural in the novel. She reminds Pavel of his ex-wife, except for an indefinable difference, explained when she turns out to be the grand-daughter of one of the farmers, who is fighting to have his land returned. Unlike Pavel's less tenacious wife, Daniela comes from tough, pre-collectivization farming stock, and has not given up, but will do anything to achieve her aim. Hájíček wants to find hope in the rural, but cannot. His difficulty is encapsulated in Pavel's inability to reconcile the unreliable historical memory of local people and the rational precision of his laptop memory.[18] Unable to find Daniela's spirit among

[16] See J. Hájíček, *Selský baroko*, Prague, 2005, pp. 21–23.

[17] Janoušek argues that Daniela could not have deceived Pavel because he would have begun researching her genealogy through the paternal line. See Janoušek, 'Co s tou kolektivizací?', p. 77.

[18] Hájíček's approach superficially recalls Graham Swift's *Waterland* (1983, in Czech 1993), in which the purpose of historiography is explored in the context of painful personal

the rural '*lumpenproletariat*' produced by industrialized agriculture, Hájíček reluctantly concludes that the task of reviving the countryside and preserving what remains of the traditional 'peasant baroque' architecture is better left to rich 'in-comers' from 'the city' with the know-how and respect.

Hájíček's ambivalence stems from his identification with Pavel, who is torn between the rural and urban. In *Peníze od Hitlera*, by contrast, Denemarková's initial proximity to the perspective of her central character, Gita, results in the demonization of the village. Gita's view of the village is shaped by her experiences, but those experiences seem merely to confirm the implied author's existing stereotypical negative urban expectations. After the German occupation of Czechoslovakia, Gita discovers her Jewish ancestry and is sent with her family to a concentration camp. When she returns home in 1945, her father's factory and the family house have been seized by local Czechs, who consider her a Sudeten German, imprison her in a barn and attempt to starve her to death, as they had her brother a few weeks before. In 2005, their descendants fiercely resist her efforts to reclaim her property. Their use of illegally obtained psychiatric reports forces Gita to tell how, in the 1950s, she was gang-raped and saw her infant son murdered by Prague youths, including one with origins in her home village. For Gita, with her idyllic memories of childhood, it is the Occupation that changed the Czech village. Denemarková, however, implies that Gita has merely been forced to abandon her naive illusions and recognize the permanent 'inherited vulgarity and callousness' of the Bohemian village.[19]

The seizure of Gita's family property amounts to a barbarian invasion of urban civilization, an implicit metaphor for the fate of Czechoslovakia from 1938 to 1989 that, for Denemarková, has yet to be fully reversed. As an adolescent in 1945, Gita wishes she could say to the villagers eating from her family porcelain:

> I am Gita Lauschmannová. The daughter of an educated mother, who was brought up in the city, wore the scent of European cafés and found it so hard to get used to life here. So my father built her this rectangular country house. In the village they called this grand building with puzzled envy the little chateau. I am Gita Lauschmannová. The daughter of a hard-working man, who employed and fed most of the grubby layabouts around here.[20]

and local history in the East Anglian Fens.

[19] R. B. Pynsent, untitled review, *Central Europe*, 4, 2006, 2, pp. 176–77 (p. 177).

[20] R. Denemarková, *Peníze od Hitlera*, Brno, 2006, p. 26. Gita's story is based on the case

Gita voices here the perceived values of the bourgeois capitalist First Czechoslovak Republic, instantly discredited in the Communist period, but notionally restored after 1989. In 2005, the elderly Gita declares: 'I don't want to be compensated as a *German*. I want to be compensated as a human being to whom an injustice has been done. Like a human being, a citizen, who has been unjustly treated.'[21] These 'civic' notions of justice, transparency and human rights, so important to the post-1989 urban intelligentsia, mean nothing to the village. Throughout the novel, urban sophistication, which is shown to breed decency, contrasts with rural coarseness — not created but nurtured by Nazism and Communism — which breeds brutality. The village is repeatedly represented by images of intimidating, Neanderthal masculinity, fleshy lips and masticating jaws; the only villager with any conscience is a terrified, bullied woman who has moved into Gita's house, but helps the adolescent Gita escape and later wants her to regain the property. Otherwise, only 'the city' is kind; a sensitive military officer saves Gita from expulsion and enables her to return to relatives in Prague. Positive characters, like Gita, speak in the standard Czech of educated people, while the villagers use dialect, littered with slang and swear-words, and are unable to understand the figurative use of language. Their cruel intransigence contrasts with Gita's planned gesture of giving up her property in return for a monument to her father.

Towards the end, however, Denemarková unexpectedly softens her position. Milena Marešová writes:

> Denemarková at first makes frank and fierce accusations. She tears out deeply rooted evil, claws open scars and makes the pain all the sharper by showing that the originators and protagonists of the very worst things were fellow countrymen, neighbours and local people. At the very end of the book, however, the author incomprehensibly and against all logic makes light of her accusations, relativizing and undermining all that had already been said and argued.[22]

Denemarková moves closer to the indecisive position of Denis, the terrified woman's son, now an orthopaedic surgeon in Prague and, like Hájíček's narrator, caught between 'the country' and 'the city'. Denis initially

of a real family from Puklice, near Jihlava. See L.Vilímek, 'Sága rodu Fischmannů' <http://www.regionalist.cz/vilimek/vil01_36.htm> [accessed 22 July 2012].

[21] Ibid., p. 222.

[22] M. M. Marešová, 'Román o nenávisti a zrazená hrdinka' <http://www.rozhlas.cz/kultura/literatura/_zprava/269794> [accessed 22 July 2012] (para. 5 of 6).

responds to his roots and becomes the village's champion against Gita, until her plan for a monument stirs the decency he has learned in the city. His feverish efforts to help Gita cause his sister to disown him, but do not achieve Gita's aims. In despair, he tells her: 'You know best of all that I am the last person who would want to defend the residents of Puklice. But… they mostly behave like this out of ignorance, the historical context confuses them.'[23] In keeping with the prevailing rhetoric in Czech society, he then emphasizes the incomparably brutal behaviour of local Germans during the occupation. Gita stops listening, all too accustomed to the village's — Czech society's — inability to understand. Denemarková, however, sympathizes with Denis; Gita dies with a new, troublesome memory of her father wearing a swastika armband 'so our lot (*naši*) leave us in peace'.[24]

Both *Peníze od Hitlera* and *Selský baroko* demonstrate what Françoise Mayer characterizes as the triumph of the 'non-political' view in post-Communist Czech efforts to 'come to terms' with their post-war history. Despite efforts to heroize, demonize, commiserate and condemn, Mayer suggests that the past has returned '"without incident" to those people, who were not Party cadres, former prisoners or dissidents, who under the Communists managed somehow not to be either for or against them and who ultimately form the overwhelming — silent — majority of the population'.[25] Hájíček prefaces his novel with an admiring dedication to his father, who worked uncomplainingly as a driver in industrial Ostrava after his father's land in South Bohemia was collectivized, and was 'rewarded' after 1989 with the chance to drive tourists round Europe. The only possible response to the past, Hájíček suggests, is to acknowledge and move on. Janoušek notes:

[23] Denemarková, *Peníze od Hitlera*, p. 221.

[24] Ibid., p. 238.

[25] F. Mayerová, *Češi a jejich komunismus*, trans. H. Beguivinová, Prague, 2009, pp. 258–59. This 'silent' majority was heard in a manner strongly reminiscent of the villagers' treatment of Gita during the 2013 Czech presidential election, when outgoing president Václav Klaus and his family sought to present the eventually defeated aristocrat, Karel Schwarzenberg, as not merely insufficiently patriotic, but insufficiently Czech to hold the office. As a child, Schwarzenberg fled to Austria with his family following the Communist takeover, and speaks Czech with a marked accent. He nevertheless supported the anti-Communist opposition and returned in 1990 to head President Havel's administration. Klaus declared that he favoured a president who had experienced recent Czech history first-hand and that he could 'never forgive' Schwarzenberg for characterizing the post-war expulsion of Sudeten Germans as a violation of human rights; his son falsely suggested that Schwarzenberg's father was a Nazi sympathizer, and his wife expressed her discomfort at the prospect of a First Lady who spoke German, but not Czech.

> The image of the village to which collectivization gave birth and which pro-Communist literary works helped to reconstruct has been more or less accepted by a large part of Czech society. It looks as though we have moved on, and many of us behave in a way that shows no desire to return to something that would cast too much doubt on our present way of life.[26]

Denemarková's novel begins with an image of digging, but eventually, like Hájíček, she chooses to compromise between the rural desire to bury, and the urban desire to investigate. The result, Pynsent argues, is enough 'to please the Czech intelligentsia; a work of self-righteous national sentimentalization'.[27]

Opening the Mind

Denemarková and Hájíček 'accommodate' the reader, rendering the past superficially attractive by emphasizing its relevance to the present and making kitsch use of popular literary forms. Topol, by contrast, is not interested in making his readers comfortable, but asks them instead to abandon shared, received opinions for the alarming, uncertain solitude of intellectual freedom, symbolized by the dangerous countryside beyond the village. His move from the city to the village in *Noční práce* appears to have been prompted by a desire to confront Czech nationalist mythology at its heart. In 2002, he praises the post-Communist media for changing Czechs' understanding of the expulsion of the Sudeten Germans:

> There is most probably the blood of twenty to thirty thousand murdered people on Czech hands. We have a victim complex: Russians are evil, Germans are evil, whereas we, with our 'sweet little village', are really nice little people, with our clean hands and Hrabalian mug of beer. By the way, [the film director] Jiří Menzel [b.1938] with his films bears his share of guilt for this unproblematic understanding of [the writer Bohumil] Hrabal [(1914–97)]. We like to erase any cruelty, any wounds or scars that we have caused anyone. That disgusts me.[28]

[26] Janoušek, 'Co s tou kolektivizací?', p. 76. Memoirs by Czech writers who grew up from the 1950s onwards tend to recall visiting rather than living in the countryside as children. For example, in *Kráčel po nestejně napjatých lanech* (He Walked Along Ropes of Different Tensions, 2007, translated into English as *Tightrope!*), Olga Walló (b.1949) nostalgically describes visits to her grandmother's farm near Hradec Králové.

[27] R. B. Pynsent, 'Conclusory Essay: Activists, Jews, the Little Czech Man, and Germans', *Central Europe*, 5, 2007, 2, pp. 211–333 (p. 331).

[28] J. Chuchma, 'Snad se v nás neprobudí démoni', *MF Dnes*, 3 May 2002, p. B8. Topol uses sarcastic diminutives to mock the cosy, sycophantic image of rural Bohemia found

For Topol, after the organized brutality, massacres and expulsions to which the Czech countryside was subjected and in which Czech rural people collaborated, the renewed idealization of the Czech village in the 1970s and 1980s Normalization evokes what Theodor Adorno called the barbarism of writing poetry after Auschwitz.[29]

In his 2000s novels, Topol shows how contemporary society seeks to petrify the past through the 'institutionalization' of twentieth-century history in education, public discourse and museums. This institutionalized identity recalls Freud's notion of the 'cultural *Über-Ich*'. Freud writes:

> It can be asserted that the community, too, evolves an *Über-Ich* under whose influence cultural development proceeds [...]. The *Über-Ich* of an epoch of civilization has an origin similar to that of an individual. It is based on the impression left behind by the personalities of great leaders, men of overwhelming force of mind or men in whom one of the human impulsions has found its strongest and purest, and therefore often its most one-sided, expression [...]. Another point of agreement between the cultural and the individual *Über-Ich* is that the former, just like the latter, sets up strict ideal demands, disobedience to which is visited with 'fear of conscience'.[30]

In Topol's novels, authorities like the police, army, religious orders, academic historians, ministries of culture, the EU and political dictatorships collaborate to protect this established identity from disruption. In *Kloktat dehet*, boys in an orphanage who 'tell lies' are made by the nuns to gargle tar. In *Noční práce*, a local state security commander orders: 'End obscurantism. To end it once and for all, to put a stop to evil, that is our night work.'[31] Topol associates this 'cultural *Über-Ich*' with the national idyll of the village. His novels since 2001 portray a flight not from the urban to the rural, but from this static, infantile dream to the 'adulthood' of 'the country' understood positively as Freud's *Es*, a place of permanent dynamic chaos and absent authority, where, through constant testing, the

paradigmatically in *Vesnička má středisková* (My Sweet Little Village, 1985), an enduringly popular Menzel film, written by Zdeněk Svěrák (b.1936) in the spirit of Menzel's earlier Hrabal adaptations. In *Noční práce*, the village neighbours Zásmuky, the birthplace of František Kmoch (1848–1912), the father of *dechovka*, patriotic Czech wind band music that shares the jolly, collectivizing sentimentality of these films.

[29] See B. O'Connor (ed.), *The Adorno Reader*, Oxford and Malden, MA, 2000, p. 210.

[30] S. Freud, *Civilization and its Discontents*, trans. James Strachey, Harmondsworth, 2002, pp. 106–07.

[31] J. Topol, *Noční práce*, Prague, 2001, p. 138.

self attains ever greater wisdom and independence. The authorities in fact seek to preserve 'obscurantism'; Topol considers it his 'night work' to resist them.

The embodiment of the 'cultural *Über-Ich*' is the village pub in *Noční práce*, an archetypal Czech setting, and the village orphanage in *Kloktat dehet*, which both act as a metaphors for a Bohemia that imprisons its people in a den of patriotic fairy-tales.[32] As in *Peníze od Hitlera*, the village in *Noční práce* is portrayed as hellishly hot. Topol writes: 'The pub was full. Old women were sitting in the hall on sacks of potatoes, chatting. In the hall it was almost dark. You could smell the lavatories there. Yellow flypaper was hanging from the pub ceiling, full of flies. The flies, buzzing, were crawling over one another, coiling up in the slime, constantly trying to fly away.'[33] The flies recall those 'shitting' on the Emperor's portrait in the pub in *Osudy dobrého vojáka Švejka za světové války* (The Fortunes of the Good Soldier Švejk in the Great War, 1921–23) by Jaroslav Hašek (1883–1923). The link is made explicit when one regular suggests that, to attract a younger clientele, a picture of Švejk should be taken down and replaced by a photograph of the singer Karel Gott, the modern embodiment of the amoral Czech survivor.[34] Like Denemarková's village, the pub and orphanage are the preserve of crass, intimidating men, who treat young boys as a captive audience for their outlandish opinions and stories, typified by Mr Cimbura in *Kloktat dehet*. His name, as Horák points out, ironically recalls the idealized Bohemian farmer in the canonical 1908 rural novel, *Jan Cimbura*, by Jindřich Šimon Baar (1869–1925).[35] A symbol of the decaying national myth, Topol's Cimbura grows increasingly infirm and deformed.

In both novels, this decay is disturbed by ill-defined external events. The images of incoming Red Army soldiers, displaced people, mass emigration

[32] In *Noční práce*, a history teacher has a comic epiphany after being struck on the head: 'I've been lyin' to schoolchildren me whole life [...] I tormented them with made-up heroic epics about our race' (ibid., p. 183). The truth about the founding of Bohemia, apparently, is that Forefather Čech was too lazy to go any further and was left with the old, the sick, pregnant whores, alcoholics with depression and children no one wanted, who somehow survived and multiplied.

[33] Ibid., p. 25.

[34] In his first novel, *Sestra* (Sister, 1994, translated as *City Sister Silver*), Topol's narrator gives this type the name 'Josef Vissarionovich Švejk'. The picture of Švejk is no doubt by Josef Lada, whose naive drawings epitomize the comforting twentieth-century myth of Czech identity, and make Hašek's protagonist and the Czech countryside almost impossible to visualize differently.

[35] O. Horák, 'Pravda o válce s pěti armádami', *Lidové noviny*, supplement 'Orientace', 8 October 2005, p. 6.

and confusion evoke two periods in post-war Czech history, May 1945 and August 1968, when the national narrative briefly descended into the flux that Topol favours. Topol maximizes the reader's disorientation with a chaotic narration designed to represent a child's 'un-institutionalized' reception of events, filtered through his imagination, the books he has read and the things he has been told. These two periods promised 'liberation', but ended in the conformity of Stalinism and the Normalization respectively. In *Noční práce*, with its epigraph from Georg Büchner's *Woyzeck*, the adolescent hero, Ondra, like his namesake Andres (Ondra in Czech) in Büchner's play, resists absorption into the madness that consumes his surroundings. By contrast, the village in *Noční práce*, and the permanent child, Ilja, in *Kloktat dehet*, bear comparison to Woyzeck, whose acceptance of ever greater degradation and brutality drives him mad, until he becomes an agent of violence himself.

In keeping with the Freudian parallel, both Ondra and Ilja are seeking their fathers, but only Ondra, a lover of 'Boys' Own'-style stories, which he lives out in the woods, learns to abandon this quest. Near the end of the novel, he rebels against the stifling mediocrity of the 'cultural *Über-Ich*', declaring in the pub: 'I don't want a life like this [...] I don't want it!'[36] Soon after, he realizes that the man driving him and his brother into emigration is not their father, but the village's leading collaborator, who is going to hand them over to the Russians. Ondra vows to change forever, to stop doing what others order him and stop expecting anything from anyone else. Martin Pilař writes: 'Ondřej is tested and leaves the blessed world of the child's imagination. His younger brother, Malej [Little 'un], remains on the level of childish amazement.'[37]

The contrast between movement and stasis in *Noční práce* is captured in the opening image of the frozen river surface, under which the water continues to flow, a metaphor for time in Communist Czechoslovakia before the 'Thaw' of the 'Prague Spring'. At the height of the 'thaw', a pub regular recalls how — during the war — parents threw their children from a train passing through the village, and the villagers drowned the children

[36] *Noční práce*, p. 226.

[37] M. Pilař, 'Bůh má pořád indiánský rysy... Kultovní román?', *Host*, 18, 2002, 1, p. 10. Several critics note the autobiographical parallel of Jáchym and his younger brother, the musician Filip (b.1965). Jaromír Slomek points out that 'while [their father, the playwright and poet, Josef Topol (b.1935)] experienced a proper rural childhood, for his sons it was already a matter of summer trips into uncertain terrain'. J. Slomek, 'Druhý pokus o paměti?', *Lidové noviny*, 3 November 2001, p. 16. Pavel Mandys claims that Josef Topol moved his family to the countryside in the wake of the Warsaw Pact intervention. See P. Mandys, 'Krvavý vesnický román', *Týden*, 19 November 2001, p. 81.

in the river for fear of reprisals if they protected them. They cannot, however, remember whether the children were Jewish or Sudeten German. The river is no longer frozen, time is flowing and liberation seems possible, until the Russians come. Like the dancer-narrator, Potok (meaning 'stream') in *Sestra*, Ondra is associated with this flow, which symbolizes endless renewal and freedom. He hides a boat, which he dreams of taking to a distant rural utopia where his tribe can start again:

> He thought of a valley, far away and cold. The snow there gleams because the sun is shining. There is snow everywhere, even on the branches. He also saw people. They were standing under trees. They were all his people, people with whom he wanted to be. He will find faces and names for them. He will not be alone there, certainly not. It will be quiet there.[38]

Ondra and Malej escape in their boat just as the river is starting to freeze again and the village is on fire. As at the end of Topol's second novel, *Anděl* (Angel, 1995), the burning village signifies purification, the eradication of evil, and the chance for a new beginning, at least for Ondra, Malej and the implied reader.

Ondra has to act as a father to Malej, who cannot walk after being hit by a car. By contrast, in *Kloktat dehet*, Ilja's handicapped brother is killed by orphans in a scene reminiscent of William Golding's *Lord of the Flies*, and Ilja thus remains a child throughout the novel. Critics routinely compare him to Oskar Matzerath in Günter Grass's *Die Blechtrommel* (The Tin Drum, 1959), but he is more like Hrabal's short, amoral waiter Jan Dítě (John Child) in *Obsluhoval jsem anglického krále* (translated as I Served the King of England, 1989), another novel influenced by Grass, because he does not 'refuse' to grow up, but is not allowed to by his institutionalized upbringing. The novel's opening — 'They called me Ilja'[39] — alludes to *Říkali mi Leni* (They Called Me Leni, 1948, revised 1959) by Zdeňka Bezděková (1907–99), in which a girl growing up in post-war Germany gradually realizes that she is really a Czech, who was selected for 're-germanization' during the Occupation after the execution of her father. Like Leni, Ilja is a Czech in a German setting, and he travels around the countryside seeking a father, just as Leni seeks her homeland. Topol thus implicitly presents Bezděková's novel — recommended reading in Czech schools under Communism — as an instrument of the nationalist

[38] *Noční práce*, p.251.
[39] J. Topol, *Kloktat dehet*, Prague, 2005, p. 7.

indoctrination it purports to criticize.[40] Given Topol's rejection of the affectionate 'domestication' of both Hrabal and Švejk, *Kloktat dehet* may be read as a radical attempt to remind the reader of the insanity of conformity at the heart of *Obsluhoval jsem anglického krále*. Just as Dítě's story follows Czech history from the First Republic to the early 1950s, so Ilja's story may be read as a fantastic retelling of that history from 1945 to 1989. In 1945 — or 1968 — Ilja, an average Czech, whose name derives from the braying of an ass and perhaps — like Leni — evokes Vladimir Il′ich Lenin, adopts a Soviet army captain as his father and collaborates with the Russians, but at the end of the novel kills the captain and returns proudly to Bohemia with plans — in imitation of old Cimbura — to write his story.

The contest between the institutionalization and what Topol calls the 'revitalization' of history returns in his fourth novel, *Chladnou zemí* (Through a Cold Land, 2009), which satirizes international efforts to transform the sites of twentieth-century atrocities into sanitized objects of consumption, 'houses of horrors' conforming to current mythologies and the needs and expectations of foreign tourists. In Bohemia, this process appears complete. Having failed to protect his home town of Theresienstadt, a transit ghetto for European Jews during the Second World War, from this fate, the narrator travels to Belarus, where the accounts of the experience of the Belarusian countryside put the Czech story of martyrdom and suffering into perspective. Here, the frozen countryside is not a place of potential liberation or renewal, but a mass grave hiding the full extent of twentieth-century Central European violence and waiting for more dead. The narrator joins a like-minded group striving to preserve this countryside as a graveyard-museum, 'The Devil's Workshop', an antidote to the pastoral idyll. The president, however, decides instead to build a motorway through it. The Belarusian campaigners do not despair: 'there is still time for a museum like this in this country. Do you know why? Because the Devil is still damn hard at work here!'[41] For them, as for Potok in *Sestra*: 'only wars lost in advance, only they are interesting.'[42] Topol and his heroes will keep moving out to the perilous periphery to continue their 'night work', and hope the reader might join them.

[40] For a discussion of this view of Bezděková's novel, see R. B. Pynsent, 'The Ideologization of the Child: Zdeňka Bezděková and Marie Majerová', *Central Europe*, 9, 2011, 1, pp. 32–58.

[41] J. Topol, *Chladnou zemí*, Prague, 2009, p. 137.

[42] J. Topol, *Sestra*, Prague, 1994, p. 452.

Opening the Heart

While Topol uses a wild, unfamiliar setting and disorientating style to dramatize the opening of the mind, in *Želary*, Legátová uses a similar strategy to test the capacity for empathy of an urban reader who has implicitly grown complacent about the fate of other human beings. Her objective is captured in the name of her fictional village, which derives from *želet*, meaning to 'pity', 'deplore' or 'grieve for'. *Želary* is set in poor, isolated south-east Moravia, where Legátová worked as a school-teacher after the Second World War, but the action is moved back to the 1930s, in Horák's view to challenge the Czech idealization of life in the First Republic.[43] In this interpretation, what Denemarková presents as a model of democracy, decency and sophistication becomes synonymous with the urban self-satisfaction that Legátová seeks to disturb. Judging by the enthusiastic reception of *Želary*, 'the city' had been longing for just such a lesson from, in effect, a new 'grandmother', a voice of ageless wisdom and truth, emanating from the pure countryside, untouched by contemporary 'civilization'. Much to Ludvík Kundera's irritation, reviewers accepted the publishers' claim that *Želary* was the eighty-two-year-old author's first work, when in fact between the late 1940s and 1970s Legátová, whose real name is Věra Hofmanová, had written several radio plays and two books of rural fiction under the pseudonym Věra Podhorná.[44]

In *Želary*, Legátová thus self-consciously continues the line of female ethnographic writing that runs from Božena Němcová (1820–62) in the 1840s through Karolína Světla (1830–99), Růžena Svobodová (1868–1920), Božena Víková-Kunětická (1862–1934) and Jarmila Glazarová (1901–77) to the 1940s Silesia-based works of Ludmila Hořká (1892–1966). Mojmír Trávníček notes that in *Želary* the 'traditional motifs of rural fiction are laid marvellously bare almost to their archetypes'.[45] This effect is achieved by shattering the chronology of the text, which reflects the experience of the grandmother in one story, whose 'world is disintegrating like the world of a child into a thousand little fragments'.[46] Each story contains pieces of a larger jigsaw puzzle, which Legátová asks the reader patiently to examine individually and put together, not only in imitation of the author's own process of recollection, but also as a gesture towards those characters

[43] See O. Horák, 'Zlí samotáři, to je balada', *Revue Labyrint*, 2002, 11–12, pp. 169–70 (p. 169).

[44] See L. Kundera, 'Rozpomenutí', in K. Legátová, *Pro každého nebe*, Prague, 2003, pp. 7–10 (p. 7).

[45] M. Trávníček, 'Pozoruhodná prvotina', *Tvar*, 12, 2001, 20, p. 20.

[46] K. Legátová, *Želary*, Prague, Litomyšl, 2001, p. 226.

and their forgotten lives. The book, which is presented as a cycle of self-contained stories, thus effectively becomes, as several critics have argued, a Modernist rural novel.[47]

Legátová pointedly distinguishes between characters that do and do not possess the will or ability to approach the villagers, especially children, without prejudice. Those that do not are typically — like the implied reader — comfortable, educated outsiders. Štěpán Vlašín highlights the juxtaposition of the 'irritable, bossy schoolteacher and the patient and understanding parish priest'.[48] The schoolteacher never loses the sarcastic sense of superiority which he brings with him: 'I got to know the village through a series of slapstick events.'[49] Legátová presents the whole educational establishment as a failure, incapable of helping those in its care. The teacher is compared unfavourably to the priest, who tells him:

> 'We make our biggest mistakes with children. The child's soul is a flower yet to blossom.' The teacher brightened. 'I'd like to know what would make Vratislav Lipka blossom.' 'Vratislav Lipka really deserves our sympathy.'[50]

The priest's sensitivity allows him to recognize the qualities and talents hidden in the children, but also exposes him to debilitating doubt, which undermines his capacity actively to help. He lacks strong faith in God and his lenience at confession makes one parishioner lose hope of absolution. Ultimately, like the teacher, he is rendered powerless by the discrepancy between his ideal of humanity and the imperfect reality. He preaches: 'Only when you cease being slaves of the world, when you find good in humility, when you prove capable of unconditional love, when faith is for you no longer a chain of burdensome duties, but a blessing and a gift of which you are not worthy, only then will you become Christians.'[51]

The implied author seems to agree with this judgement, frequently contrasting poor children's capacity to find joy in simple things with the

[47] See, for example, P. A. Bílek, 'Událost, či text?', *Souvislosti*, 13, 2002, 1, pp. 224–27.

[48] Š. Vlašín, 'Povídky z Valašska', *Obrys-Kmen*, 2002, 9, p. 2.

[49] *Želary*, p. 66.

[50] Ibid., p. 60. Lipka is the son of a mining engineer, who raped a peasant woman while drunk and has no idea of Lipka's existence. Lipka's mother dies in childbirth and, like Ilja in *Kloktat dehet*, he is sent to an orphanage run by nuns, but runs away back to his home village.

[51] Ibid., p. 124. In an interview, Legátová notes that she is not a Roman Catholic, but 'in the 1950s and 1960s I found my best friends in the villages among priests. It is a shame that their strength and moral principle is disappearing'. M. Homolová, 'Tajemství paní učitelky z kopanic', *Lidové noviny*, 11 November 2001, p. 25.

selfishness and self-pity of adults. She doubts, however, that human beings will ever change. She prefers the approach of the herbalist who, unlike the teacher and priest, has no high expectations of her fellow villagers, which liberates her to help them. The local doctor claims that his practice would fail without her. The herbalist intuitively understands her people and watches over them, almost mysteriously appearing whenever illness or injury strikes, but wise enough to use the hospital when necessary. She voices the priest's (and Legátová's) implicit advocacy of compassion rather than chastisement, drunkenly declaring to a stunned visiting churchman:

> The Old Testament God does have the qualities of a strict, punishing father. The New Testament God is a Mother [...]. Immeasurable love for that which is born from us, willingness to forgive, sacrifice and pity, that is the essence of a Mother [...]. God the Mother is the home we abandon to conquer the world and our whole lives we seek him again, call for him, hurt, humbled, burdened with guilt. We betray God the Mother in moments of Pride and call for Her in moments of Disaster because only God the Mother will take our suffering on Herself.[52]

Vratislav Lipka is not reached by authority or reason, but by intuitive experiences of empathy, whether on hearing verse by Jaroslav Seifert (1901–86), or falling asleep among barn animals. Legátová writes: 'Animals inculcated timidity in him, they taught him patience and let him see freedom as the basic principle of life.'[53] It is 'the country', not 'the city', that gives him insight into his existence. On finding a corpse in the snow, he thinks: 'The human being is nothing more than any other creature who has been swallowed by the winter.'[54] The remark may be read as Old Testament judgement, mocking the modern urban human being's illusions of superiority, or New Testament love, reminding human beings that they belong to Nature and share its vulnerability.

The Return to Nature

Bajaja and Vaculík share Legátová's view of 'the country', its animals and its physically harder way of life as a pre-eminent source of insight into human existence. For them, as for Urban, renewed experience of Nature may not only reawaken sympathy for other human beings, but also restore balance to the lives of excessively urbanized human beings, for their own sake and

[52] *Želary*, p. 192.
[53] Ibid., p. 130.
[54] Ibid., p. 132.

the sake of their environment. Bajaja and Vaculík's portrayal of Prague as inimical to a healthy, happy life follows a model established by their fellow Moravian, Vilém Mrštík (1863–1912), in his 1890s novels. In *Cesta na Praděd*, inhabitants of the city are depressed, exhausted, insomniac and physically and mentally ill, their fragile condition epitomized by a young Czech man determined single-handedly to bring about a Sorbian national revival by writing verse in Upper Lusatian. His ambition comically reflects the city's muddled yearning for authenticity and purpose. In Bajaja's *Duely*, a Moravian farmer's daughter moves to Prague after the war to marry an ardent Stalinist, develops a Prague accent and a love of Socialist fake folk songs, is divorced twice and becomes estranged from both her parents and her children. In *Zvlčení* (Becoming Wolfish, 2003), the marriage of Prague-based couple Tomáš and Markéta is in trouble, while their niece has moved from the countryside to Prague only to become trapped in an abusive relationship with a drug addict.

The narrator of *Cesta na Praděd* is accompanied on his journey by Josef Zeman, the unconventional director of a farming school, and some of his 'apprentices', a term that reflects the ideological bias of the industrialization of the countryside. He hopes to rediscover a way of life that, like Zeman, is 'older, harder and manlier'.[55] People lived 'half outside the law', survival was harder, but personal freedom was greater. Vaculík's company decide not to take supplies, because 'to travel in the awareness that every day you have to work for the next day's bread, to travel on and on because you cannot stay long in one place, that is a different story and a different responsibility! Travelling players, grinders, rag-and-bone men, pipers and tinkers did not have it easy!'[56] This plan would please the elderly farmer in *Duely*, who complains that collective farm workers are paid regardless of the quality of the harvest, when in fact 'they should come to know [hunger] while there is still time'.[57] By returning to 'the country', human beings may prepare themselves for tougher times to come, and even find the resolve to avert them.

Vaculík repeatedly rues the replacement of horses by cars, which have transformed the human being's attitude to space, time, other beings and his or her place in the world. The narrator asserts: 'One of the features of

[55] *Cesta na Praděd*, p. 20.

[56] Ibid., p. 30. This reference to the freedom and comradeship of travelling workers and players recalls the Gor′kii-influenced cycle, *O zlých samotařích* (On Evil Loners, 1913), by Ivan Olbracht (1882–1952) and the anarchism-tinged 'communism' of Vladislav Vančura (1891–1942).

[57] A. Bajaja, *Duely*, 2nd edn, Prague, 2005, p. 198.

the new Czech is an inability to orientate himself in his landscape. He can no longer imagine movement in it that is not motorized.'[58] The rider uses elements of his being that the motorist has all but forgotten. The horse, as the agent of the fastest natural speed that a European human being can experience, provides a natural limit to the human being's conception of how quickly something can be achieved. Moreover, by copying the horse's constant submission to the undulations of the earth, the human being might relearn humility. E. F. Schumacher quotes Aquinas: 'It is evident that if a man practises a compassionate affection for animals, he is all the more disposed to feel compassion for his fellow men.'[59] Vaculík writes: 'If today the number of horses and different lives in general is in decline on this, their one and only earth, then it seems to me our sense of respect for horses and other lives in general is threatened, for which we shall ultimately pay ourselves, and perhaps more heavily than horses.'[60] All contemporary human beings apparently need to do is get out of their cars and onto horses, but that, as the narrator says of his own journey, is 'a simple thing, so hard to bring about'.[61]

The interference of technology in the relationship between human beings and domestic animals features in Bajaja's pre-1989 fiction.[62] In *Zvlčení*, however, he explores the extent of the human being's separation from Nature by paralleling the lives of a human and a wolf family, brought together in the east Moravian mountains. John Berger argues that animals constituted the first 'other' for human beings:

> Animals interceded between man and their origin because they were both like and unlike man. Animals came from over the horizon. They belonged *there* and *here*. Likewise they were mortal and immortal. An animal's blood flowed like human blood, but its species was undying and each lion was Lion, each ox was Ox. This — maybe the first existential dualism — was reflected in the treatment of animals. They were subjected *and* worshipped, bred *and* sacrificed.[63]

[58] *Cesta na Praděd*, p. 158.
[59] E. F. Schumacher, *Small is Beautiful*, London, 1974, p. 89.
[60] *Cesta na Praděd*, p. 87.
[61] Ibid., p. 5.
[62] Bajaja's 1986 story 'Koleda, koleda' (Here We Come a Wassailing) wryly portrays how technical innovations steadily distance cattle from those who live and work with them. It ends with a prediction for 2002: 'Where is the world in which every cow had a name?'. A. Bajaja, 'Koleda, koleda', in J. Kostrhun (ed.), *Velké vlhké oči: Skot pro 3. tisíciletí: Sborník povídek*, Slušovice, 1986, p. 44.
[63] J. Berger, 'Why Look at Animals?', in his *Selected Essays*, ed. G. Dyer, London, 2001, p. 261.

For Berger, this symbolic relationship with animals has been lost through industrialization and corporate capitalism. In *Zvlčení*, Bajaja seeks to recreate it.

In *Zvlčení*, Tomáš and his sister, Jitka, from a Prague bourgeois family, are married to Markéta and Jiří, siblings from an east Moravian game-keeping family. Tomáš, Markéta, their lawyer-daughter, and their niece first travel east from Prague to the mountains following the death of Markéta's father, a symbol of an older way of life that has definitively passed. Their journey for them is from the tame to the wild. The wolf family, by contrast, are driven to the same mountains from Transylvania. Their migration recalls that of the ancient Czech tribes to Bohemia at the beginning of Vančura's first *Obrazy z dějin národa českého* (Scenes from the History of the Czech Nation, 1939). Like the primitive Slavs, 'the emaciated beasts are urged on by the idea of a place providing sufficient prey and peace and quiet'[64] and, as in Vančura's text, their journey is from the wild east to the tamer west.

The east Moravian mountains are one of the least developed, most peripheral Czech settings, but for the wolves, the evidence of the encroachment of 'the city' on 'the country' — vehicles, litter, stray domestic animals — is overwhelming. Jiří complains that game-keeping has become more a matter of accountancy than forestry. Like Hůlová and Topol, who go outside the Czech Republic, to Mongolia, Siberia and Belarus, to find a genuine 'rural', Bajaja voices Czech writers' frequent sense that their land lacks a sufficiently wild, exotic space, particularly since the loss of Sub-Carpathian Ruthenia, which served this purpose for writers like Olbracht, Vančura and Karel Čapek (1890–1938) during the First Republic. The wolves are greeted by a hoarding advertising beer, a symbol of both urbanization and domesticity that comes to mark one edge of their new territory. The question, however, becomes whether the modern human being is willing to live alongside them.

Bajaja suggests that the wolf fascinates human beings because they recognize so much of themselves in them. Like the human being, the wolf, on entering an environment, requires all other creatures there to adjust to its presence:

> The wild animals adapted [to the danger] through increased caution, and gradually realized that wolves also have qualities that permit co-existence,

[64] A. Bajaja, *Zvlčení*, Brno, 2003, p. 19.

> that their days are subordinated to rules and that (like the human being) do not always have the intentions of hunters in mind.[65]

Bajaja also demonstrates the likeness by describing in parallel the changing nature of love-making as the wolf and human couples grow older and more familiar with one another, and using the same words to describe each couple's attempt to come to terms with the death of offspring.

What separates the wolf from the human being, however, is its unity with its surroundings. Bajaja here gives unashamed expression to the modern human being's dream of how animals apprehend the world and their place in it. When narrating from the wolves' perspective, he conveys the continuity of their connection with their surroundings by omitting full stops and using short, indented lines to indicate their pauses to listen. As the names of several wolves — Odin, Beltane, Genghis — suggest, they continue to inhabit an ancient, mythic space and time, where dream and reality intermingle, their memories and dreams merge with the memories and dreams of all wolves, and 'wolf is also Wolf'. Bajaja uses lush lyrical passages to show how the wolves experience their environment through all their senses as a 'symphony', 'an all-pervading chord of trees, herbs, soil and mycelium, flavoured here and there with a ground beetle's musk or a wagtail's inquisitiveness'.[66] Their howl is described variously as a fugue, a canon and plainsong, rising out of and inspiring awe in the life around them. The discordant notes, alerting the wolves to danger, are provided by human beings; the young he-wolf's call for 'compassion and consonance' is answered by the sound of a chainsaw and a falling tree.

By contrast, the human being's experience of being is distanced and fragmented. In Tomáš, a psychotherapist, an intuitive relationship with Nature's mysteries has been replaced by psychoanalytical theories that attempt to explain them. The quarrelsomeness of human beings reflects their disrupted, volatile apprehension of the world, whereas even the wolves' fights serve to strengthen their bond. They are also more unthinkingly capable of empathy. In one episode, they settle down to watch, with curiosity and amusement, as the human family drinks around a campfire. When two teenagers start arguing, 'He-Wolf even panted in answer and smacked his lips; perhaps, anticipating a scrap, he had remembered the pack and begun to long for a proper chase'.[67] In their readiness to reaccept

[65] Ibid., p. 145.
[66] Ibid., p. 186.
[67] Ibid., p. 202.

human beings into their wilder existence, however, the wolves may risk the corrupting domestication — and the declining ability to coexist — that has befallen human beings.

At the end of the novel, the human and wolf families finally meet in the forest, as they hunt the same herd of deer. On coming face to face with He-Wolf, Markéta wrongly assumes that he intends to attack her, and shoots him. Her family consider her action not only a logical response, in keeping with a subconscious view of Nature as alien and potentially hostile, but also a cause for celebration. Markéta, however, finds herself suddenly distanced from this perspective. She is associated in the novel with the legendary shepherdess and martyr, Margaret the Virgin, and, according to her daughter, she seems still to retain a hereditary sense of the 'dualism' described by Berger:

> She was completely different. There was something almost defenceless in her with regard to animals [...]. Just as the Old Testament is all blood and passion, while the New proclaims love and compassion, so my mother could on the same day help to slaughter a pig or go hunting and then chat somewhere in a corner with a sick tom-cat. No split personality, just one Bible.[68]

She is drawn mysteriously to She-Wolf, whose howling she alone hears as mourning, rather than as a threat. Her eyes become honey-coloured, like the amber eyes of the wolves. Sensing that She-wolf has come to the lodge, Markéta goes out, kneels before her and looks into her eyes, unwittingly imitating a young he-wolf's earlier behaviour when seeking forgiveness and reacceptance. Tomáš, however, not seeing Markéta, and anxious to demonstrate his own prowess, fires at the she-wolf, but kills his wife. Modern human beings, Bajaja suggests, can only relate to Nature through wretched attempts to assert their dominance, which are destructive and will end in tragedy that the human being neither intends nor can imagine.

This assertion of supremacy is reflected linguistically in the title, which is taken from the verb *zvlčet*, meaning 'to go wild' — literally, 'wolfish' — a typical example of what Katy Soper calls 'negative anthropomorphism':

[68] Ibid, p. 42. Berger writes: 'A peasant becomes fond of his pig and is glad to salt away its pork. What is significant, and is so difficult for the urban stranger to understand, is that the two statements in that sentence are connected by an *and* not by a *but*.' 'Why Look at Animals?', p. 259.

> if we have turned to animals in an attempt to transcend the 'loneliness' or 'alienation' of our cultural status, we have also persistently used them to preserve the culture-nature barrier [...] by associating all our 'lowlier' characteristics and bodily functions with animality, we assert the importance of sustaining those higher or more spiritual attributes that grant us human sovereignty over the beast.[69]

In *Zvlčení*, however, it is better to be wolfish than 'civilized'. Only two human characters still attempt to co-exist intuitively with Nature and, in keeping with Vančura's view of the Czechs as irredeemably bourgeois, both are from more 'eastern' Slav tribes. Ester, a witch-like peasant woman from Slovakia, experiences reality most similarly to the wolves, aided by home-brewed alcohol, and uniquely strikes no fear in them. Jadwiga, a devout Polish Catholic and Markéta's *de facto* step-mother, urges Tomáš to accept Markéta's death with humility, because 'mourning [...] springs from immaturity and pride'.[70] She sends him the story of St Francis and St Clare, which Markéta was reading just before she died. The copy was printed from the 'infernet' by Jiří's son, who, with his equal aptitude for hunting in the forest and on-line, alone embodies the possibility of renewed balance between the modern and traditional. For Bajaja, the spirituality inherent in folk belief and traditional Christianity offers a path back to a more balanced co-existence between human beings and their environment. As Lubomír Machala writes, 'becoming lupine is a goal or a means of salvation, in the sense of a return by people to "pure" natural principles'.[71] In effect, as Urban also argues in *Hastrman* (The Waterman, 2001), only by becoming more savage may the human being be tamed.

In *Hastrman*, Urban counters the notion of the human development away from Nature to culture by arguing for the preservation of a balance between them in the human being. In the first part of the novel, set in the mid-nineteenth century, the waterman objects to the parish priest's claim that local peasants are returning to paganism, arguing: 'Perhaps they are

[69] K. Soper, *What is Nature?*, Oxford and Malden, MA, 1995, p. 86. Topol criticizes both Petra Hůlová and Tomáš Změškal (b.1966) for including in their novels stereotypical scenes in which wolves attack and kill human beings, which is actually very unusual. See J. Topol, 'Chlupatý hrdina s pořádnými čelistmi', *Lidové noviny*, 2 June 2010, p. 19. In this example of 'negative anthromorphism', which directly causes the tragic outcome of *Zvlčení*, a trait more characteristic of human beings is transferred to a creature that human beings would prefer to consider more 'savage' than they.

[70] *Zvlčení*, p. 10.

[71] L. Machala, 'Bajajovo moravské romaneto', *Host*, 2004, 4, pp. 36–39 (p. 38).

not returning to paganism. Perhaps it has always been here.'[72] The balance between Nature and culture is captured in the recurring, positive motif of amphibiousness, incarnated in the waterman, who on land poses as a coldly rational, educated nobleman, the embodiment of culture, but in water is a fierce, instinctive creature, the embodiment of Nature. In a strong attack on the Czech character, Urban has the waterman criticize the post-war expulsion of Sudeten Germans for ending the ethnic 'amphibiousness' of his lands, claiming that the Germans would never have allowed the Communists to devastate them.

In his novels, Urban frequently expresses nostalgia for the time when human beings neither dominated nor lived in passive awe of Nature, but were actively fascinated by its mysteries and power. Through a weak English pun, his waterman, Johannes Salmon de Caus, appears to be descended from the French hydraulic engineer, garden designer and polymath, Salomon de Caus (1576–1626), whose work sought to imitate the 'engineering' of Nature or, in Vaculík's terms, to submit to the undulations of the Earth. As Igor Fic argues, de Caus attracts Urban as a representative of the Baroque 'yearning to decipher the world of God's creation, to break through "to God through this world" [a quotation from the art and literary historian Zdeněk Kalista (1900–82)] and thus attain salvation'.[73] In his major work, *Les Raisons des formes et mouvements* (1615, revised 1624), de Caus sought to reveal what Luke Morgan calls the 'divinely sanctioned natural law' underlying all phenomena, natural and man-made.[74] The waterman's admiring description of his ancestors' reconstruction of their lands recalls de Caus's method:

> It was undoubtedly an artificial piece of work, but it respected the original starting-points given by Nature: they built it in a place where lakes, pools and swamps had been since time immemorial. This work made the place accessible to human beings and benefited them without taking from the marshy region its natural beauty and function.[75]

Over time, however, in Urban's account, human beings change from being admirers to being unregulated exploiters of Nature. Urban situates the waterman's lands in the region associated with the poet Karel Hynek

[72] M. Urban, *Hastrman*, Prague, 2001, p. 110.
[73] I. Fic, 'Hastrman, aneb dej o čem doma nevíš', *Tvar*, 12, 2001, 20, p. 5.
[74] L. Morgan, *Nature as Model: Salomon de Caus and Early Seventeenth Century Landscape Design*, Philadelphia, PA, 2007, p. 11.
[75] *Hastrman*, p. 12.

Mácha (1810–36), whose major work, *Máj* (Spring, 1836), is devoted to the human being's separation from Nature.[76] This separation is reflected in the human being's changing conception of God. In an 1854 play by the Norwegian writer Andreas Munch (1811–84), de Caus declares to a Catholic priest: 'Thy deity is not my God! My God is Nature!'[77] In the first part of *Hastrman*, set in the mid nineteenth century, the waterman repeatedly cites Feuerbach, who, in the foreword to his *Vorlesungen über des Wesen der Religion* (1851), asserts that the 'origin or cause' of the human being is 'not God — a mystical, vague, ambiguous word — but Nature, a clear, empirical, unambiguous word and essence'.[78] For Feuerbach, Christianity marked the culmination of monotheism and the shift in religion from Nature towards the human being. In a debate with the local parish priest, the waterman shows how these developments merely legitimize ever greater human voraciousness:

> You have taught them obedience and humility, the art of ridding themselves of responsibility for sin. And he who comes after you will teach them something else: a kind of lack of shame which he will declare the new religion.[79]

The main defender of pantheism is the local squire's rebellious daughter, Kateřina, who leads a pagan cult that conducts ancient rituals in the local countryside. She is appalled by the elaborate works undertaken by the waterman to reactivate the local mill. For her, as for her patron, St Catherine of Alexandria, the wheel symbolizes death, like the breaking wheel into whose spokes the prisoner's limbs are woven in *Máj*. The waterman, however, only later realizes that the mill 'project' marks the beginning of the industrial exploitation and destruction of his lands. A

[76] Urban states that his inspiration for the waterman was 'the land that I consider my own and which is stupidly called Mácha's. As a child I sailed in a boat around a lake covered in thick green duckweed. I imagined that trees grew under the surface. That people lived there who looked like fish. I found out much later, with a feeling of horror, that reservoirs are filled and whole villages left at the bottom of them. That my fairytale invention was actually quite real, if more romantic'. A. Horáčková, 'Urban: Jen počkejte, ztrestám vás svým románem', *MF Dnes*, 15 May 2001, p. A23.

[77] Morgan, *Nature as Model*, p. 184.

[78] L. Feuerbach, *Vorlesungen über des Wesen der Religion* in his *Sämtliche Werke*, eds W. Bolin and F. Jodl, 13 vols, Stuttgart, 1959–64, 8, p. 29. By highlighting the meaning of Feuerbach's name ('fire-brook'), Urban's waterman implies that the philosopher may himself be a waterman.

[79] *Hastrman*, p. 218.

wooden idol haunts him, warning that he is becoming too like human beings:

> Johan Salmon de Caus [...] fancies himself in the role of philanthropist and is increasingly forgetting what he was born as, who he is and who he must be till the last day of his life. Let people be people and let him be their nightmare, their cautioning finger. Because if he does not do it, then they will become the nightmare and their fingers will no longer warn, but merely break and take.[80]

At the end of the first part, the waterman impregnates Kateřina and takes her underwater, as Hades takes Persephone to the underworld every autumn. His lands are thus left to a long, destructive 'winter' under capitalism and Communism in 'a plebeian state obsessed with production and consumption'.[81]

In the second part of the novel, set in the 1990s, the pre-industrial rural utopia of the waterman's estate has been submerged (*utopena*, another pun) by a huge dam and the waterman is conducting a campaign of eco-terrorism against the politicians, bureaucrats and businessmen responsible. He takes up with a group of peaceful environmentalists called Děti vody (Water Babies),[82] led by the charismatic Tomáš Mor, the namesake of the author of *Utopia* (1516). Urban spells his surname like the Czech for 'plague', perhaps in reference to the rash of utopian ideologies that Thomas More's model inspired. Kateřina joins the Babies, and becomes a model 'friend of the Earth'. While the waterman kills his enemies, the Water Babies achieve their ends by peaceful means. They recover the village and begin establishing an Edenic community based on solidarity with and deference to Nature. Since human beings no longer need him, the waterman allows himself to be sacrificed in a carnival ritual of renewal. Should human history repeat itself, however, Kateřina is carrying his heir.

Critics disagree about how seriously to take the utopian ending. Janoušek, while praising Urban for restoring 'ideological' writing to post-Communist Czech literature, detects a familiar totalitarianism in his ecological message that scares him.[83] By contrast, Anzhelina Pencheva

[80] Ibid., pp. 154–55.

[81] Ibid., p. 287.

[82] The name may be a typically playful allusion to Charles Kingsley's pro-Darwinian 1863 novel *The Water Babies*, which Urban perhaps encountered when living in London as a child. The novel was translated into Czech in 1911 as *Vodňátka*, but is not well known.

[83] See P. Janoušek, 'Vpředvzad! (Miloš Urban a návrat ideologie do české literatury)', *Tvar*, 12, 2001, 20, p. 6.

reads *Hastrman* as a postmodernist analysis of the 'birth of a concrete ideological construct or system',[84] which exposes the danger of ideology through 'mystification' that continues in Urban's interviews. Urban seems to have written the ending like Mácha wrote *Máj*, 'a light smile on his face, deep grief in his heart'. In an interview, Urban claims that the violence reflected his anger at the state of Czech politics and public life, personified for him by the former Prime Minister and future President, Václav Klaus, an outspoken climate-change sceptic and proponent of libertarian economics. The destructive exploitation of the countryside in *Hastrman* serves as a metaphor for the dominance of corruption, greed and commercialism in contemporary Czech society, epitomized by the takeover of the Mladá fronta publishing house where Urban worked until 'in the spring of 2000 it was subjected to political and economic pressure from above and forcibly transformed into a different type of publishing house. He was the only person to leave the normalized publisher out of sheer idealism'.[85] Urban maintains that in the novel 'I am settling scores with people who made me angry a short time ago. I consider them the people who are really harming this country. I have distorted the names, but they can still be recognized'.[86] With the ending, Urban playfully realizes his sincere, but hopeless fantasies of revenge and the restoration of respectful co-existence with Nature.

The Openness of Despair

Hůlová's novels *Paměť mojí babičce* (A Memoir for My Grandmother, 2002, translated into English as *All This Belongs to Me*), set in Mongolia, and *Stanice tajga* (Taiga Station, 2008), set mainly in Siberia, satirically explore 'the city''s persistent need for 'the country' as a metaphor for the more general relationship between the self and other. Both novels play with the fashion for travel literature, which transports readers from their comfortable modern urban mediocrity to unfamiliar places that offer a richer, more colourful and intense experience of life or confirm the superiority of their own world. This fashion exemplifies Hůlová's implication in her fiction that people, including readers and writers,

[84] A. Penčevová, 'Vzadvpřed, aneb není snad všechno jinak? (Ideologie jako objekt imaginace v románech Miloše Urbana)', *Acta Universitatis Palackianae Olomucensis Facultas Philosophica: Moravica*, 4, 2005, p. 224.

[85] *Hastrman*, inside back cover. The word 'normalized' is a pointed allusion to the continuation of practices associated with the post-1968, Party-led Normalization of the 1970s and 1980s.

[86] Horáčková, 'Urban: Jen počkejte', p. A23. For a discussion of this context, see P. Matoušek, 'Utopie utopená v pomstě', *Host*, 17, 2001, 8, p. 11.

prefer not to confront their problems, but to seek ways of feeling better. In interviews, she appears amused by the perception of *Paměť mojí babičce* as an ethnographic text, and hopes that readers 'will find something more general than just a story from an exotic world that has nothing in common with our life here and now. For example, even here a clash arises between the maintenance of classical norms and their transgression. I think that they have this problem everywhere and a story set in Mongolia only puts it in sharper focus, because there they really do not bother about a whole series of things that obscure this problem for us'.[87]

Hůlová's work implicitly rejects the 'familiarity' prevalent in contemporary Czech fiction, which is commonly set in a recognizable, shared notion of Bohemia, with predictable frames of reference and opinion and narrators or main characters closely identified with the author. For Hůlová, this method, despite appearances, inhibits self-discovery in favour of self-affirmation. Instead, she favours distance and defamiliarization as the means of achieving clarity. She claims that the characters and stories in *Paměť mojí babičce* come from Prague and her own life.[88] Much of what is shown about Mongolia in the novel could equally belong to a stereotypical view of Czech society and family life, from the fatty diet, matriarchal household and internecine hostility to the 'invented' nationalism imposed on children in school and the paradoxical superiority and inferiority complexes of a lukewarmly patriotic nation caught between two larger nations that behave like colonizers.

Hůlová thus uses the exotic 'other' not to escape the self, but to analyse it more closely. She defines her writing as 'coming to terms with what has happened to me'.[89] She is not easily identified with any of her characters; instead, her novels may be read as 'experiments' in viewing existence from 'other' perspectives and life experiences, through 'other' settings, with the aim of learning more about her own.[90] She detects a similar method in another work commonly approached as an ethnographic text, the monumental two-volume novel, *Cesty na Sibiř* (Travels to Siberia, 2008), by the documentary film-maker, Martin Ryšavý (b.1967):

[87] J. Rulf, 'Na Číňana pozor!', *Reflex*, 13, 2002, 43, p. 70.

[88] See M. Janda, 'Mongolové se dívají víc do Evropy než do Asie', *Právo*, 31 August 2002, supplement 'Salon', p. 4.

[89] F. Cinger, 'Fascinuje mě energie lidí', *Právo*, 6 November 2008, p. 17.

[90] Josef Chuchma pejoratively likens *Paměť mojí babičce* to a greenhouse or laboratory. See J. Chuchma, 'Petra Hůlová: obrovský talent a řada nástrah', *MF Dnes*, 16 October 2002, p. C8.

> [*Cesty na Sibiř*] is a meditation on the search for meaning. For the narrator, this does not lie mainly in the shooting of a documentary film in Siberia, but in the longing through this work to find out something about himself [...]. Despite the extensive passages describing the local environment, *Cesty na Sibiř* is above all auto-therapy.[91]

This approach reflects Hůlová's perception, in both novels, that the other is unreachable, and that any attempt to get to know the other results only in self-delusion or, perhaps, greater self-understanding. In *Paměť mojí babičce*, Hůlová juxtaposes the perspectives of five women — three sisters, Dzaja, Nara and Ojuna, their mother, Alta, and Dzaja's daughter, Dolgorma — who have faced the choice between 'the country' or 'the city'. Several critics interpret the novel as an account of the decline of traditional rural life,[92] but the debate about the two settings is a red herring. The subjectivity of each narration means nothing can be known for sure about the quality of life in each setting, now and in the past, though both seem horrendous.

Hůlová suggests that most people are pre-determined for a particular environment, and struggle when removed from it. Nara complains of the plants Dzaja buys to make their flat more 'natural':

> Every plant likes something different, but it's not always possible to do this. If I give them too little water, the prickly ones are happy, but the flat-leaved ones wither and their stems give way. If I give them too much water, only the flat-leaved ones enjoy it and the others darken and the water in their pots smells like a sewer.[93]

Dzaja and Nara are of mixed race — the children of affairs Alta had with Chinese and Russian men associated with the city — and seem to belong wholly to neither the steppe nor the city. By contrast, Ojuna, the child of steppe parents, can, like city-born Dolgorma, only imagine life in one setting, and loathes the other. Where characters 'belong' — or perhaps hope to belong — is betrayed by their language. Even after life in the city, Dzaja persists in using similes relating to sheep and horses, a reflection of her carefully nurtured nostalgia for the steppe, whereas Dolgorma compares things to ketchup and lift-shafts.[94]

[91] P. Hůlová, 'Sibiriáda mladého muže', *Týden*, 15, 2008, 48, p. 70.

[92] See, for example, J. Rulf, 'Na Číňana pozor!', *Reflex*, 13, 2002, 43, p. 70, or Horák, 'Zlí samotáři', p. 170.

[93] P. Hůlová, *Paměť mojí babičce*, Prague, 2002, p. 200.

[94] For a discussion of the language of *Paměť mojí babičce*, see J. Svobodová, 'Lexikum

Rather than admit their inadaptability, the characters persuade themselves that their way of life is superior to the other. Each narrator strives to recast a life marked by disappointment, degradation and failure as a triumph. Dzaja presents her final return to the steppe, in middle age, as a logical, happy ending: 'When I sit in front of my *ger*, I feel like a Khan princess.'[95] Hůlová, however, disagrees: 'Dzaja may say "I am at home here and all this belongs to me", but in fact this is a bit ridiculous. She is kidding herself.'[96] Dolgorma has found out about Dzaja's life as a prostitute and abandoned her, leaving her nowhere else to go but the steppe. The same self-delusion is apparent in Alta's dreams of becoming a 'grandmother' figure like her mother-in-law, Ojuna's self-aggrandizement as a model of the traditional rural wife and mother, and Dolgorma's quest to find her father, one of her mother's clients.

The 'city''s attempt to get to know 'the country' is more comically satirized in *Stanice tajga*. In 1946, Hablund, a middle-aged, married businessman, decides to leave his Copenhagen home, the epitome of Western comfort and civilization, in an attempt to compensate for his failure to participate in the resistance against Germany. He is inspired by a popular geographical magazine, *Our World*, to travel to a remote, poor, backward Siberian village to observe the natives and report on their ways. On his arrival, 'he could feel that his heart was wide open and he was ready to be much more understanding and generous than in Copenhagen'.[97] However, when he meets his first local villager, in accordance with the advice in *Our World*, he tries to find something to praise about him, but cannot. Hablund never returns, and sixty years later, a young Danish anthropologist, Erske, goes to look for him, hoping that he might make a discovery that will earn him promotion, implicitly the only likely 'impact' of his research.

The encounter in the novel between 'the city' and 'the country' — or the West and the East — resembles that between a psychologist and a madman, in which the psychologist believes he has the knowledge and skills to understand his patient, but is easily outwitted. Hablund is an idealistic, clumsy but well-intentioned amateur, vainly struggling in the opening scene to see himself and his rucksack in the mirror in his hallway before he leaves. Erske is a professional, well-read and well-trained, but

jako prostředek charakterizace prostředí v próze Petry Hůlové *Paměť mojí babičce*', in O. Uličný (ed.), *Eurolitteraria & Eurolingua 2005*, Liberec, 2005, pp. 341–47 (p. 342).

95 *Paměť mojí babičce*, p. 235.

96 A. Horáčková, 'Já se těmi ohlasy docela bavím', *MF Dnes*, 26 November 2002, p. C6.

97 P. Hůlová, *Stanice tajga*, Prague, 2008, p. 9.

also a tubby, bespectacled man who still lives with his mother, and who took up anthropology to become manlier. Erske would no doubt dismiss *Our World*, but the anthropological theories through which he filters his experiences are even less useful because they prevent unmediated contact with the villagers, just as in Topol's *Chladnou zemí*, contemporary historiography is shown not to uncover, but to mask the past. Erske misses the opportunity of a love affair with the wife of Fedorek, a conductor on the Trans-Siberian Railway, because he views their relationship as a case study in research ethics. He eventually leaves the village, without learning Hablund's fate, disillusioned not so much by his theories as by the local people's failure to live up to them. By contrast, Hablund gradually believes he is becoming accepted; as summer turns to autumn, villagers start greeting him by cheerily squeezing his arms, apparently in the manner of a tribe described in *Our World*, and then he is invited to join the annual reindeer hunt. The hunt fails, however, and the villagers eat well-fed Hablund instead, perhaps as they had always intended.

Fedorek learns more about the village and its past than Hablund and Erske. Like Dzaja, he is genetically split between 'the city' and 'the country', since his father fled to Siberia during the siege of Leningrad and married a local villager. Unlike Denemarková and Hájíček, for whom this combination breeds weakness, Hůlová, like Urban, favours amphibiousness. In a world where answers cannot be found anywhere and the modern human being is equally alienated in all settings, the most authentic way to live, it seems, is to drift endlessly between them, like Fedorek and Dzaja, and like she does in her novels, set alternately abroad and in Prague.

Conclusion

Most writers discussed here place their hope in 'openness' as a means of coming to terms with the past, liberating human beings from dogma and restoring their compassion for one another and Nature. Hůlová's 'openness' by contrast, is bleak and daunting, Topol's dangerous, uncertain landscape without the incorrigible adventurer's optimism, and with little hope of what contemporary psychology calls 'cognitive closure' or genuine empathy. The pessimism in the 2000s 'return to the rural' can be linked not only to disillusion with the Western society and culture that the Czechs rejoined after 1989, but also a perception that post-Communist Czech society had become a continuation of late Communist society, whether in political practices, the perpetuation of post-war myths or modes of thought, the urbanization of the countryside or the seamlessness between

Marxist-Leninist materialism and late-twentieth-century capitalism. The banality of some messages in the works discussed may say as much about a perceived absence of common sense in the paths followed in recent Czech and human history as the limitations of their authors. 'Returns to the rural' often seek to slow or halt the momentum of 'the city' in a particular direction. They remind people of older truths that they appear to have forgotten or dismissed, and their repetitiveness itself seems to undermine 'urban' notions of development and progress. By contrast, the 2000s 'return to the rural' seems to crave movement and change.

The break with the post-1989 consensus is evident in the renewed fascination with the East, so soon after the departure of Soviet troops, as a source of less pampered and enfeebled, more rounded humanity. In both content and style, these works escape the narrow preoccupations of much mainstream 1990s Czech fiction, which was dominated by autobiographical, notionally 'authentic' accounts of life under Communism that, in its implicit attempt to create a post-Communist collective based on shared experiences and beliefs, recalled the poetics of first-person-narrated sanctioned realism during the Normalization.[98] For the writers discussed here, 'the country' is not only a political device, but also a rich source of creative possibilities. Their preoccupations with the state of contemporary human beings, their environment and their capacity to face the challenges of the future, moreover, resonate with those of writers, scientists, sociologists, economists, historians, philosophers, the media and wider public throughout the industrialized world. In the 2000s, most uncharacteristically in Czech literature, 'the country' becomes the source of renewed cosmopolitanism.

[98] For a discussion of this poetics, see R. B. Pynsent, 'Adolescence, Ideology and Society: The Young Hero in Contemporary Czech Fiction', in I. Wallace (ed.), *The Adolescent Hero*, Dundee, 1984, pp. 65–86.

The Return of the Photograph: Time, Memory and the Genre of the Photo-Film in Andrei Zviagintsev's *Vozvrashchenie* (The Return, 2003)

PHILIP CAVENDISH

'The reel of film is a museum full of stills'.[1]

THE epilogue of Andrei Zviagintsev's *Vozvrashchenie*, a photographic slide-show of twenty-five images which are presented on screen just prior to the final credits, is formally the most innovative device of this award-winning film. Structurally, this epilogue consists of two discrete sub-series. The first twenty-one images purport to have been taken by fictional protagonists within the diegetic present (two young brothers who have taken a camera on a fishing expedition with their father, who deserted the family some twelve years previously but has now mysteriously reappeared). The remaining four photographs ostensibly date from the early childhood of these two protagonists. These photographs, their authorship unknown, are connected to two other images in the film that belong to the same period and feature the same location: the first, a family photograph, is preserved within the pages of an illustrated version of the Bible which the two boys consult after their father's reappearance in order to confirm his true identity; the second is a snapshot of the two boys and the mother dating from the same moment which the younger of the two boys discovers

Philip Cavendish is a Senior Lecturer in Russian at UCL SSEES.

[1] Bruce Kawin, 'Time and Stasis in *La Jetée*', *Film Quarterly*, 36, 1982, 1, pp. 15–20 (p. 18). I am indebted to Vladimir Mishukov, the production photographer on *Vozvrashchenie*, for his permission to reproduce the twenty-five stills which constitute the 'coda' to Zviagintsev's film, and also eight images from his album of production stills, also entitled *Vozvrashchenie*, which he published independently in 2004. Unless otherwise stated, all translations from the Russian are my own.

behind the sun-shield above the front passenger seat of the father's car just moments before they embark on their journey home. Metaphorically speaking, the epilogue constitutes a form of time-travel in which two kinds of return are present: a return to the events of the fishing trip with the father, one that has culminated in his accidental death; and a return to the period of their childhood, one of which they appear to have no memory, just as they appear to have little or no memory of their father before his reappearance.

In view of the predictability of the family photograph, one that appears to transcend cultural differences, it is perhaps unsurprising that the critical writing on *Vozvrashchenie* hitherto has tended to neglect the significance of this elongated, mnemonic episode. One film scholar, for example, has described the images in terms of 'the fleeting moments of happiness and the forced smiles people frequently adopt when posing for a picture'.[2] The historical alignment of photography with the expansion of tourism, and the fact that the fishing expedition in the film features an 'exotic' terrain as part of its landscape (Lake Ladoga and its scattered archipelago of small islands), might be argued to lend further ammunition to the accusations of banality.[3] Such accusations would be misguided on several counts, however. The content of the images in the coda is more varied than the conventional snapshot: few of them are posed or involve subjects gazing at the camera; fewer still could be characterized as 'moments of happiness'; and hardly any evince interest in the archetypal attractions of the tourist's gaze. The manner of composition, moreover, which is sophisticated and artistic, and the fact that the images have been taken in black and white, further remove them from the contemporary family snapshot. The marked tension between diegetic (amateur) impulse and actual professional realization highlights the problem of the epilogue's authorship generally: although operating according to a conceit which stresses their genesis at the hands of fictional creations, the images in question are actually the work of Vladimir Mishukov, a professional photographer and close friend of Zviagintsev, who was invited to produce a portfolio of images

[2] Vladimir Strukov, 'The Return of the Gods: Andrei Zviagintsev's *Vozvrashchenie* (*The Return*)', *Slavic and East European Journal*, 51, 2007, pp. 331–56 (p. 332). Identical sentiments are expressed in Yana Hashamova, 'Resurrected Fathers and Resuscitated Sons: Homosocial Fantasies in *The Return* and *Koktebel'*', in Helena Goscilo and Yana Hashamova (eds), *Cinepaternity: Fathers and Sons in Soviet and Post-Soviet Film*, Bloomington, IN, 2010, pp. 169–89 (pp. 179 & 180).

[3] Susan Sontag, *On Photography*, London, 1979, p. 15.

relating to the production process.[4] In the light of this knowledge, the images which relate to the fishing expedition, because they ostensibly express the viewpoints of fictional protagonists, might be regarded as acts of photographic ventriloquy or, to borrow a literary term which applies to first-person narratives and other types of stylistic voice-play, *skaz*. Zviagintsev has confirmed that the coda was conceived as a replacement for a scene in the screenplay which showed the boys, now middle-aged adults, reading excerpts from a diary (vestiges of this concept remain in the sense that the two brothers are shown making entries in this diary during the trip).[5] Potentially, therefore, the epilogue assumes the status of a 'photo-diary' which can be analysed in terms of its register and tone, as well as its structural dynamic. At the same time, as a series of creative acts on the part of Mishukov, the coda can also be explored within a number of contexts that relate to his work as a professional photographer. The most important point of intersection lies in the portfolio of images (some five hundred in total) which relate to the production. A proportion of these were selected for exhibition at the Solianka Gallery as part of the Moscow 2004 Photobiennale;[6] and a smaller proportion, some eighty in total, were published independently in the form of an album in the same year.[7] More broadly, Mishukov's portfolio can be approached in the light of projects undertaken both before and after *Vozvrashchenie*, most relevantly the production stills from the sets of films directed by Zviagintsev since 2000 for television and cinema, but also a series of independent, non-film related initiatives, which have made Mishukov one of the leading Russian photographers of his generation.[8] Beyond these projects, the

[4] Andrei Zviagintsev and Vladimir Mishukov, 'Fil′m o fil′me: Fotografiia i kino' <http://www.fotogl.com/content/film_o_filme_fotografiya_i_kino-168/> [accessed 4 March 2012].

[5] Zviagintsev's preface in Vladimir Mishukov, *Vozvrashchenie*, Moscow, 2004, p. 5. For the scene in the original screenplay, see Vladimir Moiseenko and Aleksandr Novototskii, 'Ty', *Kinostsenarii*, 2004, 1, pp. 72–114 (pp. 113–14).

[6] Mikhail Sidlin, 'Gumanoidy i kapoeira: Piat′ samykh identichnykh vystavok fotobiennale', *Nezavisimaia gazeta*, 14 April 2004 <http://www.ng.ru/accent/2004-04-14/9_photobienale.htm> [accessed 13 April 2012].

[7] Zviagintsev and Mishukov, 'Fil′m o fil′me'.

[8] For stills produced during the making of *Busido* (2000), *Obscure* (2000), *Vybor* (2000), *Izgnanie* (2007) and *Elena* (2011), see <http://az-film.com/ru/Photo14.html> [accessed 13 March 2012]. Photographs from the production of *Izgnanie*, under the title 'Predchuvstvie', were exhibited at the Museum of Contemporary Art from 26 March to 27 April 2008 as part of the Moscow 2008 Photobiennale. The portfolio from the production of *Elena*, under the title 'Inter′er: Natura: Pavil′on', was exhibited from 6–22 April 2012 in the Moscow State Exhibition Hall 'Novyi Manezh' as part of the 2012 Moscow Photobiennale. See <http://club.foto.ru/guide/event.php?event_id=2743> [accessed 25 May 2012].

Vozvrashchenie portfolio can also be analysed from the perspective of the long-standing tradition of film-production photography generally, an eclectic genre which, although historically neglected, has always embraced artistic as well as commercial objectives, and undeniably constitutes a fundamental part of the 'archive' of international cinema since its birth.

Zviagintsev himself has acknowledged the narrative significance of the photographic coda in *Vozvrashchenie*. His description of its poetics in terms of a 'release' from the psychological tension which has accumulated during the main body of the film, and his observation, albeit tentative, that the photographs might be interpreted as a testament to the 'resurrection' of the father in the hearts and minds of the two sons after his death, hint that this coda was intended to possess a poetic rationale.[9] This is confirmed by the presentation of the material within a specific acoustic environment (the sounds of thunder and rain accompanied by fragments of a plaintive Russian folk song), which seems designed to provoke a meditative and melancholic response. The formal innovation of the epilogue has also been acknowledged. Oleg Negin, co-author of the screenplays for *Izgnanie* (The Banishment, 2007) and *Elena* (2011), Zviagintsev's subsequent feature-films, has described the coda as a 'film within a film' and a 'text within a text'.[10] In this context, it is important to emphasize that the *mise-en-film* of photographic material in *Vozvrashchenie* is a device with a rich pedigree in experimental cinema. In the sphere of the fiction-film, the most celebrated examples are French director Chris Marker's *La Jetée* (The Pier, 1962), a 'photo-*roman*' in the science-fiction genre which consists almost entirely of still images, and Polish director Andrzej Munk's *Pasażerka* (The Passenger, 1962), the contemporary section of which survives in the form of frame-stills because the director died in a car crash before it could be completed.[11] Within the realm of the documentary short, important precedents can be found in the three photo-films made by Latvian photographer Gunar Binde in the Soviet Union during the 1960s and 1970s;[12] the 'photo-essays'

[9] Zviagintsev's comment about the coda as a form of 'release' is given in *The Return: A Film about the Film*, a sixty-three minute documentary broadcast by RenTV in 2004 and included among the supplementary materials on the version of *Vozvrashchenie* released by Twentieth Century Fox. The comment about the father's 'resurrection' appears in a recent interview with Marina Nefedova. See 'Andrei Zviagintsev: Istoriia shelkopriada', *Neskuchnyi sad*, 22 May 2011 <http://www.pravmir.ru/istoriya-shelkopryada/> [accessed 27 March 2012].

[10] See Negin's afterword in Mishukov, *Vozvrashchenie*, pp. 90–93 (pp. 91 & 93).

[11] Tadeusz Lubelski, *Historia kina polskiego: Twórcy, filmy, konteksty*, Katowice, 2009, pp. 200–01.

[12] The three films in question are *Allo Moskva!*, also known as *Znakom'tes', Moskva!*

by Marker and fellow French director Agnès Varda from the late 1950s onwards;[13] and the experimental projects on the part of photographers and filmmakers during the last five decades which have sought to interrogate the ontology of the photograph from within the medium of the moving image.[14] The extent to which Zviagintsev and his inner circle of collaborators were aware of this corpus of work when realizing the scenario for *Vozvrashchenie* is unclear at present. It is intriguing to learn, nevertheless, that twice in recent years Zviagintsev, Mikhail Krichman, the director's first-choice camera operator, and Mishukov have accepted invitations to discuss the relationship between photography and film at RGGU, the Moscow-based Russian State University of the Humanities.[15]

This article seeks to investigate the dramatic and poetic significance of the photographic coda in *Vozvrashchenie*. It will examine the film as a narrative text augmented by a complex and interwoven tapestry of photographic and cinematographic materials, these including not only the coda itself, but also the production stills which chronicle the filmmaking process and the documentary about the making of the film which was broadcast by RenTV in 2004. Each of these materials offers a prism through which to interpret the main themes of the narrative. In relation to the coda's diegetic conceit, this article will speculate on its confessional character, the extent to which the photographic materials reflect the shifting emotional moods and states of mind of the protagonists, the

(1966), *Svoimi rukami* (1967) and *Saliut* (1975). For further information on these works and Binde's interest in Marker, see <http://bogemnyipeterburg.net/vocabulare/alfavit/persons/b/binderGunar.htm> [accessed 29 March 2012].

13 During his long career, Marker has made a number of documentaries which incorporate montage sequences of still images, as well as several 'photo-essays' which consist entirely of stills, among them *Si j'avais quatre dromadaires* (1966), *Level Five* (1997) and *Le Souvenir d'un avenir* (2003). For further information on these works, see Sarah Cooper, *Chris Marker*, French Film Directors series, Manchester, 2008, pp. 60–65, 156–67 & 174–77, respectively.

14 On the incorporation of photographic images in the works of Raymond Depardon, Agnès Varda, Robert Frank, Chris Marker and Hollis Frampton, see Philippe Dubois, 'Photography *Mise-en-Film*: Autobiographical (His)stories and Psychic Apparatuses', in Patrice Petro (ed.), *Fugitive Images: From Photography to Video*, Theories of Contemporary Culture series, Bloomington, IN, 1995, pp. 152–72. Many of the artists producing works in the photo-film genre have recently been the subject of a 'Stillness and Movement' conference at the Tate Modern. This conference, which was accompanied by a season of photo-films, took place between 5–14 March 2010.

15 The first occasion was a 'masterclass' given by Zviagintsev and Mishukov which took place on 1 March 2008 and was entitled 'Fotografiia i kino'. See <http://www.rsuh.ru/announcements.html?id=65781> [accessed 28 March 2012]. The second was a seminar involving Krichman and Mishukov which took place on 16 November 2010. See <http://artdesign.rsuh.ru/news.html?id=609525> [accessed 29 March 2012].

degree to which, as a form of 'photo-diary', the coda offers a competing version of events when compared to the main narrative, and the ways in which the entries in this 'diary' reflect the personalities of the respective 'authors'. The evocation of mood courtesy of the acoustic accompaniment will be examined; so, too, will the thematic and aesthetic links between the coda and Mishukov's portfolio of production stills. It will be argued that the *skaz*-style conceit of the coda in *Vozvrashchenie* constitutes its main source of originality within the tradition of the photo-film. Indeed, its complexity as photographic voice-play can be gauged by the fact that the very last image in the contemporary section of the epilogue now commonly referred to as 'Chaika' (Seagull) (Fig. 20 [**21**]),[16] was actually taken along the Adriatic coast in Croatia some two months before the start of the filming proper.[17]

This article will also investigate the coda in *Vozvrashchenie* in the light of the practices of photographic *mise-en-film* generally. As various film scholars have pointed out, the device of juxtaposing still and moving images inevitably raises questions in relation to the respective ontologies of photography and film.[18] The former has traditionally been viewed as a moment arrested in time, its cryogenic impulse acting as a preserver or embalmer of the moment, and thus the human subject contained within its frame, but also, paradoxically, a stark reminder of the inevitability of decay and mortality; as Susan Sontag has maintained, 'all photographs are *memento mori*'.[19] The filmic sequence, by contrast, because of its kinetic

[16] Henceforth, references to the photographic images discussed in this article will give both their sequence order in the article and their position within the epilogue to *Vozvrashchenie* (indicated in square parentheses and in bold type).

[17] Negin's afterword in Mishukov, *Vozvrashchenie*, p. 90.

[18] Much of this speculation has been prompted by the example of *La Jetée*. See Roger Odin, 'Le Film du fiction menacé par la photographie et sauvé par la bande-son (à propos de *La Jetée* de Chris Marker)', in *Cinémas de la modernité: Films, théories*, Colloque de Cerisy directed by Dominique Château, André Gardiès and François Jost, Paris, 1981, pp. 147–71; Kawin, 'Time and Stasis in *La Jetée*'; Peter Wollen, 'Fire and Ice', first publ. *Photographies*, 4, 1985, repr. in Liz Wells (ed.), *The Photography Reader*, London, 2003, pp. 76–80; Raymond Bellour, 'The Film Stilled', first publ. *La Recherche photographique*, 3, 1987, repr. *Camera Obscura: Feminism, Culture, and Media Studies*, 8 (September 1990), pp. 99–124; Réda Bensmaïa, 'From the Photogram to the Pictogram: On Chris Marker's *La Jetée*', first publ. *Iris*, 8, 1988, repr. (with Alison Rowe and Elisabeth Lyon) *Camera Obscura: Feminism, Culture, and Media Studies*, 8 (September 1990), pp. 139–61, and Paul Sandro, 'Singled Out by History: *La Jetée* and the Aesthetics of Memory', *French Cultural Studies*, 10, 1999, pp. 107–27. For discussion of the production stills in *Pasażerka*, see Iurii Lotman and Iurii Tsiv′ian, *Dialog s ekranom*, Tallinn, 1994, pp. 159–60.

[19] Sontag, *On Photography*, p. 15. For the idea of photography as a mechanism for 'mummification', see André Bazin, 'The Ontology of the Photographic Image', in his *What is Cinema?*, essays selected and translated by Hugh Gray, foreword by Jean Renoir, 2 vols,

drive, its relative openness by virtue of being part of an evolving series, the overt or covert narrative imperative (even within the sphere of the documentary), the sense of the images unfurling in the present (their quality of happening *now*, this instant) and the potential for symbolic connections by virtue of montage is endowed with a fugitive quality: the individual photogrammes or image-cells are invisible to the naked eye, and thus impossible to fix and contemplate in isolation without artificially removing them from the sequence as a whole.[20] In temporal terms, Peter Wollen has described the difference in terms of 'a free rewriting time' (photography) and 'an imposed reading time' (cinema).[21] With the advent of digital technology, however, as Laura Mulvey has persuasively demonstrated, this particular distinction has to some extent been erased; as she argues, 'the halted frame, the arrest, discovers the moment of immobility that belongs to the frame and allows time for contemplation that takes the image back to the brief instant that recorded the "real thing"'.[22] If the capturing of the freeze-frame brings cinema closer to the ontology of the photograph, then the presentation of a slide-show unfolding in time with supplementary acoustic material compromises even further the distinctions between moving sequence and static image. Furthermore, by exploiting a series of static images which ostensibly pertain to a purely imaginary world, *Vozvrashchenie* manages to reverse the social myth, according to which photography functions as the guardian of an authentic, private domain (its popular function as 'keepsake' or 'souvenir') and cinema serves as a form of collective entertainment which references only the fictional.[23] This article will argue that the interest in the ontology of the photograph constitutes an important theme in *Vozvrashchenie*, and that the juxtaposition between photography and cinematography by means of the coda is deliberately designed to highlight their common origins in processes (chemical and optical) which facilitate the imprinting of 'real' objects, whether alive or dead.

Berkeley, CA, 1967, 1, pp. 9–17.

[20] The classic articulation of the differences is given in Roland Barthes, *Camera Lucida: Reflections on Photography*, trans. by Richard Howard, London, 2000, p. 78. On the 'nowness' of the cinematic image, see Gilles Deleuze, *Cinema 2: The Time-Image*, trans. by Hugh Tomlinson and Robert Galeta, London, 1989, pp. 34–43.

[21] Wollen, 'Fire and Ice', p. 76.

[22] Laura Mulvey, *Death 24x a Second: Stillness and the Moving Image*, London, 2006, p. 163.

[23] Christian Metz, 'Photography as Fetish', *October*, 34, 1985, pp. 81–90 (p. 82).

'Vozvrashchenie': a 'drama of everyday life'

Despite its relatively straightforward plot, *Vozvrashchenie* has nevertheless proved itself a particularly fertile object of enquiry.[24] Its exploration of psychology and emotion within the context of a journey draws attention to its generic origins in the so-called 'road-movie'. The tensions which arise during this journey, and the increasing levels of aggression, both verbal and physical, give rise to a sensation of claustrophobia and impending catastrophe which, in turn, prompts analogies with the genre of the psychological thriller, in particular those works, such as Roman Polański's *Nóż v vodzie* (Knife in the Water, 1962), in which the tensions arise within confined spaces and primarily concern relationships between male figures. At the same time, the film's setting in a desolate and to some extent hostile environment, and the theme of character-building which gradually asserts itself in response to this environment, is strongly reminiscent of the British 'Boy's Own' tradition and the classic adventure novel. In this context, it is interesting to note that the screenplay references Robert Louis Stevenson's *Treasure Island* (1883) and Daniel Defoe's *Robinson Crusoe* (1719).[25] The survival skills acquired by the two boys during the expedition include orienteering, wood-chopping, fire-building, fishing and the erection of shelters. They also learn to repair a boat, to understand the operation of an outboard motor, to exploit natural resources for a practical purpose and to drive a car. Much in the manner of the 'Boy's Own' adventure, the brothers acquire these skills within the context of a progression from childhood to adulthood and the development of supposedly manly virtues: self-discipline, self-respect, self-reliance, self-defence, physical and mental fortitude and, by implication, bearing in mind the long-term absence of the father, acceptance of the nomadic (hunter-gatherer) principle. *Vozvrashchenie* can be read as a rites-of-passage film in which two sons, albeit with different degrees of resistance, come to accept their father's guiding role in their lives and the value of his principles and way of life. Viewed from this perspective, the mysterious reason for the father's return to the family becomes self-evident: he has returned in order to execute

[24] Apart from the two articles mentioned in note 2 above, see Elena Stishova, 'Na glubine', *Iskusstvo kino*, 2004, 1, pp. 37–42; Ol´ga Surkova, 'Ostrov neizvestnykh sokrovishch', ibid., pp. 43–46; Andrei Plakhov, 'Chistaia mistika', ibid., pp. 46–50; Birgit Beumers, 'Tarkovsky's Return, or Zvyagintsev's *Vozvrashchenie*', *Rossica*, Spring 2004, pp. 60–63; eadem, 'Andrei Zviagintsev: *The Return (Vozvrashchenie)* (2003)', *KinoKultura*, 3, 2004 <http://www.kinokultura.com/reviews/R14return.html> [accessed 12 February 2012], and Marko Zakarias [Marco Zacarias], 'Diptikhi: Ideia Ottsa v fil´me Andreia Zviagintseva "Vozvrashchenie"', in "*Vozvrashchenie*": *Diptikhi: Doroga*, Moscow, 2007, pp. 7–100.

[25] Moiseenko and Novototskii, 'Ty', pp. 93 and 104.

the traditional role of fathers in a patriarchal culture in relation to their adolescent sons — to teach them to become adult men.

As several commentators have observed, the concern with the issue of patriarchal authority and the position of the father within the family places *Vozvrashchenie* within a wide-ranging cultural phenomenon preoccupied with a perceived 'crisis in masculinity' in modern Russian society, and expressive, or so it is argued, of a 'nostalgia for the return for the father figure'.[26] Whether *Vozvrashchenie* delivers this message in an unequivocal fashion is open to debate, however. The model of masculinity offered by the father, one based on authority, discipline, physical prowess, punishment for acts of disobedience and belief in revenge is undeniably a traditional one. As several scholars have concluded on the basis of the many biblical allusions in the film, the father's behaviour in relation to his sons, and the violence of his anger when his commandments are ignored, possesses analogies with the wrathful and destructive God of the Old Testament.[27] This behaviour does not go unchallenged, however, and neither are the father's values unambiguously triumphant. The crucial resistance in this respect is offered by the younger brother, Ivan, who refuses to recognize his father's authority, confronts him at every available opportunity, explicitly disobeys his commands, and ultimately rebels by challenging him to a 'duel'. Judging by his exchanges with his father and brother at various stages in the journey, the psychological motivations for this behaviour would appear to be two-fold: first, a residual attachment to his mother and, by extension, an anxiety on his part that the father's intrusion in his life will interfere in this relationship; and secondly, doubts about his father's identity. In response to readings which stress the film's exploration of archetypal or mythic models, it is important to point out that Ivan's challenge to his father is ultimately a failure. It is prompted not by a threat to himself, but by a desire to defend his brother; it is relatively short-lived (he drops the knife with which he has threatened his father, and runs away as soon as the latter responds to this threat and confronts him);

[26] Hashamova, 'Resurrected Fathers and Resuscitated Sons', p. 170. For wider considerations of the theme in recent Russian cinema, see Helena Goscilo, 'Cinepaternity: The Psyche and Its Heritage', in Goscilo and Hashamova (eds), *Cinepaternity*, pp. 1–25; V. Mikhalkovich, 'Kuda poklazhi tianut voz? — "Vozvrashchenie", "Koktebel′", "Progulka"', *Iskusstvo kino*, 2004, 7, pp. 98-104; Aleksandr Sekatskii, 'Ottsepriimstvo', *Seans*, 21/22, 2005, pp. 198–206, and Mark Lipovetskii, 'V gnezde "Kukushki"', *Iskusstvo kino*, 2006, 4, pp. 72–77.

[27] Strukov, 'The Return of the Gods', pp. 336–45; Beumers, 'Andrei Zviagintsev: *The Return* (*Vozvrashchenie*) (2003)', pp. 1 & 2, and Zakarias, 'Diptikhi: Ideia Ottsa v fil′me Andreia Zviagintseva "Vozvrashchenie"', pp. 43–76.

and gives rise to a desire for self-annihilation in recognition of this failure (Ivan climbs a high tower and threatens to throw himself off it). The fact that Ivan initially expresses a desire to kill his father, and that the father accidentally dies while trying to coax him down from this tower, does not make this death a form of patricide, even in symbolic terms. Furthermore, the response of the two boys to the death and subsequent disappearance of the body is couched in ambiguous terms.[28] It has been universally argued, for example, that the father's death results in Ivan's acceptance of him, this evidenced by his first, heartfelt use of the word 'Papa' after his father's dead body sinks to the bottom of the lake. While the fact of Ivan's response is indisputable, it might be argued that the uttering of this word is the result not of his symbolic acceptance of the father as a role-model, or as the embodiment of the Law, to adopt a Lacanian perspective, but rather the fact that, having climbed the tower in order to save Ivan from an act of suicide, the father has unambiguously demonstrated his paternal love for him, and thus confirmed his identity as biological father (in so doing, he replicates the earlier act of the mother, who rescues Ivan from a similar kind of tower in the opening sequence). To some extent, therefore, this scene and its aftermath should be regarded as an ironic and modernist deflation of archetypal models, rather than their renewed expression.

The fact that the transition to adulthood is achieved by virtue of the father's death possesses a celebrated precursor in the form of Ivan Turgenev's *Pervaia liubov′* (First Love, 1860). The father here, a figure similarly as authoritative and disciplined as the father in *Vozvrashchenie*, reveals the nature of adult sexual passion to his sixteen-year-old son, but only inadvertently (his 'last will and testament', a note written by hand shortly before he dies, advises his son to 'beware of a woman's love'). Although the gender dynamic of the *ménage à trois* in *Pervaia liubov′* is very different, the psychological drama in *Vozvrashchenie* is no less nuanced in its examination of the emotional developments taking place beneath the surface. It is a commonplace, for example, to emphasize the different responses to the reappearance of the father on the part of the two brothers, and to seek the origin of this split in their age difference: Andrei, the older of the two, possibly around fifteen, is post-pubescent (his voice has broken); whereas Ivan, conjectured to be around twelve, is clearly pre-pubescent (his voice has not).[29] Andrei's patronizing term of endearment

[28] For discussion of Freudian and Lacanian paradigms, see Strukov, 'The Return of the Gods', pp. 346–48.

[29] Ibid., p. 331, n.2.

in relation to his younger brother, *melkii* ('shorty'), while perhaps not intended to be offensive, reinforces this difference. Nevertheless, while Andrei's maturity suggests that he might be more receptive to his father's guidance, there has been little examination of the evolution of his character during the course of the trip, his conflicting loyalties and the gradual shift in allegiance towards his brother, which culminates in the confrontation with the father on the island. It is important to bear in mind that, before the father's re-emergence, the bond between the two boys has been experiencing tension. Ivan's right to membership of a gang of friends is under threat because he has refused to jump off a high tower into water below, ostensibly as a result of his fear of heights. This scene is presented as a test of courage, and therefore to some extent a symbolic rite of initiation into 'manhood'. His failure to meet this challenge results in a public show of indifference on the part of his brother, who abandons him at the top of the tower and the next day expresses allegiance to his peer-group rather than to their fraternal bond. This rupture in their relationship remains unresolved by the time of the father's arrival. At this early stage, as revealed by a conversation the night before they depart with their father on the expedition, the only joint enterprises on which they formally embark are the keeping of a diary, which they will later be shown maintaining on a daily basis, albeit with a degree of reluctance on Andrei's part, and their recognition of the importance of taking the family camera with them.

The 'photo-diary' in 'Vozvrashchenie': concealed emotion and the dialogic dimension

It is within the context of the camera as an instrument for communication, in particular as a means of 'dialogue' between the two brothers, that the coda of *Vozvrashchenie* merits consideration. According to the film's diegetic conceit, the main impulse for the act of photography appears to lie in the desire to record moments of the journey for posterity. Within this conventional scenario, however, it might be suspected that more subtle and subconscious imperatives are present. The number of photographs dedicated to the moment of departure, for instance, suggests that it represents a moment of anxiety; indeed, it implies that the primary audience for the 'photo-diary' is subconsciously recognized to be the mother, in other words, that the existence of such a 'diary', albeit retrospectively, will allow her to participate in the events of the expedition. Six photographs in total, just under one third of the contemporary section of the coda, are dedicated to this moment of departure. Furthermore, within this prolonged episode the mother appears in the very first photograph and two of the subsequent five. Close study of the content and unorthodox methods of composition in each case indicates a burden of concealed agitation. Unusually for a family photo, the very first image (Fig. 1 [**1**]) positions the mother outside the field of focus: the opacity of the image, and the presence of an invisible barrier in the form of a window, poeticizes the moment of separation and hints metaphorically that the memory of her is perhaps already receding. The second photograph (Fig. 2 [**2**]) reinforces this theme: Andrei's right hand reaches across to the rear-passenger window and seeks to touch his mother's hand through the glass as the vehicle begins to move away. This process culminates in the sixth and final photograph of the departure (Fig. 3 [**6**]), which depicts the figure of the mother through the back window as she recedes from view. Again, her face is partially obscured, this time by the hand she raises in a gesture of farewell, and her image generally is clouded by the faint reflection of an object from within the interior of the car.

These photographs testify to a sense of residual loyalty and possible guilt in relation to the leave-taking. It might be argued that the need to conceal this underlying anxiety gives rise to the acts of light-hearted bravado that take place both during and after this episode: Ivan presses his nose against the window of the car in a classic gesture of playfulness (Fig. 4 [**5**]); Andrei leans against the bonnet of the car in an act of seeming nonchalance (Fig. 5 [**7**]); the brothers picture each other sitting behind the wheel of the car with expressions of glee on their faces (Figs 6 & 7 [**8** & **9**]); Andrei takes a picture of Ivan as he leans his head out of the car-window (Fig. 8 [**11**]), and Ivan mirrors his action (Fig. 9 [**12**]). All these images are posed and, superficially at least, fall into the category of 'snapshot'. From the psychological point of view, however, the underlying motivation for them may be more complex. In their desire to demonstrate that they are having fun, that their journey is an exciting adventure and that, by taking pictures of each other, they are testifying to the shared nature of the adventure, it might be argued that the brothers are essentially engaged in a series of performative acts designed to reassure the absent mother when she comes to consult the photographs in future. Because the boys find themselves in unfamiliar territory, both psychologically and geographically, these acts might also be interpreted as attempts to reassure *themselves*. The tensions which lie concealed beneath the superficial bravado may explain the complete absence of the father in these images and indeed in the contemporary section of the coda as a whole. This must

Fig. 1 [**1**]

Fig. 2 [**2**]

Fig. 3 [**6**]

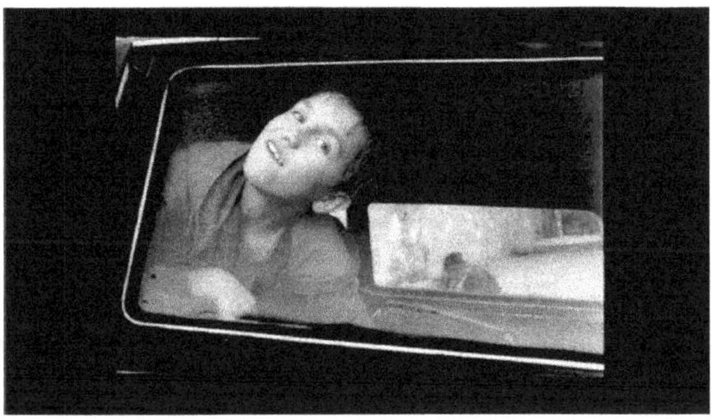

Fig. 4 [**5**]

Fig. 5 [7]

Fig. 6 [**8**]

Fig. 7 [**9**]

Fig. 8 [**11**]

Fig. 9 [**12**]

be regarded as curious in view of the interest which his reappearance has provoked prior to this moment, and which has taken the form of ocular inspection: the brothers gazing upon him while he sleeps, and consulting a photograph positioned within the pages of an illustrated edition of the Bible in order to confirm his identity. At a subconscious level, it appears that the brothers are withholding their interest in him as a potentially photographable subject until their relationship with him has become clarified.

If these early images can be argued to reflect the subtle psychological reverberations that occur as a result of the departure, it is also revealing to study them in terms of their respective 'authorship'. Although it is Andrei who is primarily identified as the 'owner' of the camera — he is shown on several occasions with the apparatus hanging around his neck — it is actually Ivan who, within the diegetic conceit of the coda, takes the vast majority of the photographs during the departure episode, and indeed who is responsible for a majority of the images in the coda as a whole. Close study of the series reveals subtle differences in the ways in which the boys approach their material. Within the diegetic conceit, the three opening shots of the mother have been taken by Ivan. This is implied by a vantage point from the back seat of the car, a position with which he is persistently associated during the main body of the narrative (one of the other photographs in the coda (Fig. 10 [**10**]) shows him asleep on this back seat), and suggests that the anxieties in relation to the imminent disruption of the maternal bond belong primarily to him. Manipulation of depth of field to suggest emotional turbulence is a device also employed in relation to an early portrait of Andrei (Fig. 11 [**4**]), which shows the elder brother looking back over his shoulder. Ivan's interrogations of his brother's moods and his sensitive handling of landscape are the hallmarks of his photographs. The portrait of Andrei as he leans on the bonnet of the car, his arms casually

Fig. 10 [**10**]

Fig. 11 [**4**]

Fig. 12 [**14**]

Fig. 13 [**16**]

folded, communicates an early mood of insouciance (Fig. 5 [7]). As the series progresses, however, his mood becomes darker and more thoughtful. The first indication of a more contemplative persona occurs in the photograph taken at the port when the father is negotiating the payment for the outboard motor (Fig. 12 [14]); in diegetic terms, this takes place after the incident during which Andrei has been injured by his father while trying to extricate the car from mud. Subsequent studies on the island show Andrei appearing to enjoy himself in the waters of the lake, knee-deep in barely rippling water, his outstretched arms and torso silhouetted against a cloudless horizon (Fig. 13 [16]). The very next shot (Fig. 14 [17]) shows him with droplets of water clinging to his nose and chin, presumably after a brief plunge into the water. These scenes of enjoyment are short-lived, however. Two shots later, he is shown during a moment of solitude as he walks along the shore, his face assuming the same pensive expression as the photograph taken at the port (Fig. 15 [19]). Because these images have clearly been taken spontaneously, and employ some interesting strategies in relation to composition and handling of light, they are far removed from the typical, beach-style snap, even if they might allude to typical, beach-style activities. In all three images, it should be noted that the body is decentred and the landscape and weather conditions accorded equal weight with the human subject.

Fig. 14 [17]

Fig. 15 [19]

Andrei's choice of subjects in the opening section of the coda offers less evidence of underlying emotional turbulence: his portraits of Ivan standing with his fishing rod (Fig. 16 [**3**]) and pressing his nose against the window (Fig. 4 [**5**]) are relatively mundane when compared to Ivan's early compositions. Nevertheless, as the series evolves, his compositional strategies become more varied and sophisticated. The portrait of his brother lying asleep in the back seat of the car (Fig. 10 [**10**]) is Andrei's first unrehearsed photograph within the coda; tellingly, the position of the body is decentred, and the aura of innocence and rest potentially punctured by encroaching shadow. This composition is followed shortly afterwards by an image of Ivan, his hair wet, and his face neatly divided by the edge of the passenger-door window, as he stares pensively into the distance (Fig. 17 [**13**]). Formally speaking, this composition is balanced between the mysterious expression on Ivan's face and the hazy outlines of trees reflected darkly in the glass and the random distribution of raindrops along its surface. Significantly, this confirmation of a shift in Andrei's lyrical sensibilities follows the traumatic episode in which he has fallen victim to the first act of violence on the part of his father. The next photograph taken by Andrei, which shows Ivan standing in the meadow on the island where the dilapidated shack with the black box is located (Fig. 18 [**15**]), sustains this interest in probing, psychological portraiture. Like the earlier images taken by Ivan, this photograph features a decentred subject. Furthermore, as with the portrait of Ivan in the car (Fig. 17 [**13**]), it reveals a sensitivity to the poetic potential of landscape (raindrops on glass are replaced by wild flowers scattered among long grass). It is important to emphasize that, in common with the images taken earlier by Ivan, this is an unrehearsed moment: Andrei has captured his brother during a moment of contemplation, his expression revealing someone who has just looked round, his thoughts disturbed.

The interest which the boys exhibit in their respective emotional moods is reflected not only in the content of their photographs of each other, but also in the ways in which the immediate impulse for the act of photography is echoed from image to image. The discrete pairing of the pictures in the contemporary part of the coda is the most obvious demonstration of this, and constitutes the visual equivalent of the practice of keeping the diary in turns. This impression is reinforced by the ways in which compositional emphases are 'rhymed' from shot to shot. Thus one pairing shows the boys sitting behind the steering wheel of their father's car, the first (Fig. 6 [**8**]) appearing to prompt the second (Fig. 7 [**9**]). Andrei's decision (encouraged by

Fig. 16 [**3**]

Fig. 17 [**13**]

Fig. 18 [**15**]

Ivan, as we learn from the main body of the narrative) to take a photograph of his brother with his head out of the window as the car travels at speed triggers the latter's response almost immediately afterwards (Figs 8 & 9 [**11** & **12**]). Although more distant in terms of their respective positions within the series, it is possible to associate the image of Ivan standing with his fishing rod during the preparations for departure (Fig. 16 [**3**]) with Andrei leaning nonchalantly against the bonnet of the car (Fig. 5 [**7**]). Elsewhere, we encounter images in which visual detail and dominant mood are echoed. Thus Andrei's interest in raindrops on glass (Fig. 17 [**13**]) may plausibly trigger Ivan's picture of Andrei with droplets of water clinging to his face (Fig. 14 [**17**]). By the same token, the portraits of a pensive Andrei (Figs 12 & 15 [**14** & **19**]) are imitated by the study of a contemplative Ivan with the dilapidated shack in the background (Fig. 18 [**15**]). As the series evolves, and the mood darkens, some of the images might be regarded as involuntary subversions of earlier shots. Thus the image of Ivan with this nose pressed playfully against the passenger-door window (Fig. 4 [**5**]) is reversed by the sombre tones of the portrait taken on the other side (Fig. 17 [**13**]). In the same way, the two images of Andrei at the port and walking along the beach (Figs 12 & 15 [**14** & **19**]) reverse the nonchalance of the portrait which shows him leaning against the bonnet of the car (Fig. 5 [**7**]). Viewed collectively and progressively, the contemporary part of the coda reveals the brothers' persistent preoccupation with each other, their sensitivity to each other's moods, and an increasing, mutual empathy, which culminates in the penultimate shot of the series (Fig. 19 [**20**]). Here, in a self-portrait ostensibly taken by Andrei, the two boys pose in an attitude of intimacy, the physical gesture by Ivan, which involves resting his head on Andrei's right shoulder and clasping his brother's left shoulder with his arm, symptomatic of their strengthening bond. As an act of solidarity, this photograph anticipates Ivan's vigorous defence of his brother in the face of the father's physical violence. The unity of photographic vision which the two boys begin to share by the end of the coda gives rise to a degree of uncertainty about the implied authorship of the final photograph within the contemporary series, the so-called 'Chaika' (Fig. 20 [**21**]).

The dialogic situation which emerges as a result of this series of photographs, while perhaps not constituting a counter-narrative as such, does nevertheless accentuate a series of themes which are only latent within the main body of the filmic narrative. It constitutes, so to speak, the third side of the triangular relationship which develops between the father and his two sons, and emphasizes the degree to which the intrusion of the former in the lives of the latter leads ultimately to a rediscovery of the fraternal bond which has previously been under threat. A crucial moment in the coda from the symbolic point of view occurs when the boys, albeit playfully, assume positions behind the wheel of the car. Psychologically, these images imply that they have grasped the car's significance as vehicle, both literal and metaphorical, for the nomadic principle and the function of the driving seat as a symbolic, paternal 'throne'. It is noteworthy that this act of subversion is instigated by Ivan, who has somehow acquired the keys and simulates the act of starting the engine (his expression betrays

Fig. 19 [**20**]

Fig. 20 [**21**]

recognition of this stunt's intrinsic blasphemy). This act functions as a repudiation of the accusation, uttered in the context of his reluctance to jump from the tower in the opening sequence, that Ivan is a 'coward' (*trus*). It is a paradox in the emotional and psychological fabric of *Vozvrashchenie* that the brother who appears to be the more resolute defender of the maternal status quo is the more 'masculine' in terms of his response to the 'invasion' of an alien figure.

Bearing in mind the significance attached to the departure, the coda also places far greater emphasis on the emotional resonance of the home as a symbolic shelter associated with the maternal principle. From this perspective, literally and figuratively, the abandoned dwelling which stands on the island and houses the mysterious black box to which the father seeks access might be regarded as its direct antipode, an insecure and vulnerable place which symbolically represents the family's shattered past. Such an interpretation would lay stress on the symbolism of the black box as a repository of memory. Like the black-box recorder of an aeroplane (the father's purported career as a pilot might be regarded as relevant in this context), this container might be interpreted as an emotional 'treasure-trove' which has long ago been buried, but which contains the secrets of the father's act of desertion twelve years earlier. By extension, the act of retrieval on the part of the father becomes an act of personal excavation or archaeology, the primary aim of which is to interrogate the self and the memories which lie within this self.

In support of this reading, it might be pointed out that the theme of the abandoned home is prominent in the screenplay in relation to the expedition. There are two references in this text to homes or communities having been evacuated or abandoned: the first concerns the dilapidated dwellings associated with the boat-repairing sequence;[30] and the second is a small settlement on the island which consists of two burnt-out shacks, a small chapel and a tiny cemetery with three graves, one of which conceals the black box.[31] In the film, while certain details have been modified, the substance of the theme nevertheless remains. In relation to the boat-repairing sequence, for example, Zviagintsev and Krichman ensure that the rickety doors of the building form part of a tracking shot which follows Ivan as he carries a bucket of pitch towards his father and brother as they stand next to the boat. Likewise, although the chapel and cemetery on the island no longer feature, and the location of the box has been moved from the grave-site to an *izba*, or hut, this building has clearly become dilapidated over time: weeds and wild shrubs have colonized its interior, and the boys estimate that it must be 'at least' one hundred years old. Furthermore, the island generally is associated with images of erosion and desertion. The boat which transports the father and his sons to the island has long ago ceased to function (it has to be repaired in order to become operational and, significantly, the outboard motor quickly malfunctions); the waters of the lake surrounding the island are populated by the relics of formerly seaworthy, but now rusting, vessels; and the lighthouse on which the father meets his death has long ago been abandoned and is unsafe (this death is caused precisely because part of its wooden structure gives way as he scrambles to reach the top). It might be regarded as significant that boxes or trunks in *Vozvrashchenie* are associated with memories, photographs and rejected household relics. The photograph of the father which Ivan seeks after his return is concealed in a large trunk in an attic filled with a multitude of discarded objects; the fact that this search raises a cloud of dust suggests that the trunk has not been examined for several years. Similarly, the black box on the island is located in a trunk, the rusty locks and buried position of which suggest an object long ago concealed. In the context of the fishing expedition as a search for mnemonic 'treasure', it

[30] Moiseenko and Novototskii, 'Ty', p. 93.

[31] Ibid., p. 103.

is worth pointing out that the term 'black box' in Russian (*chernyi iashchik*) is a colloquial term for 'camera'. In addition, the fact that the father keeps a memento of the family past with him in the form of an old photograph suggests that this past is a source of constant preoccupation for him.

The desire to retrieve or salvage a precious cargo from the past, one which ends ultimately in failure, lends the figure of the father a tragic dimension which has been ignored in the critical writing on *Vozvrashchenie* hitherto. It is possible to argue, as Zviagintsev himself has hinted, that the final photograph of the contemporary part of the epilogue (Fig. 20 [**21**]), despite its fortuitous genesis, has been included precisely in order to suggest an involuntary resurrection of the father's memory in the minds of the two brothers.[32] 'Chaika' is distinguished from the rest of the series in the sense that its location, while sea-related, is not precisely resonant with the landscape of the main narrative; for this reason, the viewer is entitled to speculate that it captures a moment in time after the events of this narrative have concluded.[33] Nevertheless, the subject of the photograph (a rowing-boat) uncannily resembles the vessel which serves as the final resting place for the father's body just moments before its disappearance, and therefore reflects a spontaneous recollection on the part of this image's 'author'. In other words, like the diary in the original screenplay, this image resurrects the ghost of the father and suggests that the events of the expedition might still haunt the minds of the young protagonists.

The persistence of the father's memory in the form of 'Chaika' suggests that the catharsis of which Zviagintsev speaks in relation to the epilogue must be approached with a degree of caution.[34] The potential ambiguity of the epilogue can be gauged by the emotional resonances of the soundtrack. This acoustic accompaniment consists of two elements: the sounds of rain and thunder, and the words and melody of a song, 'Ne iz sadu' ('It was not from the garden'), the beginning of which coincides with the appearance of the eighth photograph. The presence of thunder, initially a low rumble that develops shortly afterwards into a deafening thunder clap, and the rain, the tentative sounds of which are introduced before the coda proper begins, and which gradually increase in intensity before eventually fading away, support the idea of an oppressive atmosphere having been

[32] 'Andrei Zviagintsev: Istoriia shelkopriada'.

[33] In this context, it is worth noting that the scene of the diary reading in the screenplay takes place in New York. See Moiseenko and Novototskii, 'Ty', pp. 113–14.

[34] Specifically, Zviagintsev talks about the coda in terms of the 'unwinding' and 'cleansing' (*ochishchenie*) of the emotions, the 'distance' that can be gained over time in relation to suffering, and the possibility of retrospective 'happiness' even while recognizing that suffering has taken place. See *The Return: A Film about the Film*.

punctured. The poetic resonances of the folk song, however, are more complicated. From the cinematic point of view, it should be noted that the interweaving of natural sound with the haunting melody of a Russian folk song is a device which Zviagintsev has clearly borrowed from the coda of Andrei Tarkovskii's *Nostalghia* (1981). The song in question, heard in the background as the camera tracks away slowly from a superimposed vision of a ruined Benedictine monastery and rural Russian dwelling, is a traditional lyric, 'Oi kumushki, kumites′' ('Oh friends, let us come together'), which concerns the divining of future husbands on Trinity Sunday.[35] Unlike this song, however, only a fragment of the full text of 'Ne iz sadu' (approximately one third) is heard in Zviagintsev's film. In fact, the soundtrack of the coda in *Vozvrashchenie* features a fragment of a fragment of a fragment. Twelve lines are borrowed from the only existing recording of this song, and this version itself, as the compilers make clear, constitutes only around half of the best known variants of the text.[36]

'Ne iz sadu' belongs to the folk repertoire of the so-called Nekrasov Cossacks, descendants of Old Believer communities forcibly expelled from Russia after their participation in a rebellion in the early eighteenth century, and the majority of whom only returned to Russia in 1962.[37] The song is a ballad which belongs to the category of *protiazhnaia pesnia* (protracted song), so termed in Russian because the long, vibrating notes of the melodies lend such songs a sorrowful, meditative quality.[38] In its full version, this lyric tells the tale of two warrior-brothers who leave home and try to cross the freezing Danube. It falls upon the younger brother to cross first, but his noble steed stumbles, he falls from his saddle into

[35] The song is sung by the virtuoso (and now legendary) folk singer Ol′ga Fedoseevna Sergeeva and was released on vinyl by Melodiia in 1977 in a collection entitled *Usviatskie pesni*. See <http://kumukhi.narod.ru/sergeeva.html> [accessed 12 July 2012].

[36] The song was recorded during field trips to the Soviet Union in 1989 and 1990; its singer, Ivan Mefod′evich Banderovskii, was eighty years old at the time. It was released on CD in 1995 by Smithsonian/Folkways in a collection entitled *Old Believers: Songs of the Nekrassov Cossacks*, which was compiled and annotated by Margarita Mazo with the assistance of Olga Velichkina. Professor Mazo and Dr Velichkina explain in the booklet which accompanies this release that, because of the length of the originals, many of the songs are presented only in shortened versions. See Margarita Mazo and Olga Velichkina, 'History, Memory, Song: Voices of the Nekrasov Cossacks', ibid., pp. 2–13 (p. 2).

[37] The Nekrasov Cossacks are named after their eighteenth-century leader, Ignat Nekrasov, who participated in the uprising of ataman Kondratii Bulavin in the years 1707–09. Their peregrinations abroad included periods of settlement along the Danube delta and areas bordering the Sea of Marmara. See 'Kazach′i pesni nekrasovskie' <http://a-pesni.org/kazaki/nekrasov/Nekrasov.php> [accessed 27 January 2012].

[38] Vadim Prokhorov, *Russian Folk Songs: Musical Genres and History*, Lanham, MD, 2002, pp. 79–85.

the freezing waters below and, as he drowns, he appeals to his brother to pass on his words of lament for his tragic fate to his family and wife.[39] Although the song is unique to the Nekrasov Cossacks, it features several well-known motifs from lyrical and epic song cycles: the death of a warrior on foreign soil; a body of water which functions as a liminal boundary; death in the bosom of nature (drowning as a form of 'death-wedding'); and the testament of a dying warrior to his nearest and dearest.[40] In broad terms, the genre of the ballad (ideal for a 'road-movie') and the melancholic tone (the lyric laments the death of someone brave and fearless who has left home) must obviously have appealed to Zviagintsev. Furthermore, by interrupting the song after only twelve lines at the moment when the two brothers arrive at the river, in other words before the death has occurred, the director facilitates an obvious parallel with the photographic coda itself in the sense that the images in the contemporary section end before the death of the father. In the context of the full version of the song, however, the parallels between the *Vozvrashchenie* coda and 'Ne iz sadu' break down, since it is a 'warrior-father' who 'drowns', the submerging of his body beneath the water constituting a second, 'symbolic' death, rather than a 'warrior-brother'. Nevertheless, in the poignant lament for a loss of life far from home, and its stress on the importance of kith and kin, the song reinforces the idea of a memory which continues to reverberate in the mind.

Actual authorship and 'skaz'-style performance

The knowledge that all the photographs of the coda, both 'contemporary' and 'historical', are the work of a professional photographer renders the series highly ambiguous in formal terms. The selection of these photographs from the portfolio produced by Mishukov while working on the production clearly reveals his desire to preserve the integrity of the *skaz*-like conceit. Thus, for example, only one image in the coda shows both boys within the frame, and this has been presented in the form of a 'self-portrait' in order to preserve the conceit of authorship.[41] The need to

[39] I am indebted to Professor Anatolii Ivanov, senior researcher at the Moscow Republican Centre for Russian Folklore, who recorded a version of 'Ne iz sadu' in 1984 and has supplied me with a full text of this version and some of its variants. Private email to the author dated 19 July 2012.

[40] Private email to the author dated 23 July 2012 from Dr Vasilii Kovpik, Researcher at the Department of Russian Folklore, Faculty of Philology, Moscow State University. I am indebted to Dr Velichkina at the Sorbonne for putting me in touch with Dr Kovpik.

[41] This may well have been the case in reality, but bearing in mind the difficulty of centring the image when one is not looking directly through the viewfinder, as well as

maintain the illusion of subjectivity doubtless also explains the rationale for the positions adopted by Mishukov during the departure episode, each of which simulates the (presumed) vantage point of the brothers at the moment of leave-taking.

Although it might be assumed, bearing in mind their status as production photos, that all the images of the coda have been produced spontaneously, it is clear that some have been staged. This is a fundamental ambiguity which further complicates their formal status. Zviagintsev has confirmed that the departure scene was organized especially for Mishukov.[42] We may assume, therefore, that the positioning of the actors, the angle of perspective and the desired aesthetic were planned in advance. The 'historical' part of the coda, moreover, bears traces of a similar kind of choreographic procedure. Mishukov's contact sheets, a rare insight into the working practices of a professional photographer, reveal that, although the figures involved were not posing for the camera as such, the general situation (the arrangement of figures and the positioning of props) was staged.[43] Like the 'contemporary' section of the coda, these four photographs, selected from a series of thirty-six taken with Ilford FP4 black-and-white film stock, offer ironic commentaries on the fictional events which form the main part of the narrative. The mother (Fig. 21 [**22**]) is portrayed for the most part unflatteringly, which hints at the stress and fatigue of early-years parenthood (the absence of make-up, the pallor of her skin and the small bags under her eyes stand in stark contrast to her presentation in the main narrative). The presence of a motorbike with side-car in two of the photographs (Figs 22 & 23 [**23** & **24**]) underlines the father's symbolic association with vehicles and thus, by extension, the nomadic principle (the fact that Andrei is pictured sitting in this side-car and wearing his father's helmet — Fig. 22 [**23**] — hints that he is being 'groomed' as the future son and heir). Finally, and ironically in view of the tensions which prevail during the expedition, the final image of the sequence, the only one in the coda which features a close-up of the father, and thus retrospectively confirms his paternal identity, portrays him holding Ivan in his arms and looking towards him in a gesture of tenderness (Fig. 24 [**25**]). The tactile warmth displayed here contrasts sharply with his lack of physical affection during the expedition. In so doing, this

avoiding the tilting of the camera, it is more than likely that this image was actually taken by Mishukov, with Andrei's hand only reaching towards the camera, but not in actual fact holding it or pressing its shutter.

[42] Zviagintsev's preface in Mishukov, *Vozvrashchenie*, p. 5.

[43] Ibid., p. 92.

Fig. 21 [**22**]

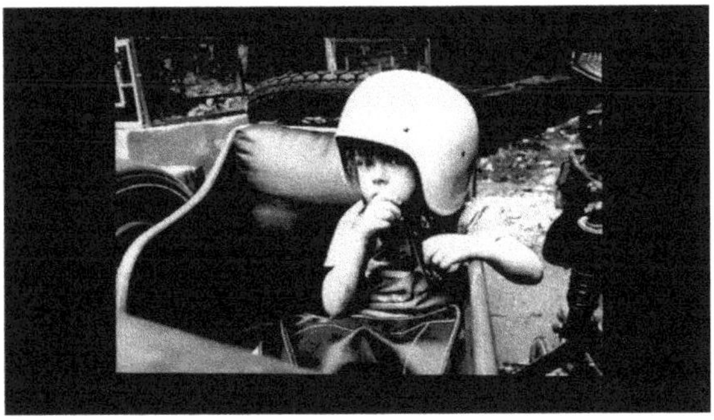

Fig. 22 [**23**]

Fig. 23 [**24**]

Fig. 24 [**25**]

portrait reinforces the film's investigation of parental desertion as an act with potentially tragic consequences which cannot be painlessly or easily reversed.

Significantly, among the eighty stills included in his *Vozvrashchenie* album, Mishukov not only decided to include nine of the photographs which featured in the coda, but also ended the album with the very same images (Andrei's 'self-portrait' (p. 88) and 'Chaika' (p. 89) with which the contemporary part of the coda concludes.[44] In view of the 'collision' between the staged and non-staged, it is tempting to speculate on the degree to which Mishukov was deliberately seeking to explore the tensions between fictional creation and documentary fact. One of the stills from the album, which shows Andrei, played by Vladimir Garin, playfully pointing the family camera towards Mishukov and either genuinely taking or simulating the act of taking a photograph (p. 22 [Fig. 25]), is a meta-photograph which reveals a degree of self-reflexivity on Mishukov's part. There are precedents for this type of creative manoeuvre in the history of Russian cinema, most notably Tarkovskii's use of purportedly genuine family photographs (in reality, production stills by Vladimir Murashko) to establish a psychological rationale for the doubling of the actress Margarita Terekhova in *Zerkalo* (Mirror, 1974).[45] Compared to Murashko's images from the sets of *Zerkalo*, however, Mishukov's portfolio is a great deal more ambitious from the artistic point of view. Along with Georgii Pinkhasov's portraits of dancers at the Bolshoi Ballet, and his other studies of performers backstage for the Magnum agency, it demonstrates the degree to which, from the late 1960s onwards, and especially after the collapse of the Soviet Union, photographers associated with the world of celebrity portraiture had graduated from the more straightforwardly commercial genres, for example fashion photography, towards statements with serious artistic pretensions.[46]

[44] Ibid., pp. 88 & 89. Henceforth, all page references pertaining to images within this album will be given in parentheses in the body of the article.

[45] Terekhova plays the role of the narrator's mother in the past and his ex-wife in the present. At one point in the film, as the ex-wife, Terekhova studies four photographs which show herself and Tarkovskii's actual mother, Mar′ia Vishniakova, who plays herself in the present, and comments on their physical resemblance. This resemblance is denied by the narrator in the exchange which follows, but in an earlier conversation with his ex-wife he comments that 'whenever I recall my childhood and my mother, for some reason my mother always has your face'. The last of the four photographs is reproduced in Natasha Synessios, *Mirror*, London, 2001, p. 90. Although these images are not authentic, it is worth noting the importance of genuine family photographs in helping Tarkovskii reconstruct the realia of his childhood in *Zerkalo*. These images were mostly taken by Lev Gornung, a family friend and enthusiastic amateur photographer. See ibid., p. 42.

[46] These photographs are currently available at <http://www.magnumphotos.com> [accessed 25 March 2012]. For Pinkhasov's artistic evolution both before and after his

Fig. 25

Even allowing for the multiplicity of forms in which film-production photographs currently exist, there are several unusual features about the *Vozvrashchenie* album. Most film-production photography tends to concentrate on the director and his or her work with the acting ensemble, and invariably captures the latter during moments of performance from a position not far removed from the motion-picture camera itself. Alternatively, it may seek to expose the artifice with which the film-industry manipulates 'reality' on screen, or reveals a fascination with the technological mechanics of contemporary filmmaking. By contrast, it is noteworthy that more than half of Mishukov's portfolio of stills consists of studies of Garin and Ivan Dobronravov, who plays the role of Ivan. Furthermore, the vast majority of these studies consists of images in which the boys are isolated from the other cast members and the crew, and indeed

decision to emigrate from the Soviet Union in 1985, see 'Georgii Pinkhasov: "Sud´ba daet fotografu dva shansa"', *Moskovskie novosti*, 30 September 2011 <http://mn.ru/newspaper?freetime20110930/303354687.html> [accessed 26 March 2012], and 'Georgii Pinkhasov: "Chem bezvykhodnei moe polozhenie, tem bol´she otkrytii ia delaiu', interview with Mitia Nesterov <http://www.photographer.ru/cult/person/4928.htm> [accessed 26 March 2012]. For the specific contributions of Viktor Dombrovskii, Georgii Ter-Ovanesov, Mikola Gnisiuk, Valerii Plotnikov and Igor´ Gnevashev to the canon of film-production photography, see, respectively, the following articles by Dzhemma Firsova: 'Sopernik samogo Moskvina (Fotokhudozhnik Viktor Dombrovskii)', *Iskusstvo kino*, 2006, 2, pp. 72–77; 'Kak molody my byli!', ibid., 2006, 4, pp. 54–59; 'V kadre i za kadrom', ibid., 2006, 6, pp. 56–61; 'Teatr odnogo portreta', ibid., 2006, 8, pp. 64–69, and 'Moment istiny', ibid., 2006, 10, pp. 44–46.

few relate directly to the filmmaking process. In a further act of subversion, the very first image in the album, one conventionally understood as the most programmatic, features an anonymous figure whose relationship to the wider production process is unclear. The portfolio consists of a number of landscapes in which no member of the production team or acting ensemble is present; several images in which the human subject is unidentifiable; and a number of portraits in which the human subject is a peripheral figure in compositional terms. In addition, Mishukov's portfolio includes five images which relate to the reception of the film at the Venice Film Festival in 2003, in other words, well after the production itself had been completed. Interestingly, as indicated above, these are not the images with which the album concludes.

The disruption of chronological sequencing, as well as the intense focus on the child actors, suggest that Mishukov's album was conceived with a different purpose in mind from the conventional film-production chronicle. In many respects, it is a highly personal and idiosyncratic vision which combines elements of continuity and parallelism in relation to the fictional enterprise from which it has been spawned. As a parallel movement, the portfolio represents Mishukov's interpretation of the script and his creative response to its themes. In terms of continuity, his portfolio constitutes an assembly of images which move beyond the film's interest in the crisis of masculinity to poeticize the perceptions and experiences of childhood generally. Several of his projects since the making of *Vozvrashchenie* confirm his interest in the universe of the child. *Kul′t sem′i* (Cult of the Family), for example, which was shown at Moscow's Central Exhibition Hall on the Manège in 2006, consisted of seventy-eight images of 'nuclear' families in their normal domestic environment. Mishukov has explained that the genesis of the idea for the exhibition was prompted by his discovery of a family photograph dating from the 1920s which had been discarded on a Moscow street and presumably forgotten by its owners.[47] His interest in challenging stereotypes in relation to children with Down's Syndrome (his fourth child was born with the condition) prompted an exhibition at the Lumière Brothers' Photographic Centre in Moscow in September 2011; entitled *Blizkie liudi* (People Close to Me), the portfolio was later published as an album.[48] Mishukov has also published an album

[47] 'Geroi nashego vremeni: Kakie oni, segodniashnie rossiiskie sem′i?', interview given by Mishukov to Marina Nefedova <http:///www.priestt.com/article/liter/_460.html> [accessed 26 March 2012] (para. 2 of 12).

[48] Mishukov's interview with Tat′iana Vladykina, 'Sindrom radosti: Kak roditeliam bol′nogo rebenka byt′ schastlivymi', *Rossiiskaia gazeta*, 23 March 2012 <http://www.

of portraits dedicated to Slava Polunin, the Russian clown, whose celebrated 'Snowshow' is regularly performed all over the world. Although primarily a study of the poetics of the clown-figure (Mishukov has spoken of the theme of 'loneliness' and the 'clown that exists within all of us'), these studies are careful to evoke the magical aura of the sets and the varied responses of the children among Polunin's audiences.[49] It may be deemed significant in this context that Mishukov's interest in photography, after graduating from the Russian Academy of Theatre Arts in the early 1990s, was prompted by the birth of his first child;[50] that his relationship with Dobronravov and Garin was sufficiently close during the production of *Vozvrashchenie* that, on his own admission, he acted as something approaching a surrogate father to them;[51] and that both he and Garin had been separated from their fathers at an early age.[52] As the actress playing the role of the mother, Natal′ia Vdovina, has also suggested, the decision to photograph the images of the *Vozvrashchenie* coda in black and white may have been prompted by the desire to evoke the photographs of the filmmakers' childhoods.[53] It may be regarded as significant in this context that the family camera which features in the film, and the manufacture of which is revealed in Mishukov's self-reflexive portrait of Andrei (p. 22 [Fig. 26]), is a Minolta 'Easy Flash' Hi-Matic 9. This is a camera which dates from 1966, only three years before Mishukov was born.

Mishukov's interest in communicating the experience of childhood can be witnessed in his choice of subjects in the *Vozvrashchenie* album and, where objects, their textures and forms and occasional, eccentric juxtaposition. The photograph which shows four walkie-talkies positioned as 'couples' on a pair of sandals left on a beach (p. 37 [Fig. 26]) is one such fruitful *trouvaille*, the amusement deriving primarily from the fact that the image serves as a visual manifestation of the name of the instrument ('walkie-talkie'). The photograph is suggestive in several other ways. When combined with the photograph of a child's toes in sand (p. 50), the rest of the body presumably buried in a classic evocation of the traditional, beach-

rg.ru/2012/03/23/mishukov.html> [accessed 29 March 2012] (preamble to interview).

[49] Vladimir Mishukov, *Slava: Polnopolunie*, Moscow, 2010. For Mishukov's comments on the album, see <http://www.paulsen.ru/catalogue/books/184> [accessed 12 June 2012].

[50] Dzhemma Firsova, 'Vozvrashchenie', *Iskusstvo kino*, 2006, 12, pp. 32–37 (p. 33).

[51] For these remarks, see *The Return: A Film about the Film*.

[52] Garin speaks briefly about his father in ibid. For Mishukov's background as the product of a broken home (he talks about his parents being divorced, and his concept of the family having thus been 'disrupted'), see 'Geroi nashego vremeni: Kakie oni, segodniashnie rossiiskie sem′i?' (para. 1 of 12).

[53] *The Return: A Film about the Film*.

related enterprise, Mishukov creates an ironic juxtaposition between the beach as a site for childhood recreation and as a working environment for a film production team. The irony is enhanced by the knowledge that, within the filmic diegesis, the fictional protagonists have embarked on a trip which has been presented to them as something akin to a holiday, but which is compromised and perpetually postponed by the machinations of the father. A similarly ironic distance can be witnessed in the image of Dobronravov and Garin rowing the boat as the sun sets behind them in the distance (pp. 46–47), a striking contrast to the scene in the film which shows them forced to take up oars in the same boat by the father in torrential rain in order to make the crossing to the island. The child-like exploration of the seaside is also reflected in the photographic interest in the textures and patterns of sand and feathers (pp. 37, 41, 50 & 71). The *Vozvrashchenie* album seeks to communicate the young child's fascination with the sensation of speed (the photographs of the boys with their heads out of the car windows (Figs 8 & 9 [**11** & **12**]). Furthermore, not only does Mishukov's camera on occasion offer child-like perspectives, such as the ground-level view of the toes in the sand (p. 50), it also seeks to communicate the child's perception of the bodily self. Initially, as illustrated by the opening image of the unidentified boy captured at a moment when he is airborne (p. 8), and the photograph of Ivan when he jumps into the air (p. 59), this takes the form of the experience of weightlessness. Later,

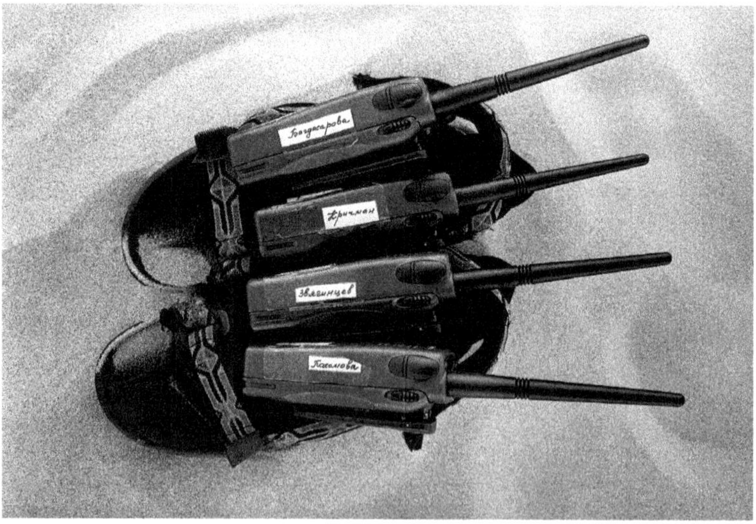

Fig. 26

in a diametrically opposed manner, this interest shifts to the experience of weight when Ivan's clothes are shown drenched in water and hanging heavily on his body for the scene in which he and his brother run towards the boat in a vain attempt to prevent their father's dead body from sinking beneath the waters of the lake (pp. 61 & 74). Mishukov's interest in evoking the pathos of childhood is also suggested by the inclusion of a photograph unrelated either to the production or the awards ceremony: this shows two toddlers feeding pigeons on St Mark's Square in Venice, one of them almost completely obliterated from view by the flock of fluttering, avian bodies (p. 86). Albeit banal, this image is a classic evocation of childhood, and one, interestingly, that also features in the childhood memory sections of Marker's *La Jetée*. Mishukov's words in his preface to the portfolio, in which he speaks of the album as an 'attempt to return to those days that will never be repeated', might be interpreted as relating to the experience of childhood as much as to the experience of the film production itself.[54]

In view of the generally sombre atmosphere of the album — the vast majority of the images have been taken in diffuse conditions, with relatively low levels of available light (even at those moments where strong sunlight prevails, compositionally the photographs privilege the areas of darkness) — it might be speculated that events occurring between the completion of the film and the publication of the album have influenced the selection of material and its sequential ordering. The death of Garin as a result of drowning in Lake Osinovetskoe, the very same lake where part of the filming had taken place, and one year exactly from the day when shooting had begun, shocked the production team and meant that he did not live to see the final version of the film (he died just two days before its première) and was absent from the awards ceremony.[55] In light of the fact that Zviagintsev dedicated his Golden Lion award to Garin, the possibility should not be excluded that Mishukov's album was conceived in part as a commemorative tribute.[56] The strategic positioning of a Garin portrait (p. 84 [Fig. 27]) within a mini-bloc of five photographs (pp. 82–85) that ostensibly marks a thematic shift from the production to the reception of the film abroad is a curious anomaly from the chronological point of view. The

[54] Mishukov, *Vozvrashchenie*, p. 3.

[55] The circumstances of Garin's death are related at the end of *The Return: A Film about the Film*. More specific information has been given by his mother, Tat'iana Vital'evna Garina. See 'Volodia byl ne ot mira sego', interview with Maksim Dynnikov, *Smena*, 9 September 2003 <http://www.smena.ru/news/2003/09/09/795/> [accessed 25 January 2012].

[56] 'Vince il film russo, delusione per Bellocchio', *Corriere della Sera*, 7 September 2003.

PROD.NO.
Отец
SCENE
7-4
TAKE
1
SOUND
DIRECTOR
CAMERAMAN
DATE
EXT.
INT.

Fig. 27

Fig. 28

urban landscape and presence of a clapper-board at the actor's feet with the sequence number prominently displayed suggest that this image refers to a moment relatively early in the production, yet it is immediately succeeded across the page by a portrait of Dobronravov (p. 85 [Fig. 28]) which, judging from his attire and haircut, dates from the time of the awards ceremony.[57] The chronological asynchrony is matched by the sartorial contrast: Garin is wearing the standard teenage recreational uniform of jeans and sweatshirt, whereas Dobronravov is wearing a pin-striped suit and tie. Furthermore, Dobronravov's pensive and slightly melancholic expression, one far removed from the other images associated with the Venice festival in the mini-series, which stress exuberance and excitement, hint that his thoughts might perhaps be directed towards his absent colleague and friend.[58] The fact that the two actors are pictured together on ten separate occasions in the album (pp. 18, 25, 30, 35, 36, 45, 46–47, 62, 74 & 88), some of these showing moments of shared frivolity and enjoyment, suggests that their growing bond off-screen is one of its many subtexts.

Although Mishukov cannot have been aware at the time that one of his human subjects would die — there is a cruel parallel between the fate of the fictional father in the film and Garin's death in the sense that, despite the efforts of divers, his body has never been located — it is striking nevertheless how many of the images in his album hint at the themes of disappearance and dematerialization. These themes assume several guises, some of them the product of subject-matter, others the result of compositional procedure. In relation to the former, there are two images in the album which consist solely of shadows (pp. 23 & 51); one in which the weather conditions (mist) impede clarity of vision (p. 48); eight in which contour (human figures presented in silhouetted form or photographed in the late evening or at night) take precedence over material substance and texture (pp. 38–39, 46–47, 60, 63, 68, 70, 80 & 81); one in which the form of the human subject loses its material solidity by virtue of being superimposed onto another object by means of reflection (p. 9); and one in which clarity of form is compromised by a screen of opaque material (p. 10 [Fig. 29]). Particular choices in relation to shutter speed and depth of field produce analogous effects. Several images display a penchant for shallow depth of field (pp. 61

[57] This can be confirmed with reference to the photographs of the ceremony. See <http://ivan.dobronravov.narod.ru/kinofestival.html> [accessed 12 June 2012].

[58] The likelihood that Garin's absence was weighing on his mind is confirmed in an interview given with the Italian newspaper *Corriere della Sera* shortly after the awards ceremony on 8 September 2003. See <http://ivan.dobronravov.narod.ru/kinofestival.html> [accessed 12 June 2012].

& 65); as a result, subsidiary objects within the frame are depicted out of focus, thus becoming intangible, and at times unrecognizable. The resort to slower shutter speeds for some of the motion studies (pp. 59 & 76), with the result that the images in question are blurred, further compromises clarity of form. Tellingly, the very first portrait of Garin in the album (p. 10 [Fig. 29]) shows his face in the form of a faintly traceable mask. The effect, which is akin to that of photogravure, produces an impression or imprint, almost an *eidoton* or ghost-like apparition.

Fig. 29

Mishukov's 'Vozvrashchenie' album as film-production photography

Traditionally, film-production photography is regarded as a body of images which possess a direct relationship with the cinematic texts from which they owe their creative genesis. It is customary, nevertheless, to note their generic amplitude. The Moscow Museum of Cinema (Muzei kino), for example, identifies a number of sub-categories within its substantial photo-library collection: portraits of filmmakers in a variety of non-film related locations (public venues, private spaces and within the photographer's *atelier*); screen tests; images pertaining to the location-scouting process and set-construction period; tests of film stock; sequences not included in the final version of a given film; photographs and frame stills offered to agencies and the mass media for publicity purposes; and 'working moments during the film-production process'.[59] Undeniably, along with

[59] See <http://www.museikino.ru/fond/photo-library.htm> [accessed 24 March 2012].

works of cinema themselves, these materials are valuable documents that belong to the historical memory of film production and thus constitute its 'archive'. From the generic point of view, however, these categories reflect different creative impulses and thus artistic procedures. Portraits of figures from the world of cinema working on set differ considerably from the meticulously choreographed and aesthetically polished, if not *retouchées*, images taken in the photographer's studio. By the same token, there are clear distinctions between studies of actors composed during moments of filming and the images which have been taken during moments of informal relaxation between takes. Another complicating factor in relation to generic models lies in the relative dispersal of film-related photography as printed or, more recently, electronically scanned material. When film-production photographs do appear in print, such as the recent collections of Valerii Plotnikov, they are invariably interspersed with other material from the author's, often wide-ranging, oeuvre and thus are not easily distinguished from it.[60]

Mishukov's album is the first publication of its kind in Russia, and very possibly the world, in the sense that it is dedicated to a single film. The sense of deliberately engineered conceptual unity places it in a different category from the random selections of production-related material which can be found in printed media or on internet websites. Furthermore, the focus on the mechanics of a single production distinguishes the portfolio markedly from informal portraits of film directors in private settings, for example those dedicated to Vasilii Shukshin, Tarkovskii and Sergei Paradzhanov, which have recently appeared despite the material dating from the Soviet era.[61] Unlike these portfolios, the *Vozvrashchenie* album interrogates explicitly the boundaries which traditionally separate the documentary 'facts' of film production from the artificial 'fiction' of the filmic text. The presence of stills from the film's coda is only one symptom of this interrogation. A second symptom lies in the tendency within the portfolio to inhabit the fictional spaces of the film and to reflect upon their poetic or dramaturgic significance. With one or two exceptions, for example the posed group-portrait of Garin, Dobronravov, Zviagintsev and Krichman (p. 35), or the few light-hearted moments between takes (for

[60] Plotnikov's most recent collections, *Chistoserdechnaia fotografiia: Momental´naia i navek* (1999), *Portret ukhodiashchei epokhi* (2003) and *Vysotskii: Taganka* (2004) would appear to have been self-published. See <http://www.fotoplotnikov.ru/albums/> [accessed 25 February 2012].

[61] A. Zabolotskii, *Shukshin v kadre i za kadrom: Zapiski kinooperatora*, Moscow, 1997; A. I. Antipenko, *Andrei Tarkovskii v ob´´ektive Aleksandra Antipenko*, Moscow, 2007, and Iurii Mechitov, *Sergei Paradzhanov: Khronika dialoga*, Tbilisi, 2009.

example, p. 43), the actors in the *Vozvrashchenie* album are for the most part presented in a 'twilight' zone where, whilst not actually performing in front of the camera, they are close nevertheless to the mental state required for filming to take place. The portraits of Konstantin Lavronenko, the actor playing the role of the father, serve as a useful illustration of this phenomenon. The eight stills in the collection in which he is featured show him either performing his role in the film (pp. 13, 31, 54, 70 & 78); or being watched by others as he performs this role (p. 14); or, as implied by his pose and expression, preparing for the imminent moment of filming (p. 68 [Fig. 30]); or appearing to contemplate his role as the father (p. 70).

Fig. 30

Mishukov's preoccupation with the psychological and emotional world of the acting ensemble is also present in some of the portraits of Garin and Dobronravov. In one still (p. 30), for example, they are shown on a bus watching a scene from the film on a digital player; in another (p. 62), they listen intently to Zviagintsev as he explains the requirements for a particular scene. In a conscious allusion to the film's 'Boys' Own' subtext, the two actors are shown exploring the physical locations of the film, the most important of which are the abandoned dwellings. Despite their scattering throughout the album, these sites feature in no fewer than thirteen photographs either as spaces inhabited by the actors or as background landscapes (pp. 35, 38–39, 40, 42, 44, 45, 52, 63, 66, 67, 70, 80 & 81). The abandoned home by the beach arouses Mishukov's particular fascination. Judging by the image of the broken gas-lamp which hangs dejectedly from the dilapidated roof (p. 42), he is keen to assert the authenticity of the building in question and thus repudiate any suspicion that it might be a set. Furthermore, his images of the structure in general are characterized by a strong interest in interior and exterior architecture: the wooden textures of its planks, its rusty ornaments and the play of light and shade within its interiors. Such is the focus on the primitive architecture of these sites that, at times, the human subjects become conspicuously marginalized. This is particularly evident in the case of the double-page spread (pp. 38–39) which shows Garin standing outside the doorway next to the 'ramp' of the abandoned building, but also the shot of Garin and Dobronravov as they wander along the beach in the distance with the vertical planks of the shack privileged in the foreground (p. 45). The importance of the interior is subsequently underlined by the images of Garin (p. 80 [Fig. 31]) and Dobronravov (p. 81) which appear opposite each other as a symbolic 'pairing'. Interestingly, the pitch-black darkness transforms the dwelling into something akin to a 'black box', this analogy reinforced by the visible presence of shutters which, like the internal mechanism of a camera, allow light to filter through into the interior. In this context, it is perhaps useful to recall that the word 'camera' derives from the Latin, meaning 'chamber'.

Fig. 31

Unlike the film, which has relatively few moments of stillness, the *Vozvrashchenie* portfolio privileges images which show the actors in a state of contemplation, either preoccupied with the film-production process or observing the landscape and appearing silently to engage with its meaning. On several occasions, Mishukov exploits the layout of the album and the directions of human gazes within the individual frames to establish informal connections between successive images. The angle of Dobronravov's head and his closed eyes as he sleeps beneath a pile of clothing (p. 49), for example, point suggestively towards the image across the page (p. 48), which shows an unidentified person rowing a boat in mist, the presence of obliterating detail in the foreground creating a ghost-like aura. The strategic positioning gives rise to the idea that the young actor is dreaming or hallucinating this image in his mind. There are other examples of images appearing to 'communicate' with each other by means of the direction of the eyes. Earlier in the series (p. 33), Garin's gaze as he stands on a jetty and stares outwards towards the sea appears to be directed towards the fishermen who are portrayed offloading their catches on the opposite page (p. 32). In the images of the abandoned dwelling-place (pp. 80 & 81), Garin gives the impression of looking across the page towards Dobronravov. In the portraits of the boys with their heads protruding excitedly from the car window, a redoubled gaze is effected: within the fictional world, the two boys are looking towards each other as takers of the photograph and subject, but in the album they are also looking at each other's portrait. Elsewhere in the album, Krichman (p. 26) appears to be observing Zviagintsev (p. 27). Through a trick of the low-angled camera, Dobronravov (p. 25) appears to be looking across to one of the other child actors (p. 24). Staring out of the rear passenger-door window in his anorak (p. 21), Dobronravov seems to be looking across towards the gang of youths who, in the filmic narrative, steal the father's wallet (p. 20). The father, as he strides towards the car (p. 13), appears to be staring towards the 'historical' portrait of the mother across the page (p. 12). In turn, the gazes of the mother (p. 19) and Ivan (p. 18) seem to meet across a page of the album, even though they are separated in time and space.

This 'dialogic' situation, one which, as we have seen, is reflected in the coda, is interesting in the light of Zviagintsev's interest in the problem of human communication, one reflected not only in *Vozvrashchenie* but just as strongly in *Izgnanie* and *Elena*. Mishukov's desire to allude to this theme can be found elsewhere in his collection, for example the aforementioned photograph which shows the four 'walkie-talkies' positioned on a pair of sandals (p. 37 [Fig. 26]). As an instrument of communication, the 'walkie-talkie' is clearly an essential item within the context of film production: the identification of the handsets in terms of their respective 'owners' (name-tags reveal them to be Genrietta Bagdasova [casting director],

Krichman, Zviagintsev and Zhanna Pakhomova [production designer]) underlines their association with a professional, working environment. At the same time, the placing together of these handsets into discrete 'couples', the two pairs of handsets in question (one 'male' and the other 'female') lying side-by-side on each sandal, implies, albeit jokingly, a more intimate type of communication, perhaps even sexual conjugation. Further 'dialogic' readings of this image are also possible. If the photograph is compared to the image across the page, which shows Dobronravov and Garin enjoying a break between shoots while sitting in a boat, the sandals might be interpreted as two little vessels inhabited by sleeping children, the wrinkled modulations in the sand conjuring up associations of ripples across the surface of water. In the context of imagistic cross-fertilization, it is tempting to comment on the juxtaposition between moments of psychological disturbance, for example the photograph which references the scene in the film in which the father's body sinks below the surface of the water and disappears (p. 74), and the moment of comforting that is displayed on the opposite page (p. 75 [Fig. 32]). The fact that this photograph features Dobronravov's actual father, who is pictured with his arms around his son's shoulders in a gesture of physical and, we might speculate, emotional support, seems calculated to increase the pathos of the moment.

'Vozvrashchenie' and the ontology of the photograph

Photographic *mise-en-film* is a standard device in Zviagintsev's films. The use of two 'family mementos' in *Vozvrashchenie* (the images that are not part of the coda) receive their later analogy in the flashback sequence in *Izgnanie* in which Vera shows black-and-white photos to Robert and explains that the child that she is carrying in her womb 'not only' belongs to her husband, and the 'family snaps' adorning the room of the eponymous heroine in *Elena*, which appear to emphasize the overriding importance of family in determining her decision to murder her husband.[62] Relatively speaking, however, neither of the two later films poses ontological questions with the same degree of radicalism as Zviagintsev's debut.

The photographic still in *Vozvrashchenie* is presented as a 'footprint' or 'fingerprint' of its referent, but at the same time its status as confirmation of 'that which has been' (*avoir été-là*), to borrow Barthes's definition, is

[62] See Julian Graffy's review of *Elena* in *KinoKultura*, 35, 2012 <http://www.kinokultura.com/2012/35r-elena.shtml> [accessed 11 February 2013] (para. 8 of 18).

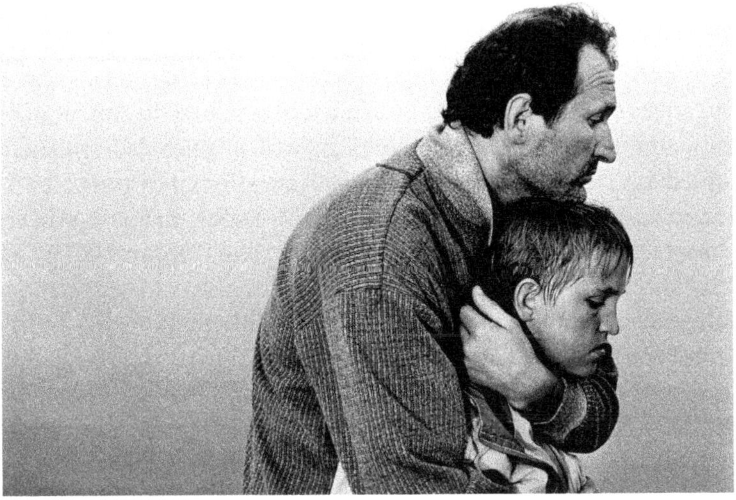

Fig. 32

questioned.[63] This can be witnessed by the treatment of the historical photo of the family which has been preserved within the pages of the Bible. This is sought by Ivan as proof of his father's identity, but the reality depicted in the photograph is sufficiently distant in time, and the father's image sufficiently indistinct, to leave the issue open to question (it certainly does not resolve the nagging doubt in his mind). After the father's death and Ivan's acceptance of his identity, it might be conjectured that, even allowing for the process of material degradation, this same photograph preserves his image 'for eternity'.[64] The question remains, however, what exactly has been preserved. In some senses, this photograph illustrates the limits of 'living resurrections', what Barthes in relation to his deceased mother describes as the difference between 'recognizing' and 'finding'.[65] Furthermore, the juxtaposition between photographic slide-show and filmic sequence raises questions in relation to which memories will take precedence in the minds of the fictional protagonists in future: the 'living memory' (the main body of the narrative), which is fuller and more complete, but inevitably subject to degradation, fragmentation and distortion; or the photographs of the coda, which will, it is implied, form part of a family album at some unspecified point in the future and thus represent tangible evidence

63 Barthes, *Camera Lucida*, p. 77.
64 Sontag, *On Photography*, p. 15.
65 Barthes, *Camera Lucida*, pp. 63–64.

of their expedition. The Proustian dichotomy, according to which the photograph lacks the 'deep discoveries' of involuntary memory, but permits a more intense scrutiny of the remembered subject than is possible in the circumstances of 'real life', might be argued to reside in this juxtaposition.[66]

Like a number of precursor works in which animated sequences are interrupted by freeze-frames, ontological questions are posed by scenes which involve direct modes of comparison. A useful analogy in this regard is the montage interlude in Philip Kaufman's *The Unbearable Lightness of Being* (1988), which restages the Warsaw Pact invasion of Prague and shows one of the main protagonists, Tereza, played by Juliette Binoche, in the act of photographing a Russian officer who is threatening her with a revolver. We see this officer directly from her point of view, and the three photographic images that she takes are shown on screen in rapid succession (the confrontation, which dramatizes her courage and seeming nonchalance in the face of external aggression, appears to have been modelled on the iconic images of the invasion taken by the Czech photographer Josef Koudelka).[67] The sequence in *Vozvrashchenie* which shows Andrei photographing Ivan as he leans out of the car window, because it shows an image of the coda (Fig. 8 [**11**]) in the process of creation, belongs to a similar category. Leaving aside the fact that the camera angles are different in the two cases, there would appear to be a clear distinction between the 'living' moment of the moving image and the 'arrested' moment of the still. The manner of composition, however, seeks to erode that distinction. By virtue of the fact that the shutter speed adopted by Mishukov attempts to simulate the effect of motion, this photograph borders on the kinetic: the contours of the trees in the background, the surface of the road, the plastic bag held above Ivan's head and the boy's face and right arm have been deliberately blurred or 'smudged'. This device characterizes a number of photographs in Mishukov's album and suggests a persistent interest in subverting the properties of the still image; significantly, the photographs chosen for the front cover of the *Vozvrashchenie* album and the final image ('Chaika' [Fig. 20 [**21**]) also belong to these motion studies.[68] Since the photograph of Ivan forms part of a series, it belongs to a narrative which, much in the manner of a filmic sequence, possesses an open system of signification. Furthermore, the relationship between the coda and the

[66] Ibid., p. 63; Sontag, *On Photography*, p. 164.

[67] Josef Koudelka, *Invasion 68*, Paris, 2008, in particular pp. 126–27.

[68] Mikhail Sidlin, 'Toska po poletu: Kniga s fil′micheskim nastroeniem', *Nezavisimaia gazeta*, 20 January 2005 <http://exlibris.ng.ru/koncep/2005-01-20/5_tosska.html> [accessed 20 March 2012].

main body of the narrative underlines this intrinsic kinship; indeed, it is the filmic precursor, rather than, for example, the presence of a narrative voice-over, as in Marker's *La Jetée* and Munk's *Pasażerka*, which supplies the necessary bridges between the images and renders them intelligible as a semiotic system.

The symbiotic relationship between the moving-picture sequences in *Vozvrashchenie* and its photographic coda confirms the proposition of the philosopher Giorgio Agamben that any still image can be regarded as a 'fragment of a lost film'.[69] The collision between the two types of images broadens our appreciation of the complex temporalities or 'aspects' that potentially pertain to the photographic still.[70] The coda in *Vozvrashchenie* functions as a flashback in the sense that it returns the viewer to the events of the recent past and invites him or her to re-experience and re-conceptualize this past. At the same time, it is a flash-forward in the sense that it envisages a moment when the images are chemically processed and assembled into an album, thus becoming part of the family's private 'archive'. Mishukov's production portfolio occupies a similarly ill-defined temporal location. While the images in question relate primarily to the events of the past, their selection and arrangement encourage them to be interpreted in the light of events which took place subsequently. This liberates the images from their original, signifying intent and accentuates the ways in which their framing within a particular context determines their meaning. In essence, Mishukov seeks to shatter the temporal 'prison' of the photograph and to underline its latent, potentially 'free-floating' modes of signification.

Conclusion

The idea of time-travel is fundamental to the science-fiction conceit of *La Jetée*. The plot is constructed around flights both backwards and forwards in time, this idea reinforced by the title and opening sequence of the film, which reference and show the observation pier at Orly airport on which travellers and visitors can watch the arrival and departure of jets. Although the means of transportation in Zviagintsev's *Vozvrashchenie* are more mundane — like the camera, the father's car, a GAZ 24 'Volga' estate, which dates from 1968, is a deliberate throwback to the Soviet-era childhood of the filmmakers — its overarching poetics, like *La Jetée*, reside

[69] Cited in Patrick french, 'The Memory of the Image in Chris Marker's *La Jetée*', *French Studies*, 59, 2005, 1, pp. 31–37 (p. 34).

[70] The term 'aspect' derives from Wollen, 'Fire and Ice', pp. 77–78.

in arrivals and departures of various kinds, both real and symbolic. The coda represents a point of departure in the sense that it heralds the exit of the characters from the diegesis, but it also constitutes a point of arrival in the sense that it signals their re-immersion into the events of the past. The potential associations of the word 'return' in the title are multiplied by this temporal paradox. *Vozvrashchenie* offers a vision of human existence in which memory and its visual adjunct, the photograph, enforce a persistent return to the events of the past, whether distant or recent. A similar process operates in relation to the viewing experience of the film itself. The augmentation of the main narrative by means of the coda, Mishukov's portfolio of production stills and the documentary on the making of the film creates a potentially endless loop which returns the viewer repeatedly to the events of the narrative and invites further contemplation and analysis. These materials are infused with an intrinsic pathos irrespective of their particular medium of expression. The portraits of Garin in the portfolio of production stills, *pace* Metz, are no more haunting by virtue of their being photographic stills than the sequences in the documentary which show his discarded out-takes and his interview as part of the casting process, during which he talks about his absent father.[71] The fact that this same documentary combines photographic and cinematic material as part of its process of memorialization serves as a triumphant demonstration of their shared ontology.

[71] Metz, 'Photography and Fetish', p. 84.

Bringing the Law Back In: Land, Law and the Hungarian Peasantry before 1848

ROBERT W. GRAY

In the spring of 1848, with the rumoured threat of a peasant army marching on Pest and much of Europe experiencing revolution, Hungary's diet emancipated the peasantry from centuries of seigneurial dependence. The hastily drafted legislation freed the peasantry from their remaining obligations to their lords and the church, and granted the peasantry full property rights to their urbarial plots, namely those that had previously been held of their lords. The emancipation of the peasantry proved one of the most enduring features of the Hungarian revolution, yet land reform had formed a central part of the liberal programme for the previous fifteen years. In the preceding years, two events had brought home the importance of the 'peasant question': the cholera uprising of 1831 and the more violent *jacquerie* in neighbouring Galicia in 1846. Ever louder voices from within the Hungarian nobility had been condemning the legally inferior and economically unviable status of the peasantry as the greatest impediment to the 'liberal society' they wished to create.[1] Prior to emancipation,

Robert W. Gray is Lecturer in Modern European History at Keele University. The author is grateful to Martyn Rady and the anonymous reviewers of *SEER* for their comments and advice on the original submission.

[1] 'Liberal society' is used here as a direct translation of '*polgári társadalom*', which was, in the early nineteenth century, defined against the existing 'feudal' social order. 'Feudal' (*feudálizmus*), a word borrowed from Voltaire, had entered Hungarian in the late eighteenth century as a term to describe all that was obsolete and in need of reform. Advocates of reform inevitably styled themselves as 'liberals', and the 'liberalization' (*polgárosodás*; a term that rose to prominence in the 1820s) of Hungarian legal, political and social structures — understood as replacing Hungary's 'feudal' order with a society based on legal and political equality underpinned by statute law — their ultimate goal. See L. Péter, 'Introduction', in L. Péter (ed.), *Lajos Kossuth Sent Word...: Papers Delivered on the Occasion of the Bicentenary of Kossuth's Birth*, London, 2003, pp. 1–14; István Barta, 'Széchenyi és a magyar polgári reformmozgalom kibontakozása', *Történelmi Szemle*, 1960,

laws passed by the diets between 1836 and 1844 had gone a long way to reconstruct the legal position of the peasantry, their relations to their lord, and the rights to the land they farmed. These followed upon measures that had been taken to define and regulate the legal position of the peasantry during 'the era of serfdom' (*a jobbágyság kora*) from the sixteenth to mid nineteenth centuries.

The relationship between the peasantry, their lords and the land they farmed had been defined, albeit imperfectly, in customary and statute law over the course of the many centuries. These laws, principal amongst them the *Tripartitum* of 1517 and the *Urbarium* of 1767, supplemented in between by a succession of *decreta* (laws of the diet published under the monarch's seal; the *Urbarium*, not ratified by the diet until 1836, was not a 'law' as such, but rather a royal patent), had established the extent of the lords' and peasants' rights to the land, their respective obligations, a framework for recording these rights, and a means to seek redress in areas of dispute. In the years between 1830 and 1848 — Hungary's 'Reform Age' — the system of land tenure would be discussed and dissected at the diets and in the press. Those who advocated reform, and there were few who rejected it outright, sought mostly to work within the established framework to place the system of land tenure on a more thorough basis, clarifying those areas where the existing law was deemed insufficient. The legislation passed during the Reform Age sought, in the first instance, to do little more than make rural relations and the system of law more accurately reflect each other: in other words, to 'bring the law back in' to rural relations. Indeed, since the legislation of the eighteenth century had aimed to more accurately record and regulate the current system of land tenure, the process of bringing the law back into rural relations can be seen to have begun much earlier. It was only, however, as the reform movement gathered momentum that a complete overhaul and, eventually, deconstruction of rural relations became the ultimate goal of reform.

Until recently, with a few notable exceptions, historians have depicted the Hungarian peasantry in the era of 'serfdom' or 'feudalism', from the Dózsa rebellion of 1514 to the emancipation of 1848, as suffering from ever-increasing exploitation by their noble landlords.[2] The landlords, benefiting

3, pp. 228–35; *A magyar nyelv történeti etimológiai szótára*, Budapest, 1967, 4 volumes, 1, p. 902; 3, pp. 242–43.

[2] See, for example, I. Szántó, 'A majorsági gazdálkodás uralkodóvá válása, a parasztság nagyarányú kisajátításának kezdetei', in G. Spira (ed.), *Tanulmányok a parasztság történetéhez Magyarországon, 1711–1790*, Budapest, 1952, pp. 221–98; I. Szabó, *Jobbágyok-parasztok: értekezések a magyar parasztság történetéből*, Budapest, 1976; I. Szabó,

from political, economic and social privileges, were able to squeeze the peasantry for all it was worth. Landlords could claim almost limitless rents or other services, relied on their serfs' free *robot* labour to farm their estates, appropriated the peasants' land without reproach, and acted as judge and executioner through the manorial and county courts. The peasant, having no legal existence and no established rights, could hope to seek no redress against the unchecked power of his lord aside from the occasional benevolent acts of the Crown. In light of this, the emancipation acts of 1848 become a moment of unrivalled historical importance, whereby nine million serfs (some 80 per cent of the population) were liberated from seigneurial dependence and servile obligations, and were granted personal, political and economic freedom for the first time. Such a view of the Hungarian peasantry has been frequently, and uncritically, adopted within English-language scholarship: when translated into English, more often than not, *jobbágyság* becomes 'serfdom', and the *jobbágy* (an individual living under *jobbágyság*) as a 'serf'.[3] Neither approach reveals the true complexity of the legal position of the Hungarian peasant, nor do they reflect the full extent of rights that derived from being a *jobbágy*.

The shortcomings of the image of Hungarian 'serfdom' that predominated until the 1990s have not, however, gone unchallenged. As early as the 1960s, János Varga, in his seminal work on the Hungarian peasantry, questioned the validity of accounts that relied solely on a simplified view of the peasants' position.[4] Varga cast doubt on the levels of landlessness amongst the peasantry and noted that, rather than being dispossessed, the peasantry extended their holdings in the century before 1848. Furthermore, Varga pointed to sufficient archival records, in the form of peasant petitions (*vallomások*), which would support his assertions although Varga never used the petitions himself. More recently, a number of localized studies, most notably for Zala, Veszprém and Bihar counties,

Tanulmányok a magyar parasztság történetéből, Budapest, 1948; I. Acsády, *A magyar jobbágyság története*, Budapest, 1944. Of those which provided a more nuanced readings of Hungarian 'serfdom', drawing particular attention to the great diversity of rights and obligations attached to the *jobbágy*, the following works should be emphasized: J. Varga, *Jobbágyrendszer a magyarországi feudalizmus késő századaiban 1556–1767*, Budapest, 1969; I. Wellmann, *A parasztság helyzete az 1767 évi úrbérrendezés előtt*, Budapest, 1955; István N. Kiss, *Bauernschaft und Warenproduktion in Ungarn vom 16. bis zum 18. Jahrhundert*, Cologne, 1974.

[3] This view is most apparent in the work of Béla K. Király, which has unfortunately been relied upon by most subsequent English-language accounts. See, for example, Béla K. Király, 'Neo-Serfdom in Hungary', *Slavic Review*, 34, 1975, pp. 269–78, and Tim Blanning's description in Blanning, *The Pursuit of Glory: Europe 1648–1815*, London, 2008, pp. 168–70.

[4] János Varga, *A jobbágyi földbirtoklás típusai és problémái, 1767–1849*, Budapest, 1967.

have sought to collate and analyse the peasant petitions. This research has provided a much more nuanced and complex picture of Hungarian 'serfdom', beginning to reveal the regional and legal variations and the myriad forms of peasant holdings that existed under the umbrella of '*jobbagyság*'.[5] In light of this recent work, I seek to provide an analysis of the laws relating to the peasantry and the land, beginning with the 1514 law that confirmed the peasants' undifferentiated legal status as *jobbágyság*, and ending in 1848 when *jobbágyság* was abolished on the eve of revolution. This paper will introduce the position of the peasantry and landed property in Hungary as defined by statute law and customary practice. In doing so, it will provide an understanding of how the reforms of the 1830s and 1840s set about to achieve the overhaul and eventual dismantling of Hungary's 'feudal' rural order.

The customary laws of Hungary had been collected in Stephen Werbőczy's *Tripartitum* of 1517. In large part dedicated to the system of land ownership and inheritance of landed property among the nobility, the *Tripartitum* is itself testament to the complex nature of land law that existed in Hungary. It remained the principal point of reference for Hungarian law until 1848, simultaneously serving as both a prop to the nobility and as a hindrance to the modernization of Hungarian society as a whole. Nevertheless, it was the ambiguities contained within the *Tripartitum* that allowed liberal reformers to challenge commonly-held truths taken from Werbőczy, and a careful re-reading of the *Tripartitum* furthered the cause of reform.

When proposals for land reform were put before the diets in the 1830s and 1840s they were viewed from a markedly 'Hungarian' position, for both the advocates of reform and more conservative forces within the nobility were thoroughly schooled in the complexities of Hungarian customary law as taken from the *Tripartitum*, specifically the Werbőczian concept of property rights. Central to this was the view, largely unchallenged before 1830, that no non-noble could 'own' landed property or, more precisely, unmediatized property. Article III:30 of the *Tripartitum* confirmed the exclusively noble nature of landed property, distinguishing between

[5] Zita Horváth, *Paraszti vallomások Zalában*, Zalaegerszeg, 2001, 2 vols; Péter Takács, *A jobbágyélet dokumentumai úrbérrendezés-kori Szatmár vármegye nyíri járásából*, Nyíregyháza, 2010; András Lichtneckert, *Veszprém vármegye köszégeinek urbáriumai, úrbéri és telepítési szerződései, 1686–1836*, Veszprém, 2009. An excellent critical overview of the Hungarian historiography can be found in Zita Horváth, 'Örökös és szabadmenetelű jobbágyok a 18. századi Magyarországon', *Századok*, 143, 2009, pp. 1063–71, with an English summary, pp. 1103–04.

a noble's right of *dominium proprium* and a peasant's limited right of *dominium utile*. It was this clause, and particularly the attempts to redefine the extent of the peasants' *dominium utile*, that proved central to the debates around land reform in the 1830s. Yet, as Ferenc Deák argued, during the diet of 1832–36, the exclusively noble nature of landed property did not, in practice, prevent the peasants benefiting from a security of tenure that amounted to little short of full ownership. Furthermore, the peasants' secure tenure, albeit limited to a perpetual right of use, served to restrict the extent of the lords' *dominium proprium*, a fact that had been long acknowledged in customary practice. For Deák and the other liberal reformers, to extend full property rights to the peasantry amounted to no more than confirming in statute what was already customary practice; to ensure that the latter was more accurately reflected by the former. Deák's reinterpretation of the *Tripartitum* thus allowed the restrictive attitude to landed property, which was seen as both a right exclusive to the nobility and a mark of their special status. This made possible a degree of land reform that was to establish the extent of the peasants' rights to the land and thus resolve what would become of the peasants' land even before the watershed year of 1848. To understand how Deák was able to reach his conclusion first requires a closer reading of the *Tripartitum* to uncover what Werbőczy had to say on the limited rights of the peasantry, before turning to the reforms of the eighteenth century that would, despite their intentions, reaffirm the importance of custom in Hungarian rural relations.

By restating the terms of laws passed in the aftermath of the Dózsa rebellion of 1514, Werbőczy had confirmed the peasants' legal status as one of 'perpetual rusticity'; a term that, lacking legal subsistence, was largely rhetorical. The peasantry were 'now subject to their lords in full and perpetual servitude [...] by which they incurred the eternal taint of infidelity'.[6] The peasants' rights to the land they farmed became dependent upon revenues and services owed to the lord, and their persons subject to the lords' patrimonial justice. This in turn defined a nobleman's lordship over his peasants as the *dominus terrestris*, as well as the right to claim such

[6] Stephen Werbőczy, *The Customary Laws of the Renowned Kingdom of Hungary: A Work in Three Parts (Tripartitum)*, edited and translated by J.M. Bak, P. Banyó and M. Rady, (*Decreta Regni Mediaevalis Hungariae/The Laws of the Medieval Kingdom of Hungary*, 5), Budapest and New York, 2005 (hereafter, *Triparitum*), III 25:2. The original Latin reads, 'ex eoque notam perpetuę infidelitatis eorum incursionem penitus amiserunt dominisque ipsorum terrestribus mera & perpetua iam rusticitate subiecti sunt', so (as was the case with the 1514 law) the peasantry were not condemned to 'perpetual servitude', rather 'perpetual rusticity'.

revenues and services from the peasant tenants, and the right to administer justice over them. By reference to this clause, it has been supposed that the peasantry of Hungary was reduced to the status of 'serfs'; the peasants became tied to the soil, were denied the right of free migration and were subject to the patrimonial justice of their lords.

Yet the status of 'perpetual rusticity' did not equate to 'serfdom', nor did it necessarily circumscribe the peasants' rights to any great degree. Whilst failing to elucidate on the matter in any great detail the *Tripartitum* hinted at a sufficient degree of rights concerning the peasantry, their landed property and their legal position that it is clear 'rusticity' did not equate to full and complete subjugation to the authority of their lord. First, the *Tripartitum* alluded to the fact that the peasants possessed strong rights to the land they farmed and, second, it affirmed that these rights were based upon long-established custom. By dealing with the inheritance of peasant property, it was made clear that the peasants' possessed hereditary, and therefore strong, rights to the land they farmed. Although the peasant could not alienate his plot from his lord, equally the lord had few legal means to deny the peasants' family the hereditary usufruct of the land: the land would only devolve to the lord if the peasant died intestate.[7] Furthermore, Werbőczy made a distinction between acquired goods, to which the peasant possessed full rights and could will or sell freely — 'the wage and fruit of his labours' — and immovable goods, to which the peasants could claim the hereditary right of usufruct extending only to the peasants' lawful heirs. This distinction had been standard in Hungarian law since the thirteenth century, but it is noteworthy that, under 'acquired goods' Werbőczy included 'the fields, meadows, mills or vineyards', including the constituent parts of a peasant plot.[8]

Werbőczy made little attempt to explore the differences between noble (dominical) and peasant-farmed (urbarial) land, and — aside from the administration of seigneurial justice — had little to say on the nature of lord–peasant relations. In this, Werbőczy acknowledged the great diversity of rights and obligations that might be attached to a peasant holding. For much of the fifteenth and sixteenth centuries, it was rare for lords to maintain a separate demesne, rather leasing the majority of their dominical land to be farmed by tenant peasants in return for rent in cash or kind. The form and amount of all rents and dues varied greatly across Hungary, established according to local custom and recorded in

[7] Ibid., III 30:1, 30:7–8.
[8] Ibid., III 29–30.

contractual agreements between lord and tenants. Before the sixteenth century, money rents tended to be more common than labour service and dues in kind, the latter two being rare and of little importance.[9] An attempt to record the peasants' obligations in written law more thoroughly was made in the aftermath of the 1514 rebellion, including a set level of labour service (*robot*) and the ninth and tenth owed to the lord and the church respectively.[10] Customary arrangements continued to predominate and the nature of peasant obligations changed only gradually after 1514, as *robot* and dues in kind slowly supplanted cash payments as the most common form of rent over the course of the sixteenth and seventeenth centuries. Even then, there remained huge variations in the form of rents, dues and labour obligations, often within the same lordship. The peasants' rights and obligations varied to such a degree that it was not possible to adequately account for them in any written law: Werbőczy could find no more to say on the matter than 'just as the conditions of tenant peasants are diverse, so are the legal customs that have to be kept in according to the ancient use of the place'.[11]

The *Tripartitum* defined both the concept of land ownership (as an exclusive noble prerogative) and the legal status of the peasantry (of 'perpetual rusticity') as these would exist until the beginnings of the Reform Age. However, in dealing with the peasants' status Werbőczy had done little more than confirm the terms of the 1514 law, which itself had provided far more detail. Indeed, by failing to elucidate what 'perpetual rusticity' entailed, Werbőczy left sufficient space for existing practice to be maintained which, in turn, provided a guarantee of the peasants' usufructary rights. This would ensure that the Hungarian peasantry were not reduced to the status of 'full and perpetual servitude', as the appropriate clauses of the 1514 law and the *Tripartitum* have so often been interpreted. Nor can it be argued that the peasants 'had no constitutional or legal personality'.[12] In fact, the diets of 1530 and 1547 reversed the limits on free

[9] Z. P. Pach, 'The Development of Feudal Rent in Hungary in the Fifteenth Century', *The Economic History Review*, 19, 1966, pp. 1–14.

[10] 1514: Articles 26–30, *Corpus Juris Hungarici: Magyar törvénytár*, Budapest, 1989–, (hereafter, CJH), 1000–1526, pp. 715–21. The ninth of the peasants' produce owed to the lord or, if a peasant had no lord, to the Crown, had been established by Articles 6 and 7 in 1351. CJH, 1000–526, p. 173; *Decreta Regni Mediaevalis Hungariae/The Laws of the Medieval Kingdom of Hungary*, 5 volumes, J. M. Bak (ed.), Salt Lake City, NV, Idyllwild and Los Angeles, CA and Budapest, 1989–2012, 2, p. 10.

[11] *Tripartitum*, III 30:6.

[12] B. K. Király, *Hungary in the Late Eighteenth Century: The Decline of Enlightened Despotism*, New York, 1969, p. 51.

movement imposed in 1514, a pragmatic concession as the restrictions had been unenforceable in the face of the Ottoman onslaught. Although the county administrations ignored these later laws, the right of the counties to determine peasant terms and conditions vis-à-vis their lords was given in 1608, after which the county court became a regular means of appeal for the peasants in disputes against their lords.[13] Despite the defeat of the 1514 rebellion, the peasants remained personally free but legally dependent tenants of their lords, in that the peasantry possessed freedom of movement, the potential to negotiate the terms of their obligations, a means of appeal against their lords and established, albeit limited, rights to the land they farmed protected by customary law.

Having been recorded in the *Tripartitum*, the peasants' rights had been enshrined in the most important text of Hungarian law. It was not until the Crown's intervention in lord–peasant relations in the second half of the eighteenth century, in the form of Maria Theresa's *Urbarium*, that a clearer concept of the peasants' rights was established in written legal provision. Even then, the protection provided by the *Tripartitum* proved significant for asserting the peasants' customary access to land that would not be accounted for sufficiently by the terms of the *Urbarium*.

The rural reforms of Maria Theresa and Joseph II, by far the most significant of which was the *Urbarium* of 1767, were, more than anything else, an attempt to accurately assess and record rural conditions. For these 'enlightened absolutists', rural reform served as a means to increase the income that could be derived from their Hungarian provinces without threatening the subsistence of the peasants. By the mid eighteenth century, the fiscal situation of the Habsburg Monarchy had become dire. The crown's debts spiralled out of control following the War of Austrian Succession and Seven Years War, made worse by the loss of Silesia, the most economically advanced province of the Monarchy, and the Habsburgs faced imminent bankruptcy. Since the Hungarian nobility had maintained their exemption from direct taxation, unlike their counterparts in the other Habsburg provinces, the need to protect the peasantry, as a principle source of the crown's revenue, became an immediate concern for the newly created Council of State. Cameralist and physiocratic thought, which had found strong support in Vienna, also laid great emphasis on the need for a prosperous peasantry to support a prosperous state. Not only were the

[13] M. Homoki-Nagy, 'A szabad költözködési jog biztositása Magyarországon', *Tanulmányok Dr Veres József 70. születésnapja: Acta Univ. Szegediensis. Acta Juridica et Politica*, 55, Szeged, 1999, pp. 121–31 (pp. 123–25).

peasantry the basis of taxation, their welfare would promote population growth and provide a source of healthy military recruits.

Plans for a far-reaching agrarian reform had been drafted under the supervision of State Chancellor Kaunitz, one of the most virulent critics of Hungarian rural conditions, and a strong opponent of the Hungarian nobility, and presented to the diet in 1764–65. The most ambitious plans for reform included the redemption of *robot* into cash payments, the division of communal lands by enclosure and the consolidation of free, peasant small-holdings: all reforms that would be adopted, in some form, by the diets in the years before 1848. In particular, Kaunitz emphasized the importance of rural reform as a means to win the support of the peasantry for the Crown, and thus break the power of the provincial nobility. The plans were, however, rejected by the nobility at the diet as they attempted to reassert their power vis-à-vis the Crown, refusing to countenance reform before a lengthy list of grievances had been answered.[14] The diet's obstinacy on the question of agrarian reform, combined with the nobility's refusal to increase the level of the *contributio* — the diet argued, justifiably, that the peasantry were already overburdened given that the state extracted more by way of taxes than the lords in the form of cash rents — tested Maria Theresa's patience to the limit and no further diet was to be called during her reign. The matter might have been put to one side had it not been that, in the summer of the following year, a rural rebellion in western Hungary forced the issue. Seeking to uncover the cause of the unrest, in December 1766 Maria Theresa commissioned reports into the current conditions of the peasantry in five western counties (Sopron, Zala, Somogy, Tolna and Baranya).[15]

The results confirmed Maria Theresa's belief that the peasantry were suffering under ever-increasing seigneurial abuses and manorial obligations: a situation made all the more shocking as the worst perpetrators of abuse were amongst the most loyal aristocratic servants of the Crown. In the spring of 1767 Maria Theresa issued her urbarial patent, extending the process of reports conducted thus far to the rest of the country. County officials were required to complete land registers, surveys and

[14] See Dezső Szabó, 'A megyék ellenállása Mária Terézia úrbéri rendeletével szemben', *Értekezések a történeti tudományok köréből*, 25, 1934, pp. 20–35; F. A. J Szabo, *Kaunitz and Enlightened Absolutism, 1753–1780*, Cambridge, 1994, pp. 320–28.

[15] Horváth, *Paraszti vallomások*, pp. 12–16, 28–29; János Barta, *Magyarország mezőgazdaság regenerálódása 1711–1790*, in István Orosz and Lajos Für (ed.), *Magyarország agrártörténete*, Budapest, 1996, pp. 33–79 (pp. 73–74); I. Acsády, *A magyar jobbágyság története*, pp. 386–96.

questionnaires of all villages within their borders, providing the first attempt to regulate and record the size of a peasant plot (*sessio*) and introducing the first comprehensive use of land registers (*telekkönyv*).[16] Once issued, copies of the *Urbarium* were printed in Vienna, in all the languages used in Hungary, and dispatched to each village for officials to conduct the necessary land surveys and record the obligations owed by the peasants. Space was left on the copies to be distributed so that, for each village, the size of a whole *sessio* could be agreed and recorded, along with the number of whole *sessiones*, the number of landed peasants and cottars and the level of obligations owed for each whole *sessio*. These agreements were then signed by the village council, representatives of the lords, and of the county. Finally, in the *telekkönyv*, the size of each individual peasant's plot and the amount of *robot* that could be claimed from each peasant, was recorded. Procrastination by county officials, who objected to the heavy-handed manner with which the patent had been handled by Vienna, combined with efforts by the peasantry to avoid committing themselves to any urbarial agreements, made the completion of surveys and concluding urbarial agreements a lengthy process: the first was completed in Sopron county by October 1767, and the last, for Bereg county, not until November 1775.[17]

At its core, the *Urbarium* sought to introduce a standardized system of dues and obligations, particularly in relation to the peasants' *robot* labour, based on what was believed to be the optimum size of a peasant holding. The terms of the *Urbarium* worked on the principle that each peasant household would be granted hereditary rights to a plot of land sufficient to support a family and for the peasant to fulfil his obligations to his lord, the church and, above all, the Crown. Each plot would consist of an internal plot for the garden and house, and a set amount of ploughland and meadow

[16] There is no full copy of the *Urbarium* in the Corpus Juris until 1836, after it had been reformed and approved by the diet in that year. There is an English translation provided in R. Townson, *Travels in Hungary, With a Short Account of Vienna, in the year 1793*, London, 1797, pp. 109–31. Although Townson does not reveal his source, the translation is true to the copies of Urbarial agreements that have survived in the archives, suggesting that Townson may have seen a copy of one such agreement during his time in Hungary. Ferenc Eckhart provided a comprehensive description of the terms of the *Urbarium* in Eckhart, *Magyar alkotmány és jogtörténet*, Budapest, 2000, pp. 178–87. Eckhart's summary was used uncritically by Béla Király, Király, *Enlightened Despotism*, pp. 51–69.

[17] F. Eckhart, 'A bécsi udvar jobbágypolitikája 1761–1790-íg', *Századok*, 90, 1956, pp. 95–100; Szabó, 'A megyék ellenállása', pp. 38–47. Extant copies of the Urbarial contracts have survived only occasionally in the archives. See, for example, Magyar Országos Filmtár, Budapest (hereafter, MOF), X4308, Urbarialia Tob. Zemplén Vármegye, A293–321.

held within the village boundary (the *határ*).[18] The size of a whole *sessio* was to be set according to the quality of the soil, divided into four categories for ploughland and three categories for meadow. In practice, this was dictated as much by population density and the availability of land as by the quality of the soil. In the densely populated counties of north-west Transdanubia a whole *sessio* varied between sixteen and twenty-two *holds* of ploughland and six and eight *kaszáló* of meadow: in the under-populated regions of the Great Plain, which contained areas of the fertile 'black earth', a whole *sessio* could be as much as thirty-two *holds* of ploughland and twenty-four *kaszáló* of meadow.[19]

Peasant households were to be divided into seven categories, with each being used to establish the level of their *robot* obligation, ranging from those who possessed more than one-and-a-half whole *sessiones* to those with only an eighth of a *sessio*: the minimum size of a plot deemed sufficient for a peasant to support his family and fulfil all his obligations. For a whole *sessio* the peasant was to owe fifty-two days' *robot* a year to be performed with his own draught animals and tools, and 104 days' labour if he possessed no animals of his own (referred to as hand *robot*). Obligations were proportionally less for a peasant possessing three-quarters, a half, or a quarter *sessio* and so on. The *robot* obligation was never to be higher than fifty-two days a year with draught animals even if a peasant possessed more than one *sessio*. All peasants possessing less land than an eighth of a *sessio* were classified as a housed cottar, if he possessed a house with an internal

[18] The *határ* consisted of all the urbarial land of any one village, including the peasants' individual *sessiones* along with the buildings of the village and, often, areas of communal meadow, woodland, vineyards and/or pasture. In some places, there could be dominical land within the physical boundaries of a *határ* but which did not form a legal part of it.

[19] When standardized in 1875, a cadastral *hold* was set at 1,200 *négyszögöl*, the size commonly used from the end of the eighteenth century, which is equal to 0.57 hectares or 1.42 acres. Prior to the *Urbarium*, there had been no attempt to introduce a uniform system of measurement: peasant land was allocated as 'strips' or 'pieces' of indeterminate size. At the time of the *Urbarium*, one *hold* was designated as enough land to produce two 'Pressburg measures' of grain. Officially, this varied between 1,100 and 1,600 *négyszögöl*, changing from village to village, or even from survey to survey for a single village. When the surveyors first tried to record the peasants' land in the 1760s and 1770s, they could encounter claims for a *hold* being anything from 600 to 2,200 *négyszögöl*. This created obvious problems for establishing the size of a *határ*, and has been seen as one of the origins of *remanencia* land. One *kaszáló* was enough meadow to produce two cart-loads of hay from a single mowing. The size of one *kaszáló* also became more uniform towards the end of the eighteenth century, from which time one *kaszáló* was the same as one *hold*, when *holds* increasingly were used to record the size of both ploughland and meadow. J. Varga, *A jobbágyi földbirtoklás*, pp. 11–14; I. Felhő, *Az úrbéres birtokviszonyok Magyarországon Mária Terézia korában*, vol. 1, Budapest, 1970, pp. 18–22.

plot, or houseless cottar, if possessed of no house of his own (*házas zsellér* and *házatlan zsellér* respectively).[20] The obligations owed by a housed or houseless cottar were significantly less than for a landed peasant, set at eighteen and twelve days' hand *robot* each, and the cottars were exempt from all other dues and services aside from the ninth of produce owed to the lord.

It was in regard to the dues owed by the peasantry, and in particular the regulation of *robot*, that the *Urbarium* most sought to protect the peasants. Significantly, the *Urbarium* was the first law to relate the peasants' obligations to the size of their holding: previously, if a peasant had performed *robot*, the amount had been set irrespective of the size of his plot, largely being dictated by his possession of draft animals. Yet, those who criticized *robot* may not have been focusing their attention on the true problem. Of far greater significance in the long term was the *Urbarium*'s impact on the peasants' rights to the land they farmed.

By requiring the completion of land surveys and land registers, the *Urbarium* sought to define and then measure the extent of the peasants' urbarial plots, confirming the strong, hereditary rights to this land that had been alluded to in the *Tripartitum*. The *Urbarium* established a lower limit on the size of a peasant's plot, based on what was deemed sufficient to provide a peasant household with its subsistence and to fulfil the obligations owed to the Crown, the church and the lord. Thus the peasant's plot was to be limited to a garden and house plot, ploughland, and an area of meadow needed to keep the peasants' draught animals so that he could perform his *robot*. Once measured, this land was then entered into the *telekkönyv*, with the individual *sessiones* collectively forming the village *határ*.[21]

The means by which the amount of land deemed sufficient for a peasant's subsistence was measured and parcelled out remains obscure. It would appear that, when completing the land registers, the surveyors simply entered the land used by the peasant at the time of surveying, with that land henceforth becoming the peasant's individual *sessio*. Suffice to say that, whilst many peasants possessed no more than the eighth of a *sessio*, thought to be the minimum required for peasant subsistence, many more peasants possessed plots larger than this, with some securing

[20] To be classified as a *házatlan zsellér* a peasant had to possess a hearth in the house of another peasant. What happened to those who did not possess even this was not made clear.

[21] Horváth, *Paraszti vallomások*, pp. 12–21; Horváth, 'Örökös és szabadmenetelű jobbágyok', pp. 1075–80.

rights to land covering many whole *sessiones*. However, not all peasant-farmed land was entered into the urbarial registers, for it could be in the interests of both peasants and landlords to withhold the true extent of such land. First, since only urbarial land — that is, land entered into the urbarial registers — was subject to tax, it was in the interest of individual peasants and the village community at large (who assumed responsibility of payment for all the villagers) to under-record the extent of urbarial land. Secondly, as the level of their obligations was determined by the size of the plot, many peasants chose to record only a portion of the land they farmed as urbarial, thus limiting the amount of *robot* that their lords could demand. Thirdly, following the *Urbarium* it would become much harder, although not impossible, for landlords to lay claim to any peasant-farmed land entered into the urbarial registers. Thus some landlords colluded with their peasants to hide the true extent of peasant-farmed land, increasing the proportion of land that could later be added to their private demesnes should they so wish.

In many cases peasant communities either under-reported the true extent of the land they farmed, or simply denied that they, and the terms of the relationship with their landlord, fell within the prescripts of the *Urbarium*. Instead, the peasants sought to maintain earlier, customary agreements with their lords as these previous agreements guaranteed access to a larger extent of land, at a lower level of rent or obligations, than the terms of the *Urbarium* accounted for. Many peasants continued to utilize land in addition to (or in place of) the urbarial plots now entered in the land surveys as various forms of 'extra-urbarial' land or 'off-holdings'. Having escaped the notice of the surveyors, property rights to all such land were inadequately covered by the terms of statute law, governed only by various and ambiguous customary rights that Werbőczy had felt unable to elucidate on. Clearing up the murky area of extra-urbarial land became one of the largest problems facing the reformers in the 1830s and 1840s, and in the years after 1848.[22]

Not all extra-urbarial land had been ignored by the terms of the *Urbarium*, but any regulation tended to be vague and left ample room for customary arrangements to retain their force. In addition to the peasants'

[22] These issues were not finally resolved until 1896, when Article XXV addressed matters relating to cottars living on the lords' demesnes. I. Orosz, 'Peasant Emancipation and After-effects', in P. Gunst (ed.), *Hungarian Agrarian Society from the Emancipation of Serfs (1848) to the Reprivatization of Land (1998)*, New York, 1998, pp. 75–91; G. Pajkossy, 'Kossuth and the Emancipation of the Serfs', in L. Péter (ed.), *Kossuth Sent Word*, pp. 71–80, (p. 72).

individual *sessiones*, the *Urbarium* had guaranteed to the peasants usufructary rights to other land, most often that land where rights were shared with the lord. These communally held lands included pasture, woodland and marsh — access to all of which formed a significant part of the peasants' economy — in addition to vineyards, which maintained their special status from earlier laws. Indeed, it was not uncommon for these 'extra-urbarial' lands to exceed the peasants' regular *sessiones*.

Of most importance were the peasants' rights to an area of communal pasture. The extent of the peasants' rights to pasture was not, however, established as clearly as to their urbarial plots. The copies of the *Urbarium* that reached the villages contained very little on the terms of the peasants' rights to pasture, leaving much of the detail to be worked out by separate arrangements.[23] The *Urbarium* stipulated that access to an area of pasture was shared with the lord, together with any priests, teachers and officials within the village if there was sufficient amount, and that the lord was prevented from dominating the communal pasture or separating any of it for his private use. The peasants were also confirmed in their right to collect wood from the lords' forests for their own use (*lignatio* or *faizás*).[24] More significantly, the peasants were also restricted in the use of the pasture, for they could only graze enough cattle for their own needs and to enable them to fulfil their *robot*. Any grazing for commercial purposes was prohibited, meaning that any peasants who possessed anything larger than a small herd or flock could not be accommodated on the communal land. Such arrangements frequently proved insufficient, failing to reflect the peasants' needs and existing practice. Particularly on the Great Plain, where animal husbandry predominated and many peasants possessed large herds of cattle, horses and sheep, many peasant communities leased areas of additional land as large as, if not greater than, their urbarial lands to supplement the communal pasture. The terms of use fell outside the regulations provided by the *Urbarium*, and instead were subject to a mixture of custom, negotiation and the good will of the lord. Defending their access to pasture land was of great importance to the peasants in the period after the *Urbarium* and it should come as no surprise that rights to pasture was a frequent cause of dispute. What is more, when urbarial relations began to be unravelled in the 1830s, the question of how the

[23] MOF, X4308, A293–321: N58, pp. 26–32; N59, pp. 156–62.

[24] These rights of access made enforcing the exclusive noble right of hunting almost impossible and, as such, some lords chose to lease hunting rights as another source of income. K. T. Mérey, *A somogyi parasztság útja a feudalizmusból a kapitalizmusba*, Budapest, 1965, pp. 36–38.

terms of the peasants' use could be converted into property rights became a central part of the debates on land reform.

Another form of extra-urbarial land accounted for, albeit imperfectly, by the *Urbarium* was cleared land, or *irtvány*. This equated to the 'acquired goods' mentioned in the *Tripartitum*, formed of virgin land that the peasants cleared from forest or scrub, or drained from swamps and marshes, and used in addition to their urbarial plots.[25] With much of the country in the first half of the eighteenth century being unpopulated and uncultivated, offering peasants incentives to clear land had been an important means of encouraging resettlement. Even by the 1760s there was still much potential for the area of cultivated land to be expanded in this way, and the *Urbarium* sought to further encourage the practice by confirming the special status of *irtvány*. The *irtvány* was to be exempt from the normal obligations owed by the peasants, including any *robot* and the ninth, aside from a one-off clearing fee paid to the lord as acknowledgement of his seigneurial rights. At the time of the urbarial surveys, many peasants chose to record almost all of their land as *irtvány* rather than as urbarial *sessiones* so as to reduce the obligations they owed. Indeed, in the early decades of the nineteenth century there appeared in the surveys whole communities of cottars or landless peasants who farmed an extensive area of *irtvány* that had been excluded from the original urbarial surveys in addition to their small household plots.[26] Yet the peasants' rights to *irtvány* were never secure, for lords could confiscate the land under the seigneurial right of *regulatio*. This permitted landlords to exchange the cleared lands in exchange of land of a similar size and quality elsewhere on their estate once the peasant had been compensated the value of his labour, or claim the land outright if the peasant was paid the assessed value of the lands. Inevitably the exercise of *regulatio* led to frequent conflict between peasant communities and estate administrations as peasants regularly challenged both the lords prerogative and the assessed value of the land through the county courts.[27]

Of other forms of extra-urbarial land, the *remanencia* or *maradvány* ('left-over') and *puszta* ('deserted') were the most common. The *puszta*, or *sessio deserta*, included peasant plots or, in places, whole village *határs*, that had once been cultivated by peasant tenants but had since been deserted. The *pusztas* were leased by peasants from nearby villages, most often as

[25] Articles II and IV of the *Urbarium*. See, Townson, *Travels*, pp. 110–11, 116–17.
[26] Varga, *Jobbágyi földbirtoklás*, pp. 33–35.
[27] B. Tenk, *A vízszabályozások Tolna vármegyében a XVIII. században*, Szekszárd, 1936, pp. 40–43.

additional pasture land, or were resettled by new tenants under agreements separate to regular urbarial relations. The origins of *remanencia* land are more obscure. Part of the *remanencia* may have come from land used by the peasants that was in excess of their urbarial allocation. This included orchards, and hemp, tobacco, and flax plantations: land deemed unnecessary for the peasants' subsistence. As noted above, not all peasant communities were willing to submit to the new urbarial agreements. Fearing that their obligations would increase under the new urbarial contracts, peasants often perceived that it would be in their interests to avoid having all or part of their land included in the surveys. Part of the *remanencia* may have been that land which had 'disappeared' from the original urbarial surveys, and was then leased from the lord in much the same way as *puszta*.[28] In places whole villages avoided being included in the urbarial surveys as peasants wished to maintain the previous system of contractual agreements, with the peasants then becoming *contractualis* or *szerződéses* through concluding separate ('extra-urbarial') agreements with their lords. The terms of rent for these peasants were concluded through periodic contracts, much as had been the situation prior to the *Urbarium*, and the land they farmed formed part of the lord's demesne.[29]

Since a principal aim of the *Urbarium* was to record the area of peasant-farmed land to protect it from further encroachment by the lords' demesne, and thus secure the tax base of the crown, it became imperative to demarcate the urbarial and dominical land more clearly than any previous law had sought to. So as to secure subsistence for the peasants, the *Urbarium* granted the peasantry indisputable rights of tenure to that land which was needed to support their family, and to fulfil their obligations to their lord, the church, and the Crown. Thus the peasants received the secure, hereditary right of tenure to their urbarial plot that had only been alluded to in the *Tripartitum*, with the land permanently separated from the lords' demesne in the written record. By recording the peasants' plots in the *telekkönyv*, an insurmountable wall had been created between the peasants' urbarial land and that of the lords' demesne. Henceforth it became much harder for lords to expropriate peasants' holdings, saving that, even before 1767, it was almost impossible for a lord to lay claim to an

[28] Varga, *Jobbágyi földbirtoklás*, pp. 11–32; E. Fél and T. Hofer, *Proper Peasants: Traditional Life in a Hungarian Village*, Chicago, IL, 1969, p. 40. The *puszta*, which was often much larger than any *remanencia*, was normally to be found surrounding the *határs* of the villages: any *remanencia* was often held either within the boundaries of the *határ* or directly adjacent to it.

[29] Varga, *Jobbágyi földbirtoklás*, pp. 104–07.

inhabited peasant plot. Of vital importance for the discussions of reform in the 1830s, the *Urbarium* made it impossible to emancipate the peasantry without land, for their usufructary rights had been protected in statute law for the first time.

Yet by restricting the peasants' hereditary rights to land included within the urbarial registers much peasant farmed land did not receive the protection that had been confirmed to the peasants' urbarial plots. The peasant-farmed land excluded from the urbarial surveys, whether recorded as dominical or extra-urbarial, existed in a legal limbo until uncovered during the process of reforming rural relations in the 1830s and 1840s. This left room for customary agreements to remain a large part of lord–peasant relations, governing the peasants' rights to extra-urbarial land, and meant that there remained potential for future disputes between lords and peasants. Whilst allowing that customary agreements could supplement the provisions of the new law, the *Urbarium* made it clear that, in any cases of dispute, the county courts were to act as adjudicators. In regulating the practices of seigneurial justice, not only did the *Urbarium* confirm the position of the county officials in lord–peasant relations, but it also reaffirmed the possibility for peasants to appeal to higher legal authorities in defence of their rights. The procedure for appeal was expanded upon in 1791 and 1792, when laws granted the right to appeal decisions made in the seigneurial courts in the county courts.[30] The peasants' right of appeal was to shape the nature of lord–peasant relations until 1848. The right of appeal confirmed that negotiation between peasants, their lords

[30] Articles 35:1791 and 12:1792. This right had long since ceased to be practised, for it proved too costly and time-consuming for many lords. According to the 1791/92 laws, the village council, aided by the village notary and jurors, first submitted a written complaint to their lord or his representative, the estate stewards and bailiffs. If any matter remained unresolved, the petition would be forwarded to the county, which then issued a summons for representatives of both parties to come before a court hearing while, at the same time, officials (either the *alispán* or *szolgabiró*) were sent to investigate the case and ensure any ruling was carried out. Both parties could then appeal to the district courts and then, by appeal, to the *curia* in Pest. Either party could also petition the chancellery in Vienna, which would, on most occasions, refer the case back to the curia. The latter had no direct legal impact on a given case but if a petition won the sympathy of the chancellery, pressure could be applied to the lower courts. These proceedings were, of course, costly, particularly if the peasants chose to send representatives to Pest or Vienna from the more remote extremes of Hungary, and relied on the village possessing a competent and sympathetic notary. Nevertheless, such obstacles do not appear to have limited the peasants' attempts to defend their rights through the courts. See I. Kalláy, Úriszéki biráskodás a XVIII–XIX században, Budapest, 1985, pp. 111–12, pp. 167–75; Eckhart, *Magyar alkotmány*, pp. 184–87; Martyn Rady, 'Judicial Organization and Decision Making in Old Hungary', *Slavonic and East European Review*, 90, 3, 2012, pp. 450–81.

and the courts would form a part of normal lord–peasant relations, and reaffirmed the peasants' legal and constitutional being. Through the negotiations, establishing the terms of the peasants' rights to the land and the dismantling of urbarial relations begun prior to emancipation was guaranteed to be a two-way process, settled between the parties involved as much as by the diets in Pressburg or authorities in Vienna.

The *Tripartitum* and the *Urbarium* together provided the legal framework in which the reformers of the 1830s and 1840s worked as they sought to reconstruct Hungarian rural society on a liberal basis. The reformers realized that their first task was 'to rectify certain imperfections and unnecessary omissions' of the previous laws, as it was put by one deputy at the diet of 1832–36, converting the ill-defined customary rights that covered so much of the peasant-farmed land into statutory rights supported by appropriate legislation.[31] This would involve placing lord–peasant relations on a firmer legal footing, whereby the mutual rights and obligations of peasants and lords would be better accounted for, and which could be grounded on a more rational basis. To this end, the laws of the 1830s and the 1840s sought to make statute and custom more aligned with rights accounted for and recorded in written law. The reforms would then serve as the basis for private property rights, the bedrock of any liberal order, and ease the civil transformation of Hungary from a 'feudal' society to one based on legal equality and economic advancement: the ultimate goal of the Reform Age.

Through the debates at the diet, and the reforms that resulted from these debates, property rights and the peasants' legal status were reinterpreted in a way that enabled the final act of emancipation in 1848. At the 'long diet' of 1832–36, proposals were put forward for the voluntary redemption of the peasants' urbarial obligations, as a consequence of which the peasants' urbarial holdings would become their permanent private property. Although these proposals were rejected in 1836, only to become law in 1840 and 1844, the lengthy discussions at the diet had asserted that the peasants' rights to their urbarial holdings amounted to full property rights. Furthermore, when addressing the allocation of rights to extra-urbarial lands, the diet established the principle that the peasants' customary use of these lands amounted to property rights that had to be acknowledged in written law. Thus the diet provided means to convert customary use into

[31] Z. Fónagy, 'Az úrbéri operátum megyei tárgyalása (1831–32)', *Agrártörténeti Szemle*, 40–41, 1992–93, pp. 20–46 (pp. 32–34); *Kossuth Lajos összes munkai* (Fontes historiae Hungaricae aevi recentioris), 7 volumes, Budapest, 1948–, 1, pp. 123–42, pp. 336–43.

statutory rights, and for peasants and lords to resolve disputes over rights to the land where these remained unclear. All that remained was to support the assertions made in 1836 with appropriate legislation, which occurred with the laws passed in 1840, enabling redemption agreements and, in 1844, granting full property rights to the peasantry.

In the first decades of the nineteenth century there had been a concerted effort by jurists, notably Károly Pfahler, Pál Szlemenics and Ignác Frank, to establish the nature of property rights in Hungary. Primarily conservative defenders of noble privileges, they had sought to reinterpret the appropriate clauses of the *Tripartitum* as a means to assert the lords' seigneurial rights over the peasants' urbarial land, thus challenging the limitations imposed on seigneurial rights by the *Urbarium*. Maintaining the distinction between *dominium proprium* and *dominium utile*, the jurists argued that the peasants' obligations were not a matter for private agreement, nor did they stem from the terms of the *Urbarium*. Rather, the peasants' obligations derived from the landlords' authority and original jurisdiction over their tenants' urbarial land. By asserting the exclusivity of noble rights to landed property, the jurists also confirmed the limitations of the peasants' usufructary rights, rendering the peasantry incapable of possessing landed property.[32] It thus followed that granting full property rights to the peasants following any redemption agreement contradicted the fundamental laws of Hungary.

In the course of the debates at the diet of 1832–36 this Werbőczian concept of property rights was turned on its head by the liberal advocates of reform. It was their purpose to secure tenancy rights for the peasantry, not only to the urbarial plots but also to the extra-urbarial land. But even this was not seen as a radical overhaul of rural relations. For the liberals, reform would merely confirm the rights of the peasants to their land as established by customary practice in written law as necessitated by the tenets of liberalism. Through reference to the *Tripartitum*, Ferenc Deák, the most eloquent of the advocates for reform, asserted that the peasants' rights to their land were not restricted to the *dominium utile*, but extended to the 'jus de substantia rei disponendi': the right to dispose of the wage and fruits of their labours. Furthermore, since the peasants' urbarial plot had been permanently separated from the lords' demesne and was 'unreclaimable', the lords' *dominium proprium* was incomplete. The peasants' rights were,

[32] A ruling in 1739 had confirmed that non-nobles were incapable of acquiring landed property. I. Orosz, *Széchenyi és a kortársai. Válogatott tanulmányok a reformkorról*, Debrecen, 2000, p. 191; Pajkossy, 'Kossuth', p. 73.

to all effect and purpose, a perpetual lease: the lords' rights, in contrast, were restricted to the dues and obligations owed. As Deák put it to the diet in 1834:

> a peasant's rights must be seen as secure ownership since [...] a peasants' plot is leased under the conditions that this rent cannot increase, that the possessor cannot be removed legally, that the plot cannot be exchanged for another, and the peasant owes no more than the stated obligation. Therefore must it not be termed his perpetual property?[33]

None saw fit to challenge Deák on this point. From then on, once the peasants' obligations had been redeemed, the peasants' land had to become their private property. It only remained to establish the terms of redemption and how far Deák's assertion could be applied to the peasants' customary use of land not accounted for in written law.

Deák's arguments were subsequently popularized by Louis Kossuth in a series of articles published in *Pesti Hirlap* during the course of 1841. In these articles Kossuth enthusiastically embraced the cause of 'free land and free men', and proposed increasingly radical ideas for land reform, including compulsory redemption partly funded by the state, and permitting the peasants to cede rights to a portion of their urbarial land to pay for redemption: an idea that had been rejected at the 1832–36 diet.[34] Most reformers believed voluntary redemption, properly supervised by the authorities, and accounting for the peasants' customary rights to the land, would be sufficient to place land tenure on a more rational basis, fully accounted for in written law. Plans for the wholesale overhaul of rural relations remained only the ideas of a radical minority, isolated from the mainstream of political opinion. It was only as the old order collapsed around them, in the spring of 1848, that the reformers seized the opportunity to complete the abolition of what was left of the 'feudal' laws, doing away with the peasants' *robot* and dues in kind, and putting an end to seigneurial justice. Once the revolutionary moment arrived, the abolition of what remained of the 'feudal' system of land tenure and the 'liberation' of the peasantry was inevitable.

[33] Magyar Országos Levéltár, Budapest, N.66, Archivum Regni Diaetae, Országgyűlési jegyzőkönyvek, 1832–26, III, p. 249.

[34] Kossuth's arguments for reform, based on increasingly direct appeals to the peasants, bear marked similarities to the wider European movement towards emancipation. See, for example, J. Gagliardo, *From Pariah to Patriot: The Changing Image of the German Peasant, 1770–1840*, Lexington, MA, 1969, pp. 24–57.

At first glance, it would seem that the reforms passed in that time achieved little. Articles IV to X of 1836 amounted to little more than a confirmation of the *Urbarium*.[35] Voluntary redemption agreements, permitting the peasants to convert all their dues into a one-off payment, had been discussed in great detail. But the proposal was narrowly defeated by the efforts of the court in Vienna, whose members had waged a campaign against liberal elements within the counties, and the conservatives of the Upper Table.[36] Laws enabling the separation of communal land, the allocation of rights to *remanencia*, and permitting peasants to incorporate any *írtvány* within their urbarial plots were passed, and the role of the counties in settling matters of disputes was enhanced. Thus Articles VII, X and XI of 1836 enabled the division of communal and extra-urbarial land, according to the terms of its use and accounting for the size of the peasants' holdings, between the peasants and their lords; confirmed that the peasants' urbarial rights extended to any area of cleared land acquired since the first urbarial surveys, and provided for the redistribution of extra-urbarial land amongst the landless cottars. In 1840, the law concerning redemption agreements that had been rejected in 1836 was accepted. Should agreement be reached, however, and the cost of redemption met, the peasants would not receive permanent rights to the land, since this continued to be restricted to the nobility. Finally, by Article IV of 1844, the peasants were granted the right of *dominium proprium* over their urbarial property once redemption payments had been met.

The immediate impact of the laws passed before 1848 was, undoubtedly, restricted. Between 1836 and 1848, less then 1 per cent of peasant villages successfully concluded redemption agreements with their lords, amounting to less than 2 per cent of peasant-farmed land. Little more than a quarter of peasant communities had established terms for the division of communal land or resolved their rights to their extra-urbarial lands before 1848 and, of these, only two-thirds had enacted any division of the disputed lands. The limited scope of the reforms passed between 1836 and 1844 should not, however, detract from their significance in redefining concepts of landed property. Notwithstanding the limits of legislation, the discussions at the diet of 1832–36, continued thereafter in the press, had successfully challenged ideas of 'property' and 'property rights' as taken from the *Tripartitum*. It was the redefinition of property rights that guaranteed the

[35] CJH, 1836–68, pp. 15–49.

[36] P. S. Sándor, *A jobbágykérdés az 1832/36-os országgyűlésen*, Budapest, 1948, pp. 84–109; Z. P. Pach (ed.), *Magyarország története 1790–1848*, Budapest, 1980, 2 vols, 2, pp. 720–29.

peasants' urbarial plots had to become their private property following the emancipation of 1848. More importantly, these rights were not confined to the peasants' urbarial land, but were to extend to a great part of the land which had been used by the peasants under customary agreement but which had not formed part of their urbarial plots.

It has often been argued that the April Laws of 1848 did no more than sweep away, with the stroke of a pen (or rather two pens), the legal status of rusticity. Article IX of 1848 ended the peasants' obligations in labour and kind to their former landlords, and Article XI abolished the lords' patrimonial justice over their former tenants. It was then left to subsequent legislation to establish whether the peasants' former urbarial plots would become their permanent private property.[37] In fact, by the spring of 1848 there was little for the reformers to do other than remove the last remnants of the peasants' rusticity. From the *Urbarium* onwards there had been attempts to codify and categorize the land as either urbarial or dominical, the respective rights of peasants and lords to the land, and the terms of lord–peasant relations. But these attempts had been flawed since the terms of codification did not reflect the existing system of land tenure or lord–peasant relations or as these had been established through custom. This is apparent in the *Urbarium*, wherein distinctions were made between urbarial and dominical land which had not existed before, and the regulation of the peasants' obligations did not account for the various local and customary practices. The matter has been further complicated as the terms of the *Urbarium* were subsequently adopted by historians to define the legal position of the Hungarian peasantry, often without reference to actual conditions. The failure of codification to adequately reflect customary practice and local conditions left many aspects of property rights and lord–peasant relations open to doubt, which could be exploited by the peasantry or their lords through negotiation or, should it be necessary, the courts. Indeed, it was precisely because the peasants' rights remained rooted in customary practice not accounted for in written law that negotiations were able to play such a large role in establishing the terms of lord–peasant relations.

The *Tripartitum* had defined the rights associated with 'rusticity', and the Urbarium defined how far these rights extended onto the land. But the extent of rights to the land was revealed more by what the Urbarium did

[37] L. Petér, 'The Aristocracy, the Gentry and Their Parliamentary Tradition in Nineteenth-Century Hungary', *Slavonic and East European Review*, 70, 1992, pp. 77–110 (pp. 81–83).

not include than what it did. Before the Urbarium, rights to the land were held in numerous and varied ways defined by local use and interpreted through customary arrangements. The Urbarium reclassified the land in two ways, as either urbarial or dominical, with a third, 'extra-urbarial' land, emerging by default. But these classifications did not reflect existing forms of use. Thus custom persevered, retaining an important role in establishing the peasants' rights and the terms of their relations to their lords. The ubiquity of custom, in turn, ensured that negotiation between lords and peasants to establish the peasants' obligations and to define the peasants' right to the land, with occasional reference to the courts, formed a central part of normal lord–peasant relations. In the course of the debates concerning land reform in the years prior to 1848 Deák argued that, once the two aspects of rusticity as defined in the *Tripartitum* had been done away with, it was inevitable — indeed, there was no other possibility — that peasant-farmed land must become the peasants' private property. It only remained to establish how far the peasants' property rights extended beyond the boundaries of their urbarial plots and the village *határs*, a task well underway before 1848, albeit one not finished until the 1890s. Yet this was not simply a matter of imposing a new rural order through the issuing of new statutes, as had been attempted unsuccessfully by Maria Theresa and Joseph II. Rather, the reforms of the 1830s and 1840s, together with the legislation passed throughout the second half of the nineteenth century, had to ensure that the law and the rights that derived therefrom reflected the reality of rural conditions.

All the grey areas concerning property rights and lord–peasant relations had to be resolved as the old rural order was dismantled in the years leading to 1848. In this period, the laws and the rights that derived therefrom were made to reflect the reality of rural conditions: a process that proved so complicated it was not completed until four years before the end of the nineteenth century. The dismantling of lord–peasant relations and the reinterpretation of property rights were not only accomplished by reformers and lawyers in Vienna or at the diet, but was also a result of almost constant negotiation between lords and peasants, and between lords, peasants and the courts. These negotiations formed a part of normal lord–peasant relations that was only occasionally interfered with by outside factors. Most importantly, even if lords and peasants were not legally or politically equal, the negotiations were two-way, in that the peasants had established means to make their voices heard, to defend their rights, and define what they believed to be just. Furthermore, through these negotiations, the dismantling of Hungarian seigneurialism and the restructuring of the rural order were well under way before the last 'feudal' diet met in the spring of 1848. Hungarian rural society before 1848 had been governed by a delicate mixture of statute, custom and consensus, where much of the practices of everyday life lay outside the provisions of statute law. This created a rural order where dispute, negotiation and mediation played a central a role in defining the terms of land use, the mutual obligations of lords and peasants, and the concept of property rights as these had been shaped by age-old practices. Thus the revolutionaries of 1848 could not simply bring the law back into rural relations: they had to bring rural relations back into the law in a more complete, comprehensive manner than ever before had been achieved. This did not constitute a revolutionary reordering of rural society but rather, as Deák successfully achieved during the diet of 1832–36, a reform of the law that would make it reflect more completely practice and conventions as they already were.

Public Perceptions of Corruption and Anti-Corruption Reform in the Western Balkans

ÅSE B. GRØDELAND

Introduction

Corruption studies usually investigate corrupt behaviour — mainly bribery — within countries, or in relation to specific institutions or sectors in these countries.[1] Considerable attention has been given to structural factors facilitating corruption. Less attention has been given to corruption as an 'expression' of culture.[2] To the extent attention has been given to

Åse B. Grødeland is a Senior Researcher at the Fafo Institute for Applied International Studies, Oslo. This article is based on partial findings from the project 'Legal Culture and Anti-Corruption Reform: The Case of the West Balkans' (2010–14), funded by the Research Council of Norway (Award 203347). The author would like to thank the anonymous reviewers of *SEER* for their useful comments on this article.

[1] For an in-depth analysis of bribery in the Western Balkans, see United Nations Office on Drugs and Crime (UNODC), *Corruption in the Western Balkans: Bribery as Experienced by the Population*, Vienna, 2011. For an analysis of the link between corruption and anti-corruption reform, see Tony Barber, 'Corruption in Way of Reform in the Western Balkans', *Financial Times*, 30 October 2007 <http://www.ft.com/intl/cms/s/0/6a5ab4e6-871c-11dc-a3ff-0000779fd2ac.html#axzz1tFKqgduO> [accessed 10 April 2012].

[2] As noted by Sandholz and Taagepera, 'few studies explicitly address cultural factors that might affect levels of corruption'. Wayne Sandholz & Rein Taagepera, 'Corruption, Culture, and Communism', *International Review of Sociology-Revue Internationale de Sociologie*, 15, 2005, 1, pp. 109–31 (p. 111). Added to this, internationally-driven anti-corruption reform rarely addresses culture. Michael, for instance, notes that 'the donors offer holistic and integrated strategies almost always ignoring the country's history and institutions'. Bryane Michael, *The Rise and Fall of the Anti-Corruption Industry: Toward Second Generation Anti-Corruption Reforms in Central and Eastern Europe*, paper prepared for the SIGMA/OECD/EU/Agentia Nationala a Functionarilor Publici conference on Public Integrity and Anticorruption in the Public Service, Bucharest, 29–30 May 2007, p. 2. Other authors warn against cultural imperialism when creating 'universal' anti-corruption instruments. See for instance Philip M. Nichols, 'Regulating Transnational Bribery in Times of Globalization and Fragmentation', *Yale Journal of International Law*, 24, 1999, pp. 257–303; Philip M. Nichols, 'The Myth of Anti-Bribery

the latter, the focus has tended primarily to be on institutional culture rather than on the link between national culture and corruption.[3] Further, anti-corruption measurements and efforts are as a rule based on Western (normative) notions of corruption.[4] Fairly little is known about how the term *corruption* is understood within different cultural contexts — and also whether, within these contexts, some types of corruption are more socially acceptable than others, even though both are of crucial importance for reform. Our knowledge about the link between legal culture, corruption and anti-corruption reform is limited.

This article offers an alternative approach to the study of corruption and anti-corruption efforts. It investigates public perceptions of i) the concept of corruption; ii) different types of corruption; iii) institutions responsible for anti-corruption reform, and iv) anti-corruption efforts in Kosovo, FYROM[5] and Serbia. The first part of the article outlines cultural[6] and structural factors thought to affect corruption in the Western Balkans. It is followed by an account of public perceptions of corruption and anti-corruption reform based on large scale qualitative and quantitative data collected amongst the general public in this region in 2010–11. The

Laws as Transnational Intrusion', *Cornell International Law Journal*, 33, 2000, pp. 627–55; Steven R. Salbu, 'Extraterritorial Restriction of Bribery: A Premature Evocation of the Normative Global Village', *Yale Journal of International Law*, 24, 1999, pp. 223–55, and Steven R. Salbu, 'A Delicate Balance: Legislation, Institutional Change, and Transnational Bribery', *Cornell International Law Journal*, 33, 2000, pp. 657–88.

[3] Some local corruption experts, notably Andras Sajó and Ivan Krastev suggest that corruption in the East is not as bad as Western corruption experts claim. Sajó argues that 'were it not for the drumbeat of external criticism, corruption would not be construed as an acute social problem'. Andras Sajó, 'Corruption, Clientelism, and the Future of the Constitutional State in Eastern Europe', *East European Constitutional Review*, 7, 1998, pp. 37–46 (p. 37); Ivan Krastev, *Shifting Obsessions: Three Essays on the Politics of Anti-Corruption*, Budapest, 2004. Others, such as Ledeneva, argue that in Russia, blat (the exchange of favours) has historical and cultural, as well as socio-economic, dimensions. Alena V. Ledeneva, *Russia's Economy of Favours*, Cambridge, 1998.

[4] Alena Ledeneva, 'A Critique of the Global Corruption Paradigm', in Jan Kubik and Amy Linch (eds) *Postcommunism from Within: Social Justice, Mobilization and Hegemony*, New York, 2013 (forthcoming), pp. 297–332.

[5] Former Yugoslav Republic of Macedonia — in the following for practical purposes referred to as the Republic of Macedonia in the main text. In quotes from focus groups conducted amongst ethnic Macedonians and Albanians, the country is referred to as Macedonia, as this is the term the focus group participants themselves used.

[6] See, for instance, Åse Berit Grødeland, 'Informal Practice in the Judiciary: A Comparison of East Central Europe, South East Europe and the Western Balkans', in William Simons (ed.), *Law in Eastern Europe*, Leiden, 2013, forthcoming; Åse Berit Grødeland, 'Culture, Corruption and Anti-Corruption Strategies in Post-Communist Europe', in Sebastian Wolf and Diana Schmidt-Pfister (eds), *Anti-Corruption Regimes in Europe: Between Corruption, Integration and Culture*, Baden-Baden, 2010, pp. 137–60.

concluding part of the article summarizes the empirical findings, linking them to the cultural and structural factors referred to in part one where relevant. We argue that (a) local perceptions of what does and does not constitute corruption, and (b) negative public perceptions of law, legal and political institutions that have developed historically in the Western Balkans, are conducive to corruption and have a negative impact on anti-corruption reform. Unless such perceptions are properly addressed by anti-corruption reform in the region, efforts to reduce corruption are likely to have limited impact.

Legal Culture and Corruption in the Western Balkans

Hofstede and Bond define *culture* as 'the collective programming of the mind that distinguishes the members of one category of people from those of another. Culture is composed of certain values, which shape behaviour as well as one's perceptions of the world'.[7] *Legal culture* may be defined as a 'way of describing relatively stable patterns of legally oriented social behaviour and attitudes'[8] — that is 'the ideas, values, attitudes and opinions people in some society hold with regard to law and the legal system'.[9] Common types of corruption such as bribery and nepotism are prohibited by law in Kosovo, the Republic of Macedonia and Serbia. Mapping the manner in which citizens in the Western Balkans perceive such practices more generally, as well as their personal experiences with them, is thus useful in terms of gaining insight into Balkan legal culture.

Legal culture in the Western Balkans has been shaped historically, in response to political and economic developments both before and during socialism. Even though legal culture, as defined above, is fairly

[7] Hofstede and Bond, quoted in Chuck C.Y. Kwok and Solomon Tadesse, 'National Culture and Financial Systems', *Journal of International Business Studies*, 37, 2006, pp. 227–47 (p. 229).

[8] David Nelken, 'Using the Concept of Legal Culture', *Australian Journal of Legal Philosophy*, 29, 2004, 2, pp. 1–28 (p. 1).

[9] Friedman distinguishes between internal and external legal culture. The former refers to the attitudes and behaviours of legal professionals, while external legal culture refers to that of lay people. See Lawrence M. Friedman, 'Is there a Modern Legal Culture', *Ratio Juris*,7, 1994, 2, pp. 117–31 (p. 118); Lawrence M. Friedman, *The Legal System: A Social Science Perspective*, New York, 1975. The concept of legal culture is controversial and has been heavily criticized. One of the most ardent critics of the term, Roger Cotterrell, argues that the term legal culture is ambiguous, difficult to measure and that it is therefore better to use other concepts. Roger Cotterrell, 'The Concept of Legal Culture', in David Nelken (ed.), *Comparing Legal Cultures*, Aldershot, 1997, pp. 13–31. Most academics conducting research on attitudes towards, and behaviour in regard to, law, however, seem to agree that it is useful to make a distinction between those working professionally with the law, on the one hand, and those being affected by the law, on the other hand.

stable, it is likely to have been affected by transition — i.e. political and economic reform, conflict, war and adjustment to the EU. From a corruption perspective, transition has no doubt provided people with more opportunity structures for corrupt behaviour. What is more, it has weakened the strength of the state and state institutions — and thus also their ability to enforce the law. Added to this, transition has weakened the ability of the state to provide citizens with their lawful rights — and also the citizens' ability to provide for themselves: difficult socio-economic conditions and high levels of unemployment have caused hardship for many people in the Western Balkans.

Do citizens respond to the challenges caused by transition with the same coping strategies (bribery, use of contacts) that they applied during socialism? Or do new challenges require new responses? Do people's attitudes and behaviour towards law (including legislation on corruption and anti-corruption reform) reflect deep-seated social norms?[10] Or do they emerge in response to current legislation, institutional settings, socio-economic and political realities? If attitudes are 'informed' by the former, facilitating change will require complex and long-term solutions. If they reflect the latter, changing negative attitudes and negative behaviour could be achieved by changing the manner in which institutions operate and/or the content of existing legislation.

Though different in many respects, the countries of the Western Balkans have similar historical experiences. For a start, they were all part of the Ottoman Empire for several hundred years (however parts of Serbia were under Austro-Hungarian rule and Kosovo was occupied by the Austro-Hungarian Empire[11] during the greater part of World War Two). Second, they have a shared socialist experience, having been constituent parts of the former Yugoslavia. Research on corruption in post-Communist states,[12] suggests that prolonged foreign rule has bred public distrust in state institutions and state law as both were perceived as illegitimate. In the Western Balkans such distrust appears to have left a significant imprint on attitudes towards politicians, state institutions and

[10] What is more, perceptions of what does and does not constitute corruption may differ from one cultural setting to another. If social norms of acceptable behaviour clash with laws seeking to regulate such behaviour, social norms may well take precedence.

[11] G. Richard Jansen. 'Albanians and Serbs in Kosovo: An Abbreviated History. An Opening for the Islamic Jihad in Europe' <http://lamar.colostate.edu/~grjan/kosovohistory.html> [accessed 3 May 2012].

[12] It could be argued that the Former Yugoslavia is post-Socialist rather than post-Communist. For practical purposes, however, this article refers to the Former Yugoslavia's successor states as post-Communist.

state laws: while moral and social norms are largely abided by, politically-driven laws and regulations are treated with some flexibility.[13]

In order to cope with the state, citizens in Eastern Europe developed various informal practices — including the giving of bribes and gifts and the use of contacts.[14] The use of such informal practices is widespread and corruption is extensive — and particularly so in countries that belonged to the Ottoman Empire.[15] Our previous research on informal practices in Eastern Europe suggests that it is largely 'informed' by social norms and thus resistant to change.[16] Data on how ordinary citizens deal with their elected representatives show that their expectations of, and behaviour towards, such people largely match those applied in interaction with Communist Party officials in the past: while the role and tasks of the elected representative have changed following the collapse of Communism, citizens' attitudes and behaviour towards them have not changed accordingly.[17] Further, the use of contacts and informal networks to solve practical problems and/or gain advantages appears to be 'informed' more by habit than by need.[18]

[13] Radaev suggests that in Russia formal rules perceived as illegitimate are informalized. Vadim Radaev, 'How Trust is Established in Economic Relationships When Institutions and Individuals Are Not Trustworthy', paper presented at the CEPR/WDI Annual International Conference on Transition Economies, Collegium, Budapest, 3–5 July 2003, pp. 1–30 <http://www.cepr.org.uk/meets/wkcn/7/756/papers/radaev.pdf> [accessed 15 April 2013].

[14] During socialism informal practice was primarily used to deal with shortages and/or to get a good job for someone, while during transition it is being used to cope with bottlenecks and financial hardship. Institutional, as well as interpersonal, trust is lower in Eastern than in Western Europe.

[15] The Ottoman Empire primarily divided people by religion, not by ethnicity. A *millet* refers to the separate legal courts pertaining to personal law under which minorities were allowed to rule themselves (in cases not involving any Muslim) with fairly little interference from the Ottoman government. All Orthodox Christians were organized into one millet, *millet-i Rûm*, up until 1870, when Bulgarians gained limited autonomy. Serbs had limited autonomy from 1557 to 1766. The religious hierarchy was dominated by the Greeks even though the millet included Orthodox Greeks, Bulgarians, Albanians, Vlachs, Macedonian Slavs, Georgians, Arabs, Romanians and Serbs. Western historians suggest that Christians were considerably discriminated against during the Ottoman Empire, whereas Muslim historians have taken a more cautious stand. See 'Millet. Ottoman Empire', <http://en.wikipedia.org/wiki/Millet_(Ottoman_Empire)> [accessed 3 May 2012].

[16] Grødeland, 'Culture'.

[17] Åse Berit Grødeland, 'Political Lobbying in Post-Communist Europe', paper presented at the workshop, 'Post-Collective Economic Lives and Livelihoods: Studies of Economy, Institutions, and Everyday Practice in Post-socialist Eurasia and Asia', Conference on Inter-Asian Connections, Dubai, UAE, 21–23 February 2008.

[18] See, for instance, Åse Berit Grødeland and Aadne Aasland, 'Civil Society in Post-Communist Europe: Perceptions and Use of Contacts', *Journal of Civil Society*, 7, 2011, 2, pp. 129–56.

Sandholtz and Taagepera claim that 'Communism created structural incentives for engaging in corrupt behaviours, which became such a widespread fact of life that they became rooted in the culture in these [transitional] societies — that is, the social norms and practices prevailing in communist societies. The transitions toward democracy and market economies have not yet erased this culture of corruption'.[19] Husted claims that corruption is 'ingrained into the political culture of a society',[20] while Uslaner suggests that 'corruption has both cultural and structural roots. *The most powerful effects are for the cultural variables* [emphasis in the original].'[21] He therefore concludes that a polity cannot be cleansed from corruption simply by replacing its leaders or even its laws.[22] People's mindsets also have to be addressed.

The countries of the Western Balkans have undergone extensive political and economic change in recent years. For a start, they have moved from authoritarian to democratic rule and from the planned economy to the market.[23] Secondly, some of them have experienced war or conflict, thus qualifying them as 'post-conflict societies'. Finally, they all aspire to EU membership and are in the process of adjusting their legislation/institutional structures to that of the EU[24] — including in the area of anti-corruption.[25] The transfer of laws, institutional structures and best practices, however, is by no means an easy and straightforward process. New legislation and new practices are not always sufficiently adjusted to the local context and local mentality into which they are introduced. Added to this, foreign concepts and poor translation cause confusion rather than clarity amongst the recipients of such transfers.[26]

[19] Sandholz & Taagepera, 'Corruption', p. 109.

[20] Bryan Husted, 'Wealth, Culture, an Corruption', *Journal of International Business Studies*, 30, 1999, pp. 339–60, cited in Uslaner, 'Trust and Corruption', p. 9.

[21] Eric Uslaner. 'Trust and Corruption', prepared for Johann Graf Lambsdorf, Markus Taube and Matthias Schramm (eds), *Corruption and the New Institutional Economics*, London, 2004, pp. 1–34 (p. 14), <http://www.bsos.umd.edu/gvpt/uslaner/uslanercorruptionroutledge.pdf> [accessed 10 May 2012].

[22] Uslaner, 'Trust and Corruption', p. 9.

[23] For an overview of the transition to the market in post-Communist states, see Anders Åslund, *How Capitalism was Built: the Transformation of Central and Eastern Europe, Russia and Central Asia*, Cambridge, 2007.

[24] Legal borrowing is by no means a new phenomenon. For an overview of EU conditionality in the fields of democracy and the rule of law, see Dimitry Kochenov, *EU Enlargement and the Failure of Conditionality: Pre-Accession Conditionality in the Fields of Democracy and the Rule of Law*, AH Alphen aan den Rijn, 2008.

[25] According to Michael, 'These awareness raising based anti-corruption programmes — for the most part — were not developed in Eastern Europe — but diffused from abroad. [The Balkans] were beneficiaries of "best practice" from other European countries'. Michael, *The Rise and Fall of the Anti-Corruption Industry*, p. 3.

[26] See, for instance, Zdenek Kühn, 'Development of Comparative Law in Eastern

While a majority of the populations in the Western Balkans see obvious economic advantages in joining the EU, they are sceptical of the West and the international community as such. Such scepticism is widespread, especially in the Republic of Macedonia, but also to some extent in Serbia. Even in Bosnia Herzegovina (BiH) and Kosovo, where the presence of the international community is perceived as necessary to avoid resumption of war or conflict, citizens feel that the international community has gained too much influence at the expense of national structures.[27] Roth observes that 'the paradox is that people in the Balkans want to become "Europeans" without really becoming "Europeans", that is they want to become members of the EU without giving up their social logic and — purportedly — losing their cultural identity'.[28]

Our mapping of informal practice and perceptions of law in seven post-Communist states[29] — including several in the Western Balkans — suggests that two parallel legal cultures exist side by side in these states. A 'fear-based legal culture' predominantly manifests itself amongst older people, but also amongst those who are not so financially well off and/or as well connected. Older people lived through socialism, when there was more state control than during the war and the initial stages of transition. At that time some laws simply had to be abided by. Older people therefore largely observe the law out of habit.[30] Poor people try to be law-abiding because they fear the consequences of breaking the law: they either lack the financial means to pay fines or bribe their way out of trouble should they

Europe', in Mathias Reitmann and Reinhard Zimmermann (eds), *The Oxford Handbook of Comparative Law*, Oxford, 2008, pp. 215–36.

[27] In BiH many people do not identify with BiH: they do not perceive it as a real state, but rather as an international protectorate. For a discussion of Bosnia's formal status, see Kimberley Coles, *Democratic Designs: International Intervention and Electoral Practices in Postwar Bosnia-Herzegovina*, Ann Arbor, MI, 2007, pp. 11–13. See also, David Chandler, *Faking Democracy after Dayton*, London, 2000. Perceptions of BiH statehood amongst citizens in BiH are discussed in Åse B. Grødeland, '"They have achieved a lot because we have paid them to do a lot": NGO and International Donor Perceptions of Each Other in Bosnia & Herzegovina, Macedonia and Serbia', *Global Society*, 24, 2010, 2, pp. 171–99.

[28] Klaus Roth, 'Trust, Networks and Social Capital in the Transformation Countries: Ethnological Perspectives', in Klaus Roth (ed.), *Soziale Netzwerke und soziales Vertrauen in den Transformationsländern*, Zürich and Berlin, 2007, pp. 7–19 (p. 13).

[29] 'Informal Relations and Corruption in Post-Conflict States: The Case of the Western Balkans' (Research Council of Norway Award 174856/S30), and 'Conditionality, Corruption and Informal Institutions: An Analysis of Corruption in the Spheres of Public Procurement, Party Funding, Lobbying and the Judiciary in East Central and South East Europe' (Research Council of Norway Award 156856/V10).

[30] Åse Berit Grødeland, 'Culture, Corruption and the Orange Revolution', in Juliane Besters-Dilger (ed.), *Ukraine on its Way to Europe? Interim Results of the Orange Revolution*, Frankfurt am Main, 2009, pp. 70–102; Åse Berit Grødeland, 'Elite Perceptions of Anti-Corruption Efforts in Ukraine', *Global Crime*, 11, 2010, 2, pp. 237–60.

break the law and get caught,[31] or do not have access to people who could get them out of trouble.

The other legal culture, a 'nihilist legal culture',[32] is based on the premise that social norms must be respected but that state laws can — and in some instances even should — be evaded. *Legal nihilism* thus refers to 'the "lightness" of the significance of law'.[33] People whose attitudes and behaviour are 'informed' by this legal culture believe that it is unacceptable to steal from other people, but perfectly acceptable to enrich oneself at the expense of the state. According to socialist ideology, state property belongs to the people. Ensuring that one gets one's share of such property was — and to some extent still is — not perceived as illegitimate in Eastern Europe. Even in countries like the Czech Republic and Slovenia, law-breaking is often referred to as a 'national sport'. People who try to abide by laws are fairly tolerant of those who for various reasons choose not to do so.[34]

Adherents of the 'nihilist legal culture' largely justify their behaviour by referring to corrupt politicians and state employees. Politicians pass 'designer laws' that serve narrow group interests rather than those of society at large.[35] Laws are generally of poor quality and they are neither

[31] Socio-economic factors seem to be significant: people who find themselves in a difficult socio-economic situation often have no choice but to break the law. They are often also not aware of the law as law changes frequently in the Western Balkans.

[32] The term 'legal nihilism' has been officially referred to in several post-Communist states in recent years. In 2008, for instance, Former Russian President Dimitrij Medvedev stated that 'Russia is a country of legal nihilism. Not a single European country can boast of such contempt for the law'. Medvedev, quoted by Daniel Rothstein in Panel Discussion, March 4, 2008 on 'The Rule of Law in Russia: Historical and Contemporary Perspectives' <http://www.danielrothstein.com/publications/The_Rule_of_Law_in_Russia.html> [accessed 3 April 2012].

[33] Suhara explains contemporary corruption in Russia as a product of a number of historical factors, including legal nihilism. See Manabu Suhara, 'Corruption in Russia: A Historical Perspective', in Tadayuki Hayashi (ed.), *Democracy and Market Economics in Central and Eastern Europe: Are New Institutions Being Consolidated?*, Hokkaido, 2004, pp. 383–403 (p. 386).

[34] Åse Berit Grødeland, 'Informal Networks and Corruption in the Judiciary: Elite Interview Findings from the Czech Republic, Slovenia, Bulgaria and Romania', paper presented at the World Bank conference, 'New Frontiers of Social Policy', Arusha, 12–15 December 2005, pp. 1–49 (p. 16) <http://siteresources.worldbank.org/INTRANETSOCIALDEVELOPMENT/Resources/informalnetworks.pdf> [accessed 15 April 2013].

[35] It could be argued that such laws are a result of 'state capture', i.e. 'the actions of individuals, groups, or firms both in the public and private sectors to influence the formation of laws, regulations, decrees and other government policies to their own advantage as a result of illicit and non-transparent provision of private benefits to public officials'. Sandholz & Taagepera, 'Corruption', p. 115.

observed by the politicians who pass them, nor by state employees and court staff responsible for implementing or applying them. Consequently, ordinary citizens have no real incentive to comply with such laws. To cope with — or rather evade — cumbersome laws and regulations, citizens resort to informal practices.[36] Nihilist attitudes towards law and general lack of trust in state institutions are deeply embedded in local culture throughout post-Communist Europe.[37]

It could be argued that the two types of legal culture identified above are essentially expressions, or manifestations, of the social logic that Roth refers to.

Ethnic minorities in the Western Balkans appear to have developed their own approach to laws and state institutions. Research on the relationship between local government officials and the general public in four post-Communist states suggests that ethnic groups who either perceive themselves to be, or who actually are, disadvantaged, compensate for their disadvantage by 'trying harder' when interacting with state institutions. Ethnic minorities in the Former Soviet Union, East Central and South-Eastern Europe do so by giving bribes and relying on contacts to a greater extent than the ethnic titular groups— though with the exception of the Roma, who simply give up.[38] It seems reasonable to assume that ethnic minorities in the Western Balkans who perceive themselves as being disadvantaged not only in terms of belonging to the 'wrong' ethnic group but also in terms of having the 'wrong' religion, apply such coping mechanisms to a greater extent than the ethno-religious majority group.

Below we will map local understandings of what does and does not constitute corruption in the Western Balkans, perceptions of different types of corruption, the institutions that deal with corruption and anti-corruption efforts. The purpose of this article is not to test hypotheses about legal culture and corruption as such. However, empirical findings will, where relevant, be linked to the theoretical observations outlined above.

[36] For an analysis of the informalization of formal rules in economic relationships within the post-Communist setting, see, for example, Radaev, 'How Trust is Established'.

[37] Mishler and Rose note that 'popular trust in political institutions is vital to democracy, but in post-Communist countries skepticism and distrust in institutions are pervasive'. William Mishler and Richard Rose, 'What are the Origins of Political Trust? Testing Institutional and Cultural Theories in Post-Communist Societies', CPS Isssue: February 2001, pp. 1–52 (p. 25) <http://www.u.arizona.edu/~mishler/TRUSTorigins.pdf> [accessed 10 August 2012].

[38] William L. Miller, Åse B. Grødeland and Tatyana Y. Koshechkina, *A Culture of Corruption? Coping with Government in Postcommunist Europe*, Budapest, 2001.

Methodological Approach

Data for the legal culture and anti-corruption reform project was collected in three stages: (i) focus groups (FGs), (ii) nationally representative surveys with booster samples amongst ethno-religious minorities (surveys), and (iii) structured, open-ended in-depth interviews (IDIs). Stages (i)–(ii) were conducted amongst *legal outsiders*,[39] whereas data for stage (iii) was recently conducted amongst *legal insiders*.[40] We commissioned professional pollsters to collect data for stages (i)–(iii), according to an FG guide, survey questionnaire and IDI guide prepared by us. This article is based on data from the FGs and from the nationally representative surveys and ethno-religious boosters.

As concerns the FGs, we conducted a total of eighteen such groups: six in Kosovo, six in the Republic of Macedonia and six in Serbia — all with citizens aged eighteen or more. To the extent possible, the pollsters sought to ensure that the FGs were mixed not only in terms of education, but also in terms of gender and age. The average number of participants per group was 8.6 people and each group session lasted for an average two hours and twenty two minutes.[41] All groups were moderated in the local language by professional moderators, and were both audio- and video-recorded. Complete transcripts were prepared both in the local language and in English. The English-language transcripts were later coded in QSR NUD*IST (v 6).

Within each country we conducted two FGs in the capital: one with higher educated and one with lower educated citizens. We also conducted one FG (majority population) in a large city/town in a wealthier region and one FG (majority population) in a large city/town in a poorer region,[42] as legal culture is likely to be 'informed' by socio-economic conditions.[43] Finally, we conducted two FGs with the largest ethno-religious minority — that is ethnic Albanians (the Republic of Macedonia, Serbia) and ethnic Serbs (Kosovo).

[39] Legal outsiders may be defined as the general public — that is those people being affected by law.

[40] Legal insiders may be defined as those dealing professionally with the law.

[41] The average length per FG was two hours and thirty four minutes in Macedonia, two hours and twenty four minutes in Serbia and two hours and seven minutes in Kosovo.

[42] The wealthier and poorer regions were identified from the social welfare index for the three countries covered by our research.

[43] World Bank figures suggest that there is a link between GDP per capita, rule of law and control of corruption: countries with high GDP per capita tend to score well on rule of law and control of corruption. See *Worldwide Governance Indicators* <http://info.worldbank.org/governance/wgi/mc_countries.asp> [accessed 10 January 2012].

Table 1. FG locations

	Kosovo	Macedonia	Serbia
Capital	Priština x 2	Skopje x 2	Belgrade x 2
Big town (wealthier region)	Ferizaj	Bitola	Novi Sad
Big town (poorer region)	Gjakova	Kumanovo	Niš
Ethno-religious minority	Mitrovica x 1 Štrpce x 1	Skopje x 1 Tetovo x 1	Bujanovac x 2

In Kosovo the regional FGs with ethnic Albanians were conducted in Ferizaj (wealthier region) and Gjakova (poorer region). Ferizaj is the third largest city in Kosovo in terms of population, after Priština and Prizren. It is located in the south, some 38 km from Priština, and is the home of several private small and medium-sized businesses.[44] Gjakova is situated in western Kosovo, close to the Albanian border and currently has a population of some 100,000 people. It was badly affected by the Kosovo war in 1999: large parts of the town were destroyed, some 75 per cent of the population was forcibly expelled and many civilians were killed.[45] The town has since been rebuilt, but at present Gjakova is suffering from high unemployment.

Kosovo's remaining ethnic Serb community is mainly located in the north, along the border with Serbia. The Serbs in this region do not acknowledge Kosovo as an independent state. They consider themselves to be citizens of Serbia and have almost no interaction with Priština. There are also smaller pockets (enclaves) of ethnic Serbs in other parts of the country. Unlike ethnic Serbs in northern Kosovo, 'enclave-Serbs' have little choice but to deal with Kosovo state institutions. There are some indications that they are more pragmatically disposed towards Albanians and Kosovo statehood than Serbs in northern Kosovo. We therefore decided to do one

[44] The US company 'Brown & Root', assisting in constructing the Camp Bondsteel is a major employer in the municipality. <http://en.wikipedia.org/wiki/Uro%C5%A1evac> [accessed 5 January 2012].

[45] While most of the internally displaced people (IDPs) and refugees have now returned to their homes, a large number of people are still missing. The actions of the government forces in Gjakova formed a major part of the United Nations' war crimes indictment of the then President Slobodan Milošević. <http://en.wikipedia.org/wiki/%C4%90akovica> [accessed 5 January 2012].

FG in Mitrovica[46] — the unofficial capital of northern Kosovo and in the past also the wealthiest part of Kosovo — and one FG in the Serb enclave of Štrpce (south).[47]

The FGs with ethnic Macedonians in the Republic of Macedonia were conducted in Skopje (one with higher, one with lower educated citizens), Bitola (large town, wealthier region, one FG) and Kumanovo (large town, poorer region, one FG). Bitola (south-west) is located on the border between the Republic of Macedonia and Greece. It serves as a transit area for trade with Greece and several of the largest Macedonian companies are located there.[48] Kumanovo (north-east) is located close to the Republic of Macedonia's border with Serbia. It has a sizeable ethnic Albanian community and quite a few ethnic Serbs also live there. Kumanovo was one of the main locations for the 2001 armed insurgency.[49]

Ethnic Albanians officially make up some 25 per cent of the Republic of Macedonia's population. However, unofficial figures suggest that up to 40 per cent of the country's population are ethnic Albanians. The Albanian community is concentrated in Skopje and in the north western parts of the country. Our two FGs with ethnic Albanians were carried out in Skopje (large town, wealthier region) and Tetovo (large town, poorer region). Ethnic Albanians account for the majority (some 70 per cent) of the population in Tetovo (north-west). During the wars in Bosnia-Herzegovina and Kosovo Tetovo provided shelter for large numbers of Muslims from both Bosnia and Herzegovina (BiH) and Kosovo.[50] In Skopje, ethnic

[46] Mitrovica, just like Gjakova, suffered badly during the 1999 Kosovo War. An estimated 71,601 ethnic Serbs currently live in the northern part of the city, while ethnic Albanians and Roma live in the southern parts. Major ethnic violence erupted in March 2004 and there was also considerable tension in 2008, following the Kosovo declaration of independence. The Serbs in the north have to this day refused to accept Kosovo's independence. They have established their own Community Assembly of Kosovo and Metohija in Mitrovica and they abide by the decisions of the Serbian parliament in Belgrade, rather than by those of the Kosovo parliament in Priština. See <http://en.wikipedia.org/wiki/Kosovska_Mitrovica> [accessed 15 January 2012].

[47] Štrpce is located in southern Kosovo and it is known for its natural beauty. A total of 12,800 people lived in the municipality of Štrpce according to the 1991 census. In 2006, some two thirds of the population of Štrpce was made up of ethnic Serbs. <http://en.wikipedia.org/wiki/%C5%A0trpce> [accessed 5 January 2012]. Štrpce is one of few Serb enclaves in Kosovo where relations between ethnic Serbs and ethnic Albanians are good. See International Crisis Group, *Kosovo: Štrpce, a Model Serb Enclave?*, Priština and Brussels, Europe Briefing No. 56, 2009.

[48] <http://en.wikipedia.org/wiki/Bitola> [accessed 5 January 2011].

[49] <http://en.wikipedia.org/wiki/Kumanovo> [accessed 5 January 2011].

[50] One of the highest ranked universities in southern Europe (South East European University) is located in Tetovo. The city is the centre of most Albanian political parties in Macedonia and it also hosts some multinational companies <http://en.wikipedia.org/

Albanians officially make up some 20 per cent of the population, though the actual number of Albanians is thought to be higher.

In Serbia, FGs with ethnic Serbs were conducted in Belgrade (one FG with higher educated, one FG with lower educated people), Novi Sad (large city, wealthier region, one FG) and Niš (larger city, poorer region, one FG). Novi Sad (north) is located in the autonomous province of Vojvodina. The province is largely multiethnic: Serbs account for some 65 per cent of the population, while some 14 per cent are ethnic Hungarians. Novi Sad is the second largest city in Serbia and also one of the country's richest. Niš (south) is one of Serbia's oldest cities and one of its most important industrial centres. Besides, it was the first city in Serbia to stand up to Milošević-rule.[51] At present it hosts a large and unofficial community of Kosovo Serb refugees.[52]

Serbia's ethnic Albanian community is concentrated in the three southern municipalities of Preševo, Meveđa and Bujanovac, which are the poorest municipalities in the country. Our two ethnic Albanian FGs (one with higher educated and one with lower educated people) were both conducted in Bujanovac. Ethnic Albanians make up the largest percentage of the population there and they were heavily discriminated against during Milošević-rule. From 1999 to 2001 Bujanovac was the battleground for an insurgency, organized by a sub-group of the Kosovo Liberation Army (KLA), known as the 'Liberation Army of Preševo, Meveđa and Bujanovac'.[53]

The nationally representative surveys and ethno-religious boosters were conducted during the second half of 2011.[54] In each country we conducted a total of 1,000 interviews with the majority population. In addition, we did 200 interviews with ethnic Albanians in southern Serbia (Bujanovac, Preševo, Medvedja municipalities), 400 interviews with ethnic Albanians in the Republic of Macedonia (Tetovo, Gostivar and Skopje regions), and 200 interviews with ethnic Serbs in Kosovo: 100 interviews in northern Kosovo[55] and 100 interviews in the Serbian enclaves of Štrpce, Gracanica,

wiki/Tetovo> [accessed 5 January 2011].

51 A collation of democratic opposition parties (Zajedno – Together) won the local elections there in 1996.

52 <http://en.wikipedia.org/wiki/Ni%C5%A1> [accessed 5 January 2011].

53 <http://en.wikipedia.org/wiki/Bujanovac> [accessed 5 January 2011].

54 The interviews were carried out in the second half of 2011.

55 In northern Kosovo recruiting and interviewing people was complicated and took more time than envisaged, given the political situation on the ground at the time: clashes began in late July 2011, when Kosovo police entered the Serb-controlled municipalities in the north to control the border — and without having consulted with KFOR (NATO

Novo Brdo and Orahovac.[56] The surveys were conducted by local pollsters and to ESOMAR standards. Interviews were conducted face-to-face and lasted for an average sixty nine minutes.[57] The quantitative survey[58] explored several dimensions of legal culture,[59] the link between legal culture and corruption, corruption and anti-corruption reform. As the size of the ethno-religious boosters was fairly small, some caution is called for when analysing findings from them — though the samples were composed in such a way that we have no reason to assume that the views expressed by the minority groups are non-representative.

Quantitative findings are presented in table form below and illustrated with relevant quotes from the FGs.[60]

Perceptions of Corruption

Since the collapse of Communism numerous anti-corruption efforts have been launched in Europe's post-Communist states. Lugon-Moulin therefore claims that 'it is hardly possible to argue that people don't

Kosovo Force) and EULEX (European Rule of Law Mission to Kosovo). The border between Serbia and Kosovo was temporarily closed and there were several clashes between ethnic Serbs and NATO forces. For details, see <http://en.wikipedia.org/wiki/2011_Kosovo%E2%80%93Serbia_border_clashes>, and Reuters, 'Ethnic Serbs, NATO troops hurt in Kosovo clash' <http://www.reuters.com/article/2011/09/27/us-kosovo-violence-idUSTRE78Q5IS20110927> [both accessed 10 January 2012]. Ethnic Serbs in the enclaves, for their part, were pleased to be contacted and many of them ended up having longer discussions with the interviewers after the actual survey interviews had been completed.

56 Several questions asked during our FGs refer to state institutions. As ethnic Serbs in northern Kosovo do not recognize these institutions and refuse to have anything to do with them — preferring instead to be ruled by Belgrade — ethnic Serbs in Mitrovica were asked to give their views on state institutions in Serbia, while ethnic Serbs in Štrpce were asked to give their views on state institutions in Kosovo. The reason for our decision was to ensure that (i) ethnic Serbs in the north would answer our questions, and (ii) that their answers would be 'informed'.

57 The questionnaire contained 253 questions — all close ended.

58 Refusal rates were fairly small: 27 per cent in Kosovo, 28 per cent in Serbia and 34 per cent in Macedonia.

59 The questionnaire replicated questions on five (of eight) dimensions of legal culture explored by another project on European legal cultures so as to map legal culture in the Western Balkans, for which quantitative and qualitative data had previously not been collected.

60 As the number of interviews with the ethno-religious minorities was smaller than with the majority populations and thus not representative of the minority groups as such, some caution is called for when comparing the views of the majority and minority populations within each country. This being said, the samples were composed in such a way as to make them as representative as possible. Added to this — and as will be shown below — some patterns could be observed for all the minority populations. Our findings thus provide a useful starting point for further research and also allow us to draw conclusions with some conviction.

know about corruption anymore, and that more awareness campaigns are therefore still needed'.[61] The World Bank definition of corruption is 'the abuse of public office for private gain'.[62] However, understandings of what does or does not constitute abuse of one's official position, as well as of what constitutes private gain are likely to vary across different cultural and/or geographical contexts. Elers, Giannakopoulos and Tänzler argue that 'there is a gap between centrally designed anti-corruption measures and public perceptions of corruption'.[63] Ledeneva, citing Stiglitz, notes that 'because the corruption measurement is undertaken by international organizations, the policies are devised (or at least strongly influenced) at the supranational level without specific attention to the country's background and the culture of the country that will implement the policies'.[64]

Some experts on anti-corruption in post-Communist states warn against universal definitions of corruption. Sajó, for instance, claims that 'the problem of contemporary corruption is that its definition almost always reflects the moral opprobrium of outsiders'.[65] In other words, behaviour that is perceived as immoral in one cultural setting may be 'informed' by social norms and thus considered to be perfectly acceptable, in another.

The exchange of favours amongst family and friends is generally accepted as part of the social logic in Europe's post-Communist states, as is giving gifts to local government officials. This may explain why Ukrainian elites associate the term 'corruption' with bribes only, not with gift-giving, patronage or nepotism, despite the fact that favourable treatment granted to relatives (and other people close to the person rendering favours)

[61] Anne Lugon-Moulin, 'Mismatches between Corruption Perception, Corruption Victimisation and Anti-Corruption Measures', in Wolf and Schmidt-Pfister (eds), 'International Anti-Corruption Regimes', pp. 125–35 (p. 133).

[62] See, for instance, Vinay Bhargava, 'Curing the Cancer of Corruption' <http://siteresources.worldbank.org/EXTABOUTUS/Resources/Ch18.pdf>, pp. 1–30 (p. 1). Corruption thus covers a wide range of different practices, notably bribery, patronage, nepotism, theft of state assets and diversion of state revenues. See Ian Bannon, 'The Fight against Corruption: A World Bank Perspective', prepared for the Workshop on Transparency and Governance, organized as part of the Consultative Group Meeting for the Reconstruction and Transformation of Central America, Stockholm, 25–28 May 1999 <http://www.iadb.org/regions/re2/consultative_group/groups/transparency_workshop6.htm#1a> [accessed 10 May 2012]. One could also add extortion, cronyism, graft and embezzlement to this list.

[63] Ben Elers, Angelos Giannakopoulos and Dirk Tänzler, 'Citizens' Participation and Anti-Corruption: The Advocacy and Legal Advice Centres of Transparency International and the EU-funded research project "ALACs"', in Wolf and Schmidt-Pfister (eds), 'International Anti-Corruption Regimes', pp. 179–94 (p. 179).

[64] Ledeneva, 'A Critique', p. 307.

[65] Sajó, *Corruption, Clientelism*, p. 38.

regardless of merit, are possibly even bigger problems in the Former Soviet Union than bribery.[66]

Our FG findings from Kosovo, The Republic of Macedonia and Serbia suggest that the general public in the Western Balkans, just like elites in Ukraine, predominantly associate the term 'corruption' with bribery. Only 3 per cent of the statements made on this issue in Kosovo referred to nepotistic behaviour, while in the Republic of Macedonia and in Serbia there were no such mentions at all.[67] Those FG participants who understood corruption as bribery, distinguished between *voluntary* and *forced* bribes, and between *bribe givers* and *bribe takers* — though often referring to both (Kosovo, the Republic of Macedonia). In their view, the bribe takers are more corrupt than the bribe givers:

> 'every person who asks for money to solve a problem for you is corrupted.' (KOS-FG4-Ferizaj-Isai);[68] 'maybe someone has money and has to (give a bribe) in order to get a job or (in order) for his child to pass a subject in school [...]' (KOS-FG5-Štrpce-Dragana); 'those who have (money) will always give. On the other hand, you have a case where the officials themselves don't want to do their job in the normal way, forcing you instead, if you want to exercise your right, to bribe.' (KOS-FG6-Mitrovica-Milos); '(corruption is) paying a bribe and taking a bribe.' (MAC-FG1-Skopje-lower educated-Zdravko); 'the patient that goes to them is maybe forced to offer some money by being afraid that the treatment is not good (otherwise).' (SER-FG6-Bujanovac-II-Sadije).

FG participants typically defined bribes as monetary payments given in exchange for a favour or service — either to obtain something to which one is entitled by law (Serbia), to get something to which one is not entitled by law (the Republic of Macedonia) or for something in between — for instance to speed up formal procedures (the Republic of Macedonia and Serbia). Obtaining one's rights is clearly a legitimate purpose while seeking

[66] Grødeland, 'Elite Perceptions of Anti-Corruption Efforts', p. 246.

[67] FG participants in the latter two countries, however, did associate the use of go-betweens (contacts) with corruption. Contacts are often involved when people gain positions for which they are not qualified. Thus, citizens in Macedonia and Serbia perceive the mechanisms that often facilitate nepotism as corrupt.

[68] FG respondents are referred to as follows: country-FG-number-location-participant name. KOS refers to FGs conducted in Kosovo, MAC — to FGs conducted in Macedonia, and SER to FGs conducted in Serbia. Thus, KOS-FG4-Ferizaj-Isai, refers to FG4, conducted in Ferizaj, Kosovo — and to a participant named Isai. In locations where we conducted more than one FG, groups are referred to as one and two: for instance Belgrade 1 and Belgrade 2.

something to which one is not entitled by law is obviously illegitimate. Speeding up formal procedures may be legitimate if a problem or an issue is not solved within the stipulated official time frame. 'Jumping the queue' for a heart transplant, on the other hand, could have devastating effects for those being 'bypassed'. One could therefore argue that such queue jumping qualifies as illegitimate behaviour regardless of whether it is accompanied by a bribe. Giving bribes to achieve legitimate as well as illegitimate outcomes, however, is illegal:

> '(corruption is) illegal acquisition of property.' (KOS-FG2- Priština -higher education-Njomza); '(corruption is) rigging tenders.' (MAC-FG2-Skopje-higher educated-Ivan); 'taking payment in order to circumvent the laws.' (MAC-FG4-Bitola-Duda); 'to pay for something that someone is obliged to do by the book [...]' (SER-FG1-Belgrade-lower educated-Dragan); 'everybody who bribes someone wants to get something which does not belong to him [...]' (MAC-FG2-Skopje-higher educated-Ljupco); 'if you want to quickly finish some kind of job in an institution, you have to pay, to give bribes. You need to find a channel to bribe someone, otherwise you will wait for days, maybe months.' (MAC-FG3-Kumanovo-Nikola); 'without giving them (money) you can find yourself waiting for two days.' (SER-FG5-Bujanovac-I-Iliri).

Writings on corruption often suggest that citizens are *victims* of corruption: greedy officials controlling important state-controlled financial and/or material resources use their bargaining strength to extract bribes from citizens. While this is undoubtedly often the case, there is also evidence that citizens are voluntary, though somewhat reluctant, bribe-givers.[69] Our own data from the Western Balkans suggest that bribery is a grey area: while 'officials' do not necessarily explicitly state to their clients that they should give them something in return for a service, citizens often do not feel sufficiently 'safe' to not do so. They therefore give bribes to ensure that they get the desired outcome. The officials, for their part, may accept the bribes because their clients insist that they take them — not because they themselves request them. Most mentions of bribery in our FGs referred to *voluntary*, rather than *forced*, bribe-giving. And there was considerable understanding towards those who accept bribes — especially towards those working in health care:

> 'people are to be blamed for all (the corruption), not the doctor or the professor. People give, people are used to that.' (KOS-FG6-Mitrovica-

[69] Miller, et al., *A Culture of Corruption*; UNODC, *Corruption in the Western Balkans.*

> Dragan); 'you see we have spoilt them this way, because it happens that you offer the money even without being asked.' (SER-FG5-Bujanovac-I-Vali); 'the goodness of individuals makes (up) the corruption, my goodness or (that of) someone else with a monthly payment of 200 euro. If you want to do something, give him 100 or 1,000 denars [...] care from the doctor costs 300 denars and he will stay to watch you, but no chance without (you) buying a coca cola, coffee or cake [...]' (MAC-FG5-Skopje-Albanians-Adnan); 'if the state doesn't pay him enough and he studied for that (job), why shouldn't he take the money?' (KOS-FG6-Mitrovica-Stojan).

Willingness to give bribes seems to be partly fear-based, partly culture-based: citizens either fear that unless they give a bribe their problems will not be successfully resolved or they give something to someone after their problems have been resolved out of habit, as an expression of gratitude. The position towards corruption held by ordinary citizens in the Western Balkans appears to be based on conflicting standards: on the one hand, citizens feel that it is necessary, and thus acceptable, to give bribes to obtain something of importance to them. On the other hand, they happily criticize government officials for being corrupt while conceding that corrupt officials are to some extent the creation of the bribe-giving citizens themselves:

> 'it is we, the common people, who tend to corrupt them even if they do not want to (be corrupted) [...]' (KOS-FG3-Gjakova-Lindita); 'earlier this year the entrance exam (took place). There were many cases when students didn't pass this test but afterwards their name appeared on the list. There is a corruption network [...] the parents find these officials, take them to lunch or pay them money just to (have them) pass their child's test, without (him/her) studying at all.' (KOS-FG4-Ferizaj-Rabije); 'we ourselves bribe and corrupt, which is very bad. And then we say that the doctors are bad, or professors or anyone. The fear itself, that we will not succeed in (doing) something or we want something in a hurry and we know that by law (it) cannot be so, makes us (engage in) bribery and corruption [...]' (MAC-FG3-Kumanovo-Suzi); 'people will, if they have to pay for something, borrow the money [...] and they won't start fighting corruption because the majority pays.' (SER-FG3-Niš-Marina); '[...] children are growing up with that notion that paying will get them through everything.' (SER-FG3-Niš-Bojana).

Transparency International's corruption perception index (CPI) for 2011 suggests that corruption in the Western Balkans is widespread.[70] The

[70] <http://www.transparency.org/policy_research/surveys_indices/cpi/2010/results>

Republic of Macedonia, for instance, is ranked as the 69th least corrupt country in the world with a score of 3.9 (countries are ranked on a scale from ten — least corrupt — to one — most corrupt). In comparison, Serbia ranks 86th (score: 3.3) and Kosovo ranks 112th (score: 2.9).[71] Even though the CPI — just like other indices — should be treated with caution,[72] there is ample evidence of corruption in all three countries.[73] Not surprisingly, therefore, a majority of the respondents surveyed in all of them (majority and minority populations) believed that their country has a serious problem with corruption.[74] In Serbia this view was slightly less widespread (11 per cent) amongst ethnic Albanians (Table 2). The difference may reflect the fact that ethnic Albanians are relatively less discriminatedagainst at present than they were during the Milošević regime. Their need to bribe officials may therefore be somewhat lesser now than it was in the past.

Table 2. Do you think (COUNTRY) has a serious problem with corruption?

	Kosovo %		Macedonia %		Serbia %	
	Majority	Minority	Majority	Minority	Majority	Minority
Yes	94	98	92	97	97	86
No	6	2	8	3	3	14

Note: Decimals rounded up or down to the nearest whole number. Totals may therefore not add up to exactly 100. Silent categories such as mix/depends/don't know are not included.

Just like the survey respondents, our FG participants also expressed serious concern about the extent of corruption in their respective countries:

> 'I don't think there is another country in the region which has a more serious problem with corruption than Kosova!' (KOS-FG4-Ferizaj-Rabije);

[accessed 30 April 2012].

[71] Transparency International, 'Corruption Perceptions Index 2011' <http://cpi.transparency.org/cpi2011/results/#CountryResults> [accessed 10 May 2012].

[72] See for instance Fredrik Galtung, 'Measuring the immeasurable: boundaries and functions of (macro) corruption indices', in Charles Sampford et al. (eds), *Measuring Corruption*, Aldershot, 2006, pp. 101–30.

[73] UNODC, *Corruption in the Western Balkans*.

[74] Our findings are this in line with those of the UNODC. A large-scale survey conducted by the UNODC in the Western Balkans show that 'the people of Albania, Bosnia and Herzegovina, Croatia, Kosovo, Montenegro, Serbia and the Former Yugoslav Republic of Macedonia rank corruption as the most important problem facing their countries/areas after unemployment and poverty'. UNODC, *Corruption in the Western Balkans*, p. 7.

> 'there is much more corruption (in the Republic of Macedonia) now than there was before […]' (MAC-FG3-Kumanovo-Jaska); 'not just Macedonia but all the Balkans have a problem with corruption […] Kosovo, Albania, Serbia, all of them.' (MAC-FG6-Tetovo-Albanians-Zeni); '(corruption is a) very serious problem, that's why nothing changes in Serbia.' (SER-FG1-Belgrade-lower educated-Dusan).

Some FG participants attributed corruption to the difficult socio-economic condition their countries are currently faced with. Others identified the areas in which corruption is particularly widespread and/or problematic — such as education (Kosovo, Serbia), health (Kosovo, Serbia), politics, the judiciary, the police (Serbia) or simply 'all spheres of society' (the Republic of Macedonia). FG participants in the Republic of Macedonia believed that corruption has caused their country considerable damage. They also believed that the problem is further compounded by lack of deterrents and corruption control mechanisms:

> 'corruption has consequences that have brought people to extreme poverty.' (KOS2-Vllaznimi); '(corruption is most widespread in) education and health care.' (KOS-FG6-Mitrovica-Stojan); 'it has entered all spheres of society, whether it's health, education, police, the judicial system. It is everywhere where the citizen should seek justice, complete some need […]' (MAC-FG4-Bitola-Duda); 'the health department, judiciary, education, the police. There are no areas of life without corruption.' (SER-FG3-Niš-Dragan); 'the entire system is corrupted, from the government to the cleaners.'(SER-FG5-Bujanovac-I-Beri).

Despite the problems with corruption, some of the FG participants from the Republic of Macedonia spontaneously noted that the level of corruption has subsided somewhat in their country in recent years.

Survey evidence suggests that corruption *increases* during transition.[75] While some studies suggest that during periods of transition corruption increases before it starts decreasing,[76] others suggest that corruption during transition is cyclical and does not follow a linear development.[77] Shedding light on the root causes of corruption is thus useful both in terms of determining how stable levels of corruption are in a given country and also whether and how corruption can best be fought.

[75] Miller et al., *A Culture of Corruption*; Leslie T. Holmes, 'International Anti-Corruption Regimes and Corruption Levels in European and Eurasian Post-Communist States', in Wolf and Schmidt-Pfister (eds), 'International Anti-Corruption Regimes', pp. 25–45 (p. 25).

[76] Miller et al., *A Culture of Corruption*.

[77] Holmes, 'International Anti-Corruption Regimes', p. 25.

Research on informal practice and corruption amongst elites in seven post-Communist states indicates that one important explanation for the use of informal contacts and informal networks — both of which act as drivers of corruption[78] — is to be found in national culture.[79] The majority populations in Kosovo, the Republic of Macedonia and Serbia, however, primarily attributed corruption to transition. By contrast, the Serb minority in Kosovo believed that national culture is primarily to blame, while ethnic Albanians in Serbia attributed the problem to armed conflict and war. Albanians in the Republic of Macedonia, for their part, perceived corruption as a result of transition and national culture in more or less equal measure (Table 3).

Table 3. Would you say that corruption in (COUNTRY) is primarily a result of...

	Kosovo %		Macedonia %		Serbia %	
	Majority	Minority	Majority	Minority	Majority	Minority
(COUNTRY) national culture	8	32	35	29	25	25
The Yugoslav period (i.e. before 1989)	19	18	10	18	9	12
Armed conflict/war	27	26	4	21	27	39
Transition	45	25	51	32	39	24

Note: Decimals rounded up or down to the nearest whole number. Totals may therefore not add up to exactly 100. Silent categories such as mix/depends/don't know are not included.

FG participants who perceived corruption as an expression of *culture* pointed out that gift-giving is a local custom, an expression of Balkan mentality. It is even customary to give presents to people who officially charge for their services if the service has been performed in a satisfactory

[78] Åse Berit Grødeland, '"Red Mobs", "Yuppies" and "Lamb Heads": Informal Networks and Politics in the Czech Republic, Slovenia, Bulgaria and Romania', *Europe-Asia Studies*, 59, 2007, 2, pp. 217–52.

[79] Åse Berit Grødeland and Aadne Aasland, *Informality and Informal Practices in East Central and South East Europe*, CERC (Contemporary Europe Research Centre, University of Melbourne) Working Papers Series, 3, 2007.

manner. Size-wise informal payments are bigger nowadays than they used to be in the past. Though part of the social logic, some FG participants questioned such informal payments:

> '(gift-giving), that's not corruption, that's giving thanks in Serbia!' (SER-FG2-Belgrade-higher educated-Mladen); 'it's part of our folklore.' (SER-FG2-Belgrade-higher educated-Srdjan); '(it is) a custom. You go to the childbirth centre and you give something to the midwife [...] everybody knows and everybody gives.' (KOS-FG5-Štrpce); '(it is) culture. I go to see a dentist, a friend of mine, she finished someone's teeth for 1,200 euros [...] he paid 1,200 euros and (still) felt the need to give champagne, a chocolate box and chocolate. Is that normal to you? You go to a car service (place), replace the oil, pay 5,000 dinars to the mechanic and 1,000 more because he replaced it. Is that normal?' (SER-FG1-Belgrade-lower educated-Dušan); '(it is) tradition. In Tito's time and in the beginning of the Milošević period it wasn't so massive [...] usually it was coffee, chocolate, whisky [...] it was always coffee and whisky for doctors.' (SER-FG1-Belgrade-lower educated-Dragan).

In Eastern Europe negative phenomena are often blamed on past foreign rule. Mungiu-Pippidi notes that in Romania, corruption is partly attributed to the Phanariotes, partly to the Ottoman legacy. The latter has become 'the favourite scapegoat of modern Romanian thinkers'.[80] The habit of circumventing official institutions and/or official procedures is also perceived as an important part of the Ottoman legacy by citizens in the Western Balkans. The same goes for bribe-giving. Even though FG participants in the Western Balkans perceived gift-giving as part of the *local* (that is Balkan) culture, some of them emphasized that bribery is essentially a legacy of the Ottoman Empire rather than a genuine feature of the local culture and traditions. The fact that Turkish words are still used by locals to describe various corrupt phenomena was taken in evidence of this.[81] Christian Serbs and Macedonians, but not ethnic Albanians (the Albanians in Kosovo, The Republic of Macedonia and Serbia are predominantly

[80] Alina Mungiu-Pippidi, 'Breaking Free at Last: Tales of Corruption from the Postcommunist Balkans', *East European Constitutional Review*, 6, 1997, 4, pp. 85–90 (p. 85).

[81] A media representative in Bulgaria interviewed for our previous projects on informal practice and corruption in seven post-Communist states made a similar observation: 'it is interesting to consider the different terms for corruption used in Bulgaria: *baksheesh* (tip), *rushvet/vzyatka* (bribe, sweetener), and *koruptsia* (corruption). The first are from Turkish, the second from Russian, and the last are used in Western Europe. The first one denotes a social system, there is no rationalization and it's simply about supporting the system. The second one stands for a means of interaction and the third — for the rational pursuit of profit.' (Bu-ME-6).

Muslim) argued that as the habit of gift-giving has developed over a long period of time, it is not likely to change overnight:

> 'corruption has existed since the Ottoman period. It was called *rushvet* (bribe). If you wanted to accomplish something, you should bring *rushvet* to the *aga*[82] or to the *kadija*.[83] So it is with us. In our country in recent years it has become a habit. We, the people ourselves, do that. You go to the doctor and bring coffee, juice [...] everyone necessarily brings with him something, no matter whether he is asked to bring something or not [...]' (MAC-FG3-Kumanovo-Nikola); 'we [...] have [...] the remains of Turkism, Turkish culture, in our genes.' (KOS-FG6-Mitrovica-Milos); 'from the Turkish times the relations towards authorities and institutions [have been bad], 500 years of grandfathers and great grandfathers, who were raised to bypass institutions, it's a lot of generations. It took root in the collective consciousness [...] it is changed slowly and not right away.' (SER-FG2-Belgrade-higher educated-Boris).

Those who blamed corruption on *socialism* emphasized that in the past, corruption occurred as 'gate keepers' demanded informal payments to provide access to limited resources. These FG participants believed that not only corruption as such, but also the size of bribes, has increased during transition as a result of high unemployment and low salaries. Following from this, if socio-economic conditions in the Western Balkans were to improve, the need for informal payments would drop accordingly:

> 'Yugoslav officials were those who, no matter which sphere of life it was (they were working in), you had to give something (to) in order to proceed. For example [...] for an ID and a passport (you were) supposed to give something... or the police on the streets: if they stopped you continuously, you had to give something [...] (from) 1987 until the war [...] the source of corruption is not post-war Kosovo. This comes from the Yugoslav regime and now it is gradually increasing.' (KOS-FG1- Priština-lower education-Violeta); 'it is a consequence of the Communist period [...] only the amounts are higher now. Before, it was (done) for the daily allowance or (for) some favour, and now people want money [...]' (MAC-FG2-Skopje-higher educated-Ljupco); 'I think that it is from the time of the Former Yugoslavia, (it) is a social problem [...] in our country the doctor has a salary of 200 euros [...]' (MAC-FG6-Tetovo-Albanians-Jaki).

[82] *Agha* is a title that was given to civil or military officers in the Ottoman Empire. It was also used by some court functionaries <http://en.wikipedia.org/wiki/Agha_(Ottoman_Empire)> [accessed 15 March 2012].

[83] *Kadija* (*qadi*) — is a title used for judges during the Ottoman Empire.

In the view of Balkan citizens *conflict/war* has had only limited impact on corruption. FG participants in Serbia thought it corrupted government and resulted in widespread disregard for the law, while FG participants in the Republic of Macedonia believed the Yugoslav and Kosovo wars caused corruption as it brought corrupt ethnic Albanians to their country. In their view, Albanians are generally more corrupt than Macedonians:

> 'during the war period there was no control, not by the government and neither by anyone else. The government was generally corrupted during this period.' (SER-FG5-Bujanovac-I-Veton); 'during war there is no respect for the law, no one takes responsibility for (their) own action, not for the corruption, and as we are the Balkans, the war is not a rare thing — it happens very often.' (SER-FG6-Bujanovac-II-Sead); 'the armed military insurgence as well in 2001 [...] when the Albanians arrived, the level of corruption increased [...] the Albanian mafia is famous. We aren't as corrupted as the Albanians [...]' (MAC-FG1-Skopje-lower educated-Dalibor).

Those FG participants who attributed corruption to *transition* believed that corruption flourishes in their respective countries because old structures have collapsed (Serbia) and been replaced by new ones (Kosovo), because the socio-economic situation is difficult (Kosovo), laws are undefined and not implemented (the Republic of Macedonia) or, more importantly, because corrupt politicians and oligarchs allow corruption to exist — that is that they make no effort to curb it (all countries):

> 'in every "after war"-country [...] corruption is expected in the transition period [...] after a period of time it is expected to be reduced.' (KOS-FG3-Gjakova-Lindita); 'this is a result of transition as Kosovo emerged from war totally destroyed, (with) very high unemployment [...] if there were (a high level of) economic development and everyone (were) employed with good wages, they wouldn't be corrupted.' (KOS-FG1- Priština-lower education-Hilmiu); 'it is a result of transition. A new culture has spread.' (KOS-FG2-Priština-higher education-Servete); 'in 92, 93 at the beginning of transition the laws were not defined and (they were not) strict, and people were not respecting them. I think transition (is to blame for corruption).' (MAC-FG2-Skopje-higher educated-Daniela); 'here the real values were lost with transition.' (MAC-FG4-Bitola-Marijan); 'I think from the 90s (onwards).' (SER-FG6-Bujanovac-II-Uros).

FG participants who believed that corruption is caused by *a mix of factors*, either attributed corruption to socialism and transition (the Republic of Macedonia) or to culture and transition (Serbia).[84]

Survey respondents were also asked what *type* of corruption they considered to be the most serious for their country. Our survey data are not clear-cut in this regard: Kosovo Albanians perceived political corruption as the most serious problem for their country while Kosovo Serbs were more concerned about economic corruption — possibly as a result of extensive smuggling across the border between northern Kosovo and Serbia.[85] Ethnic Macedonians in the Republic of Macedonia perceived judicial corruption as the most serious problem, while ethnic Albanians were more concerned with political corruption — as were Serbs in Serbia. Ethnic Albanians in Serbia viewed economic corruption as more problematic — possibly as they live on the Kosovo-Serbian border where smuggling is commonplace (Table 4).

Table 4. Which of the following four types of corruption do you consider the most serious one for (COUNTRY): administrative corruption, political corruption, economic corruption or corruption in the judiciary?

	Kosovo %		Macedonia %		Serbia %	
	Majority	Minority	Majority	Minority	Majority	Minority
Administrative corruption	10	13	25	20	14	9
Political corruption	44	24	26	39	48	31
Economic corruption	27	42	15	23	13	52
Corruption in the judiciary	20	21	35	18	26	8

Note: Decimals rounded up or down to the nearest whole number. Totals may therefore not add up to exactly 100. Silent categories such as mix/depends/don't know are not included.

84 Findings for Kosovo were not clear cut: of the three statements that were coded one explained corruption as a result of communism and transition, one — as a result of Communism, war and transition, while the final statement blamed Turkish culture and transition.

85 See, for instance, Doreen Carvajal, 'In Kosovo, smuggling fosters unusual ethnic cooperation', *New York Times*, 24 October 2011 <http://www.nytimes.com/2011/10/24/world/europe/in-balkans-smuggling-forges-a-rare-unity.html?pagewanted=all&_r=0> [accessed 15 April 2013].

As noted above, the academic literature on corruption frequently refers to the general public as *victims* of corruption. However, our data suggest that the situation is less straight forward: while in some instances the general public fall prey to greedy officials, on other occasions they themselves initiate corruption, by offering bribes to government officials in return for the speeding up of procedures, to obtain their lawful rights, or favours to which they are not entitled by law. As in other parts of post-Communist Europe[86] it is therefore more useful to refer to members of the general public in the Western Balkans not only as victims, but also as accomplices of corruption.[87]

To further explore the victims-accomplices dimension we asked our FG participants whether it is more or less acceptable to give a bribe if someone asks one to do so than if one offers to do so voluntarily. Table 5 shows that the majority populations in Kosovo, the Republic of Macedonia and Serbia, as well as the minority population in the Republic of Macedonia, thought giving bribes is never acceptable. Ethnic Serbs in Kosovo and

Table 5. Is it more acceptable or less acceptable to give a bribe if someone asks one to do so than if one offers to do so voluntarily?

	Kosovo %		Macedonia %		Serbia %	
	Majority	Minority	Majority	Minority	Majority	Minority
It is more acceptable	10	23	4	14	9	36
It is equally acceptable	13	18	12	15	8	8
It is less acceptable	15	14	17	12	11	19
Giving bribes is never acceptable	62	45	67	60	72	37

Note: Decimals rounded up or down to the nearest whole number. Totals may therefore not add up to exactly 100. Silent categories such as mix/depends/don't know are not included.

86 For a discussion of this issue, see William L. Miller, Åse B. Grødeland and Tatyana Y. Koshechkina. 'Are the People Victims or Accomplices? The Use of Presents and Bribes to Influence Officials in Eastern Europe', *Crime, Law and Social Change*, 29, 1998, 4, pp. 273–310.

87 The UNODC study of corruption in the Western Balkans show that some citizens (22%) perceive bribery as simply a common practice and also, when constituting an expression of gratitude for services rendered, actually as a positive practice (18%). UNODC, *Corruption in the Western Balkans*, p. 8.

ethnic Albanians in Serbia found it is more acceptable than the majority populations in their respective countries to give a bribe if asked to do so — thus lending some support to the 'try harder'-hypothesis.[88]

Above we noted that there appears to be a correlation between the successful extortion of bribes and the bargaining strength of the official requesting the bribe. Academic studies of corruption in post-Communist states suggest that doctors, in particular, have high bargaining strength.[89] This might explain why bribe-giving in health care is widespread and perceived as fairly acceptable in the Western Balkans. Bribes are sometimes requested by health personnel before, and sometimes given voluntarily by citizens after, medical treatment. In the former case, bribes tend to be viewed as a necessary evil. In the latter case, they are viewed as an expression of local culture — that is, as acceptable gift-giving rather than corruption. FG participants found it especially acceptable to give something to a doctor if he/she did not request a bribe before treating the patient:

> 'when it is a matter of life or death (I would give a bribe). I had a case when someone had to give a bribe for his family member to get operated (on). For such cases it is acceptable (to give a bribe), for other (cases it is) not.' (KOS-FG3-Gjakova-Sharri); 'that was the case at the surgery: "give us 1,000 euros to supply you with a bed for an operation".' (MAC-FG1-Skopje-lower educated-Zore); 'they actually force you to do it (that is to bribe them). You don't have a big choice. You will either cure (your child) or you won't.' (MAC-FG1-Skopje-lower educated-Oishe); 'it's customary (to give something to the doctor afterwards), but it's when they are asking you for something in advance (that it is not acceptable).' (SER-FG4-Novi Sad-Uros).

FG participants justified their position with regard to bribing health personnel by telling stories about people who had died because they were either not in a position to, or chose not to, pay doctors for life-saving medical treatment.[90] The stories told by FG participants in Serbia were particularly heart-breaking in terms of the cynicism exhibited by doctors and the very serious consequences their attitude had for the patients

[88] The ethnic Albanian community in Macedonia is bigger than that in Serbia and also bigger than the Serbian community in Kosovo — which may explain why the views of the ethnic Macedonians and Albanians in Macedonia are similar.

[89] Miller et al., *A Culture of Corruption*, p. 261.

[90] For an overview of bribery in the health sector in post-Communist Europe, see William L. Miller, Åse B. Grødeland and Tatyana Y. Koshechkina, 'If you pay, we'll operate immediately', *Journal of Medical Ethics*, 26, 2000, 5, pp. 303–11.

involved. FG participants even told stories about people who had died because they could not afford to pay for the required treatment, and to which they were entitled by law. Their stories were not based on hearsay, but on the personal experience of FG participants themselves or their close family members:

> 'you go to the doctor's and he says how much (to pay) in order to admit him (the patient). There are numerous examples here, some (doctors) have (even) been arrested [...] I lost my aunt because the doctor didn't want to operate (on her). She died at (the age of) fifty four, she was in good health before that. He didn't want to admit her, he said that the surgery costs 3,000 DM: "if you want me to operate on her, bring the money, we'll take care of it, if not, then nothing". We didn't have that kind of money [...] that doctor still works, unfortunately [...]' (SER-FG3-Niš-Dragan); 'it was our mistake that we didn't give them (the doctors) the money. Our child died.' (SER-FG2-Belgrade-higher educated-Ceca).

We noted above that law-breaking in the Western Balkans has developed historically in response to foreign rule — especially in those parts of the Balkans that were under Ottoman rule for some 500 years: prolonged foreign rule not only affected the relationship between rulers and ruled, but also the relationship between the ruled in that no real sense of community spirit was allowed to develop. In such societies people still distinguish between 'us' (one's nearest family, friends and acquaintances) and 'them' (everybody else). Their practical and moral obligation is primarily directed towards 'us' ('our people') rather than towards 'them'. The latter can, and should, generally not be trusted. This dichotomy can still be found to a greater or lesser extent in East Central Europe, Southeastern Europe and the Western Balkans. It could even be argued that the selfish behaviour of ruling elites throughout post-Communist Europe essentially reflects such thinking.

People's loyalty to 'our people' is likely to be particularly strong when socio-economic conditions are harsh in that financial hardship may reinforce social norms that are conducive to corruption. Our data suggest that nepotism is a major source of job distribution in the Western Balkans. Jobs tend to be passed on from parents to children and it is very difficult to obtain a job on merit alone.[91] Besides, knowing the right people is not in

[91] The UNODC study suggests that 'some 18 per cent of the region's (Western Balkans) citizens, or members of their households, have applied for a job in the public sector in the last three years, but of those whose application was successful one in eight admits to paying some money, giving a gift or doing a favour to help secure their position. Among those who failed, there is a widespread perception that factors such as cronyism, nepotism

itself always sufficient: jobs sometimes also have to be paid for. Given the high level of unemployment in the Western Balkans, prospective employers therefore have considerable bargaining strength. As with health-care, FG participants found it acceptable to pay for a job. Our findings thus seem to suggest that the higher the bargaining strength of the bribe taker, the more socially acceptable bribing appears to be:

> 'if someone has been unemployed for twenty years and if that (that is giving a bribe) is the only way in which to get the job [...] I think I approve of that.' (MAC-FG2-Skopje-higher educated-Dejan); 'you must give (a bribe) because you risk your workplace, you risk the feeding of your child, family and so on.' (MAC-FG5-Skopje-Albanians-Adnan); '(giving a bribe to get a job is) justified because people cannot find work for years [...]' (SER-FG4-Novi Sad-Uros); 'the institution of competition is lost here when it comes to work: it is either (a question of) political party affiliation or (of) some contacts.' (SER-FG3-Niš-Jovanka); 'there is no fair competition. I work for a state company. It is a public secret that it costs from 3,000 to 5,000 euro to get employed. I returned that money in six months [...] no professionals came, everybody came through connections. It's the same in every company. From politicians to secretaries.' (SER-FG2-Belgrade-higher educated-Zeljko); 'here the institution of job opening(s) has been lost...(people) inherit (jobs) like monarchs (do). The mother worked, then the son comes, or the daughter. You won't find an opening anywhere [...]' (SER-FG1-Belgrade, lower educated-Vida).

Thus, young people in the Western Balkans are taught corrupt behaviour from an early age: bribes and/or contacts provide them with access to a good school or university, good marks, a certificate and then eventually also with a job. Once they have obtained a job through someone and/or for payment, they are socialized into a work-culture in which bribery and nepotism flourish.

Employment-related corruption is problematic in that the best qualified people for the job are not necessarily those best positioned to pay for it. Local companies and businesses need well-qualified staff in order to be competitive. To the extent unqualified people are hired for jobs this negatively affects socio-economic development — which, in turn, affects corruption. Current anti-corruption measures are not broad enough to successfully target such systemic corruption.

or bribery played a decisive role in the recruitment process, while only 10 per cent believe that the selection was made on merit'. UNODC, *Corruption in the Western Balkans*, pp. 8–9.

It is useful to view corruption to secure employment from the victims-accomplices and the bargaining strength dimensions. The people who control the job market have high bargaining strength and may thus request payments in return for jobs, while those in need of a job may voluntarily (and happily) offer payments to secure a job. The problem of bribing one's way to employment should therefore not be blamed exclusively on the bribe takers — that is employers or those facilitating access to such prospective employers.

As already noted, our FGs suggest that there is considerable tolerance towards corrupt behaviour in the Western Balkans, despite the negative attitudes people have of corruption as such. Our FG participants suggested that it is acceptable to give bribes if forced to do so (Serbia), in case of necessity, that is to achieve a goal or to secure a specific outcome (Serbia, the Republic of Macedonia), if stopped by the traffic police (Kosovo) or 'in a work situation' (Kosovo). Even though in principle ordinary people in the Western Balkans believe it would be better not to bribe, they often feel they are left with no real choice. Once they have given a bribe they tend to be grateful for having solved their problems. They therefore have no real incentive to report bribery:[92]

> 'there are (situations in which it is acceptable to give a bribe) […] when (a policeman) issues a fifty euro fine I give him ten and why should I care? I'm OK, he's OK, we're (feeling) super. Drive on!' (KOS-FG6-Mitrovica-Stojan); 'when you give (a bribe) you forget (about it) because you are satisfied.' (MAC-FG5-Skopje-Albanians-Arijan); 'you will either give a bribe to obtain a permit (or you will obtain no permit) […] sometimes the laws force people to (resort) to that method to achieve some goals. Those are some higher goals […]' (SER-FG3-Niš-Dragan); 'I would do it without question, having in mind that you don't have (any) other choice and I would be very grateful.' (SER-FG6-Bujanovac-II-Sadije); 'we are aware of what is good or wrong and what (we) should and shouldn't do, but there are other factors that influence our decision-making, so we do the only thing left to do so (that) we reach our goals.' (SER-FG6-Bujanovac-II-Sadije).

Respondents who took part in our quantitative surveys were also asked how acceptable they think it is to give a bribe in a number of specific situations — some of which are legitimate, some of which are illegitimate and some which could be either, depending on the context (for a discussion of legitimate versus illegitimate requests, see discussion above). Table 6 shows that a larger percentage of the ethno-religious minority groups than the ethnic titular groups find it 'very acceptable' or 'somewhat acceptable'

[92] Ibid., pp. 31–34.

Table 6. How acceptable is it to give a bribe in any of the following situations? Is it very acceptable, somewhat acceptable, not so acceptable or completely unacceptable to… (% very acceptable & somewhat acceptable)

	Kosovo %		Macedonia %		Serbia %	
	Majority	Minority	Majority	Minority	Majority	Minority
speed up an official procedure	28	65	28	61	25	62
obtain something to which one is entitled by law	22	46	17	46	26	55
obtain something to which one is not entitled by law	16	32	18	37	12	47
avoid prosecution or secure a more lenient charge	19	37	28	42	17	53
secure a certain outcome in court	19	41	24	34	16	48
avoid a fine for speeding or having to go to court for a minor traffice offence	15	60	38	49	20	49
promote laws or influence voting in parliament	16	33	8	21	12	44
enroll someone in university/school	23	49	28	46	19	52
pass an exam or obtain good marks	18	59	24	40	13	43
secure adequate medical treatment	28	70	45	65	42	49

Note: Decimals rounded up or down to the nearest whole number. Totals may therefore not add up to exactly 100. Silent categories such as mix/depends/don't know are not included.

to give bribes in all the situations we asked about. Our findings thus lend some support to the 'try harder'-hypothesis — that is that when dealing with state employees minorities have to 'try harder' than majority populations to achieve outcomes. Further, our findings fit well with our observations on bargaining strength: the higher the bargaining strength of the service-provider, the more willing people are to give a bribe.

Giving bribes to people whose bargaining strengths are high, for instance to secure necessary medical treatment or a job, was considered the most important or second most important situation in which all ethnic groups except Serbia Albanians found bribe-giving acceptable. Our respondents also found it fairly acceptable to give bribes to speed up an official procedure. Giving bribes for illegitimate purposes such as avoiding a fine for speed-driving or having to go to court for a minor traffic offence, obtaining something to which one is not entitled by law, to avoid prosecution or secure a more lenient charge, or to secure a certain outcome in court was generally considered less acceptable — though still acceptable by a rather large percentage of people.

In the Western Balkans, bribery and nepotism are, to quite some extent, facilitated by contacts and informal networks. As noted above, these types of corruption are widespread in this region: landing a job is next to impossible without the right contacts (such contacts are often close family members) or the ability to pay. We therefore asked our FG participants whether it is acceptable to get a job through connections rather than through fair competition.

Again, ethno-religious minorities stand out: Table 7 shows that while the majority of the ethno-religious titular groups in all countries found it 'not so acceptable'/'completely unacceptable' to get a job through connections rather than through fair competition, the majority of the ethno-religious minorities claimed that it 'very acceptable' or 'somewhat acceptable' to do so. Again, our findings thus not only lend support to the 'try harder'-hypothesis. They also confirm that citizens in the Western Balkans find themselves in a prisoner's dilemma as far as jobs are concerned: while they would ideally prefer for jobs to be distributed on the basis of merit and fair competition, reality is rather different. Statements made during our FG suggest that people adjust to reality rather than trying to change it: the perceived cost of doing the latter is simply too high, given that other people are not likely to follow suit.

Table 7. And how acceptable is it to get a job through connections rather than through fair competition? Is it...

	Kosovo %		Macedonia %		Serbia %	
	Majority	Minority	Majority	Minority	Majority	Minority
very acceptable	17	20	11	33	7	48
somewhat acceptable	18	48	20	22	20	25
not so acceptable	15	14	25	16	18	7
completely unacceptable	50	20	45	29	55	20

Note: Decimals rounded up or down to the nearest whole number. Totals may therefore not add up to exactly 100. Silent categories such as mix/depends/don't know are not included.

Table 8 suggests that all ethnic groups expect Serbia-Albanians think contacts and informal networks are primarily used to obtain favourable treatment, rather than something to which one is entitled by law, fair treatment, or to secure that (formal) rules are applied properly. As noted above, ethnic Albanians in southern Serbia were heavily discriminated against during the Milošević period. While in recent years much has been done to restore the rights of the ethnic Albanian community in Serbia, there is still room for improvement[93] — which helps explain our findings.

Our FG data provide more detail as to why citizens in the Western Balkans use informal practice. FG participants in Kosovo primarily held the view that contacts and informal networks are a prerequisite for getting things done — especially for getting a job:

> '(connections are needed for) everything.' (KOS-FG6-Mitrovica-Dragan); '(there will be) no job without connections [...] there can't be any competition.' (KOS-FG6-Mitrovica-Danilo); 'if you want to find a job you will not think about preparing a test, but (about) how to find an insider. That cannot be stopped in a flash of time, but (only) gradually.' (KOS-FG2-Priština-higher education-Valoni); 'if someone wants to win a tender, then

[93] Ethnic Albanians in Serbia boycotted the 2011 census — to protest their current situation. Nikola Lazic, 'Serbian Albanians rally behind Census Boycott', *Balkan Insight*, 14 October 2011 <http://www.balkaninsight.com/en/article/serbian-albanians-rally-behind-census-boycott> [accessed 10 May 2012].

he has to find an intermediate, a liaison person, who will be the connection between both parties.' (KOS-FG3-Gjakova-Sharri).

Table 8. Why do you think people in (COUNTRY) use contacts and informal networks when interacting with government officials, politicians, judges, prosecutors, lawyers and the police? Is it primarily to ensure...

	Kosovo %		Macedonia %		Serbia %	
	Majority	Minority	Majority	Minority	Majority	Minority
that they get what they are entitled to by law	24	16	13	23	20	48
that the rules are applied properly	17	11	11	12	12	18
that they are treated fairly	27	21	14	25	25	7
favourable treatment	32	52	62	41	43	26

Note: Decimals rounded up or down to the nearest whole number. Totals may therefore not add up to exactly 100. Silent categories such as mix/depends/don't know are not included.

Citizens in the Republic of Macedonia, for their part, primarily use such informal mechanisms to solve problems because it is faster, but also because they perceive them as the only means by which to solve their problems, given that laws are often not (properly) applied. By turning to contacts or informal networks it is possible to avoid issues from getting stuck in the system and also to avoid queues — thus reducing one's discomfort to a minimum. Contacts are viewed as the (only) solution to one's problems. Useful people to approach include friends and relatives, if they happen to work in government structures, or family members/ acquaintances working in the municipality. One FG participant noted that as everybody uses contacts the benefits of doing so and the disadvantages of not doing so eventually balance out. Consequently, one should be understanding of people jumping the queue:

'if we work in public administration, we surely would help a friend or relative (so as to) not stand in line and to pass faster, before the others. I guess it's part of our tradition, because we all know each other. And we don't have to be mad with the people using their connections and moving faster than us in the line, because at a certain point we will do that, too.' (MAC-FG2-Skopje-higher educated-Igor); 'if you know a person in the municipality you can finish your work faster [...] if you wait at the desk you will have to wait for 3-4 hours. But if you know someone you will finish the job in five minutes [...]' (MAC-FG5-Skopje-Albanians-Adnan); 'there is no way you can finish a job regularly [...]' (MAC-FG1-Skopje-lower educated-Zoran).

It could be argued that culturally-based nepotism facilitates the use of contacts in state institutions: people who are not qualified for jobs in the public sector obtain them through contacts and/or purchase them for money. This, in turn, breeds inefficiency which citizens then either pay the state employees, or use connections, to circumvent.

Serbs, for their part, use informal mechanisms because it is faster and easier to achieve intended outcomes this way. By turning to contacts or informal networks queues can be circumvented and waiting to get a job done can be reduced from days to hours. If contacts are lacking, then a bribe does the trick. Informal contacts and networks help people reach their goals — and sometimes even to save lives. One FG participant, however, suggested that he would not use contacts or informal networks if he was sure that his objectives could be achieved without them. If his views are representative for citizens as such, they again find themselves in a typical 'prisoner's dilemma' situation: ideally they would like to change their behaviour, but as long as they do not believe that state institutions and other citizens change theirs, they have no real incentive to do so. Fairly low levels of institutional trust in the Western Balkans[94] further compound the problem:

'to finish a job faster, that is if you would do something in two to three days, with the informal connection you will do that in half an hour.' (SER-FG5-Bujanovac-I-Iliri); 'if you offer something to the policeman then you will get (the car plates) in five minutes.' (SER-FG5-Bujanovac-I-Vetoni); '(contacts and informal networks are essentially about) speed and security.' (SER-FG3-Niš-Bojana); 'I wouldn't use them if I knew I would finish something on time.' (SER-FG2-Belgrade-higher educated-Boris); 'at the hospital, if there is someone you know and you have good relations, you can save a person's life [...]' (SER-FG5-Bujanovac-I-Beli).

[94] See Gallup Balkan Monitor, *Insights and Perceptions: Voices of the Balkans: 2010 Summary of Findings*, Gallup Inc., 2010 <http://www.balkan-monitor.eu/files/BalkanMonitor-2010_Summary_of_Findings.pdf> [accessed 3 May 2012], pp. 26–33.

FG participants in all countries primarily blamed the use of contacts and informal networks on non-functioning state institutions. Some of them suggested that institutions do not function properly as a result of nepotism — that is that not the best qualified people are recruited to jobs in these structures. FG participants in Kosovo, for instance, claimed that state institutions are corrupt. They reiterated that the manner in which jobs are distributed in the Western Balkans is largely to blame for this state of affairs: state institutions are not functioning properly as unqualified people are recruited to work there. Such 'personalization' (or 'embodiment') of state institutions appears to be rather common in the region. Finally, people who have paid money for their jobs are likely to try to recoup the money by requesting or accepting money from their clients:

> 'if an institution doesn't work in the proper way then it is obvious that informal networks appear. Unfortunately, in Kosovo these networks are functioning really well and they are very harmful.' (KOS-FG3-Gjakova-Idrizi); 'so they didn't put the machine for passports in operation on purpose, so you can pay more expensively (for the) fast service procedure. Obviously (they do that) to make a profit out of you.' (MAC-FG1-Skopje-lower educated-Dalibor); 'if you look at the level of nepotism, in a Ministry you can find a whole family.' (KOS-FG3-Gjakova-Lindita); 'in Kosovo the majority of the places are (staffed) with people who are not from that field. No one works in a well-deserved place (that is position). The majority entered (their jobs) through a known person.' (KOS-FG1- Priština-lower education-Sanija); 'those people are not adequately (qualified) for the positions they are holding, normally those people can't finish a job in the way it is supposed to be finished [...] because they are not skilled for that task [...] this leads to the disadvantages that we are seeing in law enforcement and in the economic system, the social system, and so on.' (KOS-FG1- Priština-lower education-Violeta); 'every person who works in these institutions acts as if it is his own institution. For example, a dean thinks that it is his faculty, or a doctor thinks that it's his decision [...]' (KOS-FG2- Priština-higher education-Valoni).

Not only the use of informal practice but also citizens' perceptions of law appear to facilitate corruption in the Western Balkans. As noted above, previous research on the region suggests that two different legal cultures appear to exist side by side with regard to the law: a 'nihilist legal culture', which has emerged over time, in response to historical developments,[95]

[95] There is some evidence that citizens living in countries that were ruled by external

and a 'fear-based law-abiding legal culture'.[96] Data from our quantitative survey suggest that citizens in the Western Balkans mostly believe that people's attitudes towards laws and regulations are conducive to corruption — that is that people primarily adhere to the 'nihilist legal culture'. Ethnic Albanians in Serbia were the only ethnic group to predominantly hold the opposite view (Table 9).

Table 9. Do you think the attitude of people in (COUNTRY) towards law and legal regulations is conducive to corruption?

	Kosovo %		Macedonia %		Serbia %	
	Majority	Minority	Majority	Minority	Majority	Minority
Yes	76	81	54	75	79	44
No	24	19	46	25	21	56

Note: Decimals rounded up or down to the nearest whole number. Totals may therefore not add up to exactly 100. Silent categories such as mix/depends/don't know are not included.

Who should be responsible for Anti-Corruption Reform: Perceptions of Law-Makers and Law Enforcers

The responsibility for overseeing anti-corruption reform in post-Communist states rests with a number of different institutions.[97] A frequently heard view in such states is that anti-corruption reform is the responsibility of too many institutions and that, for this reason, it is simply not effective.[98] To enhance the impact of reform, it is often recommended

rulers over a longer period of time, developed a deep-seated lack of trust not only in their rulers, but also in state institutions and laws introduced by these rulers as such. Such skepticism continued during Communist rule and has been carried over into transition. Grødeland and Aasland, *Informality and Informal Practices*. In other post-Communist states, notably Ukraine, misconstrued understandings of what notions like 'democracy' and 'rule of law' actually entails, is also partly to blame: many Ukrainians equal 'democracy' with 'freedom' — including unlimited freedom to break the law.

[96] Åse Berit Grødeland, 'Informal Relations in Public Procurement', in E. G. Yasin (ed.), *Sbornik dokladov 'X Mezhdunarodnaia nauchnaia konferentsia po problemam razvitia ekonomiki i obshchestva'. Volume 1*, Moscow, 2010, pp. 460–73 <http://www.hse.ru/data/2010/07/02/1218932318/%D0%93%D1%80%D0%BE%D0%B4%D0%B5%D0%BB%D0%B0%D0%BD%D0%B4.doc> [accessed 15 January 2012].

[97] For an overview of anti-corruption in Eastern Europe, see Holmes, 'International Anti-Corruption Regimes', pp. 25–45.

[98] Holmes suggests that while the impact of most international organizations on corruption levels is typically low, the EU appears to be an exception in this regard. Ibid., p. 39.

that the responsibility for overseeing it should be concentrated within a limited number of institutions.

While the issue of who should be in charge of anti-corruption reform and how, is indeed important (we will return to this issue below), the starting point for any anti-corruption effort to be successful must be that the institutions responsible for supervising and implementing it themselves abide by the law. Politicians pass anti-corruption legislation; government officials implement it, while the police, prosecutors and judges enforce it. Lawyers, for their part, assist those accused of corrupt acts. It therefore gives reason for concern that neither the judiciary nor the national government enjoy much trust amongst the populations of the Western Balkans.[99]

Legal professionals are not only professionals but also citizens, socialized into, and shaped by, the same culture as the public at large. As such, they use informal practice in much the same manner and for the same purposes as other citizens — though to a somewhat lesser extent.[100] Could it therefore be that the attitudes of legal professionals towards law are not all that different from those of the public at large? Table 10 shows that the majority of the citizens in the Western Balkans (majority and minority populations) think the legal culture of (i) judges, prosecutors, lawyers and the police (that is the legal professionals) and (ii) politicians and government officials *differs* from that of ordinary citizens (ethnic Albanians in Serbia were the only ones who thought politicians and government officials essentially have the same legal culture as ordinary citizens).

[99] Gallup Balkan Monitor, *Insights and Perceptions*, pp. 30–31. Confidence in the judicial system is fairly low in all countries: only 38 per cent of the Kosovo Albanians, 18 per cent of the Kosovo Serbs, 32 per cent of the Macedonia Macedonians, just over 16 per cent of the Macedonian Albanians and 38 per cent of the Serbia Serbs had 'a lot' or 'some' trust in the judiciary in their respective countries. Trust in the national government was also not particularly high: 44 per cent of the Kosovo Albanians, 14 per cent of the Kosovo Serbs, 32 per cent of the Macedonia Macedonians, 15 per cent of the Macedonia Albanians and 35 per cent of the Serbia Serbs had 'a lot' or 'some' trust in their country's national government (2010 figures).

[100] Grødeland, 'Informal Practice in the Judiciary'.

Table 10. Do you think the legal culture of judges, prosecutors, lawyers and police officials in (COUNTRY) differs from that of ordinary citizens? And how about politicians and government officials? Do you think their legal culture differs from that of ordinary citizens in (COUNTRY)?

	Kosovo %		Macedonia %		Serbia %	
	Majority	Minority	Majority	Minority	Majority	Minority
Judges, prosecutors, lawyers and police officials						
Yes	68	72	70	54	78	54
No	32	28	30	46	22	46
Politicians and government officials						
Yes	59	72	63	53	71	46
No	41	28	37	47	29	54

Note: Decimals rounded up or down to the nearest whole number. Totals may therefore not add up to exactly 100. Silent categories such as mix/depends/don't know are not included.

While ethnic Albanians in Kosovo and Serbia perceive *legal professionals* as being *more respectful* of the law and legal institutions than ordinary citizens, ethnic Macedonians and ethnic Serbs (majority populations) find them *less respectful*. EULEX has invested much time and effort into streamlining the police force, prosecution and courts in Kosovo,[101] which may explain our findings for Albanians in that country. As regards the ethno-religious minorities, ethnic Albanians in the Republic of Macedonia perceived legal professionals as less respectful or as equally respectful, to the same extent. *Politicians and government officials*, for their part, were mostly considered to be *less respectful* of the law and legal institutions than ordinary citizens (the Republic of Macedonia — majority and minority; Serbia — majority). By contrast, ethnic Albanians in Kosovo and Serbia viewed such people as *more respectful*, whereas ethnic Serbs in Kosovo believed that they are neither more, nor less respectful of laws and legal institutions than ordinary citizens (Table 11).

[101] For details, see EULEX Kosovo's website <http://www.eulex-kosovo.eu/en> [accessed 15 April 2013].

Table 11. Do you think "legal insiders" — i.e. judges, prosecutors, lawyers and police officials — in (COUNTRY) are more respectful or less respectful of laws and legal institutions than ordinary citizens? And do you think politicians and government officials in (COUNTRY) are more respectful or less respectful of laws and legal institutions than ordinary citizens?

	Kosovo %		Macedonia %		Serbia %	
	Majority	Minority	Majority	Minority	Majority	Minority
Judges, prosecutors, lawyers and police officials						
More respectful	63	38	27	20	25	70
Less respectful	20	18	43	40	48	14
Neither more, nor less respectful	16	45	30	40	27	15
Politicians and government officials						
More respectful	52	38	22	29	17	70
Less respectful	28	20	49	51	66	16
Neither more, nor less respectful	20	42	28	20	17	14

Note: Decimals rounded up or down to the nearest whole number. Totals may therefore not add up to exactly 100. Silent categories such as mix/depends/don't know are not included.

Our FG findings indicate that in the Western Balkans the legal professions know the law but fail to apply it properly and fairly. FG participants in the Republic of Macedonia believed that legal professionals in their country have no regard for the law and that they frequently violate it altogether. FG participants in Kosovo, for their part, claimed that legal professionals violate the law despite their knowledge of it: as they are protected by their higher-ups they have no reason to fear the consequences of not abiding by the law. In Serbia the situation appears to be even worse: legal professionals not only abstain from properly applying the law. They also act in their own, private interest and are perceived to be largely corrupt:

> 'they know much more about the rules and regulations than ordinary people. But [...] those who are the most familiar with the law are (also) the biggest violators [...] those who are familiar with it use the weaknesses of the law. Maybe they don't violate the law, but they circumvent it.' (KOS-FG1- Priština-lower education-Hilmiu); 'I think they are excluded from the obligation to obey the law.' (SER-FG3-Niš-Dragan); 'they are demagogues: they say everything, agree with the laws, the EU, but personally (they) don't implement anything.' (SER-FG1-Belgrade-lower educated-Jovan).

As for law-abidingness amongst politicians and government officials, FG participants in Serbia made the largest number of negative statements on this matter. In their view these two groups not only fail to abide by the law, but create loopholes in the law from which they can later benefit. Serbian politicians were perceived as dishonest — in that they place themselves above the law. Similar opinions were expressed by FG participants in the Republic of Macedonia who found politicians and government officials to be equally disrespectful of the law. In their view, such people, just like the legal professionals in Kosovo, place themselves above the law and are 'protected' from the negative consequences of disregarding it. Politicians and government officials in Kosovo allegedly knowingly disregard the law as they have no legal culture:

> 'they have a more negative attitude towards the laws than the ordinary man because they are the ones adopting it [...] they often put themselves above the law.' (MAC-FG4-Bitola-Ruzhica); 'I think they have less legal culture because they know the laws and know (how) to avoid violating the law.' (MAC-FG6-Tetovo-Albanians-Feki); 'on every new law some politician slipped. But nothing happened.' (SER-FG4-Novi Sad-Uros); 'if there is a tomb and (it has the inscription) "here rests an honest politician" the first thing you will ask is "are there two people in this tomb?" It is impossible to have a politician who is an honest person.' (SER-FG6-Bujanovac-II-Feride).

The Western Balkans are characterized by low levels of public trust in state institutions as well as fuzzy public perceptions of law-abidingness amongst legal professionals, politicians and government officials. One might therefore expect citizens to be more favourable to foreign anti-corruption specialists or civil society bodies supervising and/or implementing anti-corruption reform, than to various state bodies engaging in anti-corruption activities. However, our quantitative data (Table 12) show that citizens in Kosovo, the Republic of Macedonia and Serbia predominantly

Table 12. Who should primarily be in charge of fighting corruption in (COUNTRY)? Should it be...

	Kosovo %		Macedonia %		Serbia %	
	Majority	Minority	Majority	Minority	Majority	Minority
the President	4	22	3	7	11	6
the Government	51	10	27	24	15	44
Parliament	8	3	4	5	3	1
special (COUNTRY) anti-corruption bodies	11	24	28	21	30	15
foreign anti-corruption experts	5	4	2	14	6	24
the Police	7	11	13	5	12	4
Prosecutors	1	14	3	1	7	2
Judges	6	3	3	6	8	1
the Media	1	1	1	6	0	1
NGOs	0	—	—	—	0	1
Ordinary people – by protesting against corruption	1	1	2	4	1	—
Ordinary people – by reporting incidents of corruption	3	2	7	7	3	1
Ordinary people – by changing their own mentality and behaviour	2	5	7	2	2	2

Note: Decimals rounded up or down to the nearest whole number. Totals may therefore not add up to exactly 100. Silent categories such as mix/depends/don't know are not included.

preferred for the government and special national anti-corruption bodies to be responsible for this task. Only ethnic Albanians in Serbia expressed any significant support for foreign anti-corruption experts taking on this task — possibly as they are highly sceptical of anything Serbian.[102]

The general public throughout much of the Western Balkans are highly suspicious of the international community in general, and its political agenda in the region, in particular.[103] Not surprisingly, therefore, our FG data match our survey data in that support for foreign specialists appears to be limited. FG participants in Kosovo, the Republic of Macedonia and Serbia preferred for anti-corruption to be some kind of shared responsibility, involving several state bodies. This preference contrasts sharply with the view of many international anti-corruption experts who claim that insufficiently defined anti-corruption measures and fragmented responsibility for overseeing and implementing them, explain why anti-corruption efforts in post-Communist states yield limited results.

FG participants in the Republic of Macedonia favoured some kind of effort involving both state institutions and citizens. In most cases they failed to specify what they had in mind: they simply referred to institutions as 'institutions', 'the authorities', 'state bodies' or 'the state'. Only three statements referred to specific institutions, such as 'the top of the state' (that is the president), 'the anti-corruption commission, the police and the financial police'. FG participants in Serbia were also fairly vague: state institutions were referred to as 'the state', 'state bodies' and 'legal bodies'. More specific references were made to 'the party in power' and 'the parliament'. Unlike FG participants in the Republic of Macedonia, those in Serbia made fewer explicit references to 'citizens' or 'people' — when discussing who should fight corruption:

> 'firstly, the institutions and then the public (should fight corruption). But above all, the institutions (should do so). They should report the corruption, not accept it [...]' (MAC-FG1-Skopje-lower educated-Oishe); 'you need to change the consciousness of the people (in order for them) not to pay bribes. Also the institutions of the system shall properly conduct their work.' (MAC-FG3-Kumanovo-Gaga); 'I think that the first ones should be the authorities, the institutions that write laws, and then the

102 The ethnic Albanian community in southern Serbia boycotted the 2011 census on the grounds that the questionnaire to be completed was only available in Serbian, not in Albanian. Ethnic Albanians were heavily discriminated against during Milošević. There are signs that discrimination still continues — but in a more subtle manner than before.

103 David Chandler, *Bosnia: Faking Democracy after Dayton*, London, 2000; Grødeland, 'They have achieved a lot'.

citizens themselves. The mentality of thinking of the citizens [...] has to change.' (MAC-FG4-Bitola-Marijan); 'people and the state institutions.' (MAC-FG5-Skopje-Albanians-Muzafere); 'state institutions, like the anti-corruption commission, the police, the financial police, must do their jobs and fight against corruption.' (MAC-FG2-Skopje-higher educated-Zdravko); 'only the state and the party in power (should fight corruption). (SER-FG1-Belgrade-lower educated-Dragan).

FG participants in Kosovo were more specific than those in the Republic of Macedonia and Serbia in terms of identifying suitable anti-corruption institutions. Quite a few of them believed legal institutions such as the 'judiciary', 'Ministry of Justice', 'courts' and 'the police' should be involved in anti-corruption efforts. Others referred to 'the media' and 'civil society', and a few FG participants — though to a much lesser extent — believed that citizens should also take part. To the extent they should be involved in such efforts citizens should either change their own attitudes towards corruption by not giving presents and bribes, or by reporting corrupt officials:[104]

'the judiciary, the court, the police.' (KOS-FG6-Mitrovica-Dragan); 'the government, in cooperation with the Ministry of Justice and the police.' (KOS-FG1- Priština-lower education-Violeta); 'competent organs, citizens should report rather than keep silent [...] report by first name and surname. To get a name in the media and not say "someone steals".' (KOS-FG2- Priština-higher education-Njomza); 'different organizations should deal with corruption, citizens also.' (KOS-FG2- Priština-higher education-Valoni); 'I think people's awareness is important to fight corruption. If one stops himself from giving and taking a bribe then no one else is going to be corrupt.' (KOS-FG4-Ferizaj-Zyrije); 'only us, ordinary people (should fight it). If we report that [...]' (KOS-FG6-Mitrovica-Stojan); 'we should start from ourselves. Everyone should be responsible for the reduction of corruption, we should change our attitude towards this issue.' (MAC-FG2-Skopje-higher educated-Ljupco); 'we have to educate ourselves not to give bribes. It is first and foremost.' (MAC-FG3-Kumanovo-Nikola); 'we should stop giving bribes.' (SER-FG3-Niš-Danijela).

The international donors have given NGOs a significant role in the fight against corruption. Yet Michael notes that:

[104] The Serbian NGO, 'Argument', for instance, published a booklet illustrated by the famous cartoonist Corax, presenting examples of corruption and providing information on what to do if asked for bribes. The publication was primarily targeting media representatives. *Uputstvo za upotrebu korupcije* (A Guide to the Use of Corruption), Argument, Belgrade, 2002.

> 'as heretical as it sounds, we still do not know if civil society participation is important in reducing corruption. Most civil society anti-corruption descriptions talk about the objectives of their programmes and activities undertaken rather than concrete outcomes [...] moreover, much of the "evidence" about civil society effectiveness is given by civil society representatives themselves. Given that anti-corruption NGOs live off of donor and government funds, not only are there incentives to exaggerate the effectiveness of NGO anti-corruption activity, but there are also incentives to design programmes sanctioned by donors instead of by the "civil society" they claim to represent.'[105]

It is therefore worth noting that civil society — which tends to be perceived as the driver of anti-corruption reform in the Western context — is by the general public not considered suitable for being in charge of anti-corruption reform in the Western Balkans.[106] Our FG data suggest that NGOs are viewed with suspicion — and throughout the entire region. Our findings are in line with those of a project on NGOs in this region, which suggests that the general public views NGOs with considerable distrust.[107] One reason for this is that NGOs in the Western Balkans are not NGOs in the traditional, civil society sense: most of them are think-tanks, functioning as salary machines for jobless academics. Others are established to generate funds for political parties or various clandestine groups. A study of informal practice amongst NGOs in post-Communist states suggests that NGO staff generally use contacts and informal networks for very much the same purposes as other citizens — including those deemed to be corrupt.[108] Consequently, even though the international community has gone to great length to involve local NGOs in anti-corruption efforts, the impact of their involvement in such activities is questionable,[109] given their lack of legitimacy amongst the public at large.[110]

[105] Michael, *The Rise and Fall of the Anti-Corruption Industry*, p. 7.

[106] NGOs in post-Communist states are generally weak compared to NGOs in the West. See for instance Marc Morjé Howard, *The Weakness of Civil Society in Post-Communist Europe*, Cambridge, 2003.

[107] Åse Berit Grødeland, 'Public Perceptions of Non-Governmental Organizations in Serbia, Bosnia & Herzegovina and Macedonia: "It really strikes me as suspicious when people buy a jeep or a luxurious car and drive around in it after two or three successful projects"', *Communist and Post-Communist Studies* , 39, 2006, 2, pp. 221–46.

[108] Grødeland and Aasland, 'Civil Society'.

[109] For an assessment of anti-corruption coalitions in post-communist states see Martin Tisne and Daniel Smilov, *From the Ground Up: Assessing the Record of Anticorruption Assistance in Southeast Europe*, Budapest, 2004.

[110] Elers, Giannakopoulos and Tänzler, *'Citizens' Participation and Anti-Corruption*, p. 180, claim that the Advocacy and Legal Advise Centres established by Transparency

Immediately after the collapse of Communism, many people in Eastern Europe turned to organized religion. The number of citizens visiting churches and mosques soared — but has since stabilized.[111] The religious establishment was 'rehabilitated' politically, and for many, religion became a substitute for an ideology deemed to be obsolete. Compared to other institutions, churches and mosques enjoy relatively high levels of trust.[112] What is more, religious people may be perceived as generally more law-abiding than non-religious people. Unlike NGO representatives, however, clergy tend to be excluded from the anti-corruption movement.

Our survey data show that citizens in Kosovo (majority and minority), the Republic of Macedonia (majority) and Serbia (majority) do *not* think organized religion has a role to play in reducing the level of corruption. By contrast, ethnic Albanians in the Republic of Macedonia and Serbia believe that it does (Table 13). It is possible that minorities in the Western Balkans identify themselves with religion to a greater extent than the majority populations given that they tend to be minorities both in terms of ethnicity and religion within the countries in which they live. It could be argued that ethnic Serbs in Kosovo have more channels of support than ethnic Albanians in Serbia and to some extent also in the Republic of Macedonia: during the Kosovo War Orthodox churches and monasteries provided shelter for ethnic Serbs.[113] At present the Orthodox Church is channelling the grievances of the ethnic Serb community in Kosovo — and especially those of the ethnic Serbs living in the enclaves — both to the authorities in Serbia and to the international community within Kosovo.[114] While the ethnic Serbs in Kosovo enjoy the active support of the Serbian government in negotiations with the international community about the future of Kosovo, they are also protected by the international community

International in various countries in recent years 'demonstrate that people do become actively involved in the fight against corruption when they are provided with simple, credible and viable citizen participation mechanisms to do so. The ALACs provide victims and/or witnesses of corruption with practical assistance to pursue complaints and address their grievances.'

[111] See, for instance, Kimmo Kääriäinen, 'Religiousness in Russia after the Collapse of Communism', *Social Compass*, 46, 1999, 1, pp. 35–46 (p. 35).

[112] Gallup Balkan Monitor, *Insights and Perceptions*, pp. 30–31: religious organizations are amongst the most trusted in the Western Balkans. In 2010, 84 per cent of the Kosovo Albanians, 76 per cent of the Kosovo Serbs, 70 per cent of the Macedonia Macedonians, 65 per cent of the Macedonia Albanians and 66 per cent of the Serbia Serbs said they had 'a lot' or 'some' trust in religious organizations in their respective countries.

[113] See for instance 'AFP — Serbian Orthodox Monks Defy Pressures in Medieval Monastery', *Serbian Orthodox Diocese of Raska and Prizren. Visoki Decani Monastery* <http://www.kosovo.net/decmonks.html> [accessed 15 April 2013].

[114] Informal communication from embassy staff to the author, Priština, 2011.

within Kosovo. For this reason, they may perceive the political role of the clergy as less important. Ethnic Albanians in the Republic of Macedonia have their own political parties and are represented in both parliament and government. However, as noted above (Table 4) ethnic Albanians in the Republic of Macedonia consider political corruption to be the most serious type of corruption in their country. This may explain why they think religion has a role to play in combating corruption — as an alternative to corrupt politicians. Ethnic Albanians in Serbia, for their part, are better represented in state bodies at present than they were in the 1990s. They mostly live in smaller towns and settlements and religion may therefore play a greater role in their lives — which may in turn explain why they are more supportive of religion having a role to play in anti-corruption than ethnic Serbs.

Table 13. Do you think religion has a role to play in reducing the level of corruption in (COUNTRY)?

	Kosovo %		Macedonia %		Serbia %	
	Majority	Minority	Majority	Minority	Majority	Minority
Yes	47	33	15	59	22	63
No	53	67	85	41	78	37

Note: Decimals rounded up or down to the nearest whole number. Totals may therefore not add up to exactly 100. Silent categories such as mix/depends/don't know are not included.

As regards the position of organized religion on corruption, FG participants either believed that religious texts prohibit corruption (Kosovo, the Republic of Macedonia) or that religion itself is not corrupt (the Republic of Macedonia, Serbia). FG participants in Kosovo and Serbia claimed that religion may in principle help reduce corruption — though they were generally vague as to whether religion could actually contribute to lowering levels of corruption: it 'may' reduce corruption (Kosovo), it 'may' prevent corruption given certain conditions (the Republic of Macedonia), or it 'can' prevent corruption (Serbia):

> 'of course (it has a role to play) because religion strictly prohibits corruption. If you are a believer and you fear God (then) you don't take a bribe. You don't fear the state authorities, but you fear God [...]' (KOS-FG3-Gjakova-

Lindita); 'religion has an impact in reducing corruption because [...] Islam, and Christianity too, (have) no written passage that promotes corruption [...] if we were more religious then I believe there would be no corruption at all.' (KOS-FG3-Gjakova-Sharri); 'corruption is forbidden in every religion and it is a harmful phenomenon to human society and therefore prohibited [...] if people were more religious they would steal less, would be less corrupted. The problem is with the Communists.' (MAC-FG6-Tetovo-Albanians-Jaki); 'it can reduce (corruption). If priests were more active, people would build healthy issues, starting from the family [...]' (SER-FG2-Belgrade-higher educated-Boris); '(it) can (prevent corruption) under the Shariat [...]' (MAC-FG5-Skopje-Albanians-Emine).

Those FG participants who believed that religion has no role to play in reducing corruption in most cases simply stated this as a fact. To the extent they provided explanations for their views, they mostly felt that religious institutions are 'corrupt', 'too insignificant', or that people in the Western Balkans are simply 'not religious enough'. They pointed out that giving something to the priest or imam is customary throughout the Balkans. Religious leaders are no different from other citizens in this regard:

'(it is) a custom to give some food (to the priest) for the baptising [...]' (KOS-FG6-Mitrovica-Dragan); 'as long as priests cut the line (that is speed things up), I don't think so.' (SER-FG2-Belgrade-higher educated-Srdjan); '(its role could be) considerable if priests were more active and normal here. Christening a child here is fifty euro for me, thirty euro for another person, and for that one it's 200 euro.' (SER-FG2-Belgrade-higher educated-Zeljko); 'no, priests also (engage in) different kinds of wheeling and dealing. Let's not mention names. They are only people.' (SER-FG1-Belgrade-lower educated-Dragan); 'even the Imams are corrupted.' (SER-FG5-Bujanovac-I-Vetoni); 'people are not religious enough to reduce corruption.' (MAC-FG5-Skopje-Albanians-Semra).

Some FG participants pointed out that religion is about forgiveness more than anything else: criminals go to church to ask God's forgiveness for their crimes, while ordinary citizens pray that acts of petty corruption be forgiven. An exchange of views between FG participants in Bitola (the Republic of Macedonia) illustrates this point rather well:

'I see many big criminals who go to church every day.' (MAC-FG4-Bitiola-Dushko); 'that's what I said just now, they are the biggest believers.'

(MAC-FG4-Bitola-Ruzhica); 'but they go to church for something else, for God to forgive them because they did some dishonest things.' (MAC-FG4-Bitola-Dushko); 'when it comes to something very important or you are in a hurry, then you forget about everything, including all the sermons you have heard. We all somtcimes rush to do something. I have said so many times "Lord, please forgive me". Regarding bribe(s) and corruption I think religion could do nothing.' (MAC-FG3-Kumanovo-Suzi).

Most FG participants did not feel that the churches or mosques are doing much — if anything at all — to encourage people to abstain from corrupt behaviour. In their opinion, corrupted priests and imams simply have neither the incentive, nor enough influence to do so:

'they neither have the influence, nor the courage and wish (to do so).' (KOS-FG6-Mitrovica-Milos); 'from the legal point, in my opinion, the Islamic community has never appealed against corruption.' (KOS-FG2- Priština-higher education-Astriti); 'when the imam gives a blessing to a deceived person he asks for a certain sum of money, for instance thirty euros. From a religious point of view that is bad. You know that it is forbidden and that you will be punished.' (KOS-FG2- Priština-higher education-Fatmiri); 'no (the church has no role to play [...] priests are corrupt and they take bribes. They are the biggest (bribe-takers) in Macedonia after the judiciary.' (MAC-FG3-Kumanovo-Zoki); 'the Macedonian people, just like all people in the Balkans, are anarchists. They don't like authorities, not even the church.' (MAC-FG2-Skopje-higher educated-Dejan).

Even though support for foreign anti-corruption experts was limited amongst those who took part in our quantitative survey and also amongst our FG participants, our survey data suggests that citizens in the Western Balkans are overwhelmingly in favour of pressure from the EU and international organizations on their respective countries to reduce corruption (Table 14). As support for foreign anti-corruption bodies and/or experts is limited in the Western Balkans (Table 12), it seems likely that people in the region prefer for Europe to exert the pressure and for national institutions to design and implement the actual anti-corruption reform.

Table 14. Do you think pressure from the EU and other international organizations on (COUNTRY) to reduce corruption is a good thing or a bad thing?

	Kosovo %		Macedonia %		Serbia %	
	Majority	Minority	Majority	Minority	Majority	Minority
It is a good thing	96	97	96	99	91	89
It is a bad thing	4	3	4	1	9	11

Note: Decimals rounded up or down to the nearest whole number. Totals may therefore not add up to exactly 100. Silent categories such as mix/depends/don't know are not included.

Public Perceptions of Anti-Corruption Efforts

Numerous anti-corruption efforts have been introduced in post-Communist states throughout Europe in recent years. Their impact, however, appears to be limited.[115] This undoubtedly has to do both with the *quality* of these efforts and the *extent to which* they are implemented. However, it is also possible that such efforts yield limited results because they fail to engage the public. Another possibility is that citizens are not aware of them in the first place. A study of awareness of anti-corruption efforts amongst Ukrainian elites indicates that they are fairly knowledgeable about national anti-corruption efforts.[116] The general public in post-Communist states may be less aware: even though awareness campaigns were introduced throughout post-Communist Europe during the first stage of internationally driven anti-corruption efforts there, such efforts have focused on limited aspects of corruption (bribery). Besides, they appear to have failed to properly translate into the local context both in terms of access to citizens and in terms of addressing specific behaviour within this context.[117]

Table 15 suggests that awareness of national anti-corruption efforts varies throughout the Western Balkans. While the majority of the ethnic Albanians in Kosovo, the Republic of Macedonia and Serbia said they were aware of such efforts, the majority of the Serbs in Kosovo and Serbia, as

[115] See for instance Michael, *The Rise and Fall of the Anti-Corruption Industry.*

[116] Grødeland, *Elite Perceptions of Anti-Corruption Efforts in Ukraine*, p. 247.

[117] Some NGOs have prepared materials on corruption with a view to creating more awareness amongst journalists on what exactly corruption is. However, it is difficult to assess the impact of such materials. See, for instance, Argument: *Uputstvo za upotrebu korupcije.*

Table 15. Are you personally aware of any anti-corruption efforts carried out in (COUNTRY) in the last few years?

	Kosovo %		Macedonia %		Serbia %	
	Majority	Minority	Majority	Minority	Majority	Minority
Yes	67	37	41	54	35	68
No	33	63	59	46	65	32

Note: Decimals rounded up or down to the nearest whole number. Totals may therefore not add up to exactly 100. Silent categories such as mix/depends/don't know are not included.

well as the Macedonians in the Republic of Macedonia, were not.[118] One reason why awareness of anti-corruption efforts is higher amongst ethnic Albanians than the other two ethnic groups may be that the international community has initiated extensive anti-corruption efforts in Kosovo (a part of this work is undertaken by EULEX)[119] and that such efforts are frequently referred to in the Albanian-language media. Ethnic Serbs in northern Kosovo do not identify with Kosovo proper. They have their own media outlets and are oriented towards Serbia proper. Ethnic Serbs living in the Serb enclaves also have their own media outlets (such as Radio KIM, Klokat Radio and Radio Kontakt Plus) that mostly focus on issues of relevance to the Serb community in Kosovo — of which corruption may not be all that important. The difference in findings between ethnic Serbs and Albanians in Serbia may be a result of ethnic Albanians watching broadcasts from Kosovo and obtaining information from local Albanian-language media outlets rather than from Serbian-language media outlets.

[118] All countries covered by our study have introduced extensive anti-corruption legislation in recent years: Kosovo has adopted the Law on Amending and Supplementing the Law on Preventing Conflicts of Interest in Exercising Public Functions. Some 40 laws aimed at repressing corruption have either been amended or adopted in Macedonia, whereas Serbia passed the Law on the Prevention of Conflict of Interests in Performing Public Functions in 2003 and a further series of anti-corruption laws in October 2008. UNODC, *Corruption in the Western Balkans*, pp. 11–12. Our own data suggest that citizens in the Western Balkans are primarily aware of anti-corruption efforts in politics (ethnic Albanians — Kosovo; Macedonia; Serbia), government administration (ethnic Macedonians - Macedonia) or in other areas of society (ethnic Serbs — Kosovo; ethnic Serbs — Serbia).

[119] EULEX Kosovo, for instance, is actively involved in the fight against corruption in Kosovo. International judges are involved in court cases addressing corruption and EULEX also organizes various activities in this area, such as roundtables on corruption. See EULEX's homepage: <www.eulex-kosovo.eu> [accessed 15 April 2012].

FG participants in the Republic of Macedonia and Serbia were overwhelmingly negative to anti-corruption efforts in their countries. In the Kosovo FGs some positive attitudes were voiced — even though the number of critical remarks in FGs there exceeded the positive ones.

Our quantitative data suggest that the media is the main source of information about anti-corruption efforts for most people living in the Western Balkans. However, ethnic Albanians in Serbia obtain such information by media and by hearsay to more or less the same extent, while ethnic Serbs in Kosovo also obtain such information through their work (Table 16).

Table 16. How did you hear about anti-corruption efforts in (COUNTRY)? Did you hear about them...

	Kosovo %		Macedonia %		Serbia %	
	Majority	Minority	Majority	Minority	Majority	Minority
through hearsay (i.e. from family, friends or acquaintances	9	12	13	31	12	50
through the media	87	50	84	52	85	49
through your work	4	38	3	17	3	1

Note: Decimals rounded up or down to the nearest whole number. Totals may therefore not add up to exactly 100. Silent categories such as mix/depends/don't know are not included.

Our FG findings largely match our survey findings. FG participants (all countries) suggested that they obtain information about anti-corruption efforts from the media (television coverage, not newspaper coverage):

> 'we have seen many commercials on TV which ask the population to denounce corruption and crime.' (KOS-FG4-Ferizaj, Rabije); '(coverage) on TV.' (KOS-FG5-Štrpce-Miroslav); 'everyone can watch on TV that the anti-corruption commission is concerned about their budget and whether they are going to have enough money for salaries in the next period. They are concerned if they start to check the government's work, the government will start to cut their budget [...]' (MAC-FG2-Skopje-higher educated-

> Ljupco); 'it is very actual and we talk about that every day. Every TV station talks about anti-corruption. I do not think there is a TV station that does not know what anti-corruption means or what corruption means. I think they are pretty much familiar with the issue [...]' (MAC-FG3-Kumanovo-Nikola); 'just the things I see on TV, Verica Barac, who was loud about the Belgrade Port and yesterday it was banned from selling. And she has been at it for the last five years even before he bought the property. There is that anti-corruption committee.' (SER-FG2-Belgrade-higher educated-Zeljko).

FG participants also believed that people are aware of actions taken against corrupt officials and/or of campaigns started with a view to reducing corruption. Some of them, however, pointed out that little effect could be observed from such efforts:

> 'yes, in Gjakova, one person was imprisoned as he was reported by the person who paid him a bribe. Before he paid, he noted the money bill number and by that number the police caught him.' (KOS-FG3-Gjakova-Astriti); 'officials declaring their wealth.' (KOS-FG1-Priština-lower education-Violeta); 'everyone knows about the anti-corruption commission.' (MAC-FG2-Skopje-higher educated-Ljupco); 'the Macedonian people are familiar (with anti-corruption efforts) but it is also familiar with the selective use of laws on corruption so there is no big effect from that.' (MAC-FG4-Bitola-Marijan); 'you have actions such as report the customs officer, report this, that, and so on.' (SER-FG4-Novi Sad-Slobodan); 'there is good information, but there is no respect for it.' (SER-FG5-Bujanovac-I-Beri).

Only a very limited number of FG participants believed that citizens are either insufficiently or not at all aware of anti-corruption efforts.

The discussion of which measures are most effective in terms of reducing corruption has been on-going for years. It appears that different approaches work differently within different contexts — that is there is no universal solution. Our survey data suggest that three measures stand out in terms of perceived effectiveness: (i) prosecuting and sentencing corrupt high-ranking politicians, government officials and others who have engaged in corrupt behaviour (this solution was perceived as the most effective by ethnic Serbs in Kosovo, ethnic Macedonians in the Republic of Macedonia and ethnic Serbs in Serbia); (ii) strengthening the powers of legal and other institutions fighting corruption (this solution was preferred by ethnic Albanians in Kosovo and ethnic Albanians in the Republic of Macedonia — and also scored high amongst ethnic Albanians in Serbia);

and (iii) introducing new anti-corruption legislation (this solution was preferred by a majority of the ethnic Albanian respondents in Serbia and also by a fairly large share of the ethnic Albanians in the Republic of Macedonia) (Table 17).

Table 17. Which of the following measures would, in your view, be the most efficient with which to fight corruption in (COUNTRY)? Would it be…

	Kosovo %		Macedonia %		Serbia %	
	Majority	Minority	Majority	Minority	Majority	Minority
to introduce new anti-corruption laws?	19	13	5	27	23	50
to strengthen the powers of legal and other institutions fighting corruption?	34	14	22	30	27	43
To prosecute and sentence corrupt high-ranking politicians, government officials and others who have engaged in corrupt behaviour?	23	51	45	18	41	5
to change people's mentality?	8	7	14	6	6	1
to increase EU pressure on (COUNTRY) authorities to actively fight corruption?	10	15	9	9	1	1
to increase international pressure on (COUNTRY) authorities to actively fight corruption	6	1	4	10	2	1

Note: Decimals rounded up or down to the nearest whole number. Totals may therefore not add up to exactly 100. Silent categories such as mix/depends/don't know are not included.

The international community has invested considerable resources in improving anti-corruption efforts through various initiatives organized by the Council of Europe, the EU, World Bank, the United Nations and various bilateral organizations. Most post-Communist states have signed the Council of Europe (CoE) anti-corruption conventions as well as the United Nations Convention against Corruption (UNCAC)[120] and put national anti-corruption legislation in line with these conventions.

A read-through of the statements made by FG participants in Kosovo suggests that citizens are not only concerned with the legislation as such but also, and perhaps even more so, with its implementation and enforcement — or rather the lack of both. The majority of those who voiced their opinion on this issue called for better laws — in combination with better law-enforcement and sanctions against those failing to abide by the laws. Similar views were expressed by FG participants in the Republic of Macedonia and Serbia. Calls for new anti-corruption legislation were typically accompanied by demands for proper enforcement of such legislation:

> 'what we need is some really strict law and some rigorous sanctioning. Like it was [...] in Kragujevac.' (KOS-FG5-Štrpce-Marica); '(one should) strengthen anti-corruption laws.' (KOS-FG2- Priština-higher education-Servete); 'every (act of) corruption should be reported and laws should be enforced.' (KOS-FG2- Priština-higher education-Vllaznimi); 'tougher laws and greater penalties (for violating the laws). For example, instead of three years (as it is now) in prison for bribing, (one should get) ten to twelve years to make people afraid — and to not even think about bribing (somebody).' (MAC-FG3-Kumanovo-Ivan); '(new) laws and non-selective application of the laws, the law should be valid for everyone, equally, and (there should be) more severe (penalties).' (MAC-FG4-Bitola-Marijan); 'there should certainly be one law, and I mean one, not a different one every five-six months with new amendments [...] and that law should really be obeyed [...] a law should be passed and implemented even retroactively, if necessary.' (SER-FG3-Niš-Dragan).

FG participants in Kosovo who favoured strengthening the powers of legal and other institutions fighting corruption emphasised the need for an 'independent' and 'good' judiciary, and the need to 'strengthen' and ensure the 'functioning' of the courts. A well-functioning police and judiciary were viewed as essential for effective anti-corruption reform. A few FG participants also emphasized the need for other well-functioning state bodies, such as 'new teams and institutions', 'good authorities' and/

[120] Serbia signed this convention in 2005 and Macedonia in 2007. See UNODC home page: <http://www.unodc.org/unodc/en/treaties/CAC/signatories.html> [accessed 10 May 2012].

or 'functioning president'. This could be achieved by 'replacing those in position' with new people. FG participants in the Republic of Macedonia were more concerned with strengthening institutions as such. They also talked about appointments — that is the need to appoint 'experts', 'responsible persons' and 'uncorrupted people' to institutions fighting corruption. Better technology might, in their view, also help. In addition to voicing their concern with institutions fighting corruption, FG participants in Serbia were also critical of the people working within them. In their view there was obviously a need to strengthen or change institutions — but also to get rid of corrupt people working in anti-corruption:

> 'when these courts get strengthened and when citizens denounce corruption and know that it will be punished, only then can it be decreased […]' (KOS-FG1- Priština-lower education-Hilmiu); 'courts have to function.' (KOS-FG1- Priština-lower education-Violeta); 'when the police functions together with the judiciary, then corruption stops.' (KOS-FG2- Priština-higher education-Astriti); 'new technologies should be used […]' (MAC-FG2-Skopje-higher educated-Dejan); 'only experts and experienced people (should be appointed) […] the political background should not be considered. ..(one should) appoint managing people from the first to the last person in the government who have a function only as experts […]' (MAC-FG4-Bitola-Duda); 'strengthen institutions and increase the standard.' (MAC-FG6-Tetovo-Albanians-Feki); 'making institutions stronger. Educating people and directing them […]' (SER-FG2-Belgrade-higher educated-Marina); 'we even have to bring down the ones that are fighting corruption which… are corrupted themselves.' (SER-FG6-Bujanovac-II-Sadije); 'we have to choose the competent people in charge.' (SER-FG6-Bujanovac-II-Feride).

Those FG participants in the Republic of Macedonia and Serbia who favoured other measures primarily advocated sanctions for engaging in corrupt activities. Some of them also believed that exposing corrupt people would be helpful. Ethnic Macedonians, for instance, pointed out that sanctions will have limited effect until the socio-economic situation in their country improves. Given people's current mentality, media exposure and harsh punishments were viewed as necessary preconditions for reducing corruption in the Western Balkans:

> 'to catch them on camera […] but let's not be so rigorous as (they are) in China and hang them on the central square.' (MAC-FG2-Skopje-higher educated-Igor); 'only Chinese methods will work here.' (MAC-

FG2-Skopje-higher educated-Mimi); 'to arrest the one who caused the corruption, to show him on TV and to convict him. That is the best way to show people that something has been done. When you see that someone is convicted for something, surely you will not do the same.' (MAC-FG3-Kumanovo-Jaska); '(to do) something similar to the Law Faculty of Niš where a professor asked for money to pass the students on an exam and the case was proven with facts and afterwards professors hesitated to take money from students [...]' (SER-FG6-Bujanovac-II-Sadije); 'if he is poor as a church mouse, there is no use in fining him. If he hasn't got a way out, he will commit a crime. So first the country should be settled, the unemployment, so everyone has a piece of bread. Then you can fine him. People don't have jobs and the fines are enormous. It isn't the way to do it [...]' (MAC-FG1-Skopje-lower educated-Dalibor).

Citizens in the Western Balkans — unlike elites in Ukraine — were less in favour of changing people's mentality. Although they acknowledged that mentality and corruption are linked and although they to some extent advocate a mentality change, they believe that it would be very difficult, though not impossible, to bring about such a change:

'change people's mentality.' (KOS-FG2- Priština-higher education-Njomza); 'the mentality of the people should be raised.' (MAC-FG5-Skopje-Albanians-Adnan); 'everything (that is all the measures) is necessary, but mostly (the) change of (people's) mentality.' (SER-FG4-Novi Sad-Saska); 'to change people's mentality takes a very long time.' (KOS-FG3-Gjakova-Sharri); 'it is hard to change the mentality (of the people).' (KOS-FG5-Štrpce-Marica).

Previous research on elites in Ukraine suggests that national institutions responsible for anti-corruption reform are not considered capable of reducing corruption.[121] Citizens in the Western Balkans, however, believe most state institutions are capable of reducing corruption. Albanians in Kosovo rank the police, special anti-corruption bodies and foreign anti-corruption experts as the most capable. The Kosovo police force has been reformed in recent years. Besides, the international community has put considerable efforts into enhancing the performance of local anti-corruption bodies — and predominantly through EULEX. In the Republic of Macedonia special anti-corruption bodies and the government scored highest amongst ethnic Macedonians, while foreign anti-corruption

[121] Grødeland, 'Culture, Corruption'; Grødeland, 'Elite Perceptions of Anti-Corruption Efforts in Ukraine'.

experts and special anti-corruption bodies scored highest amongst the ethnic Albanians. While ethnic Serbs in Serbia thought special anti-corruption bodies and foreign anti-corruption experts are the most capable corruption fighters, ethnic Albanians in Serbia believed foreign anti-corruption experts, the president and government were equally capable in terms of reducing corruption (Table 18).

Table 18. How capable do you think the following institutions responsible for anti-corruption reform are of reducing corruption in (COUNTRY) — % capable & very capable

	Kosovo %		Macedonia %		Serbia %	
	Majority	Minority	Majority	Minority	Majority	Minority
The President	60	57	33	25	52	87
The Government	72	50	61	40	46	87
Parliament	72	47	46	36	40	81
Prosecutors	75	64	46	30	55	84
Judges	74	73	46	38	52	75
The Police	85	62	53	23	56	67
Special anti-corruption bodies	85	78	60	62	71	82
Foreign anti-corruption experts	85	63	57	81	61	87
The Media	67	44	42	38	45	80
NGOs	58	9	27	30	34	76

Note: Decimals rounded up or down to the nearest whole number. Totals may therefore not add up to exactly 100. Silent categories such as mix/depends/don't know are not included.

It is one thing to have the capacity to do something and quite another to muster the will to actually do it. FG participants in Kosovo — though convinced that various bodies engaged in fighting corruption are capable of doing so — suggested that such institutions are essentially 'corrupt', 'have no will', 'make no effort', 'do nothing' or 'have no benefit from doing so' (that is fighting corruption). Similar views were expressed by FG participants in the Republic of Macedonia and — though to a lesser extent — Serbia:

> 'they are capable of fighting corruption, but they are the ones who are corrupt!' (KOS-FG4-Ferizaj-Rabije); 'how can they fight corruption when they are corrupt? They are very capable.' (KOS-FG4-Ferizaj-Arsimi); 'they have the capacities, but not the will.' (KOS-FG6-Mitrovica-Milos); 'they are capable, but they don't work.' (KOS-FG1- Priština-lower education-Avniu); 'they can (fight corruption), but they don't want to.' (MAC-FG1-Skopje-lower educated-Dalibor); 'they can fight corruption, but they do not want (to) because they themselves are corrupted.' (MAC-FG6-Tetovo-Albanians-Saranda); 'they are capable, they could (reduce corruption) if they wanted to, but it does not suit them.' (SER-FG4-Novi Sad-Slobodan).

FG participants in the Republic of Macedonia and Serbia primarily believed that the institutions responsible for fighting corruption are incapable because the people working there are 'corrupt' (both countries), because they are 'dirty', 'involved' (the Republic of Macedonia) or promote 'private interests' (Serbia). Some of the FG participants in the Republic of Macedonia were also concerned with the qualifications of their staff, suggesting that anti-corruption commission staff is either 'unqualified' or 'not hired for reasons of merit':

> 'that team there is all corrupted and cannot be anti-corrupted.' (MAC-FG4-Bitola-Mare); 'in the Government there are people that have to go directly to jail for many things, but they don't go because if they do, the Prime Minister will be left without a Government.' (MAC-FG4-Bitola-Alex); 'somehow I also think that they are unable (to do away with corruption). They are not able because the system "on merit" does not exist here [...] everything is done by appointment and where (everything) is done by appointment,(those hired) are not able (to do) the work [...] in 99 per cent of the cases [...] I believe that they are not skilful [...]' (MAC-FG6-Tetovo-Albanians-Jaki); 'I think they are not capable of putting the general interest in front of (their) personal interest [...] anti-corruption efforts are not carried out because of petty interests [...]' (SER-FG3-Niš-Caslav).

Still, statements made by FG participants in all countries suggest that the general public either does not believe it is possible to reduce corruption in their countries at all, or that it is only possible to do so in part.

The 'optimists' were cautiously optimistic: they believed that corruption could be successfully addressed, provided that certain conditions are met. Such conditions include political will, stricter laws and law enforcement (Kosovo), higher living standards, or the use of force (Serbia). From the above, however, it is clear that citizens throughout the Western Balkans held the view that law enforcement is not working in their country and also, that there is little, if at all any, political will to do away with corruption. Their statements to the effect that corruption may be addressed successfully thus come across as fairly unrealistic:

> 'yes, (it can be solved) if there's the will and strict laws.' (KOS-FG4-Ferizaj-Rabije); 'it surely is possible to change (the situation), however, much effort is needed, primarily from the key people in the country and then from the citizens.' (MAC-FG4-Bitola-Marijan); 'until the living standard improves, until we have 2,000 euro salaries, (it won't change).' (SER-FG2-Belgrade-higher educated-Zeljko); 'it's possible by fire and sword.' (SER-FG1-Belgrade-lower educated-Dušan).

The pessimists — that is those FG participants who held the view that nothing could be done to reduce corruption in their respective countries — just didn't believe corruption could be successfully fought — or that corruption has become so endemic that regardless of the amount of effort that is given to solve the problem it is unlikely to disappear:

> 'it will not (be resolved), I am a pessimist.' (MAC-FG4-Bitola, Mare); 'it cannot change.' (MAC-FG4-Bitola-Ruzhica); 'no chance!' (MAC-FG5-Skopje-Albanians-Arijan); 'even the internationals cannot help us [...] we will teach the international(s) how to steal. They'd better not come because they will become thieves like these here.' (MAC-FG6-Tetovo-Albanians-Zeni); 'I don't think anything will change, because I will be the first one to go again and give (something) if necessary, for (the sake of) my children [...]' (SER-FG3-Niš-Jovanka); 'not for the next 500 years.' (SER-FG5-Bujanovac-I-Beri).

Conclusions

Above we have investigated public perceptions of (i) corruption; (ii) types of corruption; (iii) those that should be responsible for anti-corruption reform; and (iv) anti-corruption efforts, in the Western Balkans. Our findings show that local perceptions of what constitutes corruption appears to be largely 'informed' by culture: citizens in the Western Balkans equate corruption with bribery, that is payments given for a service in advance, rather than presents given as an expression of thanks once the service has been rendered. Besides, patronage and nepotism are not viewed as corruption but rather as necessary mechanisms for obtaining legitimate goals: helping one another is considered to be part of the social logic. Transition and the problems it has brought about in terms of high unemployment, difficult socio-economic conditions, and red tape, no doubt reinforces this logic.

Data presented above suggest that citizens in the Western Balkans to some extent have contradictory views on corruption and anti-corruption reform. Citizens in Kosovo, the Republic of Macedonia and Serbia condemn bribery while being willing bribe givers. Their willingness to give bribes (and also to use go-betweens) to achieve their goals is conditioned partly by the urgency of their needs, partly on the bargaining strength of those receiving the bribes. In matters pertaining to health, education and speeding up slow official procedures citizens are more than willing to give something to ensure the desired outcome. Our data suggest that the strategies that people used to cope with government during Socialism are also used to cope with government during transition. Despite disastrous consequences for those unable to bribe doctors for medical treatment, citizens in the Western Balkans were somewhat sympathetic of corrupt doctors, blaming the authorities for not providing doctors with decent salaries. And they acknowledge the role of the public in 'creating' corrupt state employees.

Slow and poorly functioning state bodies are to some extent viewed as a result of patronage and/or nepotism: jobs are few and far between in the Western Balkans and unemployment rates are high. For this reason, jobs are inherited, that is given to 'our people', or purchased with money. Connections and ability to pay, rather than formal qualifications,[122] determine whether somebody will get a job. The hiring of unqualified personnel breeds inefficiency, which citizens then try to evade by paying for faster and/or better service (often also for favourable outcomes). What is more, expenses made to secure a job have somehow to be recovered. This is often done by soliciting informal payments from the general public. The 'personalization' of public positions is common at all levels of Balkan

[122] The problem of unqualified people is further compounded by the fact that educational institutions — both at compulsory and higher level — are plagued by corruption. A good certificate from a university in the Western Balkans does not always bode for quality. Rather, the question is how the certificate was obtained — that is whether by hard work or by means of bribes.

society — and it facilitates corruption. The ethno-religious minority groups seem to be particularly disadvantaged in this regard: while both the ethnic titular and the ethno-religious minority groups are willing to give bribes to secure specific outcomes, the latter are willing to do so to a much greater extent. This suggests that they feel a need to compensate for their perceived or real disadvantage — thus lending support to the 'try harder'-hypothesis. These factors, together with the 'nihilist legal culture' referred to above, help explain why anti-corruption efforts in the Western Balkans fail to take hold.

Citizens in the Western Balkans are fairly well aware of anti-corruption efforts. Most people receive information about such efforts through the media, and they believe that their impact is likely to be fairly limited. Further, the public mostly do not favour major involvement of foreign anti-corruption experts in their country — despite considering them (i) very capable, (ii) viewing national institutions as corrupt, and (iii) even though they are in favour of the EU exerting pressure on their countries to reduce corruption. Government is perceived as being best suited to oversee anti-corruption efforts even though state institutions in the Western Balkans are not held in high regard by ordinary citizens. Citizens in the Western Balkans are therefore rather pessimistic regarding the prospects for reducing levels of corruption in their region. Such contradictions may, in part, reflect the tension identified by Roth and referred to above between on the one hand, wishing to become 'European', and on the other, wishing to preserve one's culture and social logic: while it is permissible for the EU to exert pressure on the authorities in the Western Balkans to implement measures against corruption such measures should be developed locally and supervised by local institutions.

NGOs, which have been singled out by the international community to play an active role in facilitating anti-corruption reform in post-Communist states, are not perceived as suitable for this purpose. It could be argued that this partly has to do with the fact that NGOs are viewed as a foreign invention, partly with the fact that NGOs in the Western Balkans tend to be perceived as 'salary machines' for the middle class or as extended arms of the international community rather than as organizations working for the benefit of society at large. NGOs therefore suffer the same fate as state institutions in that they are perceived as representing 'them' rather than 'us'.

Georgia is often singled out as a post-Communist state where efforts to reduce petty corruption have been very successful. The Georgian experience seems to suggest that major and rapid improvement is possible, given political will, political capacity and public trust in the measures implemented. The Singaporean experience suggests that it is also possible to reduce grand corruption when elites translate political will into political action — by setting a good example. Data on informal practice and corruption previously collected amongst elites in seven East European countries suggest that political will to tackle corruption is absent in the Western Balkans. Politicians and government officials pay lip service to internationally driven anti-corruption campaigns — but they fail to 'convert' their verbal commitment into political action.

Our data suggest that a two-pronged approach to corruption might be useful in the Western Balkans. On the one hand, there is a need for prosecuting and sentencing corrupt politicians and officials so as to set a good example. This requires political will – which is largely absent. On the other hand, there is a need to change (i) local perceptions of what constitutes corruption; (ii) local attitudes towards bribery, patronage, nepotism, law, and state institutions; and (iii) people's willingness to give bribes, take bribes and make use of contacts.

The former task may be facilitated by means of external incentives. To give an example, the former Romanian Minister of Justice, Monica Macovej, successfully prosecuted and punished corrupt politicians and government officials during her country's run-up to EU membership. At that time Romania was under considerable pressure from the EU to reduce corruption and there were real fears within Romania that EU membership might be denied should such efforts fail. Even though Macovej was forced out of office once EU membership had been secured, her successful fight against corruption suggests that externally-driven conditionality requirements can in given situations produce results.

For real changes to take place, however, the prevailing and contradicting attitudes towards corruption amongst ordinary citizens will also have to be addressed. Changing attitudes to corruption in the Western Balkans is a difficult task that will require both time and patience, given that such attitudes have developed historically, over time, and become part of the social logic. As such attitudes are not only held by the general public, but also by those passing, implementing and enforcing the law, addressing them is a prerequisite for anti-corruption efforts to succeed. Such efforts should not be driven by the international community but rather be initiated from within and adapted to the local context.

Finally, efforts to involve the general public in anti-corruption efforts in the region should be made through other channels than local NGOs, as such organizations are not perceived as legitimate by citizens in the

Western Balkans and as they engage with the general public only to a limited degree. An alternative and better approach might be to try to mobilize the public against corruption by establishing broader anti-corruption grassroots movements, another — to approach the public directly, for instance through the new social media.[123]

[123] The role of the new social media in combating corruption was explored at the 15th International Anti-Corruption Conference (IACC) which took place in Brasilia in November 2012. For details, see <http://15iacc.org/>.

REVIEW ESSAY

Vladimir Nabokov and the Play of Art

LELAND DE LA DURANTAYE

Karshan, Thomas. *Vladimir Nabokov and the Art of Play.* Oxford English Monographs. Oxford University Press, Oxford and New York, 2011. xi + 269 pp. Notes. Bibliography. Index. £55.00.

THOMAS KARSHAN is one of the finest Nabokov critics of his generation. His work is erudite and insightful and he is certain to make many lasting contributions to the study of Nabokov's works. That said, his *Vladimir Nabokov and the Art of Play* falls short of his promise and, more to the point, the book falls short of its goal. Before this second point be judged too harshly, however, it should be noted that the goal in question could hardly be more ambitious. It is to give, through what Karshan alternately calls Nabokov's 'signature theme' and 'signature idea' of *play*, a unifying principle to the diversity of Nabokov's writings and their reception.

Karshan begins at the beginning, or near it, with a public lecture that Nabokov gave in 1925 about a then recent boxing match in which Nabokov remarked that 'everything in the world plays' (p. 1). Everything that follows, for Karshan, concerns how fundamental a declaration this was, how broadly play might be understood and what an understanding of play illuminates in Nabokov's works and their reception. The (eminently understandable) reason that *Vladimir Nabokov and the Art of Play* falls short of its goal is that it cannot give enough unity to the diversity of things that might be understood under the heading of *play*, that it cannot marry the theme of *play* with the practice of *play*. There are what virtually any reader would agree to call playful elements in all of Nabokov's works,

Leland de la Durantaye is Professor of Literature at Claremont McKenna College.

major and minor, critical and creative, English and Russian. But what is this playfulness? In what does it consist? How does it affect readers? What does it say about the relation of work to world? What, in other words, is the essence of literary play and how are readers of *Vladimir Nabokov and the Art of Play* to understand it? These are exceedingly difficult questions — and as resistant to typology as ones like *what is literary ambiguity?* Given this fact, it comes as no surprise that Karshan does not present his reader with a short systematic definition of *play*. This, however, creates a problem when this supremely slippery thing, *play*, is made to unify and to explain Nabokov's writing. When one undefined and perhaps undefinable thing is made to explain another undefined and perhaps undefinable thing there significant limits to what can be achieved.

The problem that arises for the reader of *Vladimir Nabokov and the Art of Play* is one of conceptual coherence. Karshan, for instance, notes that Nabokov wrote playful works in which sports and games are not infrequently played, that when not writing he liked to play soccer, tennis and chess and that, moreover, socially speaking he 'cultivated the image of a sportsman' (p. 3). These things are all true, but how are they related? One matter is biographical. Would we understand Nabokov's works differently if he never played any games and professed to loathe them? Probably not, or not much, and this is something of an unfair question in that while he invokes it, Karshan places little emphasis on the connection between Nabokov's play-filled life and his playful art. The point is not whether Nabokov's playful art was influenced by the playing of sports or games, and his argument is not reductively causal in this way. What the question highlights, however, is the degree of conceptual coherence that can be given to the idea of play in Karshan's study, and beyond it. It is interesting in this connection to note that when, in his *Philosophical Investigations*, Wittgenstein turns to the idea of conceptual coherence itself, he chooses as examples through which to discuss it, precisely, *play* and *games*. Wittgenstein then asks what 'family resemblance' such diverse games as soccer, chess, tennis and board games possess.[1] To his question, 'What is common to them all?', Wittgenstein, however, immediately adds a warning: 'Don't say: "There must be something common, or they would not be called "games"', as this would be 'only playing with words'.[2] Karshan is not merely playing with words in his analysis of play, but the question of conceptual

[1] Ludwig Wittgenstein, *Philosophical Investigations: The English Text of the Third Edition*, translated by G. E. M. Anscombe, New York, 1958, pp. 31, 32.

[2] Ibid., p. 32.

coherence, and the ascertaining of the degree of family resemblance between different things called play, determines how much Karshan's signature idea will be able to explain. (Given his interest in the matter I found it curious that Karshan does not discuss Wittgenstein's analysis of games and play, and all the more so as Karshan discusses Wimsatt's ideas on 'family resemblance' which were, directly and avowedly, borrowed by Wimsatt from Wittgenstein; cf. Karshan, p. 10.) Playing tennis and writing a novel are different things with, we might argue, a family resemblance, just as playing chess and playing with words are different things with some sort of resemblance, but for these family resemblances to increase our understanding they must have a certain definition. More fundamentally, *playing with words* is a way of describing what happens when we do certain literary and non-literary things with words. And so long as we do not know what *literary play* is, we are, in a certain sense, merely playing with words about playing with words.

Karshan is clearly aware of the problem which leaving *play* at an abstract level presents, and he attends to it in an interesting way. This is by pointing to the history of abstract discussions of art as play. His readers are given an initial chapter in which art — all art — is presented as play, and in which he traces the idea of free play from German Idealism to Nabokov's day (p. 25 ff.). The central philological question herein of, in Karshan's words, 'How, though, did the idea of art as play, and the doctrines which inform it in Kantian aesthetic theory, make their way into Nabokov's novels?' is given a tenuous answer (p. 34). Readers are likely to find that the question as posed is somewhat premature given that the question of *whether* these ideas are present is taken as something of a given and/or treated on the level of general resemblance rather than specific contour. What follows are a series of readings of Nabokov's Russian and English works. They are often illuminating and feature many fine insights (as in Karshan's treatments of questions of work, play and utilitarianism — cf. p. 107 ff). They have the drawback, however, of seeking to unify *game* and *play*, the theme of play and the practice of play, in ways that sometimes remain merely associative (like the parallel between Nabokov the playful writer and Nabokov the player of soccer), and occasionally move towards misrepresentation. To begin with Nabokov's most famous work, Karshan claims, for instance, that '*Lolita* centres on the tennis game that Humbert and Lolita play' (p. 2). This is at least a stretch and perhaps simply false. The scene in question is interesting, rich and important, but it is unlikely that many readers will find that it eclipses in centrality the two separate scenes of moral revelation Humbert experiences (the reunion with a seventeen-year-old Lolita and his hearing of the children's chorus), Humbert's first act of 'safely solipsizing' Lolita, their first night together, the scene where Humbert overhears Lolita and a young friend discuss death and realizes that 'there was in her a garden and a twilight, and a palace gate — dim and adorable regions which happened to be lucidly and absolutely forbidden to me',[3] or still other scenes. That is, it is possible that readers may have missed the importance of the tennis scene, but this is something they need to be shown, rather than simply told. Remaining with *Lolita*, something of this same stretching is to be found where Karshan reminds the reader that Lolita's husband's name is Richard Schiller and claims (rather than shows) that this is an allusion to Friedrich Schiller (a writer Nabokov never showed any special interest in and which we are not even sure he ever read), and which is followed by a second leap in that Karshan sees this as not only an allusion to Schiller but, more precisely, to Schiller's remarks on the free play of the aesthetic faculties (i.e. it is a stretch to see an allusion to Friedrich Schiller here, but even if the reader makes this stretch a second one is required in seeing this as an allusion to — among all that the prolific Schiller wrote — precisely this set of remarks). That Lolita's husband's name is Richard Schiller indeed may have been inspired in one way or another by the Friedrich Schiller who reformulated and popularized Kant's ideas on art and aesthetic education is possible. But that the mere name, without any further internal or external evidence, points us in the direction of play is far from compelling, especially in light of the fact that Nabokov shows little or no interest in Kantian aesthetics or in Schiller's reformulation of it. It speaks to Karshan's sensitivity that he makes such connections — and he makes many of this sort — but they do not do much to help us understand *Lolita*, the play of art or the art of play.

Were Karshan's signature theme and idea to succeed in doing what he would like it to, this would reconcile those who have found, and continue to find, Nabokov brilliant, but gratuitously so, with those critics who have found in his works an 'otherworldly' message. For those readers unfamiliar with the history of Nabokov criticism, for many years after the first flush of Nabokov's fame (in the wake of *Lolita*) there reigned a contested but nonetheless prevalent view of Nabokov as a supreme, but supremely gratuitous, stylist. This was followed by a reverse swing of the critical pendulum in which the focus was placed on an otherworld and an afterlife. The pithy version of this shift is from the metafictional to the

[3] Vladimir Nabokov, *Lolita*, New York, 1997, p. 284.

metaphysical. As is generally the case with such conceptions, both views were right in fundamental ways and both proved limiting, eventually leading to constraining critical readings and frustrated dismissals. At the moment of writing the pendulum has roughly returned to the middle, without the question really having been resolved (beyond the suggestion that it doesn't need to be). This (simplified) thumbnail history is relevant to keep in mind when considering *Vladimir Nabokov and the Art of Play*, as Karshan claims that *play* might serve as the master theme in Nabokov's work and would give a reason (albeit a circular one) for the impish, deceptive playful elements in Nabokov's work. It would do this by ennobling *play* not as something which Nabokov might have done a bit less of, but which was his theme and which is a theme worthy of him. As the reader would expect, Karshan's task is thus double — or perhaps triple. He must make *play* a theme worthy of Nabokov, and then he must show that it is in fact the central theme of Nabokov's work, that Nabokov's 'novels form the fullest, most sophisticated, and most profound treatment of play ever achieved' (p. 1). And all this with enough particular contour and focus so as to illuminate Nabokov's writing itself. The problem with the master theme of *play* is that it is too vast and amorphous to reformulate specific problems and yet too limiting to reformulate any general ones. Play is limiting in reducing art to an instance of play, a species of the genera of play. And something of a hermeneutic circle results such that art is defined by being, essentially, a form of play and, for the purposes of the study, play is artistic behaviour.

It seems to me petty to simply say this won't do without suggesting what might. And so in this vein it is my sense that still more helpful than the idea of play might be the idea of *deceptive play*, play which does not present itself as such, or which suggests that it might be play and might be serious and might be both. In a general sense this leads into the critical territories of *ambiguity* and *irony*, and concerns a significant cross-section of the most interesting criticism of the twentieth century, from Empson on ambiguity to de Man on irony. Remaining close to the texts Nabokov left, we might point to the role of *deception*. Nabokov was so uniquely deceptive that he often put off readers as a result, so deceptive that he was often asked about deception in his works and gave, as a rule, deceptive answers to the question (of deception). What then happens when we modify Karshan's question about *play* to one about *deception*? If the answer to the question of why Nabokov is playful is that he is an artist (and art is play), what is the answer to the question of why Nabokov is deceptive? Nabokov said that 'all art is deception and so is nature'.[4] Elsewhere he remarks that 'deception is practiced even more beautifully by that other V.N., Visible Nature'.[5] Nabokov is deceptive — at least by his own account — because Nature is deceptive. He is then *mimetically* deceptive, he is following nature in a unique way, and thereby presenting a rationale for deception which goes beyond the merely mischievous or the frustratingly gratuitous. There is a serious intent and a serious task in his deceptive art, and understanding it allows readers to approach and understand his work — both its unique successes and its unique failures.

Moving from play to signature there seems a connection here that also might also be made. Play may or may not be Nabokov's 'signature theme' or 'signature idea', to use the terms Karshan employs. But there is an idea and a theme in Nabokov's works of the *signature* which merits particular attention. This is the theme and idea of playfully deceptive signatures which Nabokov's readers find in his works and which Nabokov himself found in his life. The latter is one of the main themes of his *Speak, Memory* where the 'thematic trails' and 'systematic correlations'[6] of his life point Nabokov in the direction of a creator about whom we can know nothing, but whose signature can be seen in the intricate details of the natural world (such as the wings of butterflies). This is an idea with its own rich history and which involves literally every aspect of Nabokov's literary creation. And it is this sense of a signature to be read in the natural world which Nabokov describes having experienced which so many of his characters experience — from the Krug who intuits a world beyond his own nightmarish one to the mysterious patterns of fate traced in *Pnin* to the mysteries of authority spun out in *The Real Life of Sebastian Knight* and *Pale Fire*.

For the reasons and in the ways sketched above it is not my sense that *Vladimir Nabokov and the Art of Play* succeeds in its ambitious enterprise, but it nevertheless offers conclusive evidence that Karshan is capable of such success.

4 Vladimir Nabokov, *Strong Opinions*, New York, 1974, p. 12.

5 Ibid., p. 153.

6 Vladimir Nabokov, *Speak, Memory: An Autobiography Revisited*, New York, 1999, pp. 3, 248.

Reviews

Hnatiuk, Lidiia. *Movnyi fenomen Hryhoriia Skovorody v konteksti staroukraïns'koï knyzhnoï tradytsiï.* Kyiv University, Kyiv, 2010. 446 pp. Bibliography. Price unknown.

THIS volume is the first monograph to deal with the language of Hryhorii Skovoroda (1772–94), a great 'people's philosopher', and representative of the pinnacle of Ukrainian Baroque. Apart from Latin and Greek, Skovoroda used several languages (Church Slavonic, Russian and Ukrainian) in a peculiar mixture in his writings that were all virtually comments on Biblical and patristic texts. From the early nineteenth century onward his *lingua mixta* has remained a major stumbling block in numerous studies of Skovoroda's output. After George Y. Shevelov's groundbreaking article, 'Prolegomena to Studies of Skovoroda's Language and Style' (1991), Hnatiuk should be given credit for her attempt to offer, instead of entirely subjective evaluations by her predecessors, a balanced analysis of the philosopher's language.

Hnatiuk's study is premised on several postulates propagated in Eastern Slavic linguistics over the last thirty years, in particular 'linguistic awareness', 'linguistic personality' and 'linguistic' vs. 'conceptual' worldviews (pp. 13, 18, 30). The treatment of the linguistic awareness and the linguistic personality of Skovoroda in a wider social and cultural context could further, as the author rightly posits, our understanding of the language of Skovoroda, who himself identified his tongue as 'Little Russian' (*malorossiiskii dialekt*) (p. 47). The book is designed and structured accordingly. Part one covers the afore-mentioned psycholinguistic postulates applied in the diachronic perspective. Part two deals with Skovoroda's linguistic awareness projected onto the Middle Ukrainian (Ruthenian) period, while his 'language practice' is analysed in part three. Finally, part four investigates the Baroque tradition as reflected in Skovoroda's stylistic experiments and language games. The book is furnished with brief conclusions and a list of references. However, save for German-language publications, the list conspicuously lacks Western contributions which, according to the latest bibliography of works on Skovoroda published in Ukraine in 2002, count hundreds of them. The book lacks indices, which with rare exceptions is typical of Eastern Slavic linguists.

The author maintains that Skovoroda's language is rooted in the Baroque world-view, whence an alleged functional identification of Church Slavonic with *prostaja mova* (Ruthenian) (p. 86). To draw a parallel, Hnatiuk mentions a 'Common Slavonic' language created by the Croat Juraj Križanić in Russia in the late seventeenth century and Slaveno-Rusyn codified by Myxailo Luchkai in 1830 in Transcarpathia (p. 88). Yet Hnatiuk's argumentation is flawed. Church Slavonic had its own dignity in the Ruthenian lands, although no pure specimens in either Church Slavonic or Ruthenian were possible. In fact, in different genres, Skovoroda did distinguish Ukrainian and Russian from Church Slavonic rendering the Biblical connotation.

In addition to the intellectual milieu of the Kyiv Mohyla Academy where Skovoroda received his education, Hnatiuk discusses the significance of the so-called 'precedent texts' in the language of the philosopher (pp. 130–57). The analysis of his language encompasses orthography, stressing, vocabulary, 'relevant Ukrainian grammatical features', like the vocative case or the genitive of the type *vkusu* (R *vkusa*) 'taste' and derivational patterns. Only a small section (pp. 290–97) is devoted to Russian features in the language of Skovoroda because Hnatiuk does not agree with Shevelov's hypothesis that the language mix of Skovoroda was Russian, as used in Kharkiv and *Sloboda* Ukraine by the upper class in the eighteenth century. Instead, the author argues that the language of Skovoroda was not chaotic at all, rather an aggregate of Church Slavonic of Ukrainian recension and Ruthenian bequeathed from the Middle Ukrainian period, interspersed with vernacular elements (p. 80). Misconceivedly, Hnatiuk states that a particular form could hardly be treated as Russian at the time of Skovoroda if only attested previously in Church Slavonic and Old Russian (p. 372).

The latter argument is open to doubt since the relationship of different varieties of Church Slavonic (the Ukrainian and the Biblical Russian), on the one hand, and vernacular Ukrainian and Russian on the other, are not systematically accounted for. Overall, a caveat advanced some twenty years ago by Shevelov is still valid — a student of Skovoroda's language must first establish what is quoted from the Bible in order to put this material aside and consider what is the philosopher's own. This is why, despite its innovative approach and extensive research of concrete material, Hnatiuk's book is likely to remain, for the time being, a 'prolegomenon to studies of Skovoroda's language and style'.

Department of Modern Languages and Cultures ANDRII DANYLENKO
Pace University, New York

Guseva, A. A. *Svod russkikh knig kirillovskoi pechati XVIII veka tipografii Moskvy i Sankt-Peterburga i universal′naia metodika ikh identifikatsii.* Izdatel′stvo 'Indrik', Moscow, 2010. 1252 pp. Indexes. Appendices. Bibliography. Price unknown.

OF all the books published in Russia since the time of the *pervopechatnik* those printed in the Church Slavonic typeface in the eighteenth century have so far been the least studied and described. Their well-known difficulties in identification have deterred bibliographers, and even the nineteenth-century bibliophiles chose to concentrate on the earliest printed books of the fifteenth to seventeenth centuries and those in the new Petrine civil typeface rather than on those of the eighteenth century. The only exceptions were P. P. Pekarskii (*Nauka i literatura v Rossii pri Petre Velikom*, vol. 2, St Petersburg, 1862) and V.

I. Sreznevskii and A. L. Bem (*Izdaniia tserkovnoi pechati vremeni imperatritsy Elizavety Petrovny. 1741–1761*, Petrograd, 1914). To A. S. Zernova and T. N. Kameneva belongs the credit of having produced the first union catalogue of eighteenth-century Russian books in Church Slavonic (Moscow, 1968). It was followed by the catalogues of T. A. Bykova (Leningrad, 1971) and T. A. Afanas′eva (Leningrad, 1986–87); but the disfavour with which this line of bibliographical research was regarded during the Soviet period led to these works appearing in miniscule print-runs. However, since the early 1990s the situation has been happily transformed, and hence the publication, supported by the Rossiiskii gumanitarnyi nauchnyi fond, of the present volume.

The strictly bibliographical part of the catalogue is divided into two sections. The first, pp. 23–494, covers printed books and leaflets and the second, pp. 495–526, all the extant numbers of the *Vedomosti* which were printed in Church Slavonic. 992 archival documents dealing with the eighteenth-century publications in the Church Slavonic typeface of the Synod presses of Moscow and St Petersburg from two multi-volume series, which commenced publication in the seventh decade of the nineteenth century and which continued to appear right up to 1917, occupy pp. 527–1120 (Appendices 2 and 3). Finally come the indices, some of which contain information never previously assembled and are therefore of exceptional interest.

This catalogue is remarkable on several grounds. First, it contains much the fullest list of the Church Slavonic publications of the presses of Moscow and St Petersburg yet published. Compared to Zernova and Kameneva's catalogue, which has 1,485 entries, this catalogue has 1,942 entries and a further 248 relating to numbers of the *Vedomosti* (Appendix 1). Of course, no claim is made to completeness, but the very existence of this catalogue is bound to lead to the discovery of further works in provincial churches, monastic libraries and private hands.

Second, although the items it describes are preserved in the libraries, museums, universities and academic institutions of the republics of the former USSR — the groundwork for its creation was laid when the USSR still existed — it is among the first catalogues published in Russia to include some works held outside the former USSR. (One of the earliest catalogues to do so was A. S. Zernova's *Knigi kirillovskoi pechati, izdannye v Moskve v XVI–XVII vekakh*, Moscow, 1958, which lists three foreign-held copies (p. [137]), one each in Brussels, Oxford and London.) The mention of foreign-held items should stimulate librarians in Western Europe, the Balkan countries and North America to search their holdings for eighteenth-century books in Church Slavonic. They will want to pay special attention to the works whose entries the author has marked with an asterisk, meaning that, although the particular edition's existence is attested in previous catalogues and by other documentary evidence, copies of it have not yet been found and are still being searched for. It is worth recalling that, when in the eighteenth century Russian Orthodox bishops and archimandrites visited their opposite numbers abroad, they had the custom of presenting them with Bibles and service-books in Church Slavonic. Since these books were virtually never used, if they survive, they are often found to be in pristine condition.

Third, the catalogue entries contain far more descriptive material than the entries in the catalogues of Zernova and Kameneva. This has particular significance for church books, which comprise most of the entries, because so many of them are reprints distinguishable from one another only by minute, not easily perceived, differences. The concentrated, detailed study which has gone into the creation of this catalogue is barely imaginable. However, it was indispensable, because so many of the copies described are defective. Worn out by daily use in church services, their bindings have come apart, and individual leaves and whole sections have fallen out. To remedy the absence of title-pages, the author has had to search the remainder of the texts for references to contemporary events and *realia*. Precise dating is a peculiar feature of this work: hence terms like 'beginning, end, first half of the year, etc.', used in previous catalogues have been replaced by actual dates in days, months and years. Identification marks (*kleima*) are specified when they can be found. Copies used in proof-reading, or those specially prepared for presentation to senior clerics or members of the nobility or the imperial family, are singled out. Illustrations are not reproduced, but the presence of decorative elements, particularly initial letters, *zastavki* (head-pieces), *kontsovki* (end-pieces), *viaz´* (decorative script) and other ornamentation, is mentioned. The names of the persons involved in the printing of individual works are frequently given, and the locations in the texts where these details can be found are specified. The detailed investigative work which the compiler has carried out enables her to correct mistakes and confusions in the catalogues of her predecessors. In the case of 1,288 editions, represented by more than 4,000 copies, the descriptions which she gives are taken from copies preserved in the Nauchno-issledovatel´skii otdel redkikh knig of the Russian State Library in Moscow.

Although church books predominate, there is the occasional lay work, for example, Leontii Magnitskii's *Arifmetika (*Moscow, 1703, entry 535); *Manifest ob otreshenii ot prestola tsarevicha Alekseia Petrovicha* (Moscow, 1718, entry 547); Meletii Smotritskii's *Grammatika* (Moscow, 1721; entry 553) and the early numbers of the *Vedomosti.* Up to 1708, when Peter's civil typeface was launched, all works, lay included, continued to be printed in the Church Slavonic typeface, and this font was used sporadically for some years after 1708. Thus the *Vedomosti,* the first Russian printed newspaper, was printed in the Church Slavonic font until 1711 and occasionally thereafter.

There is much more to this huge volume than bibliographical data. The extracts in Appendices 2 and 3 from the two multi-volume series of reprinted documents were selected to throw light on the Church Slavonic publications of the Synod presses of Moscow and St Petersburg from 1721–1801. They provide abundant background information on many of the editions described in the catalogue's bibliographical sections. They list the different presses working in Moscow and St Petersburg, their employees and their functions, their salaries and terms of engagement, as well as much detail on the book trade itself, the selling prices of the books, sales figures and unsold stock. These are the essential facts and figures which anyone surveying the economic and sociological conditions of the book trade in eighteenth-century Russia would require, at least as far as concerns Church Slavonic books.

An unexpected feature of this work is that many of the earlier entries incorporate the texts of Church Slavonic poems which accompany iconographic illustrations. Owing to the scarcity of poetic works in Church Slavonic in the first decades of the eighteenth century these poems present great interest.

This catalogue has rescued the domain of Russian eighteenth-century Church Slavonic books from a long and undeserved neglect. Slavonic librarians and bibliographers will find in it an incomparable resource for the identification of newly discovered works as well as for improvements in the description of those already known. The compiler must be congratulated on her magnificent achievement.

Imperial College London C. L. DRAGE

Hammond, Andrew. *British Literature and the Balkans: Themes and Contexts.* Studia Imagologica: Amsterdam Studies on Cultural Identity, 16. Rodopi, Amsterdam and New York, 2010. 321 pp. Notes. Bibliography. Index. €65.00: $88.00 (paperback).

PART of the recent scholarship that considers travel literature an important source for the study of cross-cultural interaction, Hammond's book is a critical analysis of how the Balkans were represented over the past 150 years by British novelists, poets and travellers who had visited or lived in the region. Unlike Vesna Goldsworthy's earlier study, *Inventing Ruritania: The Imperialism of the Imagination* (New Haven, CT, 1998), which focused more on literary works, Hammond's book offers an extended treatment of fiction, journalism and travel literature. Thus, well known names of modern British literature, such as those of Lord Byron, Bram Stoker, Lawrence Durrell, Evelyn Waugh and Malcolm Bradbury, among others, share company with the much less famous authors of journalistic ephemera and more than three hundred travelogues.

Approaching his topic from a theoretical perspective that acknowledges the influence of Edward Said and Homi Bhabha's contribution to discussions of the encounter between the West and the East, Hammond argues in Maria Todorova's footsteps (see her *Imagining the Balkans*, Oxford and New York, 1997) that, although influenced by Orientalist perspectives, Balkanism is a discourse that emerged separately from it. As he writes, 'contrary to the Orient's role as a contiguous or exterior other, the Balkans have become [for the West] the other within, a liminal self that undermines continental stability and unity by more subtle erosion' (p. 48). However, by contrast to Todorova's focus on the intellectual genealogy and the political impact of Balkanism, Hammond is more interested in analysing how the latter shaped self-perceptions amongst the British travellers who came in contact with this region of Europe, and how their writings were shaped in turn by specific conditions in Britain, by ideas of empire, changing gender notions, a search for factual knowledge, and the emergence of different literary styles such as romanticism, gothicism, modernism, including the impact of political ideologies such as liberalism and Communism.

Thus, the first four chapters of the book discuss components of Balkanism in the writings of nineteenth-century British authors and travellers, such as their denigratory depiction of the Balkans as a place divided by frontiers and ethnic hatred; their reliance on and contribution to emerging Western typologies of the region based on superficial observations and stereotypes; their emphasis on the antithesis between civilization and savagery (as in their Gothicist depiction of the area as a place inhabited by bloodthirsty clans, with vampires and werewolves hiding in the dark); and their use of the Balkans as a pejorative political concept reflective of power struggles and hierarchies within Europe past and present. Switching tack, the next two chapters focus on the meaning of Englishness and maleness among late nineteenth-century British expatriates in the region, and respectively British women's self-empowering as a result of their active participation as soldiers and nurses in the military conflicts that ravaged the Balkans during the first half of the twentieth century. Chapter seven looks at how, especially during the interwar period, and by contrast to former Balkanist stereotypes, the Balkans were perceived by many visitors from Britain as a rural Arcadia enabling the latter to regain access to something that had been lost in their over-civilized and industrialized Western society. The next chapter offers further evidence as to how British romanticism shaped Balkanist discourses in the immediate post-World War One period, bringing to the fore a brief moment when the West fell under the spell of the Balkans, with the romance between the two soon terminated by the region's takeover by Communism and, in its aftermath, the bloodshed of the Yugoslav wars. It was these later developments (discussed in depth in the last two chapters of the book), which resurrected, according to Hammond, former Western stereotypes about the Balkans, making Balkanist discourses appear circular and repetitive when examined from a long-term perspective.

Hammond does a splendid job in contextualizing these matters from the perspective of a much broader secondary literature, stretching from an analysis of the nature of modernism in Western literature to that of different shades of British feminism in travel writing, and from the exilic construction of self-identities to the power-laden rhetoric of Western humanitarian interventions to other areas of the world, a chapter-structuring procedure which enables him to both make important points and keep the narrative continuously informed by theoretical debates conducted in a variety of other fields. In doing this, the author proves to be an apt continuator of the tradition of imagological studies, which in his own interpretation focus 'on a broader, intertextual analysis of national images in a literary culture, exploring antecedent and concurrent manifestations of those images and analysing their interdependence with extra-textual phenomena' (p. 6).

While the book excels in doing all of the above, Hammond's text is occasionally marred by historical inaccuracies. For example, in reference to the Austrian Empire in 1844, that state formation is identified as Austria-Hungary (p. 19), when in fact the latter was created only in 1867, and in a discussion of how British nurses frequently highlighted the differences in civilization between the British serving in Serbia during the First World War and prisoners from the camp of Central Powers, the military alliance between Germany and Austria-Hungary is erroneously referred to as that of the Axis Powers (p. 269). Place and persons' names are also sometimes inaccurately spelt. Regarding a corollary of the book's main argument, according to which under the period under study British culture 'retained south-East Europe as one of its most significant others' (p. 15), a brief mentioning of the Gaelic fringe, as another instantiation of another such significant other, would have been meaningful.

In spite of these minor imperfections, with its solid and sophisticated argumentation and rich findings, thoroughly grounded in primary sources, Hammond's work is an important addition to the contemporary scholarship on the Balkans, being a book that further refines our understanding of this place's role and narrative representation in British culture.

Marywood University, Pennsylvania ALEXANDER VARI

Reyfman, Irina. *Rank and Style: Russians in State Service, Life, and Literature.* Ars Rossika. Academic Studies Press, Boston, MA, 2012. xii + 315 pp. Illustrations. Notes. Index. $85.00.

IN the opening chapter, 'Liudi i chiny', of his posthumously published *Besedy o russkoi kul′ture: Byt i traditsii russkogo dvoriantstva (XVIII–nachalo XIX veka)* (St Peterburg, 1994) Iurii Lotman declared that it would be impossible to understand Gogol′'s works without knowing why it was important that the *chinovnik* who lost his nose was a major, and why Poprishchin and Bashmachkin were titular counsellors. It is an understanding of the significant resonance of the imperial rank system in the works of writers conscious of their place in the noble estate that is Irina Reyfman's new interest. A number of contributions to the present volume provide a foretaste of her next book project provisionally entitled *Ranks and Writing*. But it is also a retrospective selection, spanning the past twenty years, related to her previous pioneering work on Trediakovskii and the ritualized violence of duelling in Russian noble culture. Of the fifteen articles, three recent conference presentations appear in print for the first time.

'Rank, State Service and Literature' is the heading of the first of four parts into which the volume is divided. The second part is devoted to an examination of how Pushkin was seen by other writers and himself; Tolstoi is the subject of the third part, and the fourth is a miscellany that does not claim to have a unifying theme or method. Each section is introduced with a purposeful and illuminating preface.

There are certain dominant themes. Rank, for example, not confined to part one, is a key component of an essay in part two on the nature of the relationship between Pushkin and Gogol′, 'Kammerjunker in "Notes of a Madman": Gogol's View of Pushkin'. The sense of honour is closely allied to anxiety about rank status that so troubled Sumarokov, the subject of the opening article 'Writing, Ranks and the Eighteenth-Century Russian Gentry Experience'. Honour too is a concept that runs as a thread through this selection. Pushkin's Dubrovskii is portrayed as a man of honour in the third article, 'Writing and the Anxiety of Rank: Pushkin's Prose Fiction'. Honour is central to the selection's concluding chapter, 'Dishonor by Flogging and Restoration by Dancing: Leskov's Response to Dostoevsky', that begins with an examination of Dostoevskii's vituperative view of *Nevsky Prospekt*'s Lieutenant Pirogov dishonoured by his flogging at the hands of German tradesmen.

Even for Dostoevskii, duelling was an acceptable means of maintaining order and Reyfman's previous study of duelling in the culture of the Russian nobility resonates not only in articles examining its prevalence as a topic in Russian literature but also in real life. Her 2001 *Russian Review* article, 'Death and Mutilation at the Dueling Site: Pushkin's Death as a National Spectacle', argues that the unprecedented publicity given to accounts of Pushkin's protracted, agonizing death brought into the open the ambiguities of duelling behaviour.

Death and violence, literary topics that preoccupy Reyfman, are not confined to duelling narratives. Part three of the collection is almost entirely concerned with Tolstoi's struggle with the inevitability of death in his later works. We are reminded of Pushkin's fascination with physical brutality, floggings and hangings in his research into the Pugachev uprising. Dostoevskii, ever sensitive to the human body's vulnerability, is always prepared to portray extreme, grotesque violent behaviour. Violence is present in discussions of writers as diverse as Rzhevskii, Leskov, Tolstoi and Zoshchenko.

Another feature of the collection is the way that Russian writers are made to speak to and interact with each other. Thus in the first article Sumarokov, Bolotov and Bogdanovich are brought together in an examination of the contrasting attitudes of writers to rank and service in eighteenth-century Russia. Pushkin is linked with Trediakovskii, Lomonosov, Derzhavin and

Gogol′; Dostoevskii with Gogol′ and Leskov; Murav′ev with Bobrov; Tolstoi with Turgenev. Zoshchenko reacts to Pushkin and Tolstoi; Tolstoi to Gogol′; Leskov to Dostoevskii.

On occasion the intertextual links are boldly speculative, such as the argument for Derzhavin's 'presence' in Pushkin's *History of Pugachev*, or the contention that Zoshchenko must have been aware of Leont′ev's suggestion that Tolstoi's subject of the Napoleonic War might be rendered in the style of Pushkin. Although Reyfman admits that there is no documentary proof that Tolstoi knew Pushkin's poem 'The Wanderer', a strong argument is made that the poem was obsessively reworked by the novelist. Her insights are always well grounded, perceptive and productive.

The present selection is an impressive testimony to her range and conviction that a sympathetic understanding of the social framework underpinning Russian noble culture enriches our appreciation of Russian literature.

Bangor W. Gareth Jones

Bird, Robert. *Fyodor Dostoevsky*. Critical Lives. Reaktion Books, London, 2012. 237 pp. Illustrations. Notes. Further reading. £10.95 (paperback).

First impressions count. Reaktion Books are well aware of this maxim to judge by the name of the publisher as well as the way in which it is spelt. On opening a book in its Critical Lives series, the reader will find the paragraphs are left-aligned. This practice is uncommon in academic literature, where justification is the norm, and it gives rise to a sense of a draft, of something incomplete, ragged, in the production process. The layout is down to the editorial policy of the publishing house but, unfortunately, in the present volume what may be construed as raggedness persists in the presentation of the biography itself. A rather too relaxed style of writing sets the tone for a degree of informality that can lapse into looseness of expression. To take an example, we learn in one chapter that both Konstantin Leontyev (p. 178) and Ivan Turgenev (p. 193) were Dostoevskii's 'nemesis'. Accommodating Oscar Wilde's famous aphorism to the occasion, it could be said that to have one nemesis is a misfortune, to have two looks like carelessness… on the part of the author. More to the point, it is never made clear why either of these two contemporaries of Dostoevskii deserves this ascription. If anything, a stronger case could be made for claiming that Dostoevskii, particularly in his portrayal of Karmazinov in *Demons*, acted as *Turgenev's* nemesis. The reluctance to explore in greater detail the abrasive relationship that existed between these two giants of nineteenth-century Russian literature is one of several instances of 'raggedness', or a failure to follow a topic to the end of the line. As Joseph Frank, the doyen of Dostoevskii's biographers, has written, 'No account of *Demons* would be complete without some discussion of the malicious but masterly caricature of Turgenev in the portrait of Karmazinov' (*Dostoevsky: A Writer in his Time*, Princeton, NJ, 2010, p. 642).

Frank's five-volume biography is cited with approval at the start of the section on Further Reading as 'the best and most complete biography' (p. 233) of the Russian writer. There are few who would disagree with the assessment or dispute the important contribution to Dostoevskii scholarship that other critics listed in the Further Reading have made, but here also we find noteworthy absences. The most egregious omission in the current evaluation of the Russian novelist is the refusal to recognize the seminal contribution that Mikhail Bakhtin has made to our understanding of Dostoevskii's poetics. Bakhtin is not mentioned at all in the Further Reading and his name is studiously avoided (apart from a single reference) in the critical discussion on issues that involve the 'authorial' status of fictional characters and the problematic nature of the narratorial voice.

This review has thus far accentuated the fact of exclusion but, conversely, the temptation to elaborate is endemic in biographical works, where an author, having insufficient historical data at his or her disposal, resorts to unsubstantiated propositions introduced by an all-too-revealing 'perhaps' or 'no doubt'. It is the biographer's ability to engage that determines whether such inferences succeed in persuading the reader. In this respect, Robert Bird does not always manage to combine fact and hypothesis with conviction. Paragraphs that conclude with a rhetorical flourish — and there are many of them in the book — can confuse rather than illuminate. The following is an example: 'The pilgrimage to Optyna Pustyn′, upon reflection, represents Dostoevsky's attempt to break out of these patterns of repetition by executing a return to his origins *before literature, and beyond literature, and yet through literature*' (p. 203, italics added). Patterns of repetition are, in fact, an invaluable asset for biographers and Bird avails himself of them. Motifs drawn from Dostoevskii's life and writings lend cohesion to the documentation of events. Many of these motifs have been used in earlier studies, such as a focus on the striking physiognomy of the Russian author, the enduring effect of the last-minute reprieve from the death sentence, or the significance of the dialectic in Dostoevskii's works between image (*obraz*) and its lack (*bezobrazie*), but others are less familiar. One of the more prominent of these, central to Dostoevskii's ambition to utter what he himself referred to as 'a new word', is the inconclusive notion of a 'radical wager on form' (p. 80 and *sparsim*), which seeks to conflate the novelist's addiction to gambling with his lifelong concern for the aesthetic dimension of his craft.

Fyodor Dostoevsky provides a useful chronological survey of Dostoevskii's life and it offers good summary analyses of his creative works at appropriate moments in the biographical account. What it does it does competently, but the initial impression of raggedness is never entirely dispelled as, for example, when the discussion of *Crime and Punishment* that occupies chapter five is carried out without once mentioning Svidrigailov and his role in the novel. Surely this cannot be justified.

Department of Literature, Film, and Theatre Studies LEON BURNETT
University of Essex

Gamsa, Mark. *The Chinese Translation of Russian Literature: Three Studies.* Sinica Leidensia, 90. Brill, Leiden and Boston, MA, 2008. xiv + 430 pp. Illustrations. Notes. Annex. Bibliography. Glossary. Index. €119.00: $176.00.

Gamsa, Mark. *The Reading of Russian Literature in China: A Moral Example and Manual of Practice.* Palgrave Studies in Cultural and Intellectual History. Palgrave Macmillan, London and New York, 2010. 227 pp. Notes. Select bibliography. Glossary. Index. £54.00.

THE Russian influence on modern Chinese literature is well-known, but unfortunately remains understudied. Mark Gamsa's two book-length studies, published in 2008 and 2010 respectively, address the dearth of scholarship on the Chinese appropriation of Russian literature, and offer thought-provoking insights into the literary relationship between Russia and China.

Gamsa, who teaches modern Chinese literature and history at Tel Aviv University, provides three meticulous case studies in *The Chinese Translation of Russian Literature: Three Studies.* The three cases are: Zheng Zhenduo (1898–1958)'s 1922 translation of Boris Savinkov (1879–1925)'s *Pale Horse* (1909) and its reception in China; the Chinese translations of Mikhail Artsybashev (1878–1927) and especially the great modern Chinese writer Lu Xun (1881–1936)'s encounter with the works of this Russian novelist; and the multiple translations of the modernist fictional works by Leonid Andreev (1871–1919). Gamsa believes that 'our enquiry into the transmission, translation and interpretation of Russian literature in China is also a study of the literature that was translated' (p. 8). By focusing on the translations and interpretations of works by these three modernist Russian writers, Gamsa aims to 'tell the story of the translation of Russian literature in republican China' (p. 25; 'republican China' refers to the rule of the Republic of China from 1912 to 1949).

His three case studies revolve around what he calls 'three main aspects of translation: technique, ideology and practice' (p. 25). 'Technique' here means 'the whole range of decisions that translators take in the course of their work' (p. 25). By 'ideology,' Gamsa means 'the motivation for translating, and the choice of their work' (p. 25). Then 'practice' denotes 'translating as an occupation' (p. 25).

Corresponding to the issue of technique, chapter one focuses on Zheng Zhenduo's 1922 translation of Savinkov's novel *Pale Horse*, and draws particular attention to the fact that Zheng's rendering was not based on the Russian original but on Zinaida Vengerova's English translation (see pp. 63–68). Gamsa's emphasis on what he calls the 'intermediary' sources or 'mediated translation' (in chapter one and throughout the book) is significant, for relay translation (to use the terminology of translation studies) played a crucial role in China's appropriation of Russian literature and other foreign cultures during the first half of the twentieth century. Raising the question about translators' ideology, chapter two examines the Chinese translation of Artsybashev's *Sanin* in relation to the rise of individualism in modern China, and considers the most famous modern Chinese writer-translator Lu Xun as a reader and translator of Russian literature (not only Artsybashev's *Worker Shevyrev*, but other works such as Gogol′'s *Dead Souls*: 'Lu Xun's own last effort, *Dead Souls*, proved [...] one of the most successful among the many translation he produced', p. 188). Chapter three then shows how Artsybashev's work became a thorny case for Chinese writers as they turned further into political left in the late 1920s and onward. Then Gamsa moves on to the issue of 'practice', giving us a collective portrait of more than forty Chinese translators of Andreev during the first half of the twentieth century. Some of them practised translation out of a cultural or political commitment (see chapter four). But there were also other less familiar categories of literary translators in republican China, such as the translators from the industry of entertainment fiction of the 1910s, the translators associated with Shanghai modernism or decadence of the 1930s, and other freelance or casual translators (see chapter five). Gamsa describes his book as a 'lens': 'gradually zooming out from a close-up shot of a single translation of one novel by Savinkov, expanding to a wider angle on the translations and reception of Artsybashev, then to a group photo of the forty-two Chinese translators of Andreev' (p. 47).

Gamsa employs a methodology called 'contextual historicism' (p. 31). Cautious against the uses of translation theories, his investigation is rigorously empirical and thereby makes solid contributions to the field of the history of Chinese translation. One detail I would like to add to Gamsa's illuminating account is about Lu Xun's 'hard translation' or *ying yi*: Gamsa mentions Lu Xun's term of 'hard translation', and sees it as an ideology of translation that emphasizes the 'linguistic revolution' (p. 154). But by 'hard translation' Lu Xun initially only referred to his translations of Marxist theoretical works by Anatolii Lunacharskii and Georgii Plekhanov, and these translations were based on the Japanese renderings of the two Marxists' works. How to link Lu Xun's idea of 'hard translation' to literary translation is then a challenging question here.

It should also be noted that the three writers Gamsa focuses on all belonged to the Silver Age of Russian literature. In Russia, they had been derogatorily labelled as 'decadent' writers' in the wake of the Communist takeover, and were rediscovered after the fall of the Soviet Union. In this sense, this book can also be read as an exploration of the brief 'engagement of leading Chinese writers with Russian literature of the "Silver age"' (p. 363). As the political environment and ideological fortunes changed in revolutionary China, Chinese writers gradually lost their interests in Artsybashev, Andreev and other Russian modernists. But Gamsa argues that the importance of these Russian writers of the Silver Age lies in 'their being among the very first representatives of Russian literature in China to become associated with literary modernity' (p. 363). Gamsa's study, in this sense, makes meaningful efforts to rescue a forgotten transnational literary encounter from the shadow of history.

Gamsa sees the Silver Age as 'an interlude between two epochs of moralism' (p. 6). For Gamsa, the first epoch of 'moralism' refers to the age of the Russian classics of nineteenth-century humanistic or critical realism, and the second means the period of Soviet Socialist Realism. A value judgment can be easily discerned in Gamsa's phrasing. A sequel to his 2008 book, *The Reading of Russian Literature in China: A Moral Example and Manual of Practice*, turns to these two literary traditions of 'moralism', and questions China's uses or abuses of Russian literary classics and Soviet Socialist Realism. This 2010 book traces how works of Russian critical realism and Socialist Realism were disseminated and received in twentieth-century China, and how Russian classics and Socialist Realist works came to be read as textbooks of life. Gamsa also shows how Chinese writers and readers fell in love with Russian classics and how they appreciated the works of the Russian humanistic tradition as a moral guidance. Moreover, Gamsa tells us the journey of Socialist Realism from the Soviet Union to China: as a slogan, it was 'promulgated in USSR in 1932' (p. 103), partially accepted in China during the Chinese Revolution and 'reaffirmed after the Communist victory' (p. 104). Socialist Realism also represented a peculiar mode of literary production and consumption for the sake of revolutionary 'indoctrination' (p. 105). The popularity of the Soviet novel *How the Steel Was Tempered* in China is a very famous example in point. Gamsa argues that in China's reception of Russian-Soviet literature, 'Word' became identical to 'Deed' (see p. 116). According to Gamsa, Russian-Soviet literature became a manual of practice in China due to 'the shared, or similar, postulates in the understanding of literature' (p. 12) in both Russian and Chinese cultures. He also pays particular attention to the phenomenon of 'time lags' (see p. 8) in China's reception of Western thought. By citing Aileen Kelly's comment on Russia's tendency to 'develop Western ideas to their logical (and often absurd) extremes' (p. 6), Gamsa indicates that China's reception of Russian-Soviet literature also brought out the 'logical and absurd' extremes of the Russian teachings (also see p. 132).

Gamsa's argument and perspective in this book are nuanced, but I still find them debatable at certain points. In contrast to the ideal of 'contextual historicism' (see above), Gamsa's study of China's reception of Russian-Soviet literature sometimes leads to oversimplification of history — and some theoretical disagreements are also involved here.

First, no one would deny that Russian realist classics and Soviet Socialist Realism, on the one hand, and Russian modernism of the Silver Age, on the other, represent two different visions of literary modernity. But it seems to me a reductionist move to call the former disparagingly as 'moralism.' In fact, the two divergent visions also shared some deep-rooted premises of literary modernity, especially that of the concern with the issues or themes of humanity, individuality, self-consciousness, meaning of life and formation of selfhood. I agree that in what Gamsa calls literary 'moralism', 'literature, morality and life became conceptually connected' (p. 12), but in modernism they were also interconnected — just in a different fashion.

Secondly, Gamsa's use of such terms as 'brainwashing' (p. 12) may cause other misconceptions. There is no denying that in socialist China the reading of Russian-Soviet literature became highly ideologically oriented. But I think Gamsa would also agree that Chinese writers' and readers' encounter with Russian literature also involved a deeply literary and aesthetic engagement and appropriation. Despite the fact that some of the Russian writers were equated with teachers (as Gamsa's book demonstrate), this engagement also embodied a strong cultural, intellectual and literary creativity or agency on the part of the Chinese (how to evaluate such an agency is another question). In addition, it is also an oversimplification to indicate that all the Chinese leftist literary experiments can be categorized under the cluster of 'Socialist Realism', as Gamsa seems to imply. As many scholars in the field of China studies have pointed out, the Yan'an literary movement and the Maoist literary experiments in socialist China should be distinguished from the Soviet model of Socialist Realism — not to mention the fact that Chinese literature's endorsement of Socialist Realism was far more limited than was its embrace of nineteenth-century realist classics.

Thirdly, Gamsa's view about the time lags in cultural exchange and the '"farcical" repetitions' (p. 11) of social experiments is very thought-provoking, but can also be counterproductive. The time lag in China's reception of foreign ideas and literatures is a quite common phenomenon, but it will oversimplify the history of modern Chinese culture (and even risk over-privileging the originator and downplaying the intervention of the latecomer/recipient) if we view every Chinese imitation of Russian-Soviet culture as a 'logical and absurd' repetition of a Russian repetition of the West (see pp. 10–11 and p. 132). A more productive way to deal with the existence of time lags may require us to abandon a linear progressive vision of the history of ideas and see China's twentieth century as a historical period into which various temporalities were compressed. In this co-existence of different temporalities, I hope, the interventions and limitations in China's acceptance of the Russian influence can be discussed in a more sophisticated way.

Gamsa's 2008 book ends with a note about the Chinese writer's obsession with the 'Russian book' (pp. 368–70); his 2010 book deals with the fetishization of the Russian book as the token or icon of humanistic moral values (see p. 141). These two studies will no doubt stimulate more discussion and scholarship on the Chinese love for the Russian book.

Department of German, Russian and Asian Languages & Literature, Brandeis University Pu Wang

Fleishman, Lazar (ed.). *The Life of Boris Pasternak's 'Doctor Zhivago'*. Stanford Slavic Studies, 37. Stanford University, Stanford, CA, 2009. 210 pp. Notes. Bibliographies. Price unknown.

The word 'life' in the title may bring to mind the name and passionate concern of the novel's hero, but it refers, primarily, to the 'life' of Pasternak's novel itself: how it was born and how it has fared. These fourteen essays (eight of them in Russian), carefully assembled by the eminent Pasternak-scholar Lazar Fleishman, mark the fiftieth anniversary of the publication of *Doctor Zhivago*. They fall into three categories: personal reminiscence, historically based accounts, and literary readings.

The first of three personal recollections is that of Pasternak's nephew Nicolas Slater, who recalls the Pasternaks in Oxford ('always aware of our family in Russia, from whom we felt unfairly cut off' [p. 9]), and dwells on their epistolary closeness to the poet during the anguished period of the Nobel Prize and his novel's problematic publication. The second (a reprinted extract from V. V. Ivanov's book, *Perevernutoe nebo*) vividly describes Pasternak's moods and actions during that difficult time, with his exclusion from the Moscow Writers' Union and his rejection of the Prize. The third, by Evgenii Borisovich Pasternak (who died, alas, in the summer of 2012), begins 'Kak-to rannei vesnoi, veroiatno, v kontse marta 1959 goda, ia priezzhal k ottsu v Peredelkino…' (p. 38). He found his father upset by a review calling *Zhivago* a failure, and supports his opinion that the émigré reviewer, S. Makovskii, was too remote from Soviet reality to appreciate the book's unconventionality; reminding us, perhaps, that there remains much to be said about it.

Pamela Davidson's essay, 'C. M. Bowra's "Overestimation" of Pasternak and the Genesis of *Doctor Zhivago*', links the personal and the historical pieces. Discussing Pasternak's five 1946–56 letters to Bowra (reproduced here as a separate item), she shows how important Bowra was to the novel's genesis. She discusses in detail his 'lifelong interest in Russian poetry' (p. 44), his translating and reviewing of Pasternak's earlier works and his twice nominating him for the Nobel Prize.

A further article deals with pre-1958 attempts to get Pasternak awarded the Prize (Bengt Jangfeldt). There are studies of the reception of pre-*Zhivago*

Pasternak in Italy (Cesare de Michelis), of *Zhivago*'s reception in 'France and the French-Speaking World' (Michel Aucouturier), its partial publication in Poland in summer 1958 (Monika Wójciak-Marek), and the attempt to publish it in the Soviet Union (Konstantin Polivanov). Using Communist Party archives, Polivanov, after a highly informative survey of official hostility towards Pasternak from 1946, describes the CP secretariat's attacks on *Zhivago* and its (apparently consequent) rejection by the *Novyi mir* editorial board.

The last group of essays starts with Susanna Witte's study of the meaning of 'nature' and 'life' in *Zhivago*. Lara's being called to name life's unnamed qualities harks back to the great namer of nature, Linnaeus, and to Gumilev's 'Sixth Sense'; these culminate — after careful consideration of related poems (especially Pasternak's 'Lesnoe' and Tyutchev's 'Ne to, chto mnite vy, priroda…' — in Zhivago's 'Peredelka zhizni' outburst to those who would alter 'life' and 'nature'.

Thomas Seifrid first considers *Zhivago* as a 'modernist Künstlerroman' (the poet despairs of the new regime's inauthentic language); then as essentially a 'strange' novel: the 'unfitness of its form' is 'in a certain (historical) sense *necessary*' (p. 182). Despite amply drawing on the philosophical legacy of the early twentieth century (as Seifrid shows in this essay), it 'seems to exemplify a type of art that emerges within Russian culture in the waning years of Stalinism […] which one could label something like "dead modernism" or "hollow transcendence"'; a 'powerful work', then, 'but also an unsettling one' (p. 182).

The conclusion of Robert Bird's essay is that 'in its very untimeliness, *Zhivago* was pre-eminently a novel of its time' (p. 198). The essay is interesting on Pasternak's relation to the epoch, especially on his engagement with, yet separateness from, the 'networks of Soviet power' (p. 191). But Bird's idea of 'the aesthetic interval', while fascinating, remains somewhat opaque. 'Pasternak […] discovered a means of representing the future by narrating the very interval that divides it from the past' (p. 194). More clarification than is given is also needed of the statement that, through its 'intervallic structure', Tarkovskii's *Andrei Rublev* is 'a successful screen adaptation of *Doctor Zhivago*' (p. 196).

I found Liudmila Gorelik's 'Duratskie voprosy Eleny Proklovny kak prolog k ural´skim glavam "Doktora Zhivago"', particularly illuminating. Mikulitsyn's wife's eccentric questions to Zhivago upon his arrival in Varykino appear meaningless, but Gorelik's analysis, based on inconspicuous hints, early drafts and thoughtful research on Russian folk-tales, discovers their resemblance to typical folk-tale questionings: they embody historical/prophetic references relevant to the narrative. Gorelik's essay makes a fine conclusion to this anthology: having looked at Pasternak's novel from several external perspectives, we end up deep in an understanding of its enigmas.

Department of Literature, Film and Theatre Studies ANGELA LIVINGSTONE
University of Essex

Fleishman, Lazar. *Vstrecha russkoi emigratsii s 'Doktorom Zhivago': Boris Pasternak i 'kholodnaia voina'.* Stanford Slavic Studies, 38. Stanford University, Stanford, CA, 2009. 499 pp. Illustrations. Notes. Index. $70.00.

LAZAR FLEISHMAN states that it took him twenty-five years to collect the material for this book, but it is not only the material (he gives extensive quotations from the publications about the novel and the correspondence of the major actors of the 'Pasternak affair'), but also his exceptional ability, known from his previous work, to act as a unique sleuth in unwinding the intricate web of information, first and foremost, the confusion about the copyright and the first Russian editions, both authorized and pirated, of *Doctor Zhivago*. This includes the pirated Russian edition distributed to Russian participants of the Brussels World Fair in 1958 and the one which gives as the publisher a Soviet publishing house which closed in 1930.

Tracing highly polarized reactions to *Doctor Zhivago* among Russian émigré writers and critics, Fleishman gives precise definitions of various 'components' within the emigration. There is no doubt that his most valuable source for this information is the correspondence of Gleb Struve with his numerous correspondents, among them Pasternak's sisters in Oxford and westerners who managed to visit the poet at the time. Chapter four with its account of Pasternak's receiving the Nobel prize and the following events worldwide, can be seen as the dramatic centrepiece of the book.

The author's examination of *Doctor Zhivago*'s progress and reactions to it gives a detailed and nuanced picture of the emigration (in a very broad sense) and the changes in the official responses from the Soviet Union. *Doctor Zhivago* can be seen, and justifiably so, as a litmus paper for both sides — the range of reactions was quite wide — from total rejection to complete acceptance, with varying degrees of acceptance and rejection in between. The reasons for judgment were both political and literary. (Perhaps the most striking example is the rejection of the novel by an émigré D. Pronin, who saw it as a clever Soviet intrigue, and by Vladimir Nabokov, who rejected it both on political and literary grounds.) Fleishman, rightly, singles out the work of two scholars — Gleb Struve and Victor Frank — giving readings of the novel that get to the essence of Pasternak's achievement.

The events of the 'Pasternak affair' can be seen as a turning point in the course of the Cold War and liberalization of cultural control in the Soviet Union. We find in Fleishman's book the account of the consequences, as it were, of the 'Pasternak affair' first in the publication of Pasternak's *Avtobiograficheskii ocherk* (*Autobiography*), then a three-volume edition of his work (Ann Arbor, 1961), and in continued work of its editors, Gleb Struve and Boris Filippov, on publication of other authors not published at that time in the Soviet Union, such as Osip Mandel′shtam, Anna Akhmatova and others.

Analysis of the cultural events of the Cold War lets Fleishman consider the role of intellectual forces in the West as significantly more important than the support of the CIA. In his view, the initiative for the support of the poet and his novel came from all liberal intellectuals of Western Europe and the USA (Congress for Cultural Freedom), including émigré intellectuals and many writers who knew Pasternak and his work before *Doctor Zhivago*. In addition, Fleishman draws a convincing conclusion that beyond the defence of the poet, the 'Pasternak affair' served a far reaching role as evidence of the unity of Russian literature despite the borders and ideological control in the Soviet Union. It served as a bridge between Pasternak and the West and, in the process, uncovered and emphasized the value of Russian emigration in the West.

It is only proper that the book is dedicated to the memory of Professor Gleb Struve who pioneered the study of Russian Soviet literature in the West with his 1935 *Soviet Russian Literature*, followed by *Twenty-Five Years of Soviet Russian Literature* in 1944, *Soviet-Russian Literature: 1917–1950* (1951) and *Russian Literature under Lenin and Stalin, 1917–1953* (1971). The obverse of the page with Struve's photograph reproduces a fragment of his letter of 30 January 1958 to the Swedish Academy proposing Boris Pasternak for the Nobel Prize.

Fleishman's book is a work which will not lose its value with time: the convoluted history of the publication of *Doctor Zhivago* in the West in translation and, more critically, in Russian will remain the most valuable source for future scholars of Pasternak's work and of political play around it.

University of California, Berkeley OLGA RAEVSKY-HUGHES

Boyd, Brian. *Stalking Nabokov: Selected Essays*. Columbia University Press, New York and Chichester, 2011. xv + 452pp. Notes. Bibliography. Index. $35.00: £24.00.

THE contemporary response to the publication of James Boswell's *The Life of Samuel Johnson* definitively outlined the problems encountered by any individual who seeks to act as literary biographer. While generally considered to be one of, if not the, greatest biographies in the English language, there was consensus at the time that Boswell had acted far too presumptuously in the practice of his critical work. Although exhibiting 'the most copious, interesting, and finished picture of the life and opinions of an eminent man' (Robert Anderson, *The Life of Samuel Johnson, LL.D., With Critical Observations on his Works*, London, 1985, p. 6), wrote Robert Anderson, there still remained 'some venial exceptions on the score of egotism and indiscriminate admiration'. Less generous was Thomas Macaulay, who thought Boswell 'servile and impertinent, shallow and pedantic' (Thomas Babington Macaulay, *Critical, Historical, and Miscellaneous Essays*, vols 1–2, Boston, 1860, p. 392). Indeed, perhaps the two perennial criticisms directed towards the literary biographer is that of wilful inaccuracy on the one hand, or mawkish sycophancy on the other.

The first attempts at biographies of Vladimir Nabokov suffered a not dissimilar fate to that of Boswell's *Life*. These works, by Andrew Field, were almost universally loathed by Nabokov scholars, the general public and, most significantly, by the author himself. The Nabokov scholarly community is, perhaps slightly more so than others, intensely deferential and protective towards its subject. Following this, Brian Boyd's extensive, rigorous and compelling two-volume biography of Nabokov was welcomed with enthusiasm when it was first published. Field's work, much like Boswell's two centuries before, demonstrates for us perhaps the main problem inherent in committing one's life to documenting that of another, much greater individual. In many ways, Field's work is spiteful, prone to gossip and speculation, probably written in bad faith, certainly written in response to some perceived slight.

In *Stalking Nabokov* we see that Brian Boyd, on the other hand, having never met the great man himself, is infinitely more generous towards his subject and his works. Both perspectives, however, are to invariable degrees informed by obsession: an indispensable quality in a biographer. When one decides to make the work of another man their life's work, it may either consume them with jealousy or fill them to the brim with boundless admiration. For Boyd the latter is most certainly true. The personal relationships which he formed with the Nabokov family, which he recounts in touching detail in this collection, have evidently had a significant effect upon his scholarly work. Boyd is, without a doubt, an incredibly exacting and rigorous scholar — his tireless research and collection of a vast array of materials is something which coming generations of academics will continue to be grateful for.

Boyd is at his best when engaged in close-reading and analysis, seamlessly sifting through his vast encyclopaedic knowledge of the various materials which he has encountered over the years, making connections between seemingly disparate strands. Boyd writes well, his tone is benevolent and warm, encouraging the reader to share in the exhilaration and wonderment which the study of Nabokov evidently continues to inspire in him. Of particular note are the tenth and twelfth chapters on 'The Psychological Work of Fictional Play' and 'Nabokov's Humour', which offer some very interesting analyses on two different aspects of Nabokovian style, and also include previously unpublished archival material.

This collection, however, reveals a persistent tension which may be impossible to resolve: the incompatibility of the roles of biographer and critic. For those who are familiar with Boyd's excellent biographies, *Stalking Nabokov*, the tale of how these works came to life, makes for fascinating and highly enjoyable reading. There is, however, a sense that Boyd is so intimately, sentimentally, obsessively and personally connected with Nabokov's legacy that even his most brilliantly realized and perceptive works of analysis seem sometimes to lack a degree of critical distance.

Department of Russian and Slavonic Studies U. H. Dematagoda
University of Glasgow

Döring, Johanna Renate and Kukuj, Ilja (eds). *Leonid Aronzon: Rückkehr ins Paradies.* Wiener Slawistischer Almanach, 62. Otto Sagner, Munich, 2008. 546 pp. Illustrations. Chronology. Notes. Translations. Appendix. €25.60 (paperback).

This volume of the Wiener Slawistische Almanach, published twice annually by Professors Aage Hansen-Löve (Munich) and Tilmann Reuther (Klagenfurt), deserves particular attention for its comprehensive coverage of the life and work of Leonid Aronzon (1939–70), a relatively little known Leningrad poet who was found shot dead in the woods near Tashkent. His death was interpreted by the police as suicide, but to this day its circumstances remain unclear. That there is growing interest in Aronzon is attested by a recent English edition of Aronzon's poetry, *Life of a Butterfly: Collected Poems* (translated by Richard McKane, Brighton and Hove, 2011). Meanwhile, this collection of essays is the product of a seminar, 'Piter in the Sixties', dealing with 'Pitertexts' (Piter = St Petersburg), which ran over three terms during 2007 at Munich University. It includes original texts accompanied by translations in several languages, notes on Aronzon's diaries and early publications (samizdat), studies of his poetic technique, intertextual aspects, the poet's 'Kunstreligion' and a comprehensive bibliography.

Apart from the introduction in German followed by a four-and-a-half-page chronicle of the life and work of Leonid Aronzon, as well as a biographical survey by Il′ia Kukui, both in Russian, the main portion of the book is divided into three sections. 'Analysen', containing fourteen essays, demands a trilingual reader, one essay being in English, three in German, the rest in Russian. It opens with Thomas Epstein's brief essay, a fitting start which relates the author's own growing attraction to Aronzon, whose four-line poem, 'Litso', serves as an apt example of his art: 'Vse litso: litso – litso / pyl′ – litso, slova – litso, / vse – litso. Ego. Tvortsa. / Tol′ko Sam on bez litsa' (p. 38). These four short lines may be said to contain the essence of Aronzon's poetic universe. They also serve as a starting point for Rainer Grübel's analysis of Aronzon's poetic technique. The other essays in this section either combine personal reminiscences with biographical details from various sources, or concentrate on the avantgarde technique of Aronzon's poems and his roots in the poetic tradition, including the Piter Avantgarde. Igor′ Loshilov contributes an exhaustive study of

Zabolotskii's influence whilst Christian Zehnder researches Pasternak's influence on Aronzon's early poetry. Readers interested in gaining more insights into Aronzon's poetic universe will profit from the excellent essay by Petr Kazarnovskii, 'Prostranstvo teksta L. Aronzona', and Olga Sedova's essay, herself a well-known Petersburg poetess, 'Leonid Aronzon: Poet Kul′minatsii', which is based on a lecture she gave at Stanford University in 2007. Remo Faccani's diary-notes on his acquaintance with Aronzon in Leningrad in 1965–66 present a wonderful and instructive portrait of the poet. The last essay by Sergei Biriukov draws a straight line from the poetry of Zabolotskii and Velemir Khlebnikov, another important influence, to Aronzon's visual poetry, three examples of which are presented in the essay, characterized by Biriukov as 'Opyty neopisatel′nogo pis′ma' (p. 249). More visual poems are to be found in the second section.

This much shorter, yet fascinating section, entitled 'Publikationen', is entirely in Russian and contains poems and prose texts by the poet. Kukui's introductory essay, '*Lepta na pir*: About one *samizdat* selection of L. Aronzon', is followed by Petr Vykhodtsev's 1976 review of *Lepta*. This is complemented by the publication of Aronzon's unpublished poems of 1961 and his poetic *Attempts at Dadaism*, as well as the poet's personal notes, *I said, that I do things right now...*, followed by excerpts from his *Notebooks*. The texts of this chapter were prepared by Kazarnovskii, Kukui and Vladimir Erl′, the editors of the two-volume edition of Aronzon's works (St Petersburg, 2006), with commentaries by Kukui.

The third section, 'Übersetzungen', is devoted to translations of Aronzon's poetry by eleven translators, with the Russian originals presented in parallel with their translations. Languages include German, English, Italian, Serbian and Czech. The section ends with an essay by Anastasiia Blium and Christian Zehnder which discusses the problems faced by translators of Aronzon's poems.

An Appendix includes Vladimir Erl′'s 'Bibliography of the Works of Aronzon (1962–2006)', followed by a useful alphabetical index of Aronzon's published texts, which informs the reader in which publications a given text can be found. This volume, in addition to the above-mentioned two-volume collection, is to be recommended highly to students and scholars alike, as well as Slavic department libraries, as a welcome resource for research and teaching on Russian avantgarde/samizdat poetry in the final decades of the Soviet Union.

Alpen-Adria University, Klagenfurt Rudolf Neuhäuser

Iangirov, R. *'Raby Nemogo': Ocherki istoricheskogo byta russkikh kinematografistov za rubezhom. 1920–1930-e gody.* Russkii put′, Moscow, 2008. 496 pp. Illustrations. R252.00.

Iangirov, R. *Khronika kinematograficheskoi zhizni russkogo zarubezh′ia: v 2 t.* Vol. 1: 1918–1929; vol. 2: 1930–1980. Edited by Z. M. Zevinoi. Russkiy put′, Moscow, 2010. 544 + 640 pp. Illustrations. Filmography. Bibliography. Index. R980.00.

Iangirov, R. *Drugoe kino: Stat′i po istorii otechestvennogo kino pervoi treti XX veka.* Edited by A. I. Reitblat. Kinoteksty. Novoe literaturnoe obozrenie, Moscow, 2011. 409 pp. R325.00.

Levchenko, Ia. (comp., ed.). *Rabota i sluzhba: Sbornik pamiati Rashita Iangirova.* Svoe izdatel′stvo, St Petersburg, 2011. 314 pp. Illustrations. Notes. Price unknown.

Over the last ten years Russian humanities scholarship has lost many outstanding researchers. Looking through the list of obituaries, it is obvious that although talking about a crisis in the humanities in Russia is quite well-founded, some substantial reservations are in order. If we accept that the work of the creators of this knowledge was not in vain, then its fruits will feed the next generation of researchers for many years to come. However, this 'historical optimism' can hardly lessen the feelings of pain and sorrow for each case of irreplaceable human loss.

The death of Rashit Iangirov in 2007 was a tragedy not only for those who knew him personally, but for all his appreciative readers. His first book, the only to be published in his lifetime, *'The Slaves of the Mute': Essays on the Historical Everyday Life of Russian Film-makers Abroad, 1920–1930* (2007) was the result of Iangirov's research into the history of Russian cinema outside Russia. Its publication was an event of paramount importance. The extensive knowledge and understanding accumulated in *'The Slaves of the Mute'*, for all its undeniable merits, was seen not only and not so much as an end but as a beginning. After publishing dozens of papers, Iangirov finally seemed to be building up to some major books. *'The Slaves of the Mute'* was seen as a 'first volume' that would be followed by more.

What in fact followed was Iangirov's premature death. This, however, failed to break the sequence of important publications. This is hardly typical. The death of distinguished Russian humanities scholars usually generates a stream of memoirs and essays regarding their legacy, but in Iangirov's case, the books he had been working on for a decade appeared immediately, due to the laudable efforts of his family and colleagues.

2010 saw the publication of *A Chronicle of Russian Cinema Life Outside Russia* in two volumes. Iangirov had been preparing this edition for over twenty years. Extensive excerpts from this book had already been published in the miscellany, *The Diaspora*, but only in this edition can one fully appreciate the scale and scope of Iangirov's work. It is difficult to describe his *Chronicle* in any way other than unique. It has no analogues, no precursors (except in his own other works), and there are no alternatives and competitors to this edition. Here Iangirov assimilated a vast quantity of material, mainly from Russian émigré, domestic and foreign periodicals, memoirs, diaries and archives. To the casual observer it may seem like conventional research, but anyone who has worked with Russian émigré periodicals cannot fail to delight in Iangirov's scholarship. Iangirov's *Chronicle* collects and arranges in chronological order hundreds of details relating to the history of Russian cinema abroad, either little known or completely unknown to the general public. This work would be considered an achievement as the combined effort of any study group, but Iangirov carried out it as an independent scholar.

Iangirov had prepared his *Chronicle* for press, but it was left unfinished, and there are therefore some understandable deficiencies in the present edition. It could be seen as a first memorial edition, to be followed by at least a second, in which a proper index of films could be included to replace the present one which reads more like a filmography, presented in alphabetical order, without page references.

Another important posthumous publication is *The Other Cinema*, a collection of Iangirov's articles, compiled by Abram Reitblat and published by *The New Literary Review*. As Reitblat points out, 'the intended plan of the book remains in Iangirov's computer'. Nevertheless, he has tried to follow the plan, including the title proposed by Iangirov. The collection includes articles on the history of pre-Revolutionary, Soviet and émigré cinema. Readers will remember most of them from their first publications, but in book form the articles acquire an additional dimension.

There is one feature in Iangirov's texts that is hard to overlook. Taking into account the specificity of his subjects, they provide evocative and fruitful reading even for those who are not students of the history of cinema. Iangirov paid attention to issues that test the researcher's impartiality — Nicholas II and Lenin as moviegoers, the image of Lenin in Soviet cinema, censorship in the cinema (which, by the way, was no less invasive before the Revolution than in Soviet times), and Jewish film and antisemitism in pre-Revolutionary Russia. Iangirov also managed to maintain a high level of insight in describing the most controversial subjects. As Reitblat notes, his topics relate closely to their social and socio-cultural contexts. This allowed him to use various sources which offered an extensive, extra-cinematic analytical and methodological perspective (for example, in the article on the 'semi-literature' of cinema libretti of the 1900s).

In Iangirov there was a felicitous balance between his roles as editor of primary sources and researcher. These two elements combined in his writings in the most natural way and his texts are full of detail which make them fascinating reading. For example: 'Rejigged segments from a staged newsreel depicting a battle between the Boers and the British were shown in the North Caucasus villages in 1918, purporting to be the Bolsheviks fighting the Cossacks' (p. 131).

Or a quotation from a 1913 article by Peter Ryss: 'We shall probably live to see the day when Holy Scripture will be known via the cinema, and the Old and New Testament will be read by priests only as a professional necessity, and by lovers of various types of archeology' (p. 51). His brilliant study of the life of Alexander Drankov reads almost like a novel by the early Ehrenburg, with the famous sanguine tone he adopted as narrator of incredible stories. Drankov, by the way, was the pioneer promoter of the notorious Constantinople cockroach races that featured a favourite known as 'Love me, Trotsky!' (p. 119).

An historian by training, Iangirov was not only the foremost student of Russian cinema of the first third of the twentieth century, but also a highly professional scholar of Russian literature. Two essays in *The Other Cinema* — 'The Feeling of Film' and '"Ivan" and "Russian Slush": The Paris Controversy' — demonstrate Iangirov's acuity as a multi-dimensional historian of cinema, literature and society, enabling us to see how a discrete topic may be contextualized to enrich both the primary source and its typologically-related phenomena.

The collection dedicated to Iangirov edited by Ian Levchenko reflects another aspect of his life and activity, his gift for attracting people and inspiring colleagues. Iangirov lectured in many cities and countries, organized conferences and led a seminar at the House of the Russian Diaspora in Moscow. The collection includes articles and publications by friends and colleagues, and not only serves as a customary tribute, but also as an extension of the work Iangirov began. Many topics here were pioneered by Iangirov either personally or with co-authors, or evolved simply in conversations with colleagues, here put into final form after his death.

The State Historical and Architectural Museum MIKHAIL EFIMOV
Monrepos Park, Vyborg

Hulík, Štěpán. *Kinematografie zapomnění. Počátky normalizace ve Filmovém studiu Barrandov (1968–1973).* Academia, Prague, 2011. 475 pp. Illustrations. Notes. English Summary. Bibliography. Index. Kč550.00.

IN her introduction to *The Greengrocer and His TV* (Ithaca, NY and London, 2010, reviewed in *SEER*, 89, 2011, 3, pp. 556–58), Paulina Bren pointed out 'the glaring absence of scholarship on late communism' (p. 3). When it comes to Czechoslovak cinema this absence is even more evident, with only two specialized journals in the Czech Republic, *Iluminace* (9, 1997, 1) and *Cinepur* (11, 2002, 21), having addressed the so-called 'normalization' period, while Robert Buchar's *Sametová kocovina* (Brno, 2001) only occasionally refers to it (and mostly in anger). It is still a sensitive topic, with many of its 'actors' (both 'active' and 'passive') still alive. Štěpán Hulík, a young FAMU and Charles University graduate and scriptwriter, has boldly undertaken the task of diminishing that absence. His is, therefore, a most welcome book, and has been well received in the Czech Republic, winning the Magnesia Litera prize in 2012 as *objev roku* ('discovery/newcomer') of the year.

Bren used 'television as a prism through which to view the 1970s and 1980s' (p. 7) but Hulík, in the Czech scholarly tradition of 'literatura faktu', simply examines the facts. The aim of the book, as its English summary states, is to describe: 'the changes of the aftermath of August 1968 in Czechoslovak film on the transformation of one place — the Barrandov Film Studio' (p. 444), and the 'specific fates of individual New Wave filmmakers in the first years of normalization and to portray the creators loyal to the new regime' (p. 444).

The book is impressively researched. Hulík has had rare access to the archives at the Barrandov film studio and labs, enabling him to formulate a very clear picture of the on-going processes of 'normalization' inside the studio. More than this, he has put names to policies and actions, and also identified those unfortunate enough to be in receipt of those actions. This is a more detailed and extensive account than the work of Hames, Liehm or Žalman, for example, but it does not differ in essence from the accepted 'discourses' — that Czechoslovak nationalized cinema was purged during the 1970s, cutting short the talent that had made it famous during the 1960s, which in turn explains to a certain extent the mediocrity of film production ever since.

Another welcome feature of the book is that it includes several interviews with people on both sides of the 'normalization'; with those who implemented it, such as Jiří Purš, at the time head of Czechoslovak Film, or Jan Balzer, head of production at Barrandov, and with those whose careers virtually ended as a result of its implementation, such as the director Ladislav Helge. Without judging the 'normalizators', and without wanting to judge them, Hulík gives the reader the opportunity to read the reasoning behind their actions, casting new light on the post-'68 years.

Nevertheless, he misses an opportunity to analyse in depth the aesthetics of the period and, more disappointingly, the 'normalization' films themselves, through which a greater understanding of the period could be achieved. Hulík rightly states on several occasions that the Communist authorities reintroduced Socialist Realism to cinema in the early 1970s, but he assumes that the reader already knows what he means by this. At no point does he attempt to analyse what the characteristics of this re-introduction of Socialist Realism, or 'neo-socialist realism', were, and except for Vladimir Čech's *Klič* (1971), does little more than merely mention the relevant films. The question as to whether 1970/80s 'neo-socialist realism' differed from 1950s Socialist Realism remains unanswered and its ramifications unexplored. These questions are, after all, the 'prism through which to view the 1970s and 1980s'.

Arts University College Bournemouth CESAR BALLESTER

Skakov, Nariman. *The Cinema of Tarkovsky: Labyrinths of Space and Time.* KINO: The Russian and Soviet Film Series. I. B. Tauris, London and New York, 2012. xii + 262 pp. Illustrations. Notes. Filmography and credits. Bibliography. Index. £17.99 (paperback).

Nariman Skakov's new monograph is a highly accessible introduction to Tarkovskii's practice and inspiration. Skakov's breadth of reading — notably including Gilles Deleuze and Susan Sontag, but also Hegel, Borges, Benjamin and Foucault — interacts with the dense texture of Tarkovskii's eclectic influences and citations, ranging from Montaigne to Florenskii and Beckett (whose pseudo-quest novel, *Molloy*, may have been a seminal influence on *Stalker*). The opening paragraph, linking Tarkovskii's and Mandel´shtam's images of time as an almost-tangible object unfolding in space, hints at the wealth of associations to come.

Skakov's analysis of Tarkovskii builds on Deleuze's concept of the cinematic 'time-image' and of 'chronically non-chronological time' as fundamental markers of European neo-realism. This is film-making as *chronema* rather than *kinema*, that is, as an attempted portrayal of the movement *of* time rather than movement *in* time. Tarkovskii's major contribution to this tradition, Skakov argues, was to emphasize 'the discontinuity of the filmic experience', as his camera examines the 'imaginary, oneiric, and hallucinatory potential' of the genre and thereby casts doubt on reality itself (p. 11). Such thinking is already familiar from the recent work of Robert Bird and others; nor does Skakov seriously challenge the Deleuzian hegemony within film theory, although he does suggest that Tarkovskii's perspective on the time-image is less metaphysical and more anthropocentric than the French philosopher's. Instead, Skakov tilts his critical emphasis away from the director's famous concept of 'sculpting in time' towards the spatial co-ordinates in which time transpires; in Tarkovskian cinema, not only is time out of joint, 'space is also out of place' (p. 5). This displaced space could be the crumbling peasant hut where Ivan encounters the maddened, war-widowed peasant in *Ivan's Childhood*; or the almost anachronistically dilapidated space station of *Solaris*; or the ruined Italian churches visited by Gorchakov in *Nostalghia*. Here Skakov borrows another Deleuzian concept: *l'espace quelconque* (any-place-whatever) is any uninhabited or anonymous location, forcing characters (often repeatedly) to define and identify themselves by their situation. This idea is sustained throughout Skakov's chronological discussion of the seven full-length films. Clearly, Skakov differs from Aleksei German's description of Tarkovskii as a 'great practitioner' rather than a 'great thinker'; he argues that Tarkovskii's aesthetic labyrinth 'still has an unambiguous route to the centre', and that the ever-multiplying discontinuities experienced by characters and viewers alike 'lead towards the creation of some kind of spiritual totality' (p. 218).

Each chapter associates one film with a specific temporal device which transcends or replaces linear narrative. *Ivan's Childhood* is thus characterized by 'dreams'; *Andrei Rublev* by 'visions'; *Solaris* by its uncanny, living 'phantasies'. Skakov frequently resorts to the *OED* to justify a revealing lexical distinction: here, between 'phantasy' ('a visionary notion') and 'fantasy' (mere whimsicality). *Mirror* is linked with 'memories'; *Stalker* with 'revelations'; *Nostalghia* with 'recollections', and *Sacrifice* with 'illusions'. Throughout, Skakov nimbly interpolates relevant critical theory (Willard Quine, for instance, on the problems of translation and mutual understanding behind *Nostalghia*), extracts from Tarkovskii's diaries and screenplays, historical anecdotes on the making of the films (the disastrous long take of the burning house in *Sacrifice*), and detailed discussion of the director's visual and literary source texts (Bruegel's paintings and Cervantes's *Don Quixote* in *Solaris*). Arsenii Tarkovskii's poems are translated and cited in full. A close reading of the citation from *Inferno* in *Mirror* reveals Tarkovskii's deliberate, and consequential, mistranslation of Dante's text. *Solaris* and *Ivan's Childhood* are usefully contrasted with the original novels by Lem and Bogomolov; the Strugatskii brothers' *Roadside Picnic*, the source text for *Stalker*, is almost neglected, perhaps because the original was wholly transformed during the screenplay's multiple redactions. Skakov perpetuates a misleading opposition between the cinematic Stalker, a visionary, pacific 'holy fool', and the supposedly 'vagabond' rapscallion from the Strugatskiis' novel (dismissed by Tarkovskii even more contemptuously as a 'bandit'). In fact, the Strugatskiis' stalker-hero is an uxorious professional, who markets artefacts from the Zone to protect his family's future; hardly a vagabond.

This book is a supplement to, rather than a replacement for, Robert Bird's *Andrei Tarkovsky: Elements of Cinema* (London, 2008); both books cover the same ground, differing in detail. Presentation would be enhanced by the use of individual large captioned images rather than the relatively tiny screenshots clustered at intervals throughout Skakov's book — although these clusters do illustrate the passage of time in the evolution of characters and motifs. Insightful and classroom-friendly, *Tarkovsky: Labyrinths of Space and Time* takes a worthy place among critical attempts to verbalize the director's quixotic task: 'to utter the unutterable' (p. 132).

Wadham College, University of Oxford MUIREANN MAGUIRE

Kniazeva, Janna (ed.). *Jacques Handschin in Russland: Die neu aufgefundenen Texte.* Basler Publikationen zur Älteren und Neueren Musik, 1. Schwabe, Basel, 2011. 1045 pp. Illustrations. Index. €69.00.

IF British scholars are at all familiar with the life and work of Jacques Handschin — described in Martin Kirnbauer and Ulrich Moschs's introduction to this volume as 'zweifellos einer der bedeutendsten und originellsten Musikwissenschaftler des 20. Jahrhunderts' (p. 12) — then it is as Professor of

Music at the University of Basel from 1935 until his death in 1955, and as the author of a number of important German-language monographs on aspects of medieval music history, as well as on the psychology of music. Yet Handschin was born into a mercantile Swiss family in Moscow in 1886, and lived and worked in Russia until his emigration in 1920. There, abandoning the life in trade that his parents anticipated for him, he rapidly gained a reputation as one of Russia's leading organists (he taught the instrument at the St Petersburg Conservatory from 1909, becoming Professor there in 1916). Until the appearance of Janna Kniazeva's fundamental biographical and bibliographical study, however, little more was known about Handschin's activities in Russia. Western scholars had no access to the published and archival sources that would have painted a fuller picture of his previous life; Soviet scholars, by contrast, were unable to work on a 'foreign' musician who had chosen to emigrate to the West. Drawing on an extensive range of sources, Kniazeva establishes for the first time the breadth and significance of the Russian period in Handschin's life. Her major coup is the discovery of a vast corpus of reviews published in the German-language *St. Petersburger Zeitung* between September 1910 and December 1914. These reviews, the authorship of which was long hidden by the use of a cryptonym, are reproduced in full in the second half of Kniazeva's volume (along with reviews and articles written for other Russian, German and Swiss journals, a selection of his correspondence with Russian colleagues, and a memoir written by Handschin's first wife, Helen Agricola). These newly-discovered materials reveal that Handschin was far more central to the history of Russian music than might previously have been suspected, and will be of considerable interest to musicologists and historians concerned with concert life in St Petersburg in the early twentieth century. Although Kniazeva notes that Handschin's approach was 'eher emotional-deskriptiv denn analytisch' (p. 125), her substantial introduction (itself as long as many monographs) nonetheless discerns a number of key principles underlying his criticism. Handschin was closely associated with a generation of composers and teachers active in St Petersburg between the death of Rimskii-Korsakov in 1908 and the Bolshevik revolution of 1917. This generation often receives scant attention in music history, especially in the West, where their cosmopolitanism, conservatoire training and perceived conservatism mean that they fail to accord with widespread clichés about Russia's contribution to nationalism (as in the case of the nineteenth-century nationalists) or to modernism and the avant-garde (whether in the case of Stravinskii in Paris, or Shostakovich in Soviet Russia). To this day, leading representatives of the St Petersburg school — Glazunov, Liapunov, Liadov — enjoy less popular exposure and critical attention than their Muscovite counterparts (Rakhmaninov, Skriabin and Medtner). Kniazeva argues, however, that Handschin's commitment to the St Petersburg tradition was no instance of narrow local patriotism (an unlikely attitude for someone born in Moscow of Swiss parents), but rather that it embodied a syncretic vision of the imperial capital as a multinational, multi-ethnic and multilingual entity that had much to offer European music more generally. This idiosyncratic recapitulation of traditional Russian messianism may go some way to explaining Handschin's rather unexpected attachment to Musorgskii and — despite his initial dislike of *Petrushka* and *The Rite of Spring* — to Stravinskii, both of whom had managed to overcome the burden of romanticism. If this idea suggests parallels with aspects of musical Eurasianism, then this may be tangentially related to Handschin's contacts with younger St Petersburg modernists, including Lur′e, Suvchinskii and Asaf′ev. Even at an ideological level, Handschin appears to have been 'neutral' enough to stay on in Russia after the Revolution, working for the musical division of the People's Commissariat of Enlightenment (where he helped establish Valentin Kovalenkov's experimental acoustic laboratory). Kniazeva's thorough and scrupulous research establishes in full the details of Handschin's contribution to Russian musical life, although the influence of this period on his subsequent work in Switzerland will be clearer to those already familiar with the secondary literature on that topic. Music history has long been written along lines inherited from the Humboldtian vision of discrete national literatures, with the result that figures who cross linguistic, cultural and ethnic borders have often been written out of many accounts of artistic life in individual countries. Scrupulously annotated and referenced, lucidly written and argued, and beautifully produced by its publisher, *Jacques Handschin in Russland* restores one such figure to the historical record in exemplary fashion, and makes a crucial contribution to the contemporary study of cosmopolitanism and the comparative history of modern European culture in a way that entirely befits its subject.

Wadham College, University of Oxford PHILIP ROSS BULLOCK

Szvák, Gyula (ed.). *Gosudarstvo i natsiia v Rossii i Tsentral′no-vostochnoi Evrope / State and Nation in Russia and Central-East-Europe*. 'Knigi po rusistike' of the Joint Research Group on Russian Studies of the Hungarian Academy of Sciences and Eötvös Loránd University, 22. Russica Pannonica, Budapest, 2009. 368 pp. Illustrations. Tables. Notes. Price unknown.

THIS miscellany is the product of a conference held in Budapest in May 2008, the sixth in a series in the field of Russian studies which began in 1998. Ranging over more than a thousand years (from the ninth century to the present day), it contains thirty essays, five in English, twenty-five in Russian, twenty-three on Russia, seven, respectively, on the Varangian question and the origins of statehood among the eastern Slavs; the Ukrainian Hetmanate in the later seventeenth and early eighteenth centuries; eighteenth-century frescoes in a Serbian church in Hungary; policies towards Hungarians of leading political figures in the eighteenth-century Habsburg Empire; 'State, Language and Nation in the Habsburg Monarchy in the Second Half of the Eighteenth Century'; national minorities in Transylvania at the time of the Nazi-Soviet Pact; and Hungarian interpretations of the past and present of the Finno-Ugrian peoples in Russia. Just under half of the contributors work in Russia (all but one of them in Moscow, most of them in various institutes of the Academy of Sciences), just under half in six or seven different institutions in Hungary, three in the USA and one in the UK. Other than the relative geographical proximity of their subjects of study and the concern which nearly all the authors evince for the latest historiography in their respective fields, the essays seem at first sight to have little in common. Closer inspection, however, reveals that they all attempt, however variously, to embrace the 'State and Nation' rubric of the book. Highlights from the point of view of the present reviewer included V. V. Fomin on the relationship between the origins of statehood among the eastern Slavs and the coming of the Varangians; Maureen Perrie's appraisal of the views of Geoffrey Hosking and Serhy Plokhy on the question whether and to what extent Russia ceased to be the patrimony of a single family after the coming of the Romanovs in 1613 and began to become a nation; Endre Sashalmi's detailed discussion of the point in time at which Russia might be said to have become a 'fiscal-military' state along the lines of the the other states in seventeenth- and eighteenth-century Europe which have attracted this designation; Erzsébet Bodnar's judicious if rather indecisive review of the literature on the extent to which the early nineteenth-century reign of Alexander I of Russia can be considered an important stage in the 'modernization' of the Russian empire; A. N. Medushevskii's description of the way in which Nicholas II's criminal code of 1903 distinguished between legitimate political activity and 'political crimes', and of the difficulty which the tsar's courts experienced in attempting to put the code's provisions in this area into practice; Brigit Farley's sympathetic account of the Gorbachev-era grassroots initiative which led to the rebuilding of the cathedral of the Kazan′ Mother of God on Red Square in Moscow (an initiative which, as the author points out, is unlikely to be repeated in the strongly directive Russian state which obtains at present), and the prolific N. F. Bugai's very fully annotated discussion of some of the problems in the field of ethnic difference to which the rulers of the Russian Federation have had to turn their minds in the last twenty years. All specialists in the field of Russian history, and many students of the history of East-Central Europe, will find something to their taste in this collection.

School of History, Classics and Archaeology DAVID SAUNDERS
Newcastle University

Banyó, Péter and Rady, Martyn (eds, trans). *The Laws of the Medieval Kingdom of Hungary, Volume 4, 1490–1526*. The Laws of Hungary Series I: Volume 4. Charles Schlacks Jr and Department of Medieval Studies, Central European University, Idyllwild, CA and Budapest, 2012. lvi + 336 pp. Notes. Bibliography. Indices. Glossary and Select Subject Index. $55.00: €50.00: £45.00.

Bak, János M., Banyó, Péter and Rady, Martyn (eds, trans). *The Laws of the Medieval Kingdom of Hungary, Volume 5, The Customary Law of the Renowned Kingdom of Hungary: A Work in Three Parts Rendered by Stephen Werbőczy (The 'Tripartitum')*. The Laws of Hungary Series I: Volume 5. Charles Schlacks Jr and Department of Medieval Studies, Central European University, Idyllwild, CA and Budapest, 2005. l + 473. Illustrations. Notes. Appendices. Glossary and Select Subject Index. Bibliography. Index of Chapters. CD-ROM. $55.00: €50.00: £45.00.

LEGAL sources are important to a wide variety of historians, so collections which improve accessibility are to be welcomed. These books are volumes four and five in a five volume series covering legislation of the medieval kingdom of Hungary (vols. 1–4) and the *Tripartitum Opus* of Stephen Werbőczy, a statement of legislated and customary Hungarian law. Both volumes are parallel texts of the original Latin and English, each with an introductory essay. The volumes overlap chronologically and Werbőczy is a prominent figure in the introductory essay to volume four meaning it is profitable to read both volumes. Volume four includes a CD-ROM which features digital copies of both the volume itself and all the legislation from the Diet from 1490–1526 in the original Latin only. Both are in PDF format and the text is searchable, providing a useful resource.

It is always difficult to translate technical literature, but generally the translations are very good. Coming from a background in legal history, one or two of the translations could have been more precise or the technical difficulties identified. For example, in volume five the use of the language of ownership as a translation for Latin nouns and verbs which would usually be translated as about possession (pp. 59, 63 and 65) was not remarked upon by the translators or editors. In medieval legal thought possession was a lesser property right than ownership. Although Werbőczy himself eventually explains his use of terminology (p. 81), it would have been useful for the translators to make the point themselves. Identifying the difficulty might have drawn attention to the fact that Werbőczy never uses the Latin language of ownership (*dominium*) for the rights that nobles and others held in their land, but does refer to *dominium* in the context of chattels (pp. 145 and 147). Werbőczy's choice of language about rights in land constantly (and subtly) reinforces the political relationship between the king and nobility which he states early in the book and to which the introductory essays draw attention as important for Hungarian constitutional theory: that the nobility received their estates from the king (p. 51).

Both volumes feature glossaries which also serve as subject indices. The glossary to volume four (the final volume to be produced) also serves as a subject index to the series as a whole. It is worth noting that the spelling in the Latin texts has not been standardized with that in the glossary. If searching for material on the CD-ROM for volume four, readers should expect to search for variant spellings (for example, *congregatio* in the glossary is *congregacio* in many of the Latin texts).

Volume four is a collection of legislation from the Diet in the years 1490–1526. The introductory essay by Martyn Rady is simply entitled 'Jagello Hungary', focusing on its governance and arguing that the period was not one of decline in government, finance or institutions (including increasing assertiveness, or even authority, on the part of the Diet), even if it was different in many respects to the reign of Matthias Corvinus. Rady also presents a case for a growing national consciousness based on a developing national history.

For reasons of space volume four does not contain a complete collection of legislation from 1490–1526. The criteria for inclusion are set out on page xlviii: *decreta* are included if they are 'politically important' or contain new legal or procedural measures. Other *decreta* are omitted entirely, as are passages in the selected *decreta* which merely repeat earlier laws. Some 'overly verbose' articles have been summarized in English and omitted in Latin. Such omissions are understandable, but less than ideal. The CD-ROM is an attempt to remedy the deficiency.

Even in this reduced form, volume four demonstrates the range of activities of the Diet. One can see: recurring concern about the upholding of noble privileges as the established law of the realm; the relationship between ecclesiastical and secular jurisdictions; reactions to Lutheranism (described as a 'sect' in 1523, p. 263) and the rebellion of 1514; and perennial worries about the availability of seals to create documents with evidential value and the risk of fraud. In some respects one can trace changes in the wider context, something which is evident in the various rules concerned with tithes, a topic which apparently provoked such 'dissensions and quarrels' that the Diet struggled to decide anything (p. 75). In 1492 and 1495 the decrees about tithes reaffirmed the nobility's exemption from payment, as well as addressing a technical question about how bees, lambs and kids should be tithed (p. 77), a decree which was supplemented by even more detail in 1498 (p. 125). In the sixteenth century, decrees about tithes focused on the obligations of the recipients of tithes to provide troops, even ordering the payment of tithe income for that purpose. A topic which initially concerned matters of noble privilege and technical questions changed to become a means to try to maintain the defence of the realm in the face of military threats.

Volume five is different to the other four volumes in the series. Rather than collecting legislation, this volume is a translation of the *Tripartitum Opus* of Werbőczy, an occasionally contradictory and certainly not comprehensive work first printed in 1517. Essentially it is a work concerning the law relating to the nobility of the kingdom of Hungary, especially their special privileges and rules related to their landholding. Like other medieval collections of customary law it contains little about commercial matters, although there is some discussion of contracts related to land. The volume includes two introductory essays. The essay by László Péter is concerned with the afterlife of Werbőczy's work, particularly in relation to constitutional and political developments. Martyn Rady's introduction is a biography of Werbőczy into which is sandwiched some discussion of aspects of the *Tripartitum* itself.

The *Tripartitum* was quickly accepted as a statement of Hungarian law, but that does not mean that it is an accurate representation of the law at the time it was written. As Rady observes, Werbőczy sometimes used his power as author to express his own views of what the law ought to be (5, p. xxxvii). Werbőczy was a lawyer, but also an active politician who in the 1520s used print to produce what Rady describes as 'propaganda' (4, p. xli). Should we consider whether the printing of the *Tripartitum*, without the approval of the king or Diet, was also a tool for propagating Werbőczy's own views about the Hungarian constitution? This issue is not raised by the editors, but is important. Certainly Werbőczy used the book to set out his opinions on Hungarian history, a history which was used to justify social and constitutional arrangements. Presenting a particular political view as the old established law was not a novel technique in medieval (or early-modern) Europe. The claim in the *Tripartitum* that the text was approved by the Diet in 1514 also merits consideration: the incorporation of material about the changes to the law concerning peasants in the wake of the rebellion of 1514 suggests that Werbőczy amended the text after it had been presented to the Diet.

Rady's introduction to volume four argues that Hungary *c.*1500 can be seen as part of broader European trends in governance. One disappointment with these volumes was the general omission of consideration of non-Hungarian ideas, despite these probably being of considerable importance. For example, the Diet's decision about tithing lambs may have been due to uncertainty in the wider European canon law, where it had been disputed whether lambs were praedial or personal tithes. As personal tithes were often not collected, this was an academic question with potentially important practical effects. The influence of European ideas on Werbőczy's *Tripartitum* is acknowledged (particularly with regard to the prologue), identified as a controversial topic, but not really discussed (5, pp. xiv and xxxiv). From a historiographical perspective, Werbőczy's book raises interesting questions about how far we can see late-medieval Hungary as part of the European *ius commune*, the shared body of legal methods and ideas which developed through the teaching and study of Roman and canon laws, starting in Italy in the eleventh century. From that perspective, unanswered, even unaddressed, questions remain about whether the late-medieval Hungarian kingdom should be regarded as part of the Western European legal tradition or (like England) an unusual outlier.

Faculty of Laws, UCL IAN WILLIAMS

Fudge, Thomas A. *Jan Hus: Religious Reform and Social Revolution in Bohemia*. I. B. Tauris, London and New York, 2010. xx + 367 pp. Maps. Illustrations. Notes. Select bibliography. Index. £54.50.

WHEN English speakers, or indeed most individuals outside of the Czech Republic, think of the Czech lands in the medieval period, the subject most commonly brought to mind is the Hussites. That the popular imagination should focus upon this group is no surprise, as the period from Jan Hus's rise to prominence at Prague's Bethlehem chapel in the early fifteenth century until the battle of White Mountain in 1620 was one of the most tumultuous in the history of Bohemia. Moreover, beyond the movement's significance in its native kingdom, the fact that it can be considered as the first comprehensive Christian reformation gives it considerable importance in the history of Europe in general. Yet as important as the subject may be, it is a regrettable fact that there exist very few studies of it English, with the majority of works in either the native language of Hus and his followers, or in German.

Filling this unfortunate gap is Thomas A. Fudge's welcome work *Jan Hus: Religious Reform and Social Revolution in Bohemia*, which provides English-language readers with a comprehensive overview of Jan Hus's life, theological ideas, and the revolution and commemoration which followed his demise. Fudge's work is remarkable both for the depth in which it considers Hus's theology and the clarity and simplicity with which it is able to explain it. This notable quality means that the book is an excellent source for both theological and Czech history scholars, who will appreciate Fudge's well-contextualized approach to the subject, as well as those looking for an introduction to Hussite studies, who will find even the most complex aspects of Hus's doctrinal beliefs articulated with lucidity.

One of the most laudable and refreshing aspects of *Jan Hus* is the author's ability to discuss the life and work of Hus within his own late-medieval context. The historiography of Hus often been mired in contemporary interpretations, in which authors attempt to evaluate his ideas using modern conceptions of piety or nationalistic pride in order to save him from the ignominy of heresy. Fudge manages to side-step the pitfalls of such an approach, stating quite rightly that through stringent analysis in a medieval framework, 'Hus can be regarded both as a reformer and a heretic' (p. 4).

To prove this statement he takes readers through Hus's biography, a discussion of the socio-religious circumstances of fifteenth-century Prague and then a careful analysis of his theological ideas. In introducing the basic facts of Hus's life and surrounds readers are able to better appreciate the circumstances which may have influenced his ideas. For example, when one considers the 'preoccupation with moral behaviour' (p. 23) flourishing in Prague's reform movements at the end of the fourteenth century, one is better able to understand how it was that later Hus would argue that 'the unrighteous are incapable of following the law of Christ', and that '[s]alvation can only be accessible to humankind on divine initiative' (p. 42).

Fudge also takes care to underpin the meaning of Hus's theological ideas with a thorough discussion of the spirituality behind it, discussing the late-medieval interest in personal piety as an aspect of faith separate from formal religion. The author's careful analysis of the mystical medieval emphasis on prayer, for example, is of particular use to those seeking to understand Hus's fervent emphasis on what Fudge terms as 'proper prayer' (p. 78) and its spiritual benefits in the fight against what he saw as the three spiritual enemies of the devout: the world, the flesh and the Devil (p. 86).

Yet, perhaps the most enjoyable aspect of the book for those well aware of the Hus historiography is Fudge's chapter on attempts to rehabilitate and overturn Hus's medieval designation as a heretic (pp. 227–40). Fudge deftly argues against such attempts, stating that it is impossible to remove Hus from his medieval context, and '"unhereticate" [him] without doing violence to history' (p. 240). The author's dedication to seeing Hus as a man of his time is heartening, as is his insistence that '[a]ccording to the medieval world, Jan Hus was a heretic. There is no shame in that' (p. 240). It is this approach which makes *Jan Hus* such a valuable work, and one which should appear in any discussion of English-language works on late medieval Bohemia for some time to come.

UCL SSEES ELEANOR JANEGA

Mikes, Kelemen. *Lettres de Turquie*. Edited by Michel Marty, translated and annotated by Krisztina Kaló and Thierry Fouilleul. Bibliothèque d'Études de l'Europe Centrale, 7. Honoré Champion, Paris, 2011. 384 pp. Illustration. Map. Notes. Chronology. Bibliography. Glossaries. Index. €81.00.

FROM 1703 until 1711 the Hungarian *kuruc* forces, led by Ferenc II Rákóczi, last prince of independent Transylvania, fought against Austria in an effort to secure independence. When defeat was imminent Rákóczi and a small court left for Poland in the vain hope of raising support from Peter the Great of Russia. They eventually found their way to exile in France and then Turkey, where the prince and most of his court spent the rest of their lives. One of the courtiers was Kelemen Mikes, who in Turkey wrote a memoir in the form of 207 letters addressed to a fictitious 'Countess P. E. in Constantinople'. They tell of the life of the exiled court, comment on current affairs in Turkey and Europe, reveal the writer's *Weltanschauung* and recount many an anecdote. Discovered after his death and first published in 1794, the *Törökországi levelek* have gained recognition for outstanding literary and historical interest, and as the finest Hungarian prose work of the eighteenth century.

In 2011 the 250th anniversary of Mikes's death — and the 300th of the end of the War of Independence — has been marked by vigorous activity in the Institute for Literary Studies of the Hungarian Academy of Sciences, with Professor Gábor Tüskés, head of the Eighteenth Century department, in the forefront. A three-day international conference took place in Budapest in October, and the occasion saw the publication *inter alia* of this translation of the *Letters*, the first complete one into French.

Nothing could be better calculated to introduce the new reader to the *Letters* than Antal Szerb's account of the work in his *History of Hungarian Literature*, the full translation of which forms the introduction. That most vital, most brilliant champion of Hungarian letters is at his francophile best: 'En sa qualité d'humble membre de la cour du prince exilé, Mikes est assis là, dans l'antichambre des grands seigneurs français, il bénéficie de l'enseignement de maîtres français, va au théâtre, assiste à des solennités, flâne l'âme ouverte, comme tant de Hongrois après lui, dans les rues de Paris' (pp. 9–10). One senses from his essay, 'Nyaralás a könyvtárban' ('Holidaying in the Library'), how deeply Szerb meant those last words. Mikes is 'a grey man', no *éminence* indeed, rather one whom his French visitors record no more than he records them, who gave no sign of latent talent until he too had emerged from his Parisian Bakony.

Professor Bérenger's preface offers a very much more than adequate account of the historical and political background of the War of Independence. He considers the situation in Hungary and Transylvania, the war itself, Poland, the Ottoman Empire, Bourbon Spain, the Austro-Turkish war of 1716–18, the War of Austrian Succession and the changes in the post-1756 balance of power. This comprehensive overview of Central European history from the late Middle Ages until the early modern period deals succinctly with events before, during and after the writing of the *Letters* — an exemplary *multum in parvo*.

The translation is followed by notes from the translators on a number of practical points that they found it necessary to consider. Some of these concern specific items, such as pre-metric measurements which may have approximate French equivalents (e.g. *toise* and *lieue*), or Hungarian words that have deceptively changed meaning over the years (*ház*, *szállít*), or even fallen into disuse (*poltura*, *kéd*, *ihon*); some are the problems of a dialect that causes difficulty even for the modern Hungarian reader of the original. Mikes is often enough at pains to insist that he is not only a Transylvanian but a Székely, and his language — though that of an educated man — is flavoured with many a 'székelyism'. There is discussion of how best to treat Mikes's frequently repeated *néne*, his term of address and reference to his fictitious correspondent; they opt for *cousine,* which is a better *nom d'amitié* than *tante* might have been; in English, the opposite seems to be true. There is, however, one topic to which the translators modestly fail to refer: who they are. Dr Krisztina Kaló is a Hungarian, Senior Lecturer in the Department of French Language and Literature at Eszterházy Károly Főiskola, Eger, while Thierry Fouilleul is French and has taught French at the University of Veszprém, Eötvös Loránd University, Budapest, and the Lycée français, Budapest, and done much translation and editorial work.

These notes are followed in the book by a map showing places that Mikes is known to have visited — not only places mentioned in the *Letters* — which sadly does not record his visit to Hull; on the other hand, quarantine regulations — he had come from plague-stricken Danzig — did not allow him to land there during his stay but kept him aboard ship in the Humber estuary, so that to call this an omission is, perhaps, stretching a point. There follows a chronology listing events in politics, society, letters, science and arts from 1664 to 1794, an extensive bibliography, a glossary of Turkish terms, one of personal names (in which, to the proofreader's shame, the Frenchman Jacques de Boissimène is listed both as serving at the Porte Sublime and as the second wife of Henry VIII of England and mother of Elizabeth I *vice* the unfortunate Anne Boleyn), one of geographical names and an index of personal names.

The translation itself occupies the greater part of the book. It is excellent. The translators refer in their notes to having to decide — as is always the case in dealing with an old text — whether to offer a reproduction of the French contemporary with the original, to contrive an 'antiqued' idiolect, or whether to use modern language; after an original draft in the first was felt to be unsatisfactory they tended towards the second, modernizing their first version. This difficulty is compounded by the question of dialect — there simply is no French counterpart to Székely Hungarian, and to show partiality for some modern dialect would be at best misleading, though the dialectal nature of the original is hinted at by the use from time to time of the odd unusual word, while its archaic quality is reflected in the judicious use of high-register vocabulary and old-fashioned syntax. The result strikes a perfect balance between content and style and is a pleasure to read.

To make any sort of selection from the *Letters* is always a thankless task, but perhaps a quotation or two will not be out of place: Letter 56 reveals Mikes's yearning for home cooking:

> peu de femmes et d'hommes sont capables d'écrire d'aussi belles lettres que vous. Elles charment l'esprit comme un beau plat appétissant la bouche. Je voulais évoquer le chou, mais je n'ose pas de peur que vous disiez que je

compare votre lettre à un chou… Eh bien, je le dirai quand même: une lettre bien écrite charme l'esprit comme les yeux le chou à l'aneth couvert de crème fraîche, qui de loin semble être un monticule d'argent au-dessous duquel, une fois cette molle couverture argentée retirée, on découvre une herbe précieuse.

The prince's death, the most significant event in all the Letters, is announced in Letter 112 of 8 April 1735:

Ce que nous redoutions, nous y voici. Dieu nous a rendus orphelins, aujourd'hui il nous a enlevé notre tendre seigneur et père, ce matin après trois heures. Comme aujourd'hui nous sommes vendredi saint, il nous faut pleurer la mort de nos pères au Ciel et sur la terre. Dieu a différé la mort de notre seigneur à aujourd'hui afin de sanctifier son sacrifice par le mérite de Celui qui est mort pour nous. À voir la vie qu'il a vécue et la mort qu'il a eue, je crois qu'on lui a dit: 'Aujourd'hui tu seras avec moi dans le Paradis.

The translators provide footnotes on numerous points of interest. These shed light on some of the obscure, folksy phrases that Mikes uses from time to time, on biblical references, allusions to popular songs, historical characters and events and more besides — all evidence of extensive research. Valuable historical notes also come from Ferenc Tóth; I beg to correct him, however on page 78 — Simon Forgách was, according to Rákóczi's memoirs, not *commandant général* of the *kuruc* army; he was arrested for insubordination in late November or early December 1706 and incarcerated for the rest of the war, first in Szepes castle — where a failed attempt at escape left him with a permanent limp — then 'in honourable confinement' at Munkács. The only other negative comment that one can offer concerns the transcription of Turkish: Mikes acquired almost no Turkish in his long exile, and his spelling of Turkish words leaves much to be desired. The translators comment that they have kept these in *une orthographe unifiée*, which is neither wholly French, Hungarian nor modern Turkish; it would have been advisable, in both the text and the list of Turkish words, exclusively to use modern Turkish orthography, provide a guide to pronunciation, and italicize Turkish (and Greek) words in the text.

Such minor blemishes, however, in no way detract from the thorough excellence of the whole. *Letters from Turkey* is a splendid book which ought to be much more widely known. It is already available in German, Italian, English, Turkish, Polish, Romanian, Esperanto and Mongolian [*sic*] translations, and one is confident that this new French version will find an appreciative francophone audience and meet with the resounding success that it deserves.

Zánka Bernard Adams

Butler, William E. and Tomsinov, Vladimir A. (eds). *The Nakaz of Catherine the Great: Collected Texts*. The Lawbook Exchange, Clark, NJ, 2010. 531 pp. Texts. Bibliography of printed editions. $95.00.

KLIUCHEVSKII changed his mind about the *Nakaz*: from the view that it occupied but a modest place alike in Russian literature and legislation, he moved on to the assertion that its publication was a highly remarkable action by which a large number of people became acquainted with the best new ideas. The consensus today appears to support the latter appraisal, with very little if any support for Pokrovskii's argument that the *Nakaz* was a piece of irresponsible plagiarism notable only for its petty contribution to the burgeoning ideology of the nobility.

William E. Butler and Vladimir A. Tomsinov accept Isabel de Madariaga's assertion that Catherine the Great's use of words and the nature of her borrowings from other writers give a special significance to the translations of the *Nakaz*. They duly present texts in Russian, French, Latin, German and English. They assert that the Latin version was 'pure vanity', 'intended to reinforce Catherine's pretension to be seen as the Russian Justinian and reaffirm the link between Catherinian Russia and the Byzantine Roman Empire in matters of lawgiving'. But the other renderings suggest to them that the work 'was intended by Catherine not merely as a fulcrum for domestic discussions about possible internal reforms, but as an act of Imperial creation and provenance for consideration throughout the civilized world' (pp. ix–x).

When the Empress herself was working years later on comparative vocabularies, she expressed astonishment that words in a wide range of languages could have cognate affinities. In the narrower range of the *Nakaz* translations, however, to take one example from article 406, 'property' in English, 'Vermögen' in German, 'biens' in French and 'imenie' in Russian all have different roots linguistically. They all stem, too, from specific historical traditions. To attribute an essential meaning to this key concept is therefore difficult. As a German writing in French while closely acquainted with Russian and distantly with English, Catherine must have been aware of problems which the Butler-Tomsinov publication illumines.

In a real sense, then, this book reopens the question of the importance of the *Nakaz* at the same time as giving a significant part of the answer. Possibly, more attention needs to be given to its context in order to effect an objective appraisal. This must include Catherine's usurpation of power in 1762 and her policies in subsequent years. To agree with Pokrovskii would be going too far, but there is perhaps a case for Pushkin's dismissal of a 'Tartuffe in skirts'.

Butler and Tomsinov deserve our thanks for their multilingual edition of this significant document. But they should not have let Rousseau appear on its cover as one of its major sources.

University of Aberdeen PAUL DUKES

Kronauer, Ulrich (ed.). *Aufklärer im Baltikum. Europäischer Kontext und regionale Besonderheiten.* Akademie-konferenzen, 12. Im Auftrag der Heidelberger Akademie der Wissenschaften, Akademie der Wissenschaften des Landes Baden-Württemberg. Universitätsverlag Winter, Heidelberg, 2011. 263 pp. Illustrations. Tables. Notes. €32.00 (paperback).

In recent scholarship on the Enlightenment, its geographical distribution and national or regional variants have been much to the fore, as have the problems of core and periphery. This volume seeks to approach the Enlightenment in the 'Baltic German' provinces of the Russian Empire, nowadays effectively Latvia and Estonia, from a similar perspective. It presents selected papers from a conference sponsored by the Heidelberg Academy of Sciences and its German Jurisprudence Dictionary (*Deutsches Rechtswörterbuch, DRW*) in 2008, in conjunction with several Baltic academic institutions. The rather unexpected link stemmed initially from the *DRW*'s interest in Baltic German legal terminology; it was strengthened by the fact that one of the principal figures treated here, C. G. Jochmann (1789–1830), studied and published in Heidelberg. It is in any case quite appropriate: manifestations of the Enlightenment in Russia's Baltic provinces were more closely connected with German than with Russian culture, and were fuelled by immigrant graduates of German universities as well as the intellectual interests of the area's urban and clerical elites. The twelve papers included here range widely in character, in subject matter and in time. Thomas Taterka's magisterial account of Garlieb Merkel (1769–1850) and his German-Latvian edition of Heinrich Zschokke's widely popular *Goldmakers' Village* locates Merkel's activity clearly within the Popular Enlightenment (*Volksaufkärung*) and the 'post-colonial' post-emancipation Baltic debate on the future of Latvian and Estonian national culture. Jaan Undusk's erudite contribution places Merkel and Jochmann in the tradition of natural law and natural-history rhetoric and explores their use of these in dealing with social issues in their provinces. Aldur Vunk traces the life story of the Jochmann family in Pernau (Pärnu) and its social context, leading up to the founding in 1873, in accordance with C. G. Jochmann's will, of a school for Estonian children. In a rather idiosyncratic chapter, Hans-Peter Schütt endeavours to define the 'Late Enlightenment' and to ascribe Jochmann to it. Wilhelm Kühlmann explores the complex of personalities and attitudes around Cagliostro during his stay in Courland in 1779 and presents the well-known exposure of the charlatan magus by Elisa von der Recke (1754–1833) as the latter's attempt to escape from early enthusiastic self-deception into rational self-understanding. Uwe Japp examines the possible links between A. W. Hupel's writings on marriage and J. M. R. Lenz's use of topoi of castration and sexual engineering in his plays of the 1770s. Anuschka Tischer provides an excellent and engaging portrait of the collector and antiquarian cleric Heinrich Baumann (1716–90), well-known in his time but now largely forgotten because he published so little. On the basis of a recent large book, and with copious bibliographical notes, Klaus Garber celebrates literary and antiquarian collecting, something the Baltic provinces very much shared with the Germanies, and provides five Baltic case studies, allegedly of the eighteenth century but ranging in fact to the mid-nineteenth. Dietmar Willoweit analyses the jurisprudential stance of C. C. Darbelow (1768–1830) and his contribution to the establishment of law at the University of Dorpat, refounded in 1802. Ineta Balode anatomizes jurisprudential vocabulary in the eighteenth-century German language of Livland and Estland. The volume concludes with two pieces, by Mati Laur and Ralph Tuchtenhagen, on Catherine II's policies and their realization in the Baltic provinces, both clear and competent but neither adding greatly to the already established picture or to our understanding of Russian Enlightened Absolutism as a variant of the European phenomenon.

The focus throughout is closely on the Russian Baltic provinces, but there is material here to interest both historians of the European Enlightenment and students of German and especially Baltic German culture; and some of the chapters are impressive. Overall, however, the volume lacks cohesion, and its proposed sub-themes of European context and regional specificity are not well developed. Its time frames are confused: nobody except Schütt refers to the 'late Enlightenment', but — since coverage wanders from the late seventeenth century as far as 1873 — some clearer periodization or sharper conceptualization of 'Enlighteners' (*Aufklärer*) would have been helpful. Nevertheless, one should not ask too much of a conference volume such as this: it offers some effective contributions to the increasingly detailed scholarship on Baltic German culture and the Baltic German Enlightenment.

Ludlow ROGER BARTLETT

Bassin, Mark; Ely, Christopher and Stockdale, Melissa K. (eds). *Space, Place, and Power in Modern Russia: Essays in the New Spatial History*. Northern Illinois University Press, DeKalb, IL, 2010. ix + 268 pp. Maps. Illustrations. Notes. Index. $42.00: £28.00.

THIS volume draws together a selection of papers originally presented at a 2006 conference hosted by the Watson Institute for International Studies at Brown University. The event, held in honour of Abbott Gleason, was dedicated to the theme 'Politics, Space, and Power in Modern Russian History'. The chapters chosen for inclusion here are unified by a common concern to elucidate the significance of space, its cultural perception and representation, its political meanings and mediations, and its role in structuring and articulating group identities and power relations. As such, the volume is a contribution — and a most impressive and important one — to the 'new spatial history' of Russia.

The 'new spatial history', as the book's editors explain in a cogent and lucid introductory essay, is a growing scholarly literature that directs attention to space as a vital framework for understanding Russian political, cultural and social development. This spatial framework has sufficient conceptual breadth to encompass the key themes and issues of Russian history, from its international relations to the structures of everyday life, yet also provides sufficient clarity to illuminate specificities and to enable historical and transnational comparisons of collective and individual experience. Space, in this scholarship, is at once a physical attribute of the world, a category of subjective cognition and a heuristic concept. The 'new spatial history' directs attention, then, to the inter-connectedness of mental and material, subjective and objective, text and context, in constituting space as it is intellectually construed, emotionally experienced and morally valorized, as it is lived and reproduced through time, and as it actuates, channels and constrains human agency. Neither the wide geographies of national or imperial histories, nor the intimate sites of ordinary social interaction are taken for granted — they are no longer merely the frame of enquiry but its focus.

The ten substantive chapters of this volume are individually of the highest academic standard, and collectively offer a compelling vindication of the scholarly potential of this new spatial approach. The book's three editors, Mark Bassin, Christopher Ely and Melissa Stockdale, all distinguished North American scholars who specialize in historical geography, cultural history and political history respectively, provide an Introduction that outlines the novelty of the 'new spatial history', describes its defining features, and points to how the case studies, despite their diverse methods, sources and subjects, are united by a shared interest in the historical and conceptual 'interpenetration' (p. 10) of space and power. These studies are organized into three thematic sections, although, to the credit of authors and editors alike, all the contributions speak to one another and to the book's unifying conception and aims in a most coherent and productive manner.

Part One, 'Geopolitical Constructions of Space', opens with an intriguing, stimulating essay by Stockdale on the concepts of 'fatherland' (*otechestvo*) and 'motherland' (*rodina*) in the first half of the twentieth century, and the ways in which the tsarist and Communist states mobilized these notions and in which society understood and responded to them. In the next chapter, Bassin brings insights developed in his classic early studies of Russian environmental determinism to bear on his more recent engagement with Eurasianism, viewed as a geopolitical ideology, a vision of history and a philosophy of national life. He offers a subtle and cogent account of the Eurasianists' ambivalence about the relative significance for Russian development of material drivers of change and spiritual or sociocultural factors.

Part Two, 'Place, Space, and Power', comprises four chapters. John Randolph contributes a enthralling article on the political and cultural role of the Petersburg-Moscow highway in the eighteenth century, which he examines as a demonstration of state power, a structuring axis of national space, and a site of subversion by a stubbornly disordered, mobile society. This is followed by an equally fascinating micro-study by the late Richard Stites of the space of the ballroom as a locus of upper class interaction, where social relations, gender hierarchies and individual identities were articulated, enacted and reproduced. The next two chapters address the Russian state's colonization of its periphery. Patricia Herlihy discusses how American diplomat Eugene Schuyler's travel accounts of Central Asia reflected and reshaped colonial practices in the region. Robert Argenbright considers the Bolsheviks' deployment in the Civil War of agitational trains and boats to exercise a 'revolutionary gaze' (p. 145) over recaptured territories, and the interaction between central schemes and local realities.

The four essays of Part Three, 'Place, Identity, and Memory', offer engaging insights into the perception and experience of place in wider political, religious and cultural contexts. Christopher Ely examines the St Petersburg streets in the period of Alexander II as venues for autonomous social expression and political performance, as well as of state regulation and repression, demonstrating how burgeoning street life shaped the emergence of urban culture and a nascent civil society. The next chapter, by Sergei Zhuk, turns to rural Ukraine, and to Orthodox anxieties about the perceived appropriation of this 'sacred landscape' (p. 198) by Protestant sectarians. Cathy A. Frierson also addresses the role of sacred space in centre-periphery relations, tracing how the Stalinist regime transformed religious buildings in the Russian North into kulak prisons, and how, following the Soviet collapse, local efforts to restore the churches to their proper use revealed evidence of state crimes, prompting new debates about regional identity, collective memory and control over space. The final essay, by Lisa A. Kirschenbaum, also addresses questions of local and civic memory in a study of late Soviet and post-Soviet campaigns to restore historic place-names in Leningrad-St Petersburg.

The chapters of this volume are consistently excellent. They are all based on extensive research and sensitive critical readings of a wide and diverse range of sources. Their conceptualization of space in its interactions with politics, society and culture, in both discourse and practice, is sophisticated and intellectually invigorating. The writing throughout is elegant, expressive and free of jargon. The three editors are to be strongly congratulated on producing a volume that is so rich in both historical insight and methodological and conceptual innovation, and that will be required reading for any scholar or advanced student interested in the new spatial approach to history.

Department of History
University of Nottingham

NICK BARON

Leonard, Carol S. *Agrarian Reform in Russia: The Road from Serfdom.* Cambridge University Press. Cambridge and New York, 2011. xiv + 402 pp. Figures. Tables. Notes. Appendices. Bibliography. Index. £50.00: $90.00.

THIS is an impressive book. Leonard analyses agrarian history from the prelude to the serf emancipation of 1861 and up to the present day. The book is necessarily a synthesis, although it draws on current economic data as well, and is divided into three manageable parts: waves of reform, law and property relations and the economic performance of the agrarian sector. It is packed with detail on property laws, censuses, outputs and employment and, more generally, the state of the field of agricultural history.

This is all good news for scholars of Russian, economic and agrarian history because our tendency to focus on narrow time-periods deprives us of the hindsight, foresight and historical perspective we need. We benefit when we make sense of 1861 against 2010, and vice versa, and identify long-term patterns. The book introduces the expert and the novice alike to the debates in Russian agrarian policy, and delivers the first overall picture we have had since Lazar Volin; it is also a good companion to David Moon's socio-economic overview of the Russian peasantry.

Leonard's book reflects the specific questions of outcomes and outputs that occupy economic historians today. It is also more policy-driven, since history is channelled to address the choices facing current Russian policy-makers. What we are not given in this book are the debates about human organization, social consequences and the overtly political dimensions of policy — emancipation as autocratic prerogative, Stolypin as a liberal, Stalin as human engineer and Putin-Medvedev as a vision of capitalist reordering. Then again, not all books need do this and it would be inappropriate to insist that all historians address the same questions with the same set of concerns. Instead Leonard succeeds in her goal, and is the only writer to have attempted to achieve it: the entire period is subjected to an economic perspective and measured in terms of accepted economic imperatives. The intelligent reader can agree or disagree with the premises because they are explicit. Reform, and presumably human progress, should be about 'enabling and expanding choice', a process by which 'individuals [*sic*] gain rights, or powers, to consume, obtain income from, and transfer landed assets' (p. 7). By this measure Russian reform and the trajectory of Russian agrarian development has been bumpy, with mixed conclusions on the emancipation, Stolypin, Stalin, Khrushchev, Brezhnev and Gorbachev. And Leonard offers persuasive evidence that the current government (Putin-Medvedev) has delivered more in terms of positive reform than the rhetorically rich El′tsin administration.

Leonard finds patterns that have endured to the present day. Strict individual or private property was always moderated by household, communal and collective property. Large-scale forms like collective farms and the current corporations often tempered the household, the commune and the individual, whilst state interest could trump them all. Stolypin might have promoted the individual homesteader but he settled for the household and accepted both commune (tacitly) and the nobiliary estate (explicitly). Stalin destroyed the commune, but in some respects its functions survived in the kolkhoz. The household plot and marginal quasi-formal occupations never went away; on the contrary, as Leonard points out, small plots have been present and essential to every system under consideration, the necessary supplement to one or another gigantomania.

The enduring economic weaknesses owe more to the inertial tendencies in the Russian and Soviet systems of administration and self-government, especially at the local level, than to failed policies. Reform has always been stimulated by one or another crisis, and these crises have been exploited to promote various reform programmes: Crimea, 1905, war scares in the late 1920s, rural depopulation after 1945, the collapse of the USSR. At such moments it seemed possible to overcome the vested interests of local administrators, local communities, benevolent statesmen and farmers who believed they benefited from the status quo. And yet those interests, for worse according to Leonard, have tended to triumph in the long term and dilute the new measures. With an eye on policy recommendations, Leonard asks that political leaders remain focused on agriculture even when it seems to be doing adequately, use central power to overcome local resistance and measure social questions, in the first instance, in economic terms. Strong centralized governments, she suggests, do have their advantages; an economic lens does have a clarifying effect.

There is a case to be made here and Leonard makes it very well. There is also a debate to be had, and this book may well initiate it, straddling as it does economics, policy and history.

New York University YANNI KOTSONIS

Soroka, Marina. *Britain, Russia and the Road to the First World War: The Fateful Embassy of Count Aleksandr Benckendorf (1903–16)*. Birmingham Studies in First World War History. Ashgate, Farnham and Burlington, VT, 2011. xix + 312 pp. Map. Illustrations. Figure. Notes. Bibliography. Index. £65.00.

THIS book examines the Russian side of Anglo-Russian relations through the career and activities of tsarist Russia's ambassador in London, Count Aleksandr Benckendorf. Marina Soroka's study differs from typical treatments of the subject that emphasize the British side of the equation based on British documents. Rather than seeking to explain how British policy-makers manoeuvred Russia to conform with British goals, this study uniquely assesses

Russia's role in the eventual alliance based on Russian archival holdings and the personal papers of Benckendorf. Soroka argues that Benckendorf's Anglophilia meant that Russia lost him as an agent of tsarist policy because in effect he adopted the role of explaining and justifying London's policies towards Russia rather than advocating St Petersburg's positions to the British. Thus, the Count's success in ingratiating himself in British high society proved a personal victory for him, but did not translate into a more positive reception to Russia and its policies by British officialdom. Fundamentally, Benckendorf had 'gone native' and ceased to carry out his job as advocate for Russia in Britain.

While the core portion of the work is devoted to the decade following the Russo-Japanese War (1904–05), the author also covers the period under Foreign Minister Vladimir Lamsdorf and Benckendorf's early career preceding his posting to London. Soroka begins her story with the Benckendorf's family background and his biography. She spends a fair amount of time detailing his career under Lamsdorf. Along the way the author covers the familiar events of Russian policy in the Far East leading to the war with Japan. In a novel telling of that story, instead of focusing on Russian Finance Minister Sergei Witte, Soroka stresses the primacy of Lamsdorf's role in trying to coordinate official policy among the Foreign, Finance and War Ministries and their ultimate defeat at the hands of the unofficial Bezobrazov clique. Although a full-blown analysis of the Lamsdorf foreign policy is beyond the scope of the author's purpose, the book indirectly challenges conventional interpretations of the primacy of Witte in Russian Far Eastern policy. At the same time, this study confirms the conventional interpretations highlighting the lack of a strong, controlling hand guiding tsarist foreign policy back in St Petersburg. It becomes clear that Benckendorf was just one of many tsarist ambassadors who pursued their own agendas without being subject to direct control of the Foreign Minister or Tsar Nicholas II.

Soroka's work serves as an interesting blend of biography and diplomatic history. Readers already familiar with the major diplomatic crises in tsarist foreign policy in the decade prior to the Great War will appreciate some of the fresh insights into the interplay of personalities revealed by this study of Benckendorf. Non-Russian specialists and those readers less familiar with this period will not benefit so much and will probably find the scope too narrow.

Department of History
Florida State University

J. A. Grant

Korpisaari, Harri. *Itsenäisen Suomen puolusta. Sotilaskomitea 1915–1918.* Bibliotheca Historica, 124. Suomalaisen Kirjallisuuden Seura, Helsinki, 2009. 394 pp. Illustrations. Notes. Bibliography. English Summary. Index. €29.00 (paperback).

THE struggle between Left and Right for control of the newly-emergent independent Finland in 1918 has dominated much of the research about this period of Finnish history. However, in Harri Korpisaari's study the theme is one of the internal and external configurations that presented themselves to the Right before it plunged into civil war in January 1918.

These were not straightforward choices. Struggling ultimately for Finnish independence, the Right had to contend with a set of powerful industrialists who wanted to maintain the lucrative contracts that a Russia still at war with Germany in the autumn of 1917 was bringing Finland. Had Korpisaari dwelled in his analysis a little more closely on the deep summer of 1917, he might have found that the Minister State-Secretary for Finland in Petrograd, Carl Enckell, used (or misused) a note of the Russian Prime Minister, A. F. Kerenskii, to secure the dissolution of a Finnish parliament with a Social Democrat majority. Ari Rasilainen's doctoral dissertation on this fatal aspect of Finnish politics came out in 2004 and does not seem to have caught the eye of Korpisaari when writing his own doctorate.

All in all, however, the Finnish Right was increasingly haunted by Germany. Various groups had been for years endeavouring to make out a case for a military liaison with Germany. Since 1915 young Finns had been training in Germany as Jaegers in a German army battalion. On 28 August 1917 a Svecoman Finn called Nikolai Mexmontan and a captain in the Swedish army by the name Carl Bennedich drafted, in Stockholm, a proposal for a confederative relationship between Finland and Germany. This recognized the independence of Finland and would have brought in Sweden to do likewise and give aid to Finland's freedom. Finland would then have worked with the Central Powers against the West. Mexmontan was to be the head of the Finnish armed forces.

This proposal seems hitherto to have been saved from oblivion by Korpisaari. In itself, it appears to have been an attempt to answer the German emissary, Major Werner Crantz, who had asked the Finns in the previous month to speak with one voice and had himself chosen Mexmontan to be that voice. Alas, Colonel Mexmontan was now losing the pitch. For some time, he had been trying to persuade the German military forces to invade his Finnish homeland, generally in connection with a rising there. The chances of the latter he initially exaggerated. Because the German invasion of Russian-held territory slowed down in 1915, Mexmontan had to wait till 1917 to get his apparent chance.

In 1915, Mexmontan began to face another problem. In that year a group of former Finnish officers from the old suppressed Finnish army joined with a number of civilian sympathizers to form a Military Committee in Finland. Immediately, it did very little, but by 1917, the events in Russia spurred it into action. So, too, it seemed, did the Stockholm proposal of Mexmontan and Bennedich.

Edvard Hjelt, the Chancellor of the University of Helsinki, crossed the water to Stockholm to find out what was going on. A month later, at the end of September 1917, a further meeting was held in Stockholm between Hjelt, Mexmontan, Crantz and two Finnish activists. To Mexmontan's chagrin, there was no discussion of the original plan for some kind of a confederation with Germany. Nor is there any evidence that the Swedes were coming in (Korpisaari has stressed that Swedish official policy was now changing in the direction of greater sympathy for the British cause). But what Crantz did bring this time was the support of General Erich Ludendorff for the *Finnish* cause. Ludendorff had taken his time and kept his silence even from many of his colleagues. Crantz also brought news of improvements in the training of Finnish Jaegers in the German army. They were brought back in February 1918. The Germans themselves came in April.

After the Stockholm meeting of September 1917 there were other changes in store. The head of the Military Committee in Finland was a former cavalryman from the suppressed Finnish dragoon regiment. His name was Hannes Ignatius. He disliked Mexmontan and he equally disliked those he termed 'Russian officers', that is, those Finns who had served in the Russian army until 1917. By the autumn of 1917, Mexmontan was already on his way out. Ignatius had, however, to eat humble pie, when two 'Russian officers' became heads of the revived Finnish army. The first was General Claes Charpentier. He became somewhat lethargic and had to be replaced by General Gustaf Mannerheim.

A Military Committee had turned itself into a general staff. When the civil war began, Ignatius served faithfully on Mannerheim's staff. There were then other kinds of enemies to counter, but mostly the enemies were still Finnish.

University of Turku GEORGE MAUDE

Edele, Mark. *Stalinist Society 1928–1953.* Oxford Histories. Oxford University Press, Oxford and New York, 2011. xiv + 367 pp. Figures. Tables. Notes. Bibliography. Index. £53.00; £20.00.

THE historiography of the Stalin period is extensive, the field crowded. As Mark Edele reminds us, the publication of many archival studies during the last twenty years followed decades of sustained and multi-disciplinary scholarship during the Cold War. Some of the attempts to synthesize this complex mass of material have in their own right been works of great distinction, but no one has written anything quite like Edele's memorable and challenging new book.

Edele does not just offer a synthesis, although his book makes coherent sense of hundreds of secondary works and published primary sources. He also articulates an original, clear and compelling vision of what Stalinist society was and what historical investigation of it has amounted to. This is a rare achievement. Edele's interpretation of Stalinism is founded on a trenchant and rigorously historicized engagement with the concept of totalitarianism. He argues that the Bolsheviks had totalizing aspirations, but the party and state machines they created lacked the capacity to realize the dreams of utopia. The economy might have been planned in theory, but it was planless in practice. He writes of a 'limping behemoth, able to thrash about, destroy, and spread fear, but not to control and engineer complex social change' (p. 5). Soviet society was fractured. Some rejected Soviet ideology, many avoided political meetings whenever they could, others preferred family life or national solidarity to the enticements of the Soviet collective. But, Edele argues, one force united everyone: 'the iron grip of economic necessity'. The argument, by the end, is for a 'totalitarian political economy' of Soviet society: that the basic engine of Soviet life was an economic one, that the economy was fundamentally different in its everyday operations from the declarations of the planners, and that it is by understanding the economic transactions which allowed people to survive that we are most likely to understand Stalinist life. In order to make this argument coherent, Edele posits that 'state' and 'society' were not separate and antagonistic phenomena, but that the state was a part of society. This seems a fruitful way of analysing the interaction of Soviet citizens, planners, and ideologists — in fact, the present reviewer makes a similar point with reference to housing in *Property of Communists: The Urban Housing Program from Stalin to Khrushchev* (DeKalb, IL, 2010) — and Edele successfully makes accessible a conceptual approach that he developed in his earlier, more specialized research.

This is a thematic survey. Edele has selected seven principal themes: violence and terror; geographical and social mobility; family life; the state (although he convincingly theorizes the state as a part of society, not as something in conceptual opposition to it); ideology; social stratification and identity (nationality, gender, status); and the economy, especially those aspects which Edele sees as dominant, the unofficial and the 'mutual'. For all their richness, these seven thematic chapters cannot consistently account for change over time, and the problem of late Stalinism (1945–53), though at the heart of Edele's own research and the subject of a growing literature to which Edele refers, is, surprisingly, never quite explained. In chapter one, Edele tells the story of a single Stalinist life, the film director Grigorii Chukrai, and chapter nine is a provocative historiographical discussion. The whole book, however, fizzes with provocations.

The author characterizes his book as an essay, in that it probes existing evidence and scholarship in order to develop a distinctive if provisional interpretation that by definition lacks detail. Edele makes a good case for the sometimes secondary role ideology played in people's lives, but he does not provide a careful summary of Stalinist ideology; he shows how politics and everyday life might have interacted, but he does not rehearse the course of high politics; he places the economy at the centre of his argument, but the book is light on the theory and data that drive economic history. Edele will perhaps only have succeeded in his task if every specialist throws the book across the room before coming back to finish it. The experts will enjoy the wit: on ideological conviction, Edele posits: 'Stalinism is not graduate school and just learning to converse in the latest jargon will not do' (p. 136). They might or might not enjoy the occasional descent from academic register: Marx is 'old Karl' and 'the bearded prophet' in the same paragraph (p. 125). This book, however, has been written for more than one audience. Students of all levels will find it stimulating, and higher-level undergraduate and graduate students will thrive on the extensive bibliography and historiographical discussions. General readers should find the book invigorating, but might be foxed by the 133 pages of notes, bibliography and index (there are 243 pages of text). Both these audiences might struggle in the absence of an opening chapter that establishes a basic narrative (the life story of Grigorii Chukrai in chapter one is an interesting but idiosyncratic substitute). As such, the book differs from a classic work with which it ought to be compared, the more instantly accessible 'textbook' written by Sheila Fitzpatrick (*The Russian Revolution*, Oxford, 1982, 2001, 2008). If OUP ever give Edele the chance to revisit the demands of his conflicting audiences in a second edition, he might yet live up to his mentor. Written with fluency, passion and charm, however, this book is already the boldest introduction to its subject.

Department of History MARK B. SMITH
University of Leeds

Balogh, Béni L. *The Second Vienna Award and the Hungarian-Romanian Relations, 1940–1944.* Translated by Andrew Gane. Atlantic Studies on Society in Change, 139; EEM, 779. Social Science Monographs and Atlantic Research and Publications, Inc., Boulder, CO and Highland Lakes, NJ, 2011. vii + 580 pp. Notes. Bibliography. Indexes. $65.00: £45.00.

NOTHING is guaranteed to charge Romanian and Hungarian emotions more vigorously than the subject of Transylvania and the situation of the Hungarian minority there. The province is regarded by both Romanians and Hungarians as an integral part of their ancestral home and in the minds of both peoples their own survival as a nation is linked to the fate of Transylvania. For the Hungarians Transylvania remains part of the homeland which was unjustly amputated at the Paris Peace Settlement after the First World War and they show a natural concern for the fate of their 1.6 million minority in the province. Yet concerns about the treatment of the minority are equated by the Romanians with territorial ambitions on the part of Hungary to detach the province from Romania. It is this contiguity of Hungary, coupled with the size of the Hungarian minority, which made, and continues to make, the treatment of the Hungarian minority such a sensitive issue for both states, and distinguished it from the problem of other minorities, such as the German one.

When Transylvania was transferred from Hungarian to Romanian rule after the First World War the Hungarian and German minorities there hoped for some form of federal or devolved association with the new polity. Instead, centralized rule from Bucharest was imposed. This vitiated the chances of a possible accommodation between the government and those of its citizens who now found themselves a minority. It also fuelled Budapest's ambitions to regain the lost territory.

Hungary's revisionist ambitions were closely linked with those of the Third Reich. Like Hitler, Hungary's leaders had never accepted the 'injustices' of the Paris Peace Settlement and therefore Hitler's advocacy of revision of the Versailles Treaty encouraged Hungary to press her claims to her lost territories. The first success of Hungary's pro-German policy was gained in November 1938 when, under the terms of the First Vienna Award, Hungary acquired part of southern Slovakia from Czechoslovakia. In March 1939, she was awarded Carpatho-Ruthenia and then concentrated her attention on Transylvania. Hungarian strategy was to coordinate the claim to Transylvania with Soviet agitation over Bessarabia. A month after the issue of Bessarabia was raised in the Soviet press, the Hungarian chief of staff, General Henrik Werth, advised his government in a memorandum dated 12 December 1939 that in the case of a Soviet attack on Romania, Hungary should act to recover 'the whole of Transylvania'. He also instructed General Gábor Faragho, the Hungarian military attaché in Moscow, to discuss with the Soviet authorities the possibility of a coordinated attack against Romania.

Not content with its amputation of Romania by annexing Bessarabia and northern Bukovina in June 1940, the Soviet Union backed Hungary's claims to Transylvania. On 11 July, the Hungarian minister to Moscow sent a report to Budapest of a discussion he had had with Molotov during which the Soviet Foreign Minister had made clear that the USSR considered Hungary's territorial demands towards Romania to be justified, and offered its support for them should a conference be called to resolve them.

Hitler's stance over Transylvania was dictated by his need for stability in preparing Operation Barbarossa, which was conceived with both Hungarian and Romanian participation. Whilst warning the Hungarian Prime Minister on 10 July not to expect any help from Germany should Hungary attack

Romania, Hitler was worried about a joint Russian-Hungarian move against Romania which would threaten the oilfields and thus endanger his plans in Russia. He therefore offered his offices as mediator and negotiations between Hungary and Romania began on 10 August at Turnu-Severin. After ten days of stalemate Hitler imposed a settlement. The German Foreign Minister Joachim von Ribbentrop and his Italian counterpart, Count Galeazzo Ciano, invited both sides to Vienna and told them to accept the result of their arbitration.

Studies by foreign historians (non-Romanians or non-Hungarians) on the Vienna Award are rare. The work of Andreas Hillgruber, C. A. Macartney and, more recently, Holly Case, stands out. The contribution of Ottmar Trașcă, a Cluj historian, to the debate on the Award suggests that there is hope for an academic dialogue between Romanian and Hungarian specialists. Balogh, a graduate of history at Cluj's Babeș-Bolyai University, and former secondary school teacher in Orăștie in Transylvania, left for Hungary in April 1989, since when he has been an archivist at the Komárom-Esztergom County Archives. He is therefore admirably equipped to gain a deep familiarity with the primary and secondary literature in Romanian and Hungarian on the subject of the Award. He adds a discerning mind to this qualification, offering the reader a relatively balanced account and analysis of the events leading up to the Award, of the circumstances and consequences of arbitration, and of relations between Hungary and Romania in the subsequent period until Romania's volte-face of 23 August 1944. It is, on the author's own admission, 'first and foremost a diplomatic history', and focuses on the evolution of bilateral relations. A meaningful analysis of such relations cannot ignore, however, the minority issue and Balogh accords due importance to it throughout his book. That said, it is unfortunate that given the contentious issues of border revisions and population, there are no maps or demographic tables to guide the reader and to offer reference points.

On the question of the future of Transylvania, Romanians were virtually unanimous that it was in political, cultural and economic terms more important to the cohesion of the Romanian state than Bessarabia, notwithstanding the painful consequences of the loss of the province in June 1940. King Carol and his ministers were concerned that rejection of arbitration would lead to a Hungarian attack and German occupation of the oilfields, which might in turn provoke a Russian invasion of eastern Romania. The King convened a Crown Council in which members of the Iron Guard, and other pro-German ministers were now present, and it voted 19 to 10 with one abstention for the acceptance of arbitration. Those against preferred defeat to disgrace, those in favour stressed the need to prevent the complete disintegration of Romania. Carol cast his vote with the latter.

Ribbentrop was instrumental in drawing up the terms of the Award and he was driven by German strategic interests in doing so. By pushing the border of Hungary, which at this time was more closely linked to Germany than Romania, to the south-east Carpathian ridge, he gave the German army a natural defensive wall. At the same time, the new frontier ran only a few kilometres from the Romanian oilfields around Ploieşti, which were vital to Hitler's plan to attack the Soviet Union. On the announcement of the Ribbentrop-Ciano adjudication on 30 August 1940, Mihail Manoilescu, the Romanian Foreign Minister, fainted on the table. Under the terms of the Second Vienna Award, as it came to be known, Transylvania was virtually partitioned. Hungary received an area of roughly 43,000 square kilometres in the north of the province representing roughly 40 per cent of its area and a population of 2.6 millions.

The partition triggered an exodus of Romanians from northern Transylvania. According to figures compiled by the official body in Romania set up to give assistance to these refugees, some 110,000 passed through its hands up to September 1943. Most were former employees of the Romanian state who overnight found themselves without jobs, including university and school teachers. Many were soon placed in the respective ministry and in the educational system. Others were sent before local committees formed from the prefect, mayor and representatives of the Red Cross who were given the authority to requisition dwellings to house them. According to Balogh, in the immediate aftermath of the Award, 'Hungarians living in Romania were dismissed from their jobs and driven from the country. [...] In response, in early October 1940, the Hungarian government expelled several hundred Romanians from Northern Transylvania in cattle trucks. The measure proved to be a mistake and was contrary to the relatively tolerant minority policy (the "Saint Stephen" minority policy) of Hungarian governments, which emphasized — at least in theory — the importance of reconciliation between the peoples of Transylvania' (pp. 528–29). In describing Hungarian minority policy as 'relatively tolerant', even more so with regard to Hungarian rule in northern Transylvania, Balogh runs the risk of losing the confidence of his informed reader, in the same measure as any historian who described Romanian minority policy in interwar Transylvania in identical terms.

As Balogh points out, the competition between Hungary and Romania for Hitler's favour increased following the Award. We might add in this regard that the principal reason of Ion Antonescu, Romania's wartime dictator, for not wishing to annex Transnistria, the Ukrainian territory between the Dniester and the Bug, stemmed from a desire to restore the *status quo ante* in the summer of 1940, which would see the return to Romania of all the territories annexed by foreign powers during 1940, not only Bessarabia and northern Bukovina, but northern Transylvania as well. He made this clear in talks with Hitler held on 11 February 1942 when he told the German leader that he did not regard the 1940 Vienna award as definitive and that, whatever the German position, he would seek to reverse it.

There was also competition between Hungary and Romania to exit the war. Hitler was made aware of the continuing Romanian overtures to the Allies and ordered plans to be drawn up for the occupation of the country. Similar plans had already been prepared for the occupation in March 1944 of Hungary, whose reliance as an ally had been long shown to be wanting. Before taking action against Antonescu, the Führer decided to give him one last chance. The two leaders met at Klessheim on 23–24 March 1944 where Hitler railed against the duplicity of the Hungarians, declaring to Antonescu that he had irrefutable evidence of their intention to withdraw from the war (see *Antonescu-Hitler. Corespondentă şi întîlniri inedite (1940–1944)*, vol. 2, edited by Vasile Arimia, Ion Ardeleanu and Ştefan Lache, Bucharest, 1991, p. 144). Unaware that his future hung in the balance, Antonescu pledged continued loyalty to Hitler. Not for the first time, Hitler was impressed by Antonescu's sincerity and decided not to remove his friend. Balogh writes that Hitler told Antonescu 'during a private meeting on March 23, 1944, that he no longer considered the Second Vienna Award to be valid. Hitler's statement was never made public, and around that time Soviet troops reached Romanian territory'. Balogh gives neither the location of the meeting — presumably Klessheim — nor a source for Hitler's statement, although there is no reason to doubt its veracity.

With the Red Army in occupation of Romania after King Michael's successful coup against Antonescu on 23 August 1944, Stalin had a unique opportunity to bend internal developments there according to his will, especially as the pre-war social systems had been completely disrupted. The Award was declared null and void in the Allied (Soviet) Armistice Convention, concluded in Moscow on 12 September 1944, and after Soviet and Romanian troops had cleared Transylvania of Axis forces, the province was handed over to the control of the Communist-dominated government of Petru Groza in March 1945. Romanian sovereignty over Transylvania was ratified by the Paris Peace Treaty of February 1947.

UCL SSEES & Georgetown University, Washington D.C. DENNIS DELETANT

Kuromiya, Hiroaki. *Conscience on Trial: The Fate of Fourteen Pacifists in Stalin's Ukraine, 1952–1953*. University of Toronto Press, Toronto, ON, Buffalo, NY and London, 2012. x + 212 pp. Maps. Illustrations. Notes. Index. $60.00.

DURING the night of 17–18 November 1952, the Soviet police arrested seven men and six women, Ukrainians of peasant origin and members, allegedly, of an 'illegal sect', in and near the Ukrainian town of Bila Tserkva. This was followed, nine days later, by the arrest of their 'ringleader', Vasilii Federovich Belokon′. On the second and final day of their trial one month later, the fourteen were sentenced to ten or twenty-five years. The General Prosecutor's Office in Moscow initiated their exoneration in 1955, and again in 1989. Using the archival record from the central archives of the Security Service of Ukraine, 852 archival folios filled on both sides and densely written in longhand, Hiroaki Kuromiya offers a solid reconstruction of a Stalinist show trial against religious believers. Despite all our knowledge about the crimes of Stalin's regime, it remains shocking to see up close the relentless and spiteful persecution of poor and harmless people.

The accused resemble the sixteenth-century 'heretical' miller known from Carlo Ginzburg's book, *The Cheese and the Worms*, for they allow us to discern a particular spiritual world: that of pacifist Christians who broke no law, but who did not conform to the Soviet mainstream in avoiding both military service and work on Saturdays. This new book stands out amidst a literature on private lives under Stalin that generally ignores religious subcultures. Kuromiya convincingly presents the case as a microcosm: the state terror against the accused (and those around them) was not exceptional but symptomatic of the relationship between regime and society under Stalin.

Hiding behind a legalistic cover of investigations and court hearings, a host of state employees spent hours and hours on the case. Kuromiya ultimately explains it by Stalin's concern about ideas: 'there was always the possibility of even a deeply held private faith becoming public', and 'no one could completely control ideas themselves: ideas have a way of spreading in one way or another' (p. 189). He argues that the interrogators disdained the arrestees and most likely considered them enemies — simply because of their belief in divine law. Because the Soviet constitution offered freedom of conscience, the prosecution had to invent an 'organization' of 'Reformed Adventists' spreading subversive propaganda (and as authoritarian as the Communist Party). But the inventors were not cynics: they actually believed in their own mirage. The same duality existed with the judges: their harsh verdicts stemmed both from instructions from Kiev and from a genuine belief in the guilt of the accused.

The book shows very well that the 'organization' had been monitored before in many ways. Kuromiya concludes after some hesitation that the alleged ringleader, who answered no questions at the trial and who does not appear on any of the 'mug shots' in the case file, was an agent provocateur.

'The formality of the process mattered, but its substance did not' (p. 135). Thus a women also described as an Adventist was not arrested because her role was to testify against the others. The accused were not allowed legal counsel before the trial, and no witnesses for the defense during it. When a courageous defense lawyer by the name of Perel′muter told the court that the accused had harboured no malice toward the Soviet state, he was ignored. It is not even clear if the indictment was read out to them. Still, not all went smoothly. Defendants retracted earlier confessions and pleaded not guilty. But those earlier confessions themselves might have been fictional, Kuromiya argues.

Overall, well-argued scepticism about the archival record, both of the trial and the prior investigation, is one of the great strengths of the book. No one knows how violent and threatening the interrogators were, but they certainly distorted statements so as to make speakers appear more hostile. (It is highly unlikely that an illiterate woman would have used the term 'anti-Soviet'.) Far from everything spoken during the interrogations was recorded. The indictment falsely stated that all the accused had been found to possess religious literature. The court failed to record statements that it disliked, or simply passed them over in silence, such as when a defendant mentioned his military service. Still, Kuromiya demonstrates in this moving book that a highly problematic source can reveal much about Stalin's regime and the people it wished to control.

NIOD Institute for War, Holocaust and Genocide Studies, Royal Netherlands Academy of Arts & Sciences

KAREL C. BERKHOFF

Patterson, Patrick Hyder. *Bought and Sold: Living and Losing the Good Life in Socialist Yugoslavia.* Cornell University Press, Ithaca, NY and London, 2011. xvii + 351 pp. Illustrations. Tables. Notes. Select bibliography. Index. $39.95.

ARE consumerism and socialism entirely antithetical? Can a consumerist mass culture exist and flourish under state socialism? These are the questions guiding Patrick Hyder Patterson's *Bought and Sold: Living and Losing the Good Life in Socialist Yugoslavia*. Through a thorough investigation of consumerism, advertising and marketing in Yugoslavia, Patterson concludes that the strict binary often drawn between consumer culture and socialism is a false one. *Bought and Sold* thus makes a valuable intervention into the literature on consumption and advertising by 'testing the traditional identification of consumer society with capitalism' (p. 12).

The flourishing mass consumer culture that Patterson describes in Yugoslavia had crucial ramifications for both the country's rise to relative affluence and its descent into ethnic warfare. Patterson argues that through the common participation of all ethno-national groups in the Yugoslav 'Good Life,' consumerism played a key role in cementing a national, Yugoslav identity, and easing over lingering ethnic tensions. With the economic crisis of the 1980s however, the heightened expectations of Yugoslav consumers could no longer be fulfilled. Patterson suggests that this frustration, and the attendant loss of stable consumer identities, was to some degree responsible for the rebirth of ethnic nationalism in the 1990s and the conflict which followed. Taking us up to the present moment, he argues that when citizens of the Yugoslav successor states look back fondly on the former socialist republic — engaging in what has come to be termed Yugo-Nostalgia — their most cherished memories are those of the consumerist plenty that characterized the 'Yugoslav Dream.'

Patterson's work is supported by an impressive variety of archival research, tracing the growth of consumerism through advertising and marketing journals, advertising conferences proceedings, women's and lifestyle magazines, advertisements in the popular press, television series and statistical sources. He also charts the backlash and opposition to consumerism produced by party officials, Marxist humanist intellectuals and officials within the advertising industry itself. The bulk of the book's narrative is thus dedicated to recounting the intricacies and controversies, as well as the pleasures and disappointments, of Yugoslavia's consumer society through its rise in the 1950s, its heyday in the 1960s and 1970s and its decline in the 1980s.

This rich empirical detail, however, is not always matched by conceptual or theoretical consistency. Though Patterson's main thesis is that Yugoslav consumer culture represented a 'hybrid form' (p. 12), his treatment of Yugoslav consumerism often maintains the stark binaries between socialism and consumerism that he putatively aims to break down. This is most apparent in chapter three, where Patterson argues that the socialist values with which Yugoslav advertisers attempted to legitimize their craft were simply an ideological 'cloaking' (p. 135) or 'socialist spin' (p. 146) on an inherently capitalist practice. For Patterson, what made Yugoslav consumerism so unique was not its ability to fuse with socialism, but rather that the socialist context generated much greater resistance to consumer culture. In these formulations, the familiar portrayal of socialism as diametrically opposed to consumerism reappears. In this respect, Patterson's position ironically mirrors that of the conservative, anti-market critics of consumerism he describes in chapter four, who feared that with consumerism, socialist Yugoslavia was importing the capitalist culture of the West wholesale. This is clearest in Patterson's claim that Yugoslav advertising carried a 'subversive', capitalist influence that 'challenged the reigning principles of Yugoslav political life' (p. 58).

Patterson claims that his work demonstrates the folly of the orthodox Marxist conception of culture as a mere superstructure resting atop the economic base (p. 13), arguing that consumerism 'need not necessarily be grounded upon capitalist economic relations' (p. 57). Yet in Patterson's own account of the economic context of Yugoslav consumerism, and indeed throughout the book, he argues that it was socialist Yugoslavia's unique political-economic system (its economic base) — specifically its mix of socialism and market mechanisms, as well as its openness to the capitalist West — that allowed its consumer culture (its superstructure) to flourish. Though Yugoslavia remained putatively socialist, Patterson's contention is that its consumer culture was made possible by its 'non-socialist' economic relations. Whatever one thinks about the base-superstructure model (and many Marxists have questioned its reductive determinism), Patterson's account is seemingly faithful to it, despite his attempt to submit it to critique.

For all of Patterson's remarks against Marxism, it is surprising his book contains no references to Marx's work. Rather, he argues against the tired Marxist stereotypes and straw men, frequently claiming that the Yugoslav state was run according to 'Marxist-Leninist governance', without elaborating on what made it a Marxist-Leninist state. Patterson's own accounts of the flexibility and pragmatism of the supposedly ardent Marxists in Yugoslavia would suggest that such unelaborated stereotypes as 'Marxist-Leninist governance' are not appropriate for historical accounts of Yugoslav socialism. Here we would do well to follow the insistence of Susan Woodward — cited extensively in *Bought and Sold* — that instead of focusing on the dogmatic or totalitarian impulses of Marxist-Leninist parties, we pay attention to how their strategies were not 'fixed beforehand, but shaped by the time and conditions in which they were formed' (*Socialist Unemployment*, Princeton, NJ, 1995, p. 31).

Bought and Sold is an important intervention into the study of consumerism, socialism and Yugoslav history. While many of its specific arguments are open to debate, Patterson convincingly shows that that no account of the socialist experience in Yugoslavia can ignore the centrality of consumerism, while no robust theory of consumer culture can blithely assume it is either a purely capitalist phenomenon or an impossibility in socialist societies.

Department of Geography and Program in Planning Zev Moses
University of Toronto

Chodakiewicz, Marek Jan. *Intermarium: The Land between the Black and Baltic Seas.* Transaction, New Brunswick, NJ and London, 2012. 568 pp. Maps. Notes. Appendices. Bibliography. Index. $59.95.

In this impressively ambitious, panoramic examination of a substantial part of Central and Eastern Europe roughly equivalent to the lands which constituted the Polish-Lithuanian Commonwealth of the sixteenth to eighteenth centuries, Professor Chodakiewicz accentuates their rich diversity in ethnic, economic, religious and political terms. He is concerned to demonstrate that despite the often cataclysmic vicissitudes experienced by that region, the concepts and practice of freedom, enterprise and independence that were epitomised by the Commonwealth were not extinguished, and provide in the post-Soviet and post-Communist era some of the essential ingredients for its longer-term prosperity and security.

By creating a broad historical framework featuring the Intermarium's genesis and development over time, with particular reference to Poland, the Baltic States and Ukraine, and to the period of the twentieth-century's World Wars, it is argued that it is equally important for the United States, with its unrivalled resources as the world's only remaining superpower, to pursue a new, emboldened strategy of economic, political and moral support for the newly liberated countries. This approach is not only in its own national interest, but also is necessary to defeat post-Communism and to oppose a Russian neo-imperialism that aims ultimately to re-establish the Kremlin's totalitarian hegemony over them, if not even their military re-occupation. For the United States to play such a role, however, a fundamental change in its traditionally somewhat dismissive view of the Intermarium states will be required. In adducing this perceptive and compelling hypothesis, the author has combined to an admirable degree a profound knowledge of the Intermarium with a vigorous prose style, which is further complemented by a plethora of extensively-detailed and largely bibliographical notes.

The central point of reference for the narrative and analysis is the wholly destructive, dehumanizing impact of twentieth century totalitarian regimes on the Intermarium, especially the much more enduring Soviet version, which virtually obliterated the variegated heritage of its captive peoples in favour of a manufactured 'false consciousness' of lies and deceit (p. 476ff). However, it is rightly emphasized that despite the formal collapse of Communism and the implosion of the Soviet Union itself by the early 1990s, the path to genuine freedom, free-market capitalism and democracy for the former satellite states was defiantly opposed by surviving post-Communist elites, including the secret police, who often continued to be in thrall to Moscow, and by leftists of varying hue in Western political, media and academic circles. In Poland, for example, the much-celebrated 'Round Table Talks' between the Government/Communist Party and the left-wing of Solidarność — the 'constructive opposition', as it was dubbed by the Communists — was a compromise whose most significant outcome was to permit Communism to be peacefully 'transformed ' rather than overthrown root-and-branch. Consequently, Communist-era crimes went unpunished as did ongoing corruption because much of the old Communist *nomenklatura* and, subsequently, its progeny, continued to occupy high-level official posts from which they wielded major influence in government, the security services and armed forces, the economy, education, judiciary and academia. Their commitment to democracy and to a new, open society was and continues to be a sham. Their opponents, especially those labelled 'right-wing' and 'nationalist', are marginalized and vilified, while the retention of most Communist public monuments and symbols, invariably glorifying Lenin and the Red Army, in Poland and throughout the Intermarium is testament to the enduring strength of the post-Communist *milieu.*

This pattern, which characterized the rest of the Intermarium, illuminates the themes of personal, intellectual and, above all perhaps, institutional continuity and discontinuity there over the last few decades. The same Soviet-era practices of deception and mendacity were once again deployed for political advantage and the securing of power and riches: only the terror was missing. The overall outcome has been a hybrid form of democracy that is susceptible to nefarious internal and external manipulation. The Intermarium is vulnerable, therefore, and must be helped and protected, particularly by the United States, but also by scholars who are prepared to objectively consider the hard archival and other documentary evidence of the past and thus assist the people of the Intermarium to re-discover an authentic sense of national identity that is devoid of Communist and neo-Stalinist myths and wilful distortions of the historical record.

This brilliantly conceived, always fascinating and richly documented study is, incontrovertibly, an outstanding scholarly contribution, which should be mandatory reading for all with a serious interest in the history of Central and Eastern Europe and in American and broader international politics.

Research Centre for Modern Polish History PETER D. STACHURA

Wipperfuerth, Christian. *Russlands Aussenpolitik*. Elemente der Politik. VS Verlag, Wiesbaden, 2011. 145 pp. Bibliography. €16.95 (paperback).

IN this relatively short monograph, Christian Wipperfuerth offers a concise overview of Russia's foreign policy from 1991 to 2011. His book opens with an introduction and a chapter in which he analyses the world-view as well as the hard and soft power approaches which underlie Moscow's foreign policy. This is followed by one chapter each on Presidents Boris El′tsin, Vladimir Putin and Dmitrii Medvedev. After this, an interpretation of Russia's foreign policy is provided in which domestic as well as foreign policy factors are discussed. The book ends with a forecast until 2020 and a conclusion. The appendix contains three short reviews of important monographs on this topic as well as a short, but interesting bibliography.

The author rightfully argues that it is sensible to present Moscow's foreign policy in chronological order, divided into presidential terms, as Russia's 1993 constitution grants the president extensive powers in domestic as well as foreign policy (p. 7). As this was put into practice more often than not Wipperfuerth succeeds in giving a comprehensible overview of the Kremlin's changing views and priorities.

The author's methodology is characterized by a focus on Russia's relations with the West. Although this is not explicitly discussed, this choice seems justified given that the book is targeted at a German-speaking audience. Apart from this, the monograph contains basic details, including about Russia's GDP, its population and its defence spending as well as the price of oil on the international market. Most of the time, this data is presented in an enlarged international context which allows the reader to make useful comparisons.

Furthermore, it makes sense to point out the connection between domestic and foreign policy, as Wipperfuerth does, because it is quite reasonable to argue that Putin fuelled certain conflicts abroad in order to achieve the desired results at home, for example, victory for United Russia and his chosen successor Medvedev during the 2007/08 electoral cycle. This interconnection has not been explained as thoroughly in other high quality publications on this topic, such as Robert Donaldson's and Joseph Nogee's *The Foreign Policy of*

Russia: Changing Systems, Enduring Interests (Armonk, NY, 2009), and Nicolai Petro's und Alvin Rubinstein's *Russian Foreign Policy: From Empire to Nation State* (New York, 1997).

It is quite natural that in a book of this size only a relatively rough overview of Russia's foreign policy can be achieved. However, Wipperfuerth's monograph is excellently suited as an introduction to this topic due to the above-mentioned strengths as well as its clarity. It is therefore particularly useful for students who have little prior knowledge of Russian politics. With this in mind the previously mentioned basic details, the three book reviews and the bibliography in the appendix are also helpful as they make suggestions for further reading. In this context, a positive assessment of the introduction to the Kremlin's changing world-views, which closes another gap in this existing literature, should also be given.

Two critical comments cannot, however, be avoided. Firstly, Wipperfuerth is not entirely convincing in his argument that the Russian Federation no longer pursues imperial interests in the former Soviet republics. On the one hand, he is not wrong when he writes that Moscow does not wish to isolate itself internationally by pursuing imperial policies and that economic factors play the dominant role in Russia's relations with the so-called 'near abroad'. On the other hand, he himself expresses the view that the process of separation of the former Soviet republics from Russia is still on-going (p. 93). In my opinion, this can be understood as the legacy of the USSR's imperial past which can still be felt in the Kremlin's foreign policy.

Secondly, Wipperfuerth overlooks the fact that it is hardly possible to speak about 'the' Russian foreign policy. On the contrary, there are several foreign policy actors whose ambitions, gestures and deeds are not coordinated and even contradictory at times. Some of their acts can be classed as imperialist, especially towards the states in the former Soviet space. Also, a critical reader might ask why the final chapter makes predictions for the future. Would it not have been more sensible to use this space for further analysis of the events which have already taken place?

Despite these drawbacks, it is obvious that Wipperfuerth has fulfilled the task he has set himself. His book provides the reader with a well structured, accessible and balanced overview of the different facets of Russia's foreign policy. Due to this, I would recommend its translation into English. A longer and more detailed volume written with the same precision and clarity, in German as well as English, would also be desirable and would certainly be well received by more advanced students and scholars.

University of Erfurt KATJA RICHTERS

Satter, David. *It Was a Long Time Ago, and It Never Happened Anyway: Russia and the Communist Past.* Yale University Press, New Haven, CT and London, 2012. xii + 383 pp. Notes. Bibliography. Index. £25.00.

THE main premise of journalist David Satter's eminently readable, if sometimes disturbing, collection of essays is that 'the failure to acknowledge and atone for the mass crimes of Communism has contributed to a situation in which the average Russian is as powerless before the apparatus of the state as was a citizen of the Soviet Union' (p. 300). Satter argues that there is a lack of concern for human life in today's Russia because 'the individual is seen by the state as a means to an end' (p. 305), and that 'the failure to memorialize the victims of Communist terror has contributed to the moral corrosion of Russian society' (p. 6). Unlike post-Nazi Germany, Satter posits, the post-Soviet state and its citizens have not accepted the 'metaphysical guilt' of collectively having failed to stop the horrors of Communism (p. 5). The book thus presents a moral rather than a scholarly argument, setting Soviet remembrance against the normative ideal of post-Holocaust memory and finding the post-Soviet Russian successor state as well as its citizens sorely lacking in their remembrance of the crimes of the Stalin era.

Satter connects this failure to remember with contemporary Russian indifference to human life, and his evidence of contemporary Russian state callousness is memorable. It includes the reckless behaviour of Russian special forces during hostage crises, killing hostages along with terrorists; Russian officials and businessmen killing innocent people in traffic accidents with impunity; and a man trapped in a garbage truck whom the emergency services failed to help even after he made repeated frantic calls from his cell phone. How these horrific events are connected to failed remembrance is never quite made clear, however, as Satter is content with pointing to the Russian population's general moral deficiencies.

The episodic chapters are also steeped in horrors, as Satter recounts a number of the greatest crimes of the Stalin era including the career of Feliks Dzerzhinskii, the massacre of Polish officers in the Katyn forest, the brutal regime at the concentration camp in Vorkuta, and the killing regimes at a number of execution sites all across Russia. Many of the stories he tells will be familiar to specialists, though he recounts them with skill. There is also no doubt that he is correct in his assertion that contemporary Russian society has neither made the investigation of Stalin-era executioners, nor the quest to identify victims its top priority. Satter seems frustrated with Russian citizens who fail to see their moral duty in his terms. In several chapters, Satter concedes that various memorial efforts were underway in the early 1990s but were stopped by both the shock of the economic collapse and the practical issue of a lack of funds to build permanent monuments. Yet he fails to seriously consider the concrete contexts in which memorializers worked in assessing the reason for their failures, instead reverting back to the general moral argument. He also does not cite Kathleen Smith's important scholarly work on the efforts to memorialize Stalin's victims in the late Soviet era.

One of the most curious essays recounts the capture and execution of a Soviet-era KGB agent turned informer for the CIA, Andrei Poleshchuk, and the quest of his son to find his body. Poleshchuk was one of the agents that Aldrich Ames betrayed to the KGB. While the tale is certainly compelling and well-told, Satter concludes that the contemporary Russian state should honour this former Soviet spy because he helped to destroy the Soviet Union. He suggests that it was the moral duty of all Soviet citizens to resist the corrupt Soviet state and so Poleshchuk deserves credit for his work for the CIA. The Russian state's reluctance to rehabilitate treasonous KGB agents, he argues, is yet another example of Russians failing to recognize a higher moral authority than the state. This chapter is especially revealing of the tendentious nature of Satter's argument and his imposition of his own particular Cold War, anti-Communist moral framework on Russian society. He cannot seem to understand why Russian nation-builders seeking to construct a new identity are reluctant to embrace Soviet traitors or to jettison the entire Soviet past.

I agree with Satter that nostalgia for Stalinism and the muting of the voices of Stalin's victims have the potential to undercut the development of democracy in the new Russian state, and that Putin's authoritarian tendencies are facilitated in part by a kind of political passivity that was fostered under the Soviet political order. However, I would argue that the failure to memorialize the victims of Communism needs to be understood through a much denser analysis of the social, political and economic contexts of the 1990s and the 2000s. This kind of detailed scholarly analysis is yet to be written.

Department of History
University of Kentucky

KAREN PETRONE

Publications Received

Alladaye, René. *The Darker Shades of 'Pale Fire': An Investigation into a Literary Mystery.* Michel Houdiard Éditeur, Paris, 2013. €20.00 (paperback).

Ashby, C., Gronberg, T. and Shaw-Miller, S. (eds). *The Viennese Café and Fin-de-siècle Culture.* Austrian and Habsburg Studies, 16. Berghahn Books, New York and Oxford, 2013. $95.00: £60.00.

Bagshaw, Hilary B. P. *Religion in the Thought of Mikhail Bakhtin: Reason and Faith.* Ashgate New Critical Thinking in Religion, Theology and Biblical Studies. Ashgate, Farnham and Burlington, VT, 2013. £50.00.

Bhattacharjee, Anuradha. *The Second Homeland: Polish Refugees in India.* Sage Publications, New Delhi, Thousand Oaks, CA, London and Singapore, 2012. $50.00.

Bugan, Carmen. *Seamus Heaney and East European Poetry in Translation: Poetics of Exile.* Legenda, Oxford, 2013. £45.00: $89.50.

Chatterjee, Choi and Holmgren, Beth (eds). *Americans Experience Russia: Encountering Enigma, 1917 to the Present.* Routledge Studies in Cultural History, 19. Routledge, London and New York, 2013. £80.00.

Costlow, Jane T. *Heart-Pine Russia: Walking and Writing the Nineteenth-Century Forest.* Cornell University Press, Ithaca, NY and London, 2013. $36.50.

Cross, Anthony (ed.). *A People Passing Rude: British Responses to Russian Culture.* Open Book Publishers, Cambridge, 2012. £15.95 (paperback).

Donia, Robert. *From the Republika Srpska Assembly 1991–1996: Excerpts from Delegates' Speeches at the Republika Srpska Assembly as Body of Evidence for the International Criminal Tribunal at the Hague.* University Press, Sarajavo-Tuzla, 2012. €29.00 (paperback).

Drace-Francis, Alex. *The Making of Modern Romanian Culture: Literacy and the Development of National Identity.* I. B. Tauris, London and New York, 2012. £25.00 (paperback).

Elsie, Robert. *A Biographical Dictionary of Albanian History.* I. B. Tauris in association with the Centre for Albanian Studies, London and New York, 2013. £50.00.

Elsie, Robert and Destani, Bejtullah (eds). *The Cham Albanians of Greece: A Documentary History.* I. B. Tauris in association with the Centre for Albanian Studies, London and New York, 2013. £59.50.

Etkind, Alexander. *Warped Mourning: Stories of the Undead in the Land of the Unburied.* Cultural Memory in the Present. Stanford University Press, Stanford, CA, 2013. $25.95 (paperback).

Fairclough, Pauline (ed.). *Twentieth-Century Music and Politics: Essays in Memory of Neil Edmunds.* Ashgate, Farnham and Burlington, VT, 2013. £65.00.

Gellately, Robert. *Stalin's Curse: Battling for Communism in War and Cold War.* Oxford University Press, Oxford and New York, 2013. £20.00.

Glazov-Corrigan, Elena. *Art after Philosophy: Boris Pasternak's Early Prose.* Ohio State University Press, Columbus, OH, 2013. $79.95; $14.95.

Hewitson, Mark and D'Auria, Matthew (eds). *Europe in Crisis: Intellectuals and the European Idea, 1917–1957.* Berghahn Books, New York and Oxford, 2012. $95.00: £56.00.

Hildermeier, Manfred. *Geschichte Russlands. Vom Mittelalter bis zur Oktoberrevolution.* Historische Bibliothek der Gerda Henkel Stiftung. C. H. Beck, Munich, 2013. €49.95.

Hunt, Priscilla and Kobets, Svitlana (eds). *Holy Foolishness in Russia: New Perspectives.* Slavica, Bloomington, IN, 2011. $34.95 (paperback).

Ioffe, Dennis G. and White, Frederick H. (eds). *The Russian Avant-Garde and Radical Modernism: An Introductory Reader.* Cultural Syllabus. Academic Studies Press, Boston, MA, 2012. $59.00 (paperback).

Ivashkin, Alexander and Kirkman, Andrew (eds). *Contemplating Shostakovich: Life, Music and Film.* Ashgate, Farnham and Burlington, VT, 2012. £65.00.

Kamiński, Antoni A. *Michaił Bakunin. Życie i myśl. Tom 1: Od religii miłości do filozofii czynu (1814–1848); Tom 2: Podpalacz Europy (1848–1864).* Uniwersytet Ekonomiczny we Wrocławiu, Wrocław, 2012–2013. Zł85.00; 65.00.

Kappeler, Andreas. *Die Kosaken. Geschichte und Legenden.* C. H. Beck, Munich, 2013. €8.95 (paperback).

Kleberg, Lars and Semenenko, Aleksei (eds). *Aksenov and the Environs.* Södertörn Academic Studies, 52. Södertörns högskola, Huddinge, 2012. SK195.00 (paperback).

Kleespies, Ingrid. *A Nation Astray: Nomadism and National Identity in Russian Literature.* Northern Illinois University Press, DeKalb, IL, 2012. $48.00.

Klejn, Leo S. *Soviet Archaeology: Trends, Schools, and History.* Translated from the Russian by Rosh Ireland and Kevin Windle. Oxford Studies in the History of Archaeology. Oxford University Press, Oxford and New York, 2012. £85.00.

Klid, Bohdan and Motyl, Alexander J. (comps, eds). *The Holodomor Reader: A Sourcebook on the Famine of 1932–1933 in Ukraine.* CIUS Press, Toronto, ON and Edmonton, AL, 2012. $34.95 (paperback).

Kravchenko, Elena. *The Prose of Sasha Sokolov: Reflections on/of the Real.* MHRA Texts and Dissertations, 86. Modern Humanities Research Association, London, 2013. £19.99: $29.99: €24.99.

Kunicki, Mikołaj Stanisław. *Between the Brown and the Red: Nationalism, Catholicism, and Communism in 20th-Century Poland — The Politics of Bolesław Piasecki.* Ohio University Press Polish and Polish-American Studies Series. Ohio University Press, Athens, OH, 2012. $44.95.

Kuxhausen, Anna. *From the Womb to the Body Politic: Raising the Nation in Enlightenment Russia.* University of Wisconsin Press, Madison, WI, 2013. $29.95 (paperback).

Lackman, Matti. *Sotavankien pako. Muurmannin ratatyömaalta 1915–1918.* Historiallisia Tutkimuksia, 261. Suomalaisen Kirjallisuuden Seura, Helsinki, 2012. €38.00.

Lyandres, Semion. *The Fall of Tsarism: Untold Stories of the February 1917 Revolution.* Oxford University Press, Oxford and New York, 2013. £35.00.

Maurer, Trude. *Diskriminierte Bürger und emanzipierte 'Fremdstämmige'. Juden an deutschen und russishen Universitäten.* Vorlesungen des Centrums für Jüdische Studien, 5. Grazer Universitätsverlag, Leykam, 2013. €12.50.

Moon, David. *The Plough that Broke the Steppes: Agriculture and Environment on Russia's Grasslands, 1700–1914.* Oxford Studies in European History. Oxford University Press, Oxford and New York, 2013. £65.00.

Muckle, James. *James Arthur Heard (1798–1875) and the Education of the Poor in Russia.* Bramcote Press, Ilkeston, 2013. £16.95.

Neuberger, Mary C. *Balkan Smoke: Tobacco and the Making of Modern Bulgaria.* Cornell University Press, Ithaca, NY and London, 2013. $39.95.

Nicolai, Giorgio Maria. *La Russia di Caterina II allo specchio della satira. Dalle pagine delle riviste di Novikóv.* Biblioteca di Cultura, 729. Bulzone Editore, Rome, 2013. €20.00 (paperback).

Olson, Laura J. and Adonyeva, Svetlana. *The Worlds of Russian Village Women: Tradition, Transgression, Compromise.* The University of Wisconsin Press, Madison, WI, 2012. $39.95 (paperback).

Peschio, Joe. *The Poetics of Impudence and Intimacy in the Age of Pushkin*. Publications of the Wisconsin Center for Pushkin Studies. University of Wisconsin Press, Madison, WI, 2012. $29.95 (paperback).

Pilke, Helena. *Korsu-uutisia! Rintamalehtien jatkosota*. Historiallisia Tutkimuksia, 260. Suomalaisen Kirjallisuuden Seura, Helsinki, 2012. €39.00.

Pyzhikov, A. V. *Grani russkogo raskola. Zametki o nashei istorii ot XVII veka do 1917 goda*. Drevlekhanilishche, Moscow, 2013. R 525.00.

Plokhy, Serhii. *The Cossack Myth: History and Nationhood in the Age of Empires*. New Studies in European History. Cambridge University Press, Cambridge and New York, 2012. £65.00: $99.00.

Pontieri, Laura. *Soviet Animation and the Thaw of the 1960s: Not Only for Children*. John Libbey, New Barnet, 2012. £22.50 (paperback).

Portuges, Catherine and Hames, Peter (eds). *Cinemas in Transition in Central and Eastern Europe after 1989*. Temple University Press, Philadelphia, PA, 2013. $94.50.

Pushkin, Alexander. *Love Poems*. Edited and translated by Roger Clarke. Alma Classics, Richmond, 2013. £7.99.

Pushkin, Alexander. *The Captain's Daughter and A History of Pugachov*. Translated by Paul Debreczeny. Alma Classics, Richmond, 2012. £7.99 (paperback).

Pushkin, Alexander. *The Queen of Spades and Other Stories*. Translated by Paul Debreczeny. Oneworld Classics, Richmond, 2011. £8.99 (paperback).

Raška, Francis D. *The Long Road to Victory: A History of Czechoslovak Exile Organisations*. EEM, 799. Columbia University Press, New York, 2012. $55.00: £38.00.

Rey, Marie-Pierre (ed.). *1812, la campagne de Russie: Historie et representations. Revue des études slaves*, 83, 2012, 4. L'institut d'études slaves and Centre d'études slaves, Paris, 2012. €28.00 (paperback).

Rofe, Michael. *Dimensions of Energy in Shostakovich's Symphonies*. Ashgate, Farnham and Burlington, VT, 2012. £60.00.

Rubin, Dominic. *The Life and Thought of Lev Karsavin: 'Strength Made Perfect in Weakness...'*. On the Boundary of Two Worlds: Identity, Freedom, and Moral Imagination in the Baltics, 33. Rodopi, Amsterdam and New York, 2013. €83.00: $112.00.

Šarić, L., Gammelgaard, K. and Rå Hauge, K. (eds). *Transforming National Holidays: Identity Discourse in the West and South Slavic Countries, 1985–2010*. Discourse Approaches to Politics, Society and Culture (DAPSAC). John Benjamins, Amsterdam and Philadelphia, PA, 2012. €99.00: $149.00.

Schippan, Michael. *Die Aufklärung in Russland im 18. Jahrhundert*. Wolfenbütteler Forschungen, 131. Harrassowitz, Wiesbaden, 2012. €88.00.

Schober, Anna. *The Cinema Makers: Public Life and the Exhibition of Difference in South-Eastern and Central Europe since the 1960s*. Intellect, Bristol and Chicago, IL, 2013. £24.95: $40.00 (paperback).

Shore, Marci. *The Taste of Ashes: The Afterlife of Totalitarianism in Eastern Europe*. William Heinemann, London, 2013. £20.00.

Smith, Kenneth M. *Skryabin, Philosophy and the Music of Desire*. Royal Music Association Monographs, 19. Ashgate, Farnham and Burlington, VT, 2013. £45.00.

Stańczyk, Ewa. *Contact Zone Identities in the Poetry of Jerzy Harasymowicz: A Postcolonial Analysis*. Peter Lang, Oxford, Bern and New York, 2012. €50.00: £40.00: $64.95 (paperback).

Starova, Luan. *The Time of Goats*. Translated by Christina E. Kramer. The University of Wisconsin Press, Madison, WI, 2012. $24.95 (paperback).

Steinby, Liisa and Klapuri, Tintti (eds). *Bakhtin and His Others: (Inter)subjectivity, Chronotope, Dialogism*. Anthem Series on Russian, East European and Eurasian Studies. Anthem Press, London, New York and Delhi, 2013. £60.00: $99.00.

Stolarik, M. Mark. *Where is My Home? Slovak Immigration to North America (1870–2010)*. Immigration from Europe to North America, 1. Peter Lang, Oxford, Bern and New York, 2012. €76.50: £61.00: $99.95 (paperback).

Trousdale, Rachel. *Nabokov, Rushdie, and the Transnational Imagination: Novels of Exile and Alternate Worlds*. Palgrave Macmillan, New York, 2010. £58.00.

Yeomans, Rory. *Visions of Annihilation: The Ustasha Regime and the Cultural Politics of Fascism 1941–1945*. Pitt Series in Russian and East European Studies. University of Pittsburgh Press, Pittsburgh, PA, 2013. $35.00 (paperback).

Zadoff, Mirjam. *Next Year in Marienbad: The Lost Worlds of Jewish Spa Culture*. Translated by William Templer. Jewish Culture and Contexts. University of Pennsylvania Press, Philadelphia, PA, 2012. $49.95: £32.50.

Zaleska Onyshkevych, Larissa M. (comp., ed.). *An Anthology of Modern Ukrainian Drama*. Canadian Institute of Ukrainian Studies Press, Edmonton, AL and Toronto, ON, 2012. $39.95 (paperback).

Abstracts

The Morphosyntax of Causative Relations in Czech and Upper Sorbian: A Contrastive, Descriptive Analysis by Gary H. Toops
The article provides a contrastive, descriptive analysis of the morphosyntax of causative relations in two closely related West Slavic languages — contemporary Czech and Upper Sorbian. Four types of causative constructions are identified: (a) contextual causatives, (b) causative 'give'-constructions, (c) synsemantic causative constructions (incorporating the Czech causative auxiliaries *nechávat*/*nechat* and *dávat*/*dát* and the Upper Sorbian causative auxiliary *dać*), and (d) autosemantic causative constructions. It is concluded that Upper Sorbian shares with Czech only causative constructions (b), (c), and (d) and that the two languages differ most from each other in their instantiation of synsemantic causatives. The potential influence of German on causative expression in Czech and Upper Sorbian is considered alongside occasional comparisons with Russian. The analysis also incorporates data from colloquial varieties of Upper Sorbian and takes into account problems of ambiguity and obsolescence as well as the syntactic exponency of Direct Agents in certain Czech causative constructions.

The Return of the Photograph: Time, Memory and the Genre of the Photo-Film in Andrei Zviagintsev's *Vozvrashchenie* (The Return, 2003) by Philip Cavendish
This article examines the photographic coda of Andrei Zviagintsev's film *Vozvrashchenie* (The Return, 2003). The images which constitute this coda are approached in terms of their diegetic and poetic significance, but also within the context of the 'Photo-Film', an experimental genre which explores the respective ontologies of still and moving images. As the work of the production photographer, Vladimir Mishukov, the images of the coda are analysed in terms of the ambiguous relationship between documentation of the film-production process and the fictional reality which this process seeks to create on screen. They are examined within the context of the history of film-production photography generally in Soviet and post-Soviet Russia, and also as illustrations of Mishukov's particular thematic and aesthetic concerns as one of Russia's leading contemporary photographers.

A Need for Greater Openness: The Countryside in Czech Fiction since 1989 by Rajendra A. Chitnis
This study explores the return to the theme of the countryside in early twenty-first century Czech fiction. It argues that, whereas previous Czech 'returns to the rural' marked a retreat from openness to the security of national tradition, in the 2000s, the countryside is used not only to criticize the nature of Western capitalist society, which the Czechs rejoined after 1989, but also to open up post-Communist Czech society and literature, which are seen to have preserved the myths, attitudes, behaviour and introversion of the preceding decades. It includes close reading of works by Antonín Bajaja, Radka Denemarková, Jiří Hájíček, Petra Hůlová, Květa Legátová, Jáchym Topol, Miloš Urban and Ludvík Vaculík.

Bringing the Law Back In: Land, Law and the Hungarian Peasantry before 1848 by Robert W. Gray
This article investigates the legal position of the peasantry in Hungary prior to their emancipation during the revolution of 1848. It uses earlier legal texts, principally Stephen Werbőczy's *Tripartitum* of 1517 and Maria Theresa's *Urbarium* of 1767, to explore the nature of peasant rights to the land they farmed and the terms of their relations with their lords. In doing so, it argues that the Hungarian peasantry did not fall under a harsh form of 'serfdom', as has previously been supposed, but rather enjoyed strong rights protected by various and complex customary arrangements, a fact that severely limited the effectiveness of Maria Theresa's attempts to reform rural conditions. The reformers of the nineteenth

century, in contrast, were more attuned to the particularities of Hungarian customary law and thus framed their arguments for reform in reference to existing local customs.

Public Perceptions of Corruption and Anti-Corruption Reform in the Western Balkans by Åse B. Grødeland

The article investigates public perceptions of the concept of corruption; different types of corruption, institutions responsible for anti-corruption reform, and anti-corruption efforts in Kosovo, FYROM (Republic of Macedonia) and Serbia — linking such perceptions to some observations on legal culture in the Balkans. Drawing on large-scale qualitative and quantitative data collected in the Western Balkans in 2011, it is argued that local perceptions of what constitutes corruption as well as negative perceptions of law and state institutions are conducive to corruption and negatively influence anti-corruption reform.

THE SLAVONIC & EAST EUROPEAN REVIEW

The Slavonic and East European Review, the journal of the UCL School of Slavonic and East European Studies, is published quarterly by the Modern Humanities Research Association (MHRA). Issues are numbered serially, the four annual issues constituting a volume. Up to and including 1965 an even-numbered issue (published in December) together with the following and odd-numbered issue (published in June) constituted a volume.

Scholarly contributions are invited on all subjects related to the field of Slavonic and East European Studies. Articles should be between 8,000 and 12,000 words, although contributions falling outside this range may also be considered. Book reviews should be no longer than requested. Other contributions (marginalia, obituaries, summary notes) should aim at a corresponding and proportionate brevity. Original documents are specially welcome. No correspondence is published in the *Review*.

Contributions should be submitted in English in a form ready for publication and in the final state intended. Contributors should study the leaflet, 'Guide for Contributors', obtainable on request from the Deputy Editor, SEER Office, UCL SSEES, Gower Street, London WC1E 6BT (seer@ssees.ucl.ac.uk), or online at www.ssees.ucl.ac.uk/seer.htm. All contributions must adhere to the *Review*'s house style.

Contributions and other editorial communications should be sent to the Deputy Editor. While the editors take every possible care with regard to typescripts, they advise authors to retain duplicate copies. The editors do not consider themselves responsible in the event of the loss of a contribution.

Disclaimer: Statements of fact and opinion in the content of *The Slavonic and East European Review* are those of the respective authors and contributors and not of the journal editors, UCL SSEES, or of the MHRA. MHRA makes no representation, express or implied, in respect of the accuracy of the material in this journal and cannot accept any legal responsibility or liability for any errors or omissions that may be made.

Online access to *The Slavonic and East European Review* for individual members of the Modern Humanities Research Association is included in the annual subscription. Further information about the activities of the Modern Humanities Research Association and individual membership can be obtained from the Honorary Secretary Dr Barbara Burns, School of Modern Languages and Cultures, University of Glasgow, Hetherington Building, Bute Gardens, Glasgow G12 8RS, UK, or from the website at www.mhra.org.uk. For institutional subscription rates and information, please contact JSTOR (http://about.jstor.org/csp). Orders and enquiries relating to back numbers (from Vol. 48 to date), should be directed to Periodicals Service Company (http://www.periodicals.com).

ISSN 0037-6795 (print); ISSN 2222-4327 (online)

www.ingramcontent.com/pod-product-compliance
Ingram Content Group UK Ltd.
Pitfield, Milton Keynes, MK11 3LW, UK
UKHW020136290926
15471UKWH00003B/529